REREADING *Women*

Thirty Years of Exploring Our Literary Traditions

REREADING WOMEN

Thirty Years of Exploring

Our Literary Traditions

SANDRA M. GILBERT

W. W. NORTON & COMPANY   NEW YORK · LONDON

For information about permission to reproduce
selections from this book, write to Permissions,
W. W. Norton & Company, Inc.,
500 Fifth Avenue, New York, NY 10110

For information about special discounts for bulk
purchases, please contact W. W. Norton Special Sales
at specialsales@wwnorton.com or 800-233-4830

Manufacturing by Dana Sloan
Book design by Courier Westford
Production manager: Julia Druskin

Library of Congress Cataloging-in-Publication Data

Gilbert, Sandra M.
Rereading women : thirty years of exploring our
literary traditions / Sandra M. Gilbert. — 1st ed.
    p. cm.
Includes bibliographical references.
ISBN 978-0-393-06764-4 (hardcover)
1. American literature—Women authors—History and criticism.
2. Women and literature—United States—History.
3. Feminism and literature—United States—History.
4. Feminist literary criticism. I. Title.
PS152.G55 2011
810.9'9287—dc22
                                        2011000698

W. W. Norton & Company, Inc.
500 Fifth Avenue, New York, N.Y. 10110
www.wwnorton.com

W. W. Norton & Company Ltd.
Castle House, 75/76 Wells Street, London W1T 3QT

1 2 3 4 5 6 7 8 9 0

For Susan Gubar, with love and friendship

CONTENTS

PREFACE

On Hybridity and Rereading

To reread is both to read again and to read anew—that is, to read in another way what is already familiar, as if it has been read yet *not* read before. To read, unread, *re*read: feminist literary critics, many whose practice was summarized by Adrienne Rich's crucial "When We Dead Awaken: Writing as Re-Vision," have undertaken this procedure for decades now, as have others who work in the ever more complex areas of gender studies. And their labors have been immensely productive to all of us, personally as well as collectively. Indeed, it can be argued that although there's more to be done, we women have historically unprecedented domestic and professional prospects because of a massive, quietly revolutionary project of cultural reinterpretation that began with feminist readings, unreadings, and rereadings a half century ago. In compiling the essays in this volume, I'm constructing an oblique narrative of a career devoted to that project, even while, in rereading some of my own writings, I'm reviewing my years of rereading women's thoughts and arts from a perspective that (I hope) I've gradually been revising. But for me this book isn't just an account of solo rereading. As I explain in my opening chapter on collaboration and identity, it is the fruit of a curiously hybrid literary life, one in which I often functioned simultaneously as an author and a coauthor, an editor and a coeditor, a teacher and a team-teacher. Even within these categories, however, I was and am a kind of hybrid: to quote the dictionary, a creature bred from two or more "distinct varieties," "a composite" formed "of heterogeneous elements."

I should note here that I'm not employing the term "hybridity" in the theoretical fashion that has come into use among postcolonial thinkers as a means of defining intersections of race and culture. Nor do I allude to hybridity as a coerced crossbreeding. Rather, I intend the word to stand in for more cumbersome phrases like "open pollination" or "cross-fertilization." For although I myself am a sort of ethnic mongrel (of Sicilian, Ligurian, Russian, and French ancestry), I'm seeking to define my literary rather than "literal" identity, which I realize, reflecting on the contours of my career, has been pollinated from a number of different directions. Because I'm the product of such multiple origins, therefore, I'm in effect an intellectual or aesthetic hybrid.

As an author and editor, I've not only worked collaboratively (almost always with Susan Gubar but also on projects with Diana O'Hehir and Wendy Barker), I've also written on my own in various genres, mainly in verse and critical prose but now and then in memoir and prose fiction. Even as a teacher and public speaker, I've been a hybrid, regularly teaching creative writing, on the one hand, and both literary history and women's studies on the other; mostly teaching alone but occasionally with Susan; and speaking in public sometimes with her but often by myself, at poetry readings (on my own) and lectures (both individual and collaborative).

What has been the impact of such hybridity on my creative life and work, and in particular on my commitment to feminist processes of rereading? From my point of view, the signs of multidisciplinarity and collaborative thinking are, for better or worse, everywhere, although they may not be as evident to others as they are to me.

To begin with, before I was any kind of intellectual, I was a little girl making up poems. "Zip zip, through the air, / goes a fearful bear," I intoned to my mother one dark and stormy night. "His name is lightning, / and when he comes you can see the whole sky brightening." When my mother dutifully copied these words into a notebook, I must have sensed that I had her hooked. Never again would I need to struggle for her attention at bedtime by begging for a glass of water. Instead, all I'd have to do would be repeat triumphantly, "I have a poem!"

Writing poems leads to reading poems (or sometimes vice versa), as most poets know, and then in many cases to writing *about* poems. In high school, I worked my way through popular fifties anthologies by Louis Untermeyer and Oscar Williams, and devoured such delicacies as the verses of Edna St. Vincent Millay and T. S. Eliot, and by the time I was a college freshman—bent on becoming a physician with a specialty in psychiatry—I produced a lyrical "Elegy for *Rana Pipiens*" when confronted with the gruesome task of dissecting a common garden-variety frog in Zoology 101. Soon, instead of cutting up frogs, I was dissecting Wordsworth and Milton under the magisterial tutelage of the great M. H. Abrams. I was still scribbling poems and laboring on the editorial boards of two wonderful Cornell magazines—*The Writer* (an undergraduate enterprise) and *Epoch* (a professional literary quarterly). But I had already become one kind of hybrid: a poet-critic.

In graduate school, I immersed myself in investigations of Romanticism and modernism while also savoring the oeuvres of Yeats, Stevens, and Lawrence, three of the great writers of my century, and finally I decided to focus my dissertation on Lawrence's poems, a then-understudied subject and one that would suit some of my revolutionary tendencies: during what Robert Lowell called the "tranquillized Fifties" (and early sixties), Lawrence, though admired as a novelist, was considered a sloppy outsider poet by many of the New Critics who reigned supreme.

But reading and studying Lawrence as a late Romantic poet propelled me toward a fascination with Harold Bloom's *Visionary Company* and began to reshape my own poetic style. I was now a hybrid modernist-Romanticist-poet-critic besides being a hybrid scholar-teacher-wife-mother (for I'd married before graduate school and started having children early, as people did in those days). And all those forces informed my thinking even before feminism electrified and—shall I say it?—hybridized me even further. But once I met and team-taught with Susan Gubar in the early seventies, I became not just a poet-critic-modernist-Romanticist-author-editor and wife-mother but also a feminist-theorist-coauthor-coeditor.

I don't think I can overestimate the impact of such hybridity on the essays collected in this volume. I discuss the problematics of collaborative versus individual authorial identity in the first chapter of this book, but I should note here that everything I've written since the seventies has been inflected by the multiple, multifaceted mind-set of feminism, both the two-in-one of my collaboration with Susan and the many-in-one of the movement out of which our partnership evolved. And even before I was inspired to read and reread, and write and rewrite, through the lens of gender I was also composing as the two-in-one of the poet-critic and teacher/speaker-writer/scholar. To be sure, all these pieces were researched and composed solely by me. As the usual formulation puts it, I alone am to blame for flaws in scholarship or argumentation, faults of style, political or poetical excess, and/or significant omissions. Yet as the thirty-five-year chronological span of this book suggests, I wrote this material after the scales fell from my eyes on the way to, and in, Bloomington, Indiana, where I did my first really serious feminist critical thinking, team-teaching a class with Susan Gubar that would quickly evolve into our collaborative *Madwoman in the Attic* as well as such other collaborative works as *Shakespeare's Sisters, No Man's Land* (three volumes), and *The Norton Anthology of Literature by Women* (three editions).

Surely it was inevitable (for both of us) that a life-altering intellectual transformation—what I'd call, quoting Emily Dickinson, a "conversion of the mind"—would issue in individually authored as well as collaboratively written texts. And surely it is equally inevitable that, just as jointly authored works are shaped by the two participants in their production, any individually written works by those who are collaborators must be indelibly marked by the mutual "mind" of the collaboration. These individual productions, indeed, might be said to become what Walt Whitman called "sparkles from the wheel"—ideas flashing out from a complex center—or, to revert to the metaphor of hybridity, flowers and fruits offering themselves on branches flaring in new directions from an originary trunk.

What are my motives for producing this selection of my essays at this time? To begin with, following my retirement from my post at the University of California, Davis, preceded by a long excursion into memoir writing (in *Wrongful Death,* 1995) and extended analyses of the literature of grief (in *Death's Door,* 2006), I've found myself rethinking (rereading!) the modes of feminism defined in the second half of the twentieth century. Why and how did these ideas become so urgently necessary to women in the sixties and seventies? Are those feminist concepts and practices still relevant today? Although these questions have been much addressed both in the media and by academics, they still compel attention from women and men alike, and for all of us, and our children, they retain their primordial urgency.

Over the last few years such matters have been brought to the forefront of my mind by collaborative work with Susan Gubar on two anthologies: the much-expanded, two-volume third edition of *The Norton Anthology of Literature by Women: The Traditions in English,* published in 2006, and an entirely new collection, entitled *Feminist Theory and Criticism: A Norton Reader,* published the following year. Assembling and editing those books reminded me (as if I needed reminding!) of the ever-increasing richness and sophistication of women's writing and feminist critical thinking. But other recent developments in my professional life also inspired me to review my decades as a feminist thinker and scholar.

First, when I was invited to join the Cornell University English Department in the spring of 2007 as the first M. H. Abrams Distinguished Visiting Professor, I was particularly asked to teach courses in feminism and gender theory, encouraging me to begin a retrospective examination—quite literally a rereading—of the feminist movement, the critical projects it energized, and my own relationship both to the movement and its enterprises. As I undertook such overviews in both undergraduate and graduate seminars at Cornell, my engagement with feminist history was greeted with more enthusiasm than I had anticipated. Although my courses in women's studies and the female literary tradition have always drawn significant student audiences, I was delighted by the interest my Cornell classes generated. In the late eighties, perhaps as part of a backlash against what came to be called "seventies feminism," students would sometimes join seminars on gender issues with the deprecating (and depressing) explanation that "I'm not a feminist but . . . I wanted to see what it was all about" (and then add that of course they believed in equal pay for equal work, reproductive control for women, political and professional advancement for female candidates, and other traditional feminist causes). But that spring no one apologized for wanting to learn about feminist politics and poetics!

And again, in the spring of 2009, when I was honored by an invitation to teach at the California State University, San Jose, as the Lurie Distinguished Professor of Creative Writing, I paired my poetry workshop with a seminar in women's literary traditions and was not only pleased but galvanized by student excitement. As we explored female-authored works from *Jane Eyre* and *Wide Sargasso Sea* to *The Bluest Eye* and *Top Girls,* I sensed again the urgency of excavating the poetics and politics defined by what the great Renaissance feminist Christine de Pizan called a "City of Ladies." Because my companions in this adventure—male and female, undergraduate and graduate, regular and "re-entry"—live not too far from my home in Berkeley, we've already had one reunion in my living room, and are looking forward to others. The motto of each and all in the class hasn't been "I'm not a feminist but . . .": instead, it's "I *am* a feminist, and . . . !"

Another motive: in these same years, a prominent editor invited me to write a keynote essay on collaboration for a special issue of his journal—an essay in which I would review not just the dynamics of my own long-term feminist collaboration with Susan Gubar but, more generally, the collaborative nature of the feminist project itself as well as the decades of research engendered by the so-called Second Wave of feminism that hit the beachheads of our culture in the late sixties and early seventies. A grave personal loss deflected me, for a while, from his challenge, but more recently I returned to my contemplation of his proposal, in the hope that such a piece could function as a historical overture to a collection of representative feminist essays that I've written over the years. Some of these have been published in periodicals and anthologies, some (because they're very recent or because I've always wanted to do further work on them) haven't appeared in print, but none have yet been assembled in a book of my own. Now, as I sense a mounting interest in the past and future of the feminist movement that evoked these writings, I'm eager to enter what I hope will be a lively public dialogue on women's achievements in the past and present along with feminist criticism's potential for the future.

Mother rites: the final section of this volume is a kind of mini-book conceived as an extended example of feminist critical analysis; it explores the ways in which nineteenth- and twentieth-century anthropological and medical redefinitions of matriarchy and maternity paralleled or were reflected in texts by authors from Elizabeth Barrett Browning to George Eliot, Emily Dickinson, Edith Wharton, D. H. Lawrence, and Sylvia Plath. But that title also, of course, alludes to Virginia Woolf's famous observation that as women we think back through, and in effect reread, our mothers. The potential for biological maternity— "legitimate" or "illegitimate," chosen or forced—is both the blessing and the curse of the female body: whether or not anatomy need be "destiny," it's obvious that the "facts of (female) life" as determined by women's sexuality have countless social and cultural consequences around the world. But the metaphoric and metaphysical implications of the very concept of *mothering* are also literarily as well as literally various. How does the mind *mother*—that is, originate—ideas? How have our intellectual mothers authored or authorized our own thoughts? These questions have been crucial to the feminist project for centuries. But how, too, has feminism itself functioned as a matrilineal enterprise, in which many women over time and space join to birth and nurture new thoughts, in particular new propositions about "the feminine" itself?

If the final section of this book traces revisionary imaginings of maternity in the last two hundred years, the first section, "Finding Atlantis—and Growing into Feminism," represents my own intellectual development as I sought to come to terms with the many modes of feminist thinking in a series of general essays I published from the seventies to the present. More pragmatically, the book's second section, "Reading and Rereading Women's Writing," demonstrates ways of examining the dynamics of gender and genre through analyses of poems and novels by a number of artists, including Charlotte Brontë, Emily Dickinson, Frances Hodgson Burnett, and Sylvia Plath, along with a range of recent poets. With the exception of the two opening essays, intended to define and justify the material that follows, the pieces in the first two sections are organized chronologically according to the dates on which I first composed or published them, in an attempt to offer an overview of my own evolution as a feminist thinker. The essays in section three appear more or less chronologically in the historical sequence of their subject matter.

This book itself is in some sense a hybrid. A creature of the past (I have allowed each selection to stand in its original form, as first published or written), it is at the same time a product of the present, shaped by the retrospective reflections that helped me choose and organize its parts. Various in style and subject (some essays are more academic than others, all the productions of a "hybrid" poet-critic), it is nonetheless unified by my earnest wish to commemorate and celebrate the feminist thinking that strengthened so much of my intellectual life. And speaking of strength: I hope the ideas investigated here will manifest the vigor of a poetics openly borne and nourished by many mothers, not bred by hyperspecialization.

For contributing to my own energy as I assembled these essays, I must thank many friends and mentors, foremost among them my longtime editor Jill Bialosky and my always supportive agent Ellen Levine, both of whom encouraged me to embark on this project, as well as a series of hardy research assistants who helped put everything together—John Beckman, Augustus Rose, Francisco Reinking, Micha Lazarus, and Seulghee Lee—and Amy Robbins, a wonderfully meticulous copy editor. Among those who fostered my most recent works, I offer my deepest gratitude to M. H. Abrams at Cornell, along with others who made my time in Ithaca very special—notably Molly Hite, Gail Holst-Warhaft, my son Roger Gilbert, and all the students in my seminar on topics in women's literature. For facilitating my wonderful seminar at San Jose, I thank Alan Soldofsky and John Engel, along with the members of English 181.

Over the years, as I researched and drafted the works collected here, I was aided, abetted, and inspired by many other editors, friends, and colleagues: the late John Benedict and Julia Reidhead (at Norton), Ellen Graham (at Yale University Press), and, among others around the world, Penny Allen, Leah Asofsky, Gianfranca Balestra, Millicent Barish, Wendy

Barker, Shuli Barzilai, Michael Bell, Margo Berdeshevsky, Elyse Blankley, Chana Bloch, Jacqueline Vaught Brogan, Sheila Lahiri Chaudhury, Kevin Clark, H. M. Daleski, Marysa Demoor, Joanne Feit Diehl, the late Moneera Doss, Linda Gardiner, Dorothy Gilbert, Gerald Graff, the late Robert Griffin, Marlene Griffith, Marilyn Hacker, the late Carolyn Heilbrun, the late Masako Hirai, Paula Harrington, Jennifer Hoofand, Diane Johnson, the late Ilinca Johnston, Claire Kahane, Shirley Kaufman, Don Lazere, Marilee Lindemann, Herbert Lindenberger, Toni Morrison, Joyce Carol Oates, Diana O'Hehir, Ruth Rosen, Betty and Ted Roszak, Ginette Roy, Kirsten Saxton, Joan Schenkar, Peter Dale Scott, Elaine Showalter, Amrit Singh, Martha Nell Smith, Garrett Stewart, Ruth Stone, Phyllis Stowell, Brenda Webster, Alan Williamson, and Alex Zwerdling. For life-strength I thank my enduringly brilliant and patient children—Roger, Kathy, and Susanna, along with their families, especially my daughters-in-law Robin and Gina and my splendiferous grandchildren: Valentine, Aaron, Stefan, and Sophia. In the beginning, and still, my beloved intellectual mentor was and has always been my late husband Elliot Gilbert, but in more recent years I was deeply enriched by the passionate energy of my late much-cherished partner David Gale. Today, I am intensely thankful for the loving companionship of Albert Magid. But most of all, as I reflect on the provenance of the works included here, I am grateful for the inspiration of my longtime friend and collaborator Susan Gubar, to whom this book is dedicated.

ACKNOWLEDGMENTS

Portions of this book were originally published, sometimes in different forms, in the following journals and volumes:

"Finding Atlantis: Thirty Years of Exploring Women's Literary Traditions": as part of the Introduction to Part I of *Feminist Theory and Criticism: A Norton Reader,* ed. Sandra M. Gilbert and Susan Gubar (New York: W. W. Norton, 2007)

"What Do Feminist Critics Want? Or, A Postcard from the Volcano": *ADE Bulletin* (Winter 1980)

"The Education of Henrietta Adams": *Profession '84* (New York: Modern Language Association, 1985)

"A Tarantella of Theory: Hélène Cixous' and Catherine Clément's *Newly Born Woman*" (Minneapolis: University of Minnesota Press, 1986)

"Reflections on a (Feminist) Discourse of Discourse, or, Look, Ma, I'm Talking!": *The State of the Language,* ed. Christopher Ricks and Leonard Michaels (Berkeley: University of California Press, 1990)

"'My Name Is Darkness': The Poetry of Self-Definition": *Contemporary Literature* (Autumn 1977)

"'A Fine, White Flying Myth': The Life/Work of Sylvia Plath": *The Massachusetts Review* (Autumn 1978)

"The Wayward Nun Beneath the Hill: Emily Dickinson and the Mysteries of Womanhood": *Feminist Critics Read Emily Dickinson,* ed. Suzanne Juhasz (Bloomington: Indiana University Press, 1983)

"*Jane Eyre* and the Secrets of Furious Lovemaking": *Novel* (Summer 1998)

"The Key to Happiness: On Frances Hodgson Burnett's *The Secret Garden*": Afterword to Frances Hodgson Burnett, *The Secret Garden* (New York: Signet Classic, 2003)

"'Dare You See a Soul *at the White Heat*?': Thoughts on a 'Little Home-keeping Person'": *A Companion to Emily Dickinson,* ed. M. N. Smith and M. Loeffelholz (Oxford, UK: Blackwell Publishing, 2008)

"From *Patria* to *Matria*: Elizabeth Barrett Browning's *Risorgimento*": *PMLA* (March 1986)

"'Life's Empty Pack': Notes Toward a Literary Daughteronomy": *Critical Inquiry* (Spring 1985)

"Potent Griselda: Male Modernists and the Great Mother": *Centenary Essays on D. H. Lawrence,* ed. Peter Balbert and Philip Marcus (Ithaca, N.Y.: Cornell University Press, 1985)

I am grateful to all of these journals and presses for their support of my work.

Part I

FINDING ATLANTIS

—AND GROWING

INTO FEMINISM

BECOMING A FEMINIST TOGETHER—AND APART

Notes on Collaboration and Identity

What people don't realize is that in collaboration, if it works, you form a single writer who is different from either writer alone.

—W. H. AUDEN[1]

Awakenings in the Dorm Room, Loneliness in the Pantry

What was it like to be or "become" a feminist in the bad, sad old days of the fifties, sixties, and seventies? Students and interviewers often ask such questions, eagerly wondering "How did you . . . ?" "Why did you . . . ?" and "When did you . . . ?" Many of them, participants in the Riot Grrrl Revolution that's part of what's now known as Third Wave feminism, have some stereotypical ideas about those of us who rose to consciousness as the Second Wave crested and flung new ideas about gender all over the world. The friendly ones think we were Amazonian warriors, marching for freedoms some of which we won and some we didn't achieve: abortion rights (yes—so far), greater access to education and the professions (yes), sexual freedom (yes), stronger representation in national politics (well, maybe), salary equity (no), the ERA (no), child

3

care for all (no). The unfriendly ones—perhaps blaming us for what we didn't manage to do or perhaps veering away from our priorities—frequently caricature us as strident, hairy-legged, man-hating, bra-burning wild women who prioritized activism over aesthetics, propaganda over pleasure, anger over love, freedom over family.

A lot of us are thought to have sat around in Wiccan circles worshiping the Goddess and refusing to let male contemporaries join in. Many of us are supposed to have said "Click" in outraged tones at moments of heightened gender consciousness. Others are believed to have insisted that sexual intercourse was a way of "physiologically making a woman inferior: communicating to her cell by cell her own inferior status . . . by shoving it into her, over and over, pushing and thrusting until she gives up and gives in."[2]

But of course, as our generation of feminists knew and as most of the younger generation of feminists has clearly begun to understand, every woman's feminism is unique, with its special ideals and images, politics and poetics, fears and fantasies—many fostered by sisterhood but some evolved in isolation. My own sense of an overarching sexual politics, for instance—to use a phrase Kate Millett made famous in the late sixties—developed early, but slowly, gropingly, along with a perception of what Betty Friedan, just as famously, called the "feminine mystique."

To begin with, as a child growing up in the forties and fifties I'm pretty sure I thought girls were just as important as boys. At home, certainly, I was encouraged to aspire to artistic achievement and professional success. Unlike many of my female contemporaries, I wasn't groomed to go to college for what we women undergraduates called an "M.R.S." degree. My parents thought, in fact, that I should become a psychoanalyst or anyway some sort of doctor, a lawyer, or a professor. Nor did they ever hint to me that there were any obstacles to my success in such fields. To be sure, my mother—a fifth-grade teacher who took doctoral-level courses in psychology—did most of the housecleaning. But then my father—a civil engineer with a master's in his subject—did most of the cooking for our little family.

When did my feminist awakenings begin? Or should I even call them "awakenings"? For in comparison to what was to become the phenomenon of "consciousness-raising," my experiences were more akin to lowerings—to perceptions of forces moving gravely and ominously underneath the surface of my life as an adolescent girl, an aspiring poet, and an increasingly serious student of literature.

Was it in my sophomore year at Cornell that someone lent me a copy of Simone de Beauvoir's *Second Sex*? It was out in the States by then, in a massive English translation we now know to have been both truncated and inaccurate, and perhaps it was being passed from room to room in my dorm. Or maybe it was the following year. I have a blurry memory of struggling with it, then finally reading enough to know that it was uncovering a strain of such deep unpleasantness in the world that I gave up on it, nauseated. Had no one ever hinted to me that I was second, not first, other, not central? Maybe someone had, at camp, at home, at school, and now, as my consciousness was *lowered* into the chasms under my dutiful schoolgirl life, I was having for the first time to come to terms with gender dynamics that were going to shape my future in ways I'd never before imagined.

Darkenings, forebodings: I had an undergraduate affair, got pregnant, was scheduled for an abortion, had a miscarriage, had to stay home from college for a month or two while my boyfriend went cheerily back to campus. Where was my transcendent, poetry-making self now? But I returned, recovered, wrote poems again, got a B.A. with high honors and a fellowship to graduate school, just like any boy my age. There were memories of pain and fear, but everything was okay now, wasn't it?

I went to a shrink who told me that I wouldn't really want to write poetry once I became a proper wife and mother. My poetry writing was probably a bad consequence, he said, of my father's cooking. Were the sex roles somehow askew in my household?

I won a highly prized guest editorship at *Mademoiselle* and entered the world that Sylvia Plath would delineate with such sardonic brilliance in *The Bell Jar*. We lucky winners met in seminar rooms full of plaid skirts and cute blouses, carried home treasure troves of linens and cosmetics, partied in penthouses, were beautified at Helena Rubinstein's salon. I was the guest Managing Editor (as Plath had been before me) and charged with thinking up a clever "theme" statement—something to do with telephones—for our special College Issue. Direct Line to Campus? Dialing Up Success? Calling All Coeds? Busy Signals in the Dorm? Phoning Fashion? Straining after winsome ideas, I dissolved in tears every morning before boarding the bus to Madison Avenue.

Several of our victorious group left: one was pregnant, one had a nervous breakdown. I filled in temporarily for the guest editor-in-chief, writing an office gossip column. My stylishly dressed, soignée new bosses liked me and asked me to stay on, even though I didn't fit into the mostly size 6 skirts and blouses that hung on racks in our meeting rooms.

But no, I married another boyfriend and put off graduate school when he was unexpectedly drafted. Off to Germany we went, to live not far from a U.S. Army kaserne near Nürnberg. And now I was "legitimately" pregnant. On a visit to England, we went to see a Cornell professor of ours who was spending a year in residence there, and I told him how eager I was to get back to graduate school. *But now you're married,* he told me, eying my tummy, *and you won't be eligible for that fellowship anymore! After all, you have a husband to support you!*

My baby was born prematurely, and died after three days (no fault of the professor's), and I went into a deep depression that no one really recognized. (*That baby wasn't "real" anyway,* said my mother-in-law.)

I wore lipstick, shaved my legs, went back to the shrink, who told me lots of jokes and tried to explain to me that I needed to stop writing poetry, learn to cook, and have appropriate vaginal orgasms.

I worked in publishing, had another baby, went to NYU for a master's, had another baby, then went to Columbia (where my husband was an instructor) for a Ph.D. At an English Department party, one of my seminar directors wondered at my presence. *Aren't you married to someone teaching in the college? Why, you're part of an academic couple! You'll never get a job!*

I had another baby and won a doctoral fellowship that was supposed to be followed by a year as a lecturer at Columbia. *You'd better go across the street* (to Barnard or General Studies), said the director of Graduate Studies; *those lectureships are only for men.*

I wore lipstick, shaved my legs, wept in the pantry, went back to the shrink, finally got a job teaching remedial writing at Queens College. *We love mommies,* said the composition director when I explained (who knows why?) that I had three children. *They're always willing to work harder for less money!*

I wore lipstick, shaved my legs, decided to write a dissertation on D. H. Lawrence's poetry, took my children to the playground, taught remedial composition, wrote poems of my own, typed my husband's dissertation, began writing short stories, bought a copy of *The Feminine Mystique* and a copy of *Mastering the Art of French Cooking*. We lived in an old house in Kew Gardens few of our Manhattan-based friends wanted to visit, but we went to the opera, museums, even on summer vacations, thanks to kindly parents, grandparents, and in-laws, who also provided babysitters and housekeepers.

Why did I weep in the pantry? I didn't suffer from what Betty Friedan grimly called "the problem that has no name." My husband shared child care. I had serious literary aspirations and almost as serious professional ambitions—though no real job prospects. But in any case, what did I really think I was going to do for a living? Though my goal was to become a professor, I had never *had* a female professor! Indeed, so far as I could tell, professors were always pipe-smoking men in tweed jackets.

I wore lipstick, shaved my legs, reread *The Second Sex,* and wept in the pantry, I even wrote a story called "Weeping" about a young mother of three who irrationally, inexplicably, weeps in the pantry.

We moved to California, where my husband's university department wouldn't hire me because of "nepotism" rules. After teaching part-time at a nearby state college, I earned my doctorate and took what was defined as an inferior full-time job at another nearby state college, where lots of faculty wives taught. We were entering the seventies—riots on campuses, Kent State, anti-war marches, sit-ins, strikes, constant controversy.

My revolutionary gestures? I proposed a new kind of survey course in English and American literature as part of my department's major, helped implement it, fought to save a friend's job (marching, striking), and was fired. Someone told me to call Bob Treuhaft, the famously radical lawyer who was married to Jessica Mitford. When I told him I'd been unjustly fired without cause, he said, *Are you a Communist?* And when I said *no,* he said, *Are you a feminist?* I said, *Oh no, this was just awful department politics.* Then he said, *Sorry, I can't help you.*

The English department of the UC campus nearest to where we lived (in Berkeley) advertised what sounded like a suitable assistant professorship. I wrote a letter of application explaining that though I'd earned my degree from Columbia, I just happened to live in the vicinity because I was married to a faculty member at another UC campus and was granted a polite interview. The chair, a kindly Southerner, inquired, as Treuhaft had, whether I was a feminist. I replied that I was a student of modernism, a D. H. Lawrence scholar. He grew confidential. *These young women,* he complained in his gentle Tidewater tones, *they just want to throw out a thousand years of Western culture!*

Later I heard from a friend who went to an academic dinner party in the hills that another professor had expressed some surprise at my candidacy. *Why, she's just a Berkeley housewife!* this scholar was reputed to have remarked.

Jobless, I worked on turning my dissertation into a book, and in my spare time reread "girls'" classics—*Little Women, Jane Eyre, Wuthering Heights*—with my youngest daughter. She loved the "wonderful tea" Miss Temple offers Helen and Jane in Charlotte Brontë's novel. I was fascinated by the attic where Jo takes refuge and scribbles Gothic tales in Alcott's book, and the one that Bertha haunts in Brontë's, and the demonic figure of Heathcliff.

I started looking for jobs around the country, wore lipstick and dress-for-success suits. I had begun to realize that I might not be able to find work in Northern California, where my husband taught and my kids went to school. Could we relocate, land two jobs in the same place? Or what if I had to move to another town, by myself, to pursue my career? Should I take the children? Could we live apart? We no longer had a pantry, so I wept in our California laundry room as my consciousness sank toward a new level of darkness that I knew had something to do with gender.

Collaboration as Confirmation, Collaboration as Conversion

Reader, I accepted a job in Indiana, in the heart of the heart of the country where I had never been, far from the bustling East Coast and the "happening" West Coast. My husband and children moved to Bloomington with me—he for a fall sabbatical and a spring quarter's leave (but with a canny plan to return to blossoming California in the winter)—and they for the whole school year. Would my new department develop an interest in him? Would his longtime department relent and show an interest in me? We couldn't think beyond the 1973–74 academic year, the year in which we were living a life that felt tenuous, unreal.

The kids got settled in new and different schools. We explored the surrounding area—drank remarkably soothing sassafras tea in Brown County to the south, went to operas at the great Indiana Musical Arts Center, dined with new colleagues, lived in a big stone house with white-carpeted floors and a backyard that had a sloping cellar door (the kind from "Slide down my cellar door") and a real old-fashioned alley ("Sally in my alley").

Acts of Attention, my study of Lawrence's poetry, had been published by Cornell University Press, and—enthralled by some of his last poems—I began planning a book to be called "Different, and Luckier: Death as Metaphor in Nineteenth- and Twentieth-Century Poetry." I taught a seminar in this subject, which seemed somehow pointless and left everyone, especially me, feeling gloomy, though my students were fond of me and I of them. I met more and more new people, most of whom were sweet and supportive, but I felt uneasy in this strange midwestern community. From a bicoastal perspective, people sometimes seemed to be *too* nice! One night I dreamt that a group of guests at a local dinner party began intoning, *Drink the sassafras tea! Drink the sassafras tea!* And I feared I myself would become rather too nice.

Among all these kindly colleagues, I was especially drawn to two wild-haired women, neither of whom had quite the decorum the others had. Ruth Stone, a widowed poet in her fifties, was only a one-year visitor in the department despite her literary distinction. She had a mane of tangled bright red hair and a laugh that was a cross between a cackle and a screech. Her poems, I quickly discovered, were works of genius, and she herself was a sibylline presence with fierce eyes, fiercer thoughts, and fiery words. Susan Gubar, younger than I, was a tenure-track professor and the tall, skinny breast-feeding mother of an eight-month-old girl. She had a mane of unruly pitch black hair, a Brooklyn accent, and a laugh that was also a cross between a cackle and a screech. Her office was down the hall from mine, and because she mostly wore clogs, I could hear her quick clattering steps from quite a distance. Ruth and I bonded as poets, Susan and I bonded as New Yorkers. But all three of us bonded, too, as academic women each of whom was in a somewhat anomalous position.

To be sure, the IU department had a fairly good representation of women. But most were either single and childless, or women who had met and married men in the department after each member of the couple had been hired separately. Ruth, Susan, and I were different. Ruth was a literary vagrant who had been journeying from campus to campus as she fought to support her three daughters after the mysterious suicide of her husband, the novelist and poet Walter Stone. Susan, whose then-husband was a writer and stay-at-home dad, was the sole breadwinner in her family—a role that was then quite unusual. I myself was the only person around who was in what's now called a "commuting marriage"— today, like the role of female breadwinner, a relatively common phenomenon, but then also quite unusual.

We didn't discuss these matters all that much, but they surely shaped our thinking. At one of her incandescent readings, Ruth introduced us to her hilarious monologue of "Absinthe Granny," a sage old lady who's been through it all and wryly moralizes her triumph:

> *Those were long hot summers,*
> *Now the sun won't tarry.*
> *My birds have flocked,*
> *And I'm old and wary,*
> *I'm old and worn and a cunning sipper,*
> *And I'll outlive every little nipper.*

And with what's left I'm chary,
And with what's left I'm chary.

I dimly understood that, as Ruth herself clearly and deeply knew, these words were uttered in the shrewd mode of a classic feminist survivor, but I wasn't quite ready to theorize that mode yet, although I had begun to reflect on the vagaries of my situation, and Susan's, and Ruth's.

Nonetheless, I continued my research into death and metaphor, but while I labored in a desultory and gloomy way on my gloomy project, it turned out that just as Ruth was exploring the quirky female psyche, Susan was working on something to do with female monsters. I was rather befuddled by all this, at first. Though at this point I'd read and reread Millett, Beauvoir, and Friedan, and did finally define myself as a feminist, I didn't think that feminism ought to mean *studying* women— their works and images. Back in California, my husband had been codirecting a dissertation by someone who was writing about female-authored novels (she was a Ph.D. candidate named Elaine Showalter, who was now living on the East Coast), and I remember announcing with a certain superiority that it didn't seem to me I ought to be writing about women just because I happened to *be* a woman! On the contrary, I affirmed smugly, I felt more than capable of writing about *men*—for instance, D. H. Lawrence. Yet it was intriguing that Susan—so smart, such a New Yorker, so quick in her clogs!—was writing about female monsters. I told her about my interest in the Brontës and Louisa May Alcott: I'd begun to suspect that I should at least *think* more about them, about Jo, for instance, who seemed somehow to live in what I privately called "Heathcliff's other house," and Jane, who was such a surprisingly rebellious governess and seemed to inhabit yet another one of "Heathcliff's houses" (note that I ascribed the possession of all these homes, even those belonging to Little Women, to a male character).

But in the beginning of what was going to become a long friendship, we confined ourselves mostly to department gossip—including our mutual admiration for the poems of Ruth Stone—and to shared stories of our lives. Born and bred New Yorkers, we were also first-generation Americans, the children of immigrants—Susan's parents refugees from Nazi Germany, mine a mongrel combination of Sicilian, Ligurian, Russian, and French—with all the convoluted narratives and unspoken secrets such backgrounds imply. Then, as the year wore on, there were some professional issues to worry about. It began to be clear that neither my husband's department in California nor my department in Indiana was going to appoint an academic couple. He and the children would go back to Berkeley in the summer, and I'd go with them too, but then I'd have to come back to Bloomington, this time (we decided) by myself.

The children were still young: thirteen, eleven, and nine. How would we manage? Well, perhaps I could take a leave in the spring, but I'd have to be away for the fall term—and Indiana semesters were long, seventeen weeks. I could "commute" but such a prolonged absence would be hard on the kids.

Then, amazingly, our deparment's director of undergraduate studies, a savvy woman with a budding interest in feminism, decided that the curriculum ought to include a course in literature by women. Would Susan and I be willing to team-teach it—and do so in a special, "intensive" eight-week format? Miraculously, our (male) chair knew of my dilemma and, equally important, of our growing interest in a field we'd never studied, so he supported the plan. For Susan was an eighteenth-century literature specialist, and I was a scholar of Romanticism and modernism. Yes, some of "our" writers would be in our own areas but many, especially the classics (the Brontës, Dickinson, George Eliot, Louisa May Alcott) were icons of Victorianism or nineteenth-century American literature.

Neither of us hesitated for a minute. Had we been secretly preparing for this decision, with our separate preoccupations—not just the Brontës, Alcott, and female monsters but also Beauvoir, Friedan, Millett? We hadn't attended many marches, didn't belong to consciousness-raising groups, but the spirit of the age, what our graduate school professors called the *Zeitgeist,* was irresistible. We wanted to learn something about this new wind called feminist criticism that was blowing through the corridors of academe, and we sensed that it would be better to study together rather than separately.

Still, we fumbled for an understanding of what we were doing because there were few books to guide us. Mary Ellmann had already published *Thinking About Women* (1968) and a few essays by Ellen Moers had begun to appear in print. Her *Literary Women* wouldn't be published until 1976, however, and Patricia Meyer Spacks's *The Female Imagination* wouldn't come out until 1975. Snippets of work by critics who would become our feminist contemporaries—Elaine Showalter, Wendy Martin, Lillian Robinson, Rachel Blau DuPlessis, Nina Auerbach—appeared here and there, but we barely knew how or where to look for them.

We went out for pizza one afternoon and started to compile a syllabus of the most famous female-authored books we knew: *Frankenstein, Pride and Prejudice, Jane Eyre, Wuthering Heights,* "The Yellow Wallpaper" (just recuperated for feminism by Elaine Hedges), the poems of Elizabeth Barrett Browning, Christina Rossetti, and Emily Dickinson, *Mrs. Dalloway, A Room of One's Own, Ariel, Diving Into the Wreck. . . .* And we had begun collecting other writings by women whose work we were just encountering: poems by Anne Finch and Margaret Cavendish, verse by modernists and contemporaries, including our inimitable colleague Ruth Stone. And then we began arguing about what to call our course.

We had attics and monsters in common, together with lots of thoughts about ladies in parlors, and—increasingly—ideas about madness and sanity.

I suggested "Upstairs, Downstairs" in honor of the then-popular *Masterpiece Theatre* series, but Susan scoffed that it was "vulgar."

She was right. We could do better.

We brooded further on attics and monsters, nibbling sausage and mushroom pizza, then finally came up with "The Madwoman in the Attic."

We were anxious about the class: the new subject matter was risky, we hadn't studied it *anywhere,* and then it was strange and maybe embarrassing to team-teach, even with a friend. How could we orchestrate discussions? Would we (would *I—never mind about Susan!*) feel shy with another authority in the classroom? How *did* one divide pedagogical authority?

We parted for the summer planning to reread every text on all our lists, and to search out any secondary sources that might help us make sense of these works individually or as a group. But even after several months of scholarship, we were unprepared for the ways our new syllabus —our new *field*!—would astonish, enthrall, and transform us.

Fall in Bloomington. Slow hot golden days, sometimes too muggy still, with leftover summer. And a double-sized seminar of twenty-four undergraduates—mostly women but including a few men—all excited about this unprecedented class (for such a subject had never before been taught in the department). In the late heat, the classroom was molten with energy.

We began by filling ourselves in on women's history, dittoing (there were no Xeroxes then) numerous extracts from conduct books, advice manuals, classic poems (*Paradise Lost, The Princess, The Angel in the House*). *A woman's whole duty is to please. Her "power is not for rule, not for battle, and her intellect is not for invention or creation, but for sweet orderings." "He for God only, she for God in him."* Tracing social caveats from Milton and Ruskin to the Victorian precepts of Mrs. Sarah Stickney Ellis and the contemporary columns of Ann Landers, Dear Abby, and Miss Manners, we were shaken by how little had changed. Well, but wasn't that Betty Friedan's point? Simone de Beauvoir's?

Translating morals into manners, life into literature, history into what some feminists had started calling "herstory," we were even more shaken. Books we had always read one way—*how, though?*—turned out to have more layers of meaning and more interconnections than we had realized. As we delved more deeply into texts and contexts, we and our students were increasingly fascinated by recurrent images of madness, confinement, rage, fire-and-ice, disease and dis-ease. At first our insights felt weird or even crazy. How could we have spent years as diligent undergraduates and graduate students without learning anything about this body of work we were suddenly encountering, with its compelling motifs and extraordinarily brilliant writing? And how could we not have perceived some of the more disturbing aspects of beloved classics?

Our classroom collaboration saved Susan and me (and our students as well!) from feeling *too* crazy, substituting a sense of what Emily Dickinson called "divine insanity"—really a thrilling clarity of vision—for anger, denial, repression. Indeed, as we experienced Dickinsonian "conversions of the mind," each of us was able to confirm the other's insights, as a shared set of ideas began to build in the room.

Once a major contemporary woman poet visited our campus, and because I was a member of the creative writing faculty I was charged with hosting her. Of course, I immediately arranged for her to make an appearance in our class, and we prepared the students for her arrival with detailed readings of her verse. One young woman artist in the group even made a "soft sculpture"—a beautiful wall hanging—based on a poem we'd read.

Chatting about her work, the poet casually disclosed her obsession with a number of the themes and motifs we were exploring daily. So in response, we eagerly outlined a few of the notions about women's writing that we were beginning to develop. But "I don't write as a woman!" declared our visitor, in a tone half plaintive, half angry.

Then, when the artist knelt before her to present her lovely "sculpture," the poet crankily handed it back, commenting, "I can't see what *that* has to do with my poetry!"

The eye contact in the room was dramatic. And feminists though we were, after our visitor left we began our analysis of her behavior with a reference to one of D. H. Lawrence's most famous adages: "Never trust the artist, trust the tale."[3]

To be sure, we all disagreed now and then on minor exegetical points, but as we planned our classes, Susan and I rehearsed our central perceptions over and over again to each other, testing them, trying them out in different forms. And we were ever more sure that ours was no *folie à deux* but rather a new way of *reading*—through the lens of gender—that was transforming our critical practice.

Within weeks, in fact, we were torn away from our earlier projects in a kind of ekstasis—an escape from the stasis of the usual—that astonished and delighted us, despite the considerable pain and oppression we were unearthing as, for the first time, we studied in detail the lives and works of women throughout history.

What's the use of recounting here the countless things we learned? If you've read *The Madwoman* you know what some of them are, and anyway they're among many things that all the feminist critics of our generation learned. That Jane Austen wasn't a decorous spinster but a complex and subversive thinker. That Elizabeth Barrett Browning wasn't an opium-addicted invalid with cocker-spaniel curls but rather an impassioned feminist and political revolutionary. That the Brontës weren't a trio of lovelorn sisters stranded on a moor but Byronically burning rebels too. That George Eliot wasn't always the paragon of morality and maturity introduced by our professors but herself as conflicted as her often tormented heroines. That Emily Dickinson wasn't "a little home-keeping person" as John Crowe Ransom thought and as we'd been taught, but rather—in Adrienne Rich's words—a kind of "Vesuvius at home."

But if it was exhilarating to confront all this for what felt like the first time (although we weren't by any means the first to learn it), it was also unnerving. History as we had been taught it had been *men's history*: in the words of Austen's Catherine Morland, it was all about "the quarrels of popes and kings, with wars or pestilences in every page, the men all so good for nothing, and hardly any women at all." But now we were uncovering an often oppressive narrative underneath what might be defined as the "master plot." That there were other narratives of oppression too—the histories of slavery, anti-Semitism, economic exploitation, social hierarchy, religious strife of all kinds—we certainly knew. But here were tales of ourselves and our sisters of every race, class, and color, all of whom had been subordinated in one way or another by the very dynamics that shaped gender, family, and society.

Were we crazy? Well, if we were we were glad to be maddened outsiders—like the suffragists or the Amazonian women of many a feminist's dreams. We knew, after all, that we were part of a movement larger than ourselves, one that had been building for centuries. But it helped to have each other: our collaboration confirmed the conversions of the mind we were experiencing.

Collaboration as Risk, Collaboration as Safety

Needless to say, collaboration was risky and strange. For one thing, coauthorship was, and is, rare in the humanities, though it's quite routine in the sciences. How would colleagues, promotion committees, editors, publishers receive a cowritten work? Yet how could either of us manage on her own what had expanded into an enormous project? We'd been jointly electrified by the material we encountered in our class and were seized by thoughts we had evolved together. Together, therefore, we outlined a book titled *The Madwoman in the Attic,* elaborating our argument chapter by chapter. And then, as our special, intensive course came to an end, I started packing up for California, where my husband and children—and ultimately a new job at UC Davis—awaited me.

But even as we wound up our class and began drafting a prospectus for our book, we applied for aid from the NEH and several other granting organizations in an access of hope and excitement, naïvely sure that ideas we ourselves found inspiring would elicit support from major foundations. But two obscure young women scholars proposing to write on a strange new subject (a *female* literary tradition?) must have seemed odd to the readers of our impassioned applications, so no grants were forthcoming and eventually we resigned ourselves to annual appeals for assistance from our own campuses (both of which, to their credit, did come through with clerical help, prompt sabbaticals, and summer research stipends). And in the meantime, our collaboration itself acted as a kind of safety net, helping us to risk and survive a round of rejections.

Thus, uncertified by the NEH or the ACLS, we embarked on our book immediately, two thousand miles away from each other, exchanging drafts by tedious snail mail (no email then) and accumulating, as well, huge phone bills. We wrote on typewriters (no computers then) in between changing diapers (Susan) and ferrying children to after-school programs (me), while our husbands pitched in at supermarkets and softball games. We traveled from the West Coast to the heart of the country to the East Coast and back west, seeking places to meet and edit our work. Finally we finished the book, in a fever of discovery, just a few years after we began it.

In the meantime, we had become official (public) feminists, speaking on campuses and at a range of conferences. And that too was sometimes risky. I remember feeling anxious—even shyer than I had when I began team-teaching with Susan—the day I first identified myself openly, in a class or a meeting, as a *political* thinker on the subject of sexual poetics. Scholars of my generation had been trained by the New Criticism to believe in the neutrality of literary interpretation; now I was confessing to partisanship and to an especially controversial belief that the personal and the poetical are both political, indeed a belief that gender politics shapes culture. But I felt sure the work we were doing was worth any risk—and besides, there was an exhilarating safety in the collaborative way we could shield, guard, and nurture each other as we developed our mutual thoughts.

Feminists on the road, both literally and figuratively: were we anything much like the Second Wave stereotypes we've read about? Well, we weren't seventies fashion plates, though we wore our share of miniskirts and pantsuits. I used lipstick, Susan didn't. She used eyeliner, I didn't. I still shaved my legs but don't remember whether she did. A picture on an old copy of *The Madwoman* shows two serious, bespectacled, long-haired scholars with mugs of coffee, pens, and notebooks. Still no computers! But becoming a feminist together.

Collaboration as Performance, Collaboration as Play

When collaboration "works," commented W. H. Auden in a line I've used as an epigraph here, "you form a single writer who is different from either writer alone." But who is that writer and how does she come into existence? Such a process of development is what I'm referring to when I speak of "becoming *a* feminist together." Still, to those who haven't done collaborative work, this phrase may appear needlessly cryptic or even mystical. What does it mean, how does it *feel*, to be "inside" the collaboration?

Even my use of the preposition "inside" has a mystical edge, doesn't it? And yet, as Auden's sentence suggests, a collaboration is a kind of costume or mask out of which two voices speak as one, and it isn't surprising that those "outside" the mask should wonder how two individual thinkers unite within it, even if—or perhaps especially when—they disagree.

I'm thinking, of course, about collaborators working in the same genre. Those who work in different genres—Gilbert and Sullivan, Rodgers and Hammerstein, Strauss and von Hofmannsthal, Picasso and Cocteau—have their own problems juggling the priorities of words and music or text and images. But at least each can claim a separate expertise. Two writers writing together are stranger still, and it is they who have to become "a single writer who is different from either writer alone" (for Auden was clearly reflecting on the opera libretti and translations he produced in collaboration with Chester Kallman).

I can't know how Auden and Kallman became "a single" librettist and translator together, but I have some ideas about how Susan and I became a feminist together. To begin with, team-teaching was vital because it meant getting over the inhibitions so many instructors, especially beginning ones, have about colleagues in the classroom. To plan a class together was in a way to plan a performance together, surfacing intellectual premises and orchestrating pedagogical strategies, agreeing in advance on at least a few overall arguments. But to *teach* a class was of course, as it always is, to *improvise* while performing, thinking things out together and with our students as we went along. Then, given the overwhelming sense of discovery the course was generating, it was perhaps inevitable that we would begin by teaching—that is, performing and improvising—for each other, outside the classroom. Over coffee or drinks, lunch or dinner, while driving or shopping, we would interrupt each other with new sentences, new chapter ideas, new beginnings or endings of paragraphs. Sometimes after class a conversation would just keep on going as I accompanied Susan to the supermarket and back to her house for a meal with her, her husband, and baby Molly. Sometimes when we were back home we'd call each other with another insight, a different point to make.

Inevitably, once I returned to California and we began serious work on our manuscript, a lot of our collaboration was textual. Separately we drafted chapters we'd outlined together, then edited each other's writing, scribbling in revisions and marginalia. For teachers of writing, this was a familiar process, although it was significantly less familiar to be editing the words of a colleague. But by now we had slowly begun to realize that these were words for which we were both going to be responsible, words of the feminist critic that we were becoming together.

And then, when we were in the same place at the same time, the mutual editing gradually evolved into joint composition, a change in the creative mode that at first seemed subtle but was ultimately quite radical. Of course, introspection on such a matter isn't only difficult, it can be deceptive, so a lot of what I observe here is hypothetical, though it feels real.

Hypothesis: we weren't just team-teaching to and for each other, we were performing for each other, and playing with ideas together. Sometimes, when our work went well, the piling up of paragraph-after-paragraph might feel almost comically exhilarating. We were a vaudeville act, performing privately for an audience of two! But sometimes, when argumentation was a struggle, research was painful, our subject matter deeply disturbing, we were two analysands analyzing each other's words, therapists doing therapy together and for each other.

Hypothesis: the mask of collaboration that settled over us—the two-in-one of Gilbert-and-Gubar—was both enabling and constraining, fun and scary. Now we were both to blame for what either of us said, now we would succeed together or fail together. Yet by the time we finished *The Madwoman in the Attic* and began work on new volumes—especially *The War of the Words,* volume one of *No Man's Land,* but also several period introductions in *The Norton Anthology of Literature by Women*—we were producing long texts together, as a "single writer" quite "different from either writer alone."

Collaboration as Complicity? As Loss? As Gain?

Dictionary definitions of "collaboration" begin with the obvious "to work, one with another; cooperate, as on a literary work"—but as is well known they also include, more ominously, "to cooperate, usually willingly, with an enemy nation, esp. with an enemy occupying one's country"; the Vichy government of France during World War II is the most dramatic example of such collaboration. But how, after all, could Susan and I be considered collaborators in that second, malevolent sense? Neither was an enemy nation, neither "occupied" the other in a military sense. Nor were we in any way "collaborating" with an external foe.

Or were we? From the point of view of some feminist activists, especially young Third Wave women, academic feminism itself might seem to be a contradiction in terms involving some sort of "collaboration" with the patriarchal system of which the institutionalized "Ivory Tower" is a part. Writes Jessica Valenti, the author of *Full Frontal Feminism,* "When I started coming home from grad school with ideas and theories that I couldn't talk to [my mother] about, academic feminism ceased to be truly useful for me. I think feminism should be accessible to everybody, no matter what your education level. And while high theory is pretty fucking cool, it's not something everyone is going to relate to."[4]

Well, we *were* trying to write for our mothers—and our daughters—as well as each other, and we were writing books about books in the belief that not only is the poetical the political and the personal, but, more generally, the textual is the cultural and the cultural is the textual. The academy, after all, is where minds are shaped, consciousnesses expanded—raised or (as I earlier rather bleakly wrote) lowered. That said, however, I do remember feeling that the risks and rewards of feminist literary collaboration, like those of feminist teaching, were serious. On the one hand, we risked cooptation by what we ourselves had learned to call (following Gertrude Stein) the "patriarchal poetics" of the academy: its mystifications, its jargon, its elitism. On the other hand, though we might not have been marching and chanting, we were definitely offending some colleagues, mostly male but a few female, just as if we were waving placards in the classroom. The mildest reproof I got came from a famous woman philosopher on my campus who took me aside and murmured, "What's a smart girl like you doing writing about Charlotte Brontë? Why don't you study *Wordsworth*?!"

The hostility of male academics was more actively belligerent, and boiled down, as my husband observed at the time, to two main complaints:

MY wife doesn't feel that way!

and *MEN suffer too!*

We were academics, yes, but we weren't collaborating with those particular colleagues, and we felt a lot like political activists, even though our subversive efforts were centered in our studies and in the countless restaurants and coffeehouses where we met to draft our ideas.

Of course, collaboration was also a risk because both took the blame for anything our judges or critics disliked whereas we weren't always separately credited for some of our ideas because, as I've noted, humanists weren't used to collaboration while promotion committees heavily weighted with scientists tended to ask (as is the custom in the sciences), *What percent of this did YOU contribute and what percent of this did SHE contribute?* We both wanted to say *one hundred percent!* but had to content ourselves, alas, with what I might here call the patriarchal mathematics of *fifty percent.*

And as Jennifer Baumgardner and Amy Richards write in their coauthored *Manifesta: Young Women, Feminism, and the Future*, collaboration is still professionally problematic: *plus ça change, plus c'est la même chose?* "Important books aren't cowritten, you know," Baumgardner reports a well-known "Second Waver" admonishing her.[5]

But seriously, putting aside questions of career management. What is the "loss" in collaboration? Clearly, if we go back to my epigraph from Auden, it's the sacrifice of the *single* voice of "either writer alone." Solitude has its privileges and prizes, both for the ego and the imagination. To sacrifice those is to sacrifice, at least temporarily, part of the self, as one merges with the other. And some gender theory suggests that male writers have more difficulty with such sacrificial merging in collaborative writing. Nancy Chodorow's well-known work on the "fluid" boundaries between mothers and daughters implies, for instance, that women might find the process rather less threatening than men do.[6] But women are competitive too, needless to say, so perhaps a peril of collaboration is not so much the loss of ego satisfaction as it is the danger of conflict between the individual ego that longs for praise and the newly created "third" self that seeks its own gratifications. And if the single ego loses something, what does the collaborative self gain? And what does the single ego gain as it fuses with the collaborative self?

Another hypothesis: in becoming "a single writer who is different from either writer alone" one has the unique and astonishing opportunity to step out of the staleness of the self and become an *other,* together with an other, in a new and constraining but paradoxically also liberating mask. Susan and I didn't become ineradicably Gilbert-and-Gubar. We have always written separately, are doing so now, and always will. But whenever we reach back into the different, complex self of our thirty-year collaboration, we're enriched, ineradicably in fact, by the surprising person we were, for a while, able to become. And in our apartness? This may sound speculative, even mystical, but I suspect each of us is still somewhere inhabited by that third self—a kind of Gilbert-Gubar ghostwriter—who sometimes inspires and sometimes criticizes our individual writings: a collaborator who has become, now and then, a muse for each of us, the one who reminds us of how we two became a feminist together.

FINDING ATLANTIS

Thirty Years of Exploring Women's Literary Traditions in English

They were drowned for centuries, yet, in the long sleep of the drowned, women of letters never stopped whispering to each other, whispering and calling, each in her own shell, with their secret undersea voices, though often in different languages or accents and distinctive grammars. And their conversations, debates, discussions, often turned to the same, ancient questions. *When will we see the light of day? How shall we rise to the surface?* Should *we rise or should we remain hidden, in these shadowy depths?*

Here, in an early place on the lost continent, was Christine de Pizan, one of the first to speak. Passionate in the *Querelle des femmes,* she took the side of women from the start of her career and earned a good living doing that. Indeed, a widow at twenty-five, she supported her family with (among her other writings) polemics denouncing the misogyny of Jean de Meun, whose continuation of Guillaume de Loris' *Roman de la Rose* shadowed Guillaume's mystical idealization of the flower of femininity with scurrilous attacks on woman as vile, vulgar, corrosively shrewish.

How to combat such vituperation? How, even, to argue against idealization that transported woman to the stars, denying her the full

24

humanity of her complex mind, her yearning flesh? In the end, thought Christine, the only thing to do was to build a *Cité des Dames*—a City of Ladies—as the spirit of "Reason" whom she met in a vision commanded her to do, declaiming, "Get up, daughter! Without waiting any longer, let us go to the Field of Letters. There the City of Ladies will be founded on a flat and fertile plain, where all fruits and freshwater rivers are found and where the earth abounds in all good things." And as Christine "began to excavate and dig," following the marks of Reason "with the pick of cross-examination," she decided that "the more women have been wrongfully attacked, the greater waxes the merit of their glory." Still, she couldn't help wondering why so many "different authors have spoken against women in their books," and why, she wondered too, were so many girls denied the education that would strengthen them for combat against misogynistic onslaughts. "I realize," declared Christine,

> that women have accomplished many good things, and that even if evil women have done evil . . . the benefits accrued and still accruing because of good women—particularly the wise and literary ones and those educated in the natural sciences . . . outweigh the evil. Therefore, I am amazed by the opinion of some men who claim that they do not want their daughters, wives, or kinswomen to be educated because their mores would be ruined as a result.

But her shrewd counselor replied that "not all opinions of men are based on reason," for why should anyone suppose that "*mores* necessarily grow worse from knowing the moral sciences, which *teach* the virtues"? (emphasis added). Indeed, observing that "moral education amends and ennobles" its pupils, Reason reminded Christine of historical women whose thoughtful fathers ("Quintus Hortensius, a great rhetorician," "Giovanni Andrea, a solemn law professor") educated their daughters (respectively Hortensia and Novella) and thereby made them into models of womanhood, or what came to be called "women worthies."[1]

Like many other female rebels who were to come after her, Christine amassed a dream army of such women "worthies," with whom she planned to populate the city-state she longed to build. And, like most of her other writings, the pages on which she transcribed her carefully justified plans for this utopia were widely read for more than a century in their stately antique French. Until somehow—but why?—her words sank into the sea of seeming oblivion that we could define as the West's cultural unconscious and lodged on the edge of the lost continent where her literary sisters were also to leave their hopes and protests.

Yes, women seeking precursors did search those depths and hear echoes of Christine's speech, as if through some sort of feminist radar. "The [early Renaissance] revival of learning had its influence upon woman," noted the American suffragist Matilda Joslyn Gage in the nineteenth century, adding that "we find in the early part of the fourteenth century a decided tendency toward a recognition of [female] equality. Christine of Pisa, the most eminent woman of this period, supported a family of six persons by her pen, taking high ground on the conservation of morals."[2] Yet for some five hundred years after Christine's death, the visionary work in which she outlined her scheme for illuminating the hidden history of a female Atlantis was out of print. Indeed, with considerable hauteur the magisterial Gustave Lanson omitted her from his classic *Histoire de la littérature française,* explaining in 1923 that

> *We will not stop to consider the excellent Christine de Pisan, a good girl, good wife, good mother, and moreover a veritable bluestocking, the first of that insufferable lineage of women authors . . . who have no concern but to multiply the proof of their tireless facility, equal to their universal mediocrity.*

In her own country and elsewhere, therefore, the prolific and richly learned author of the *Cité des Dames* was, as a more recent critic has put it, labeled "a second-rate bluestocking" until "the last few decades" when her "now admired" works have come to "occupy their deserved place in the literary canon."[3]

This reevaluation began when in 1975 Maureen Curnow, a student at Vanderbilt University, offered an Old French version of *The Book of the City of Ladies* as her Ph.D. dissertation. The work then appeared in an English translation in 1982 (but not in French until the millennial year

2000). Ironically, then, the *Cité des Dames* may be considered, in a way, the capital of exactly the sunken continent its author longed to bring to light, and whose streets she had sought to fill with distinguished citizens. At the time when Christine was writing most of these women came from classical and biblical history, but if this utopian thinker had been able to peer into the future she would have seen that many others were to emigrate to her *cité* from English-speaking nations across the channel or the ocean.[4]

These more recent émigrées are the women of letters whose works my coauthor and coeditor, Susan Gubar, and I first analyzed in *The Madwoman in the Attic,* a book we began to research thirty years ago, in 1975 (coincidentally, the year Curnow completed her pioneering dissertation on *The City of Ladies*). After *The Madwoman* appeared in print Susan and I started collecting texts by an even greater range of literary women, and we represented many of these in successive editions of *The Norton Anthology of Literature by Women: The Traditions in English.* Now, even while we're completing a third edition of this anthology, we're in the midst of compiling a sister collection entitled *Feminist Literary Theory and Criticism: A Norton Reader.* Perhaps, therefore, after decades of work, we can note with some confidence that the contours of at least one lost continent of literature by women have been (if only tentatively) mapped.

If that is so, we certainly haven't been the only explorers of this continent. In fact, we are deeply indebted to countless intrepid poets, novelists, essayists, scholars, and critics who have charted paths for us and for others like us. In a sense, Christine might be considered one of the very first of these. The nature of her feminism has been much debated; indeed a few historians doubt that she was in any significant sense what we would now consider a "feminist." Some advocates for women, for instance, wonder whether Christine overemphasized the more suffocating qualities of female "virtue" and if her notions of the proper education for women were stiflingly dutiful. Yet as Maureen Quilligan has perhaps most definitively shown, Christine was surely as proto-feminist in her search for literary authority as in her yearning to wield that authority in defining a company of women who could properly populate her dream city. And the very dream of such a city is surely a feminist one, even if some of the qualities Christine attributed to its citizens occasionally seem problematic from a contemporary perspective.[5]

In fact, I want to argue here that over the last three decades, as the canon of literature by women has gradually emerged from subaqueous shadows, it has become increasingly clear that one of its special characteristics is precisely a sometimes conflicted consciousness of its own specialness. For better or worse, in other words, almost all of the women writers who make up what we would consider a canon of literature by women are notably aware that they inhabit a canon (or continent or city) of literary *women,* a corporate body about which they may have positive or negative feelings but about which they always have *feelings.*

In comparison to this female canon, the mainstream (or shall I say *male* stream or maelstrom?) canon of literary *master*pieces—and that last word is one I use advisedly—is not as a rule marked by such self-consciousness. To be sure, as Harold Bloom has taught us, male writers may understand themselves to be agonistically engaged in struggles with a community of strong paternal precursors, but it's hard to imagine that, for instance, one of Christine's masculine contemporaries would seek to found a City of *Men* in order to justify the propriety of male education to a readership of judgmental *women.* Yet ambivalent justifications of the very idea of a literary canon authored by educated women have certainly long characterized the canon of literary women writing in English, giving it, indeed, its distinct contours *as* a canon. The canon of women's literature is thus a self-reflexive canon that continually attempts to *theorize itself,* a canon formed by a consciousness of its own vexed and often vexing canonicity. And it's for this reason that Christine, a speaker of Old French, can be said to function for English-language women writers (and for her French descendants) as a paradigmatic theorist of "our" canon.

But now I want to complicate my argument a bit by turning to an account of the ways in which my own understanding of the canon of women's literature has evolved over the years as Susan Gubar and I have worked on a series of different projects focused on delineations of this body of writing. I say "my" understanding but I should of course note that so many of my explorations of the emerging continent of female-authored literature have been undertaken in collaboration with Susan that my own grasp of the material is really almost impossible to disentangle from what I have learned with and from her. And I should note further that although I use the word "evolved," I don't necessarily mean to imply a teleology, as if our present sense of literature by women constitutes a "divine event" toward which the whole of academic "creation" has inexorably moved over the last thirty years. On the contrary, like everyone else who has reflected on the concept of canonicity, I realize that what we consider a canon of "great" or "enduring" works is always provisional and problematic. As the history of Christine's critical reception suggests, however, some canons are usually more provisional and problematic than others—and those are usually the canons of writing produced by women (although they are often, too, the canons of literature by other socially subordinated groups, for instance—in the United States and Britain—non-white, immigrant, and working-class writers).

As might be expected when one first catches sight of a lost continent, our first view of the sunken Atlantis that is the female literary tradition was itself provisional and problematic—or, to press the metaphor further, so dimly lit and fragmentary that we didn't actually understand that what we were looking at might be figured as a continent. But here and there in the darkness of our own ignorance we saw flares of light along with faint lines—hidden roadways?—connecting them, and slowly realized, with considerable surprise and excitement, that we were studying what might be considered a new geography.

If I translate this imagery into a practical account of how Susan and I perceived the canon of women's literature in English when we began researching and writing *The Madwoman in the Attic,* I'd have to remind you that in the seventies the continent of this canon had barely been mapped by any serious contemporary scholars. We ourselves first came to the job because in those days, when the so-called Second Wave of the women's movement had just begun to gather strength, English departments were being pressured by interested students and faculty to offer courses in the "new" subject of literature by women. The two of us volunteered to team-teach such a class, and since we were as unfamiliar with the very idea of a female literary canon as almost everyone else, we chose to organize our syllabus around "major" works by "major" authors—i.e., the best-known works by the best-known women writers, works that would seem already to have been canonized, albeit in the male stream/maelstrom of "master"pieces. And it was in the light cast by these works that we knew they constituted the outline of an *other* different canon, even while they also belonged to one or more male-dominated "main"streams.

The women of letters whose novels and poems we taught, researched, and analyzed in these early years were obvious choices for any neophytes: Jane Austen (*Emma, Persuasion, Northanger Abbey*), Mary Wollstonecraft (*Maria, or The Wrongs of Woman, A Vindication of the Rights of Woman*), Mary Shelley (*Frankenstein*), Charlotte Brontë (*Jane Eyre*), Emily Brontë (*Wuthering Heights*), George Eliot (*The Mill on the Floss*), Emily Dickinson (*Selected Poems*), Christina Rossetti (*Goblin Market*), Charlotte Perkins Gilman ("The Yellow Wallpaper"), Virginia Woolf (*A Room of One's Own*), Tillie Olsen ("Tell Me a Riddle"), Sylvia Plath (*Ariel*), Adrienne Rich (*Diving into the Wreck*). As one of the first reviewers of *The Madwoman* rather caustically remarked, we had concentrated on the literary giants who could be considered the mountain ranges of our emerging continent, ignoring the plains, the foothills, the valleys, so our sense of topography was incomplete.

Yet even within this incomplete topography we could discern significant patterns, recurring themes, and obsessive motifs that brought our authors together in a coherent landscape. We discussed these in *The Madwoman*: a preoccupation with raging fire and repressive ice that a number of women writers shared; a repeated psychodrama of enclosure and escape that many persistently outlined, in verse and prose, fiction and meditation; a trope or plot of uncontrollable madness that often disrupted even the smoothest, seemingly "sanest" of texts; and perhaps most interesting, a frequently reiterated "anxiety of authorship" that continually put the whole female literary project in question. In fact, as I look back now on the ways in which our study of the canon produced by English-speaking women of letters has expanded over the years, I'd say that this last "anxiety" has all along indicated the self-reflexive need of this special canon to continually theorize itself and its own specialness.

What do I mean when I refer to this need for some sort of female self-theorizing as it manifests itself in the writings of such women as Austen, Brontë, Dickinson, and the other "mountainous" figures I listed earlier? To begin with, I don't mean to suggest that many of these writers were producing what we would now consider sophisticated literary theory of the sort that, forming a canon of its own, has been collected recently in *The Norton Anthology of Literary Theory and Criticism,* although two authors I've mentioned here—Christine de Pizan and Mary Wollstonecraft—are indeed included in that text. But I do mean to say that even our earliest and most tentative efforts to define a female canon were facilitated by the ways in which, as we soon saw, *all* the women writers we studied were always struggling to define their own identity as *women* writers. In private writings and public texts, for instance, many of the apparently mainstream poets and novelists we studied frequently commented—sometimes defensively, sometimes apologetically, sometimes angrily—on their status as writers and thus, either explicitly or implicitly, on their relationship to what Elaine Showalter has called (following John Stuart Mill) "a literature of their own"—which is to say, *a canon of their own.*

To begin with, when we first tried to analyze the effects of authorial anxiety on women writers, we noticed that, not surprisingly, many were engaged in a search *for* rather than a struggle *against* precursors. Matilda Joslyn Gage, whose homage to Christine de Pizan I noted earlier, was of course a feminist activist, but even before there was a significant women's movement women of letters were seeking to uncover and justify a history of their own through meditations on both genre and tradition. Early in the nineteenth century, for instance, Jane Austen exuberantly defended the largely female-authored novel in a self-reflexive scene in *Northanger Abbey,* denouncing a hypothetical young lady who comments "with affected indifference or momentary shame" that she is "only" reading a novel: "It is only Cecilia or Camilla or Belinda; or, in short, only some work in which the greatest powers of the mind are displayed, in which the most thorough knowledge of human nature, the happiest delineation of its varieties, the liveliest effusions of wit and humour, are conveyed to the world in the best-chosen language." More wistfully, in the mid-nineteenth century Elizabeth Barrett Browning confessed her hunger for the words of poetic precursors, declaring, "England has had many learned women . . . and yet where are the poetesses? . . . I look everywhere for grandmothers and see none." A few decades later, Emily Dickinson defined Barrett Browning herself as such an empowering ancestress, confessing that "I think I was enchanted / When first a sombre Girl / I read that Foreign Lady." And of course in the twentieth century Virginia Woolf was to theorize such yearnings as these in her famous observation that "we think back through our [literary] mothers, if we are women."[6]

Like Christine's search for women "worthies" with whom to populate her city, these efforts at self-validation through the construction of a sufficient literary community were obviously straightforward attempts at canon-formation. Yet they were often shadowed by rather different and surprisingly negative visions of a female literary tradition that were, I think, equally significant as efforts to comprehend and comment on a canon of literature by women, a canon that was sometimes more troubling than it was triumphant. Among the nineteenth-century authors we examined, many were sometimes notably self-deprecating in their often brief and hesitant statements of their own aesthetic aspirations, and this was even true of writers like Austen and Dickinson who had recorded their fascination with a community of precursors.

Best known, perhaps, are comments from Austen and Charlotte Brontë, both of whom on one occasion or another diplomatically downplayed literary ambition. Austen referred to her own work as "a little bit (two Inches wide) of Ivory, on which I work with so fine a brush as to produce little effect after much labour," satirized the novels of Mrs. Radcliffe and other Gothic romancers in *Northanger Abbey,* and cast her high-spirited imaginative Emma as a self-deluding weaver of flighty, self-indulgent fantasies. In response to Robert Southey's infamous assertion that "literature cannot be the business of a woman's life; and it ought not to be," Charlotte Brontë assured him, "I have endeavored . . . to observe all the duties a woman ought to fulfill," although, she added, "in the evenings, I confess, I do think, but I never trouble any one else with my thoughts." And even in her own journals she was uneasy about her imaginative compulsions, noting in her Roe Head Diary that she longed to "quit for a while" the "burning clime" of what she elsewhere called the "infernal world" of Angria, where she had "sojourned too long." By implication, both these writers were recording their sense that the female-authored canon was, on the one hand, comically Gothic or infernally desirous, and, on the other hand, modest, miniature, self-effacing.[7]

Similarly self-deprecating apologies for authorship, sometimes coupled with efforts at affiliation with *masculinity* rather than *femininity,* marked aesthetic statements by such other major writers as Shelley, Eliot, Dickinson, and Rossetti. Shelley, as you'll recall, introduced an edition of *Frankenstein* by nervously attempting to explain "how I, then a young girl, came to think of, and to dilate upon, so very hideous an idea." Writing to her brother William, Christina Rossetti conceded that "the world you and yours frequent" is "delightful, noble, memorable," but insisted that she herself was "well content in my shady crevice: which crevice enjoys the unique advantage of being to my certain knowledge the place assigned me." Dickinson, of course, claimed that "Publication" was as "foreign" to her "as Firmament to Fin," implicitly defining herself as a creature of subaqueous shadows rather than soaring ambition, while also expressing scorn for "Publication" as an "auction" of the mind. To her earliest intellectual mentor, Dr. Robert Brabant, Mary Anne Evans— eventually to become George Eliot—the magisterial novelist-to-be humbly defined herself as "Deutera" (which, she explained, "*means* second and *sounds* a little like daughter").[8]

Among the seventeenth- and eighteenth-century poets we researched as we worked on *The Madwoman* and with whom we became increasingly familiar in the next phase of our scholarship as we sought texts for inclusion in *The Norton Anthology of Literature by Women,* we uncovered comparably—and in some cases even more excessively—modest aesthetic self-definitions. Anne Bradstreet, though defined by her publisher as *The Tenth Muse, Lately Sprung Up in America,* anxiously assured her readers that she asked only for a domestically savory "thyme or parsley wreath," rather than manly "bays," modestly arguing that "this mean and unrefined ore of mine / Will make [men's] glist'ring gold but more to

shine." The aristocratic Anne Finch, Countess of Winchilsea, while pro-
testing the "mistaken rules" that had cast women poets in a subordinate
role, nevertheless apologized for her "crampt Numbers" and resolved
that she would "with contracted wing, / To some few friends, and to
[her] sorrow sing." Another aristocrat, Margaret Cavendish, Duchess of
Newcastle, noted that "it cannot be expected" that she "should write so
wisely or wittily as men, being of the effeminate sex, whose brains nature
has mixed with the coldest and softest elements."[9]

Similarly, though Aphra Behn's plays were the toast of Restoration
England, she complained that "poor woman" has been "debarred from
sense and sacred poetry." Even in the twentieth century this implicit
description of a female literary canon as modestly subordinate persisted.
Virginia Woolf—arguably the first major modern feminist critic—
decided that "a woman's sentence" has yet to be written while also noting that among women writers poetry "is still denied outlet." Three
decades later, the brilliant and ambitious poet Sylvia Plath informed
her mother that she was "happy" her poet-husband Ted Hughes had
"*his* book . . . accepted *first*." Taken together as a kind of corporate self-
definition, these guarded statements subtly say: Yes, we want to write,
we *do* write, but don't worry, because we're women we don't want to
write *that* much, and we certainly can't write that *well*. Just as woman
is a secondary creature, created from Adam's rib, ours is a secondary
canon, always as aware of its own inferiority as of its own potential
impropriety.[10]

Explicit definitions of the canon were equally problematic. Where
early feminist polemicists had followed Christine in urging women to
educate themselves by reading texts that would educate them in morality (as opposed to sentimental romances, most of which were presumably penned by women) a number of women writers defined a female
literary canon by attacking it. Most famously, perhaps, George Eliot
mounted a scathing assault on "Silly Novels by Lady Novelists." Here,
much as Austen had done in *Northanger Abbey* and in an even earlier,
parodic *Plan of a Novel,* the author of such ambitious works as *The Mill
on the Floss* and *Middlemarch,* comically demolished what she called
"the mind-and-millinery school" of romance in which "the lover has

a manly breast; . . . hearts are hollow . . . friends are consigned to the tomb; . . . the sun is a luminary that goes to his western couch [and] life is a melancholy boon." Even more strikingly, however, this deeply philosophical writer commented with special acrimony on "the *oracular* species" of novel, a genre produced by women who consider themselves equipped to address "the knottiest moral and speculative questions":

> *Apparently, their recipe for solving all such difficulties is something like this: —Take a woman's head, stuff it with a smattering of philosophy and literature chopped small, and with false notions of society baked hard, let it hang over a desk a few hours every day, and serve up hot in feeble English . . . You will rarely meet with a lady novelist of the oracular class who is diffident of her ability to decide on theological questions . . . and pity philosophers in general that they have not had the opportunity of consulting her.*

A century later, in the same mode, Plath, who claimed that she wanted to be "the Poetess of America," insisted that her verse wouldn't be "quailing and whining like Teasdale or simple lyrics like Millay." Rather, she wished to be "drunker than Dylan, harder than Hopkins, younger than Yeats in my saying" (even while she presumably wanted her husband to be still "drunker," "harder," and "younger").[11]

Again, implicit in these assertions is a definition of the female literary canon as secondary and even—here—*polluted* or *contaminated* by an inescapable, and inescapably *feminine,* weakness. For both of these women, the only resolution of this dilemma is a flight into masculinity. In Eliot's case (as in those of George Sand; Currer, Ellis, and Acton Bell; and countless other women writers), this flight was literalized in the adoption of a male pseudonym, while Plath metaphorized such a flight in the rhetoric of her aspiration to be "harder than Hopkins, younger than Yeats," etc. But in either case, like so many other women of letters, these writers were defining themselves as secretly male, assuming that the masculine *is* the "human" while the feminine is somehow, as Dorothy Sayers once sardonically put it, "the human less than human." With Aphra Behn, all were longing for a space in which to express the creativity of what Behn called "my masculine part the Poet in me." In this mode, Emily Dickinson too frequently postulated a fictive but powerful male self, at one point defining herself as "Uncle Emily" and at another remembering a childhood when "Ourself" was "a boy." Indeed, in her theory of imaginative androgyny, even Virginia Woolf suggested that she too felt the "masculine part" somehow necessary to the "poet" in any woman, and it's not insignificant that her radiant *Orlando* incarnates English literary history in a figure who is male from the originatory age of Shakespeare to the eighteenth century, even though "he" becomes a "she" in the era of Pope. The primordial artist, Woolf's narrative suggests, is masculine.[12]

To be sure, especially in the twentieth century there have been quite a few women writers who firmly insisted on the genderlessness of the artist's mind. In working on *The Norton Anthology of Literature by Women*, Susan and I have in fact been required to publish statements by two notable poets declaring their disapproval of the very concept of a *female* literary tradition or canon. Elizabeth Bishop's executor asked us to include a statement the poet made in a letter to a friend declaring that "undoubtedly gender does play an important part in the making of any art, but art is art and to separate writings, paintings, musical compositions, etc., into two sexes is to emphasize values in them that are *not* art." More recently, the estate of Laura Riding Jackson, noting that an anthology of women's literature was "a type of compilation" Riding found "demeaning," has requested that we print the following assertion:

> *I regard the treatment of literary work as falling into a special category of women's writing as an offence against literature as of a human generalness, and an offence against the human identity of women. I refuse every request made of me to contribute to, participate in, such a trivializing of the issues of literature, and oppose this categorization in public commentary, as I can.*[13]

Reviewing this range of female stances toward the very notion of a female literary tradition, it seems to me that, paradoxically enough, *all* together—even, or perhaps especially, in their confusions and contradictions—define a distinctive canon of women's literature. Again, here, let's imagine if any of these positions toward a gendered community of art could have been or could still now be adopted by *male* writers.

Would Robert Browning worry that he "looked everywhere" for poetic grandfathers and "found none"? Would James Joyce need to assert that "we think back through our fathers, if we are men"?

Would Percy Shelley have felt obliged to explain why *he*, "then a young man," "came to think of, and to dilate upon, so very hideous an idea" as a play depicting the travails of a hero condemned to have his liver eternally devoured by vultures? Would Walt Whitman have claimed that the idea of "Publication" was "foreign" to him? Would Dryden, Pope, or Tennyson have apologized for "crampt Numbers"?

Would Dickens or Carlyle have complained about *men* who try to solve knotty philosophical questions by noting that if you "take a [man's] head" and "stuff it with a smattering of philosophy and literature chopped small," you'll end up with a bunch of "silly novels" by "gentleman novelists"?

Harold Bloom's notion of the male poet's dependence on a female muse notwithstanding, would Milton or Wordsworth have declared that their verse was produced by their "feminine part the Poet in me"?

And indeed would Pound or Eliot, Lawrence or Hemingway have refused to be represented in anthologies of entirely male-authored literature (as they often were) on the grounds that such representation was "an offence against literature as of a human generalness, and an offence against the human identity of *men*"?

I need hardly note that these rhetorical questions about the authors of masterpieces whose works are customarily considered staples of the English-language literary canon suggest once again the singularity of a *female*-authored canon whose contours are shaped by anxieties, apologies, and protests. So far, however, I've pointed to few moves by English-speaking women critics and writers that could be considered, like Christine's establishment of a *Cité des Dames,* conscious attempts at canon formation. But as Susan and I progressed from work on *The Madwoman* and *The Norton Anthology of Literature by Women* to research for *Feminist Literary Theory and Criticism: A Norton Reader,* it became increasingly clear to us that the vintage 1970s feminist critics like ourselves who were flung onto the shores of academe by the Second Wave of the women's movement were by no means unique in our *own* canon—i.e., the canon of feminist theorists and critics. Looking everywhere for grandmothers as Barrett Browning had, thinking back through our mothers as Virginia Woolf did, and seeking women worthies the way Christine had, we can now discern four crucial strategies through which women of letters have historically attempted to define, study, and *expand* the canon of literature by women. And, interestingly, all are tactics Christine employed in her proto-feminist polemics.

I'll briefly summarize these while suggesting not only how they've been historically useful to women but also how they remain crucial to contemporary feminists in and out of the university.

First, women of letters have historically struggled to define and strengthen their own literary canon by proposing not just the education but the *re*education of women. Basic education—fundamental literacy —is of course a right for which feminists since Christine have fought. But *re*education not just in basic letters but in rational thought has been equally significant to a long line of feminist thinkers. Christine, as you'll recall, urged that all women should have the kind of access to education that wise fathers gave to such learned women as Hortensia and Novella, arguing that "moral education amends and ennobles" those fortunate enough to be graced with it. In addition, however, the very construction of a *city* or community of women worthies was a radically ambitious pedagogical project designed to inculcate in both women and men the merits of a luminous female history.

From the seventeenth century to the twentieth, Christine's English-speaking descendants outlined similar projects. In 1694 the learned essayist Mary Astell presented in "A Serious Proposal to the Ladies" a plan for "a religious retirement"—really a sort of women's college—where, though men "may resent it, to have their enclosure broke down," women would be "invited to taste of that Tree of Knowledge [men] have so long unjustly *monopoliz'd*." Similarly, in 1792 the polemicist, journalist, and novelist Mary Wollstonecraft contended that women's "faculties" should "have room to unfold," deploring the "folly which the ignorance of women generates." In a somewhat different vein, the African-American writer and educator Anna Julia Cooper argued in the late nineteenth century for "the higher education of women" as an antidote to the "greed and cruelty" of a male-dominated Western culture.

Perhaps most prominently, in 1929 Virginia Woolf devoted much of her classic *A Room of One's Own* to a meditation on female education, famously comparing the poverty and austerity of an Oxbridge women's college to the wealth, ease, and smugness of its brother institution for men. In an earlier work, too—the wistfully utopian essay "A Woman's College from Outside"—Woolf recorded an ecstatic vision of the "miraculous tree [of knowledge] with the golden fruit at its summit" (the same tree toward which Astell was also drawn) that would offer itself to women in a "good world," a "new world."[14] And if we translate this range of sometimes combative, sometimes nearly mystical feminist visions of female education into the recent history of feminism, we can see that the interdisciplinary academic project known as Women's Studies constitutes a comparable effort to teach women (and men too) to understand not only their own dilemmas but also their own potentialities, on the assumption that such instruction is urgently necessary to correct a skewed social order.

But Christine's selections of women worthies for inclusion in her canonical City of Ladies also pioneered a second (and perhaps even more obvious) strategy through which feminists past and present sought to define a canon of their own: by specifically recovering and reevaluating individual women of letters. Again, such recovery of individual "grandmothers" and "mothers" was an enterprise in which, as it turns out, women from the Middle Ages onward were engaged in one way or another, with Margery Kempe recording a life-changing visit to the aging Julian of Norwich, Anne Finch expressing a mixture of admiration and envy toward her precursor Katherine Philips ("the Matchless Orinda"), Jane Austen celebrating the works of Fanny Burney and Maria Edgeworth, and even the sometimes anti-feminist George Eliot affirming the intellectual contributions of Margaret Fuller and Mary Wollstonecraft.

Once more, though, Woolf's ambitions most vividly reiterate Christine's aspirations. Not only in *A Room* but also throughout *The Common*

Reader this exemplary twentieth-century feminist critic excavated and analyzed countless works by women, among them not just canonical novels by Eliot and the Brontës but also such writings as Anne Finch's ode on "The Spleen" and the plays of Aphra Behn—works that had largely fallen into obscurity when Woolf began (re)evaluating them. In offering such readings (not all celebratory but all seriously attentive), she pioneered another significant canon-reforming strategy that has been persistently deployed by contemporary feminists who have sought to reconstitute a canon of literature by women through painstaking research, including the scholarly recovery of forgotten texts and the scrupulous rehabilitation of reputations. Indeed, Christine herself, as I've already noted, was a beneficiary of precisely such recovery and rehabilitation.

Yet even while feminists have long struggled to define a female literary canon by reeducating and rehabilitating women as readers and writers of their own destinies, their efforts have necessarily involved them in a third strategy for canon (re)formation: reeducating readers in general, but especially (it should go without saying) misogynistic male readers. Arguably, almost all of the writings I've discussed so far have been in some sense addressed to men, with the overt or covert goal of—as the Quaker admonition puts it—speaking truth to power. Like the simultaneously apologetic and defiant assertions of such poets as Anne Bradstreet and Anne Finch, a number of these addresses to what female authors fear is an unsympathetic audience tend to be plaintive, even frankly melancholy. Bradstreet, for example, cynically noted that "if what I do prove well, it won't advance, / *They'll* say it's stol'n, or else it was by chance" (emphasis added), even as, remember, she ingratiatingly suggested to male rivals that her "mean and unrefined ore" would make your "glist'ring gold but more to shine." In the same mode, Finch argued that women may be misread because "mistaken Rules" label them "fallen" so that feminine art is inevitably and unhappily considered "insipid, empty, uncorrect."

More recently, however, feminist thinkers have begun to characterize the censorious male reader as himself somehow "fallen" and even, in fact, something of a fool. Virginia Woolf's infamous "Professor von X.," the red-faced and brutal villain of *A Room of One's Own* who investigates "The Mental, Moral and Physical Inferiority of the Female Sex," is perhaps the paradigmatic image of the male reader-as-buffoon, but even before Woolf caricatured this especially obnoxious whipping boy, her precursors had parodied the misogyny of some male reviewers with comparably bitter verve. The nineteenth-century American humorist Fanny Fern (Sarah Willis Parton) was especially adept at such salutary send-ups. Her "Male Criticism on Ladies' Books," together with her mock self-review "*Fresh Leaves,* by Fanny Fern," comically demolished what she called the "shallow, unfair, wholesale, sneering criticism" produced by "*male* spleen" while satirizing the self-satisfied solipsism of masculine authorities who thank "heaven" that "there are still women who *are* women . . . who do not waste floods of ink and paper, browbeating men and stirring up silly women" since woman "never was intended for an irritant" but should be "soft and amalgamating, a necessary but unobtrusive element."[15]

To recognize the need for reeducating male readers, however, is to understand that the apparently *main*stream *male* canon has long been dialectically engaged with a shadowy (because not clearly outlined) *female* canon. In other words, just as the female canon is defined by its own uncertainties and ambiguities, it is also defined by "male spleen." That spleen (which evoked, of course, the answering "Spleen" from which Anne Finch and other women poets suffered) goes back at least as far as Jean de Meun's misogyny and, more specifically, Alexander Pope's splenetic assertion that the "wayward Queen" of spleen rules women "to fifty from fifteen," a comment followed by countless other masculine denunciations of what Nathaniel Hawthorne called "a damned mob of scribbling women."

But to perceive that this dialogue between a foregrounded male canon and a backgrounded female canon has such a long history is to understand, suddenly, how in some sense everyone always secretly or not so secretly realized that the lost continent of the women's literary canon was already *there,* not just in the collective unconscious of our civilization, not just in our civilization's discontents, but also in the more conscious contents of the mind with which both sexes theorize their "cultural capital." Thus, a fourth major strategy through which women critics—especially recent ones—have sought to define their own literary canon has been an excavation and reexamination not just of individual women writers, not just of a female tradition, but of an intricate female and male history reimagined to factor in an overlooked but powerfully influential female-male dialectic. In such revisionary historicizing, the "mainstream"/male stream canon appears as new and different as the formerly subaqueous female canon does. And just as Christine's retorts to her antagonists in the *Querelle des Femmes* suggest the complexity of the conversation in which she was engaged, so quite a few Second Wave feminist writers have long since dramatized their understanding of the ways in which the engendering of our literature is shaped by at least two interlocking canons.

"Diving into the Wreck," a major early work by the American feminist poet-theorist Adrienne Rich, can stand here for a range of writings that seek to explore such a drowned history. In this brilliant quest poem, the speaker describes her exploration of a sunken world in which, unprecedented (carrying "a book of myths / in which / our names do not appear"), she explores "the wreck" peopled by the lost dead bodies of her ancestry: "the mermaid whose dark hair / streams black, the merman in his armored body," and understands that her history—and, implicitly, that of her culture—is constituted out of the dialectic of the two. Noting the necessity of definitional words ("The words are purposes. / The words are maps"), she concedes that "I am she: I am he" yet seeks to surface the mysterious cargo that must still be exhumed. Some of the questions with which I began my own exploration here of a hidden Atlantis might be hers too, or those of her mermaid and merman: *Shall we rise to the surface? Should we rise or should we remain hidden, in these shadowy depths?*[16]

Perhaps, Rich's poem implies, after all this time of sleeping and forgetting we can perceive the underwater continent that is the canon of women's literature as neither wrecked nor lost. Rather, what once seemed to be a wrecked and sunken geography has risen as a "Field of Letters"— a "fertile plain . . . where the earth abounds in all good things."

—2007

WHAT DO FEMINIST CRITICS WANT? OR, A POSTCARD FROM THE VOLCANO

At the risk of revealing something that will be bad for all feminist critics everywhere, I must confess that I have hardly been able to make up my mind what aspect of feminist criticism to discuss for the ADE. I have therefore decided to offer you not a single, unified paper but what may well seem to be three mini-essays, complete with three different (and I think rather impressive) titles: (1) "The Revisionary Imperative: Feminist Criticism and Western Culture"; (2) "Redundant Women: The Economics of Feminist Criticism"; and (3) "Feminist Mysteries: Male Critics and Feminist Criticism."[1]

Before I launch into the first of these "essays," however, let me take a moment to explain my odd self-division, for I'm sure you'll agree that so bizarre a rhetorical strategy does require some justification. To begin with, I should note that when I was first asked to participate in this seminar, I felt not only honored but extraordinarily pleased and excited. I knew that as a feminist critic I was going to have an exceptional opportunity, an opportunity to tell an important audience (which would consist largely of chair*men* rather than of chair*persons*) about the work I do and the field I represent. Few feminist critics have such chances. Indeed, as I complain below, we seem lately to have been left to speak more and

43

more to one another rather than to those of you "out there" whose minds we passionately wish to reach. Thus, flushed with comfortable anticipation, I accepted this opportunity in the most optimistic mood.

Alas, however, my mood soon darkened. For when I began thinking about what I ought to say—discussing the matter with friends, organizing priorities, considering possible titles—my confusion grew. As a representative feminist critic, I must make this occasion count and therefore, so my feminist friends told me and so I heartily agreed, I must not only outline a theory of literary criticism but also summarize a number of crucial moral and political points. Here, in brief and in no special order, are some of the suggestions that were urged on me:

Tell them what we can do for them.
Tell them what they can do for us.
Tell them to hire feminists.
Tell them not to fire feminists.
Tell them about the case of X or the fate of Y (feminists who were
    fired or feminists who weren't hired). Tell them to come to our
    talks.
Tell them to read our books.
Tell them what we do.
Tell them we don't do what they think we do. Tell them why they
    think we do what we don't really do.
Tell them why they think we are what we really aren't. Tell them
    who we really are and what we really do.

Well, I'm sure you can see that such a bewildering proliferation of points made three distinct essays almost inevitable. Each would deal in some sense with a pair of central questions—namely, What do feminist critics want? and, How can English departments give it to them?—or with the converse of those questions—namely, What do English departments want? and, How can feminist critics give it to them? But one of these presentations, the most important in the long run, would have to outline a theory of what feminist critics want philosophically, as a way of thinking about literary texts. A second, perhaps more immediately pressing discussion would have to analyze the politics of what feminist criticism wants from the structural realities of English departments—that is, what jobs and courses it imagines for its proponents. And a third, the most interesting to a social and literary historian like me, would try to bridge the gulf between the first two. This last little essay would have to present, in other words, a kind of sociology or psychohistory of feminist criticism as it has functioned in today's academy, explaining why and how the philosophy underlying this particular critical "ism" has so far had comparatively little effect on such political realities of English departments as hiring, promotion, and curriculum development.

Of course, all these potential discussions do have even more in common than their concern with different aspects of feminist criticism. As some of you may know, an axiom of the women's movement is that the personal is the political: the very title of Kate Millett's influential analysis of feminism and masculinism today—*Sexual Politics*—insists on an inescapable connection between private relationships (bedroom or parlor politics, as it were) and public ones. For feminist critics, however, the axiom can be modified and expanded: not only is the personal the political, the aesthetic is the political, the literary is the political, the rhetorical is the political. In other words, even what appears to be the theoretical cannot easily be disengaged or abstracted from the practical, for every text can be seen as in some sense a political gesture and more specifically as a gesture determined by a complex of assumptions about male-female relations, assumptions we might call sexual poetics.

Perhaps you can most readily see that this is so if you look back and notice the form in which both I and my feminist colleagues conceived of the points my presentation should make: "Tell *them* what we can do for them . . . Tell *them* what we do . . . Tell *them* who we really are." On reflection, doesn't my constant reiteration of the word "them" seem odd? Wouldn't it have been more natural not to dwell so obsessively on the otherness of my audience? Couldn't my friends and I have devised a list that would read, for example, "Describe what we do, explain who we are, analyze our assumptions, defend our poetics," and so forth? Yet I think we all felt it inevitable to list things in terms of what I, representing us, should say to you, representing them. For women's alienation from the sources of power is profound, and I want to argue here that it is not just a personal or a political alienation but that—at least until quite recently—it has also been a philosophical alienation, an aesthetic alienation, a literary alienation.

Ultimately, in fact, it is women's ubiquitous cultural alienation that necessitates what I have called a "revisionary imperative." Thus, as both a problem and a perception, women's otherness is the intellectual center around which my first discussion revolves. For of course women—especially educated women like me, a representative feminist critic—do not seem obviously alienated. On the contrary, in our use of academic tools—texts, techniques, terminology—I imagine we must appear as deeply implicated in cultural/intellectual styles and subjects as our male colleagues are. What, then, do I mean when I speak of the cultural alienation of women and what is this revisionary imperative I insist on as a solution to the problem? I can best begin to answer these questions by telling you one of many stories about my own feminist "conversion."

Ten years ago I had a job interview with an English department chairman who quite unexpectedly confided in the middle of an otherwise ordinary conversation that he was alarmed by the demands of some female graduate students. These radical young women believed that classes ought to be devoted to the study of women—women in literature, literature by women!

"They want to throw out a thousand years of Western culture," he suddenly said.

I was shocked. "Surely not!" I exclaimed.

Looking something like the majestic procession that passes through the third act of *Die Meistersinger,* a thousand years of Western culture paraded across my mind: grave monkish scholars, impassioned poets, thought-worn philosophers, and beautiful stately ladies, all dimly glowing, all holding out faintly imploring hands to me, their heir and guardian. Remember us, they seemed to signal as their noble robes swept by. Don't throw us out!

"Surely," I added (a bit priggishly, I now realize), "we're all equally committed to the preservation of Western culture."

But of course I was wrong. For what feminist criticism and scholarship have taught me in the last ten years is that although we obviously can't "throw out a thousand years of Western culture," we can and must redo our history of those years. Nothing may have been thrown out of that record but something has been left out: "merely," in Carolyn Kizer's ironic understatement, "the private lives of one-half of humanity"—the private lives of women and sometimes their public lives, too.[2] When I say we must redo our history, therefore, I mean we must review, reimagine, rethink, rewrite, revise, and reinterpret the events and documents that constitute it.

I should note here, incidentally, that words beginning with the prefix "re-" have lately become prominent in the language of feminist humanists, all of whom feel that if feminism and humanism are not to be mutually contradictory terms, we must return to the history of what is called "Western culture" and reinterpret its central texts. Virginia Woolf speaks of "rewriting history"; Adrienne Rich notes that women's writing must begin with a "re-vision" of the past; Carolyn Heilbrun observes that we must "reinvent" womanhood; and Joan Kelly declares that we must "restore women to history and . . . restore our history to women."[3] All, I would argue, are articulating the revisionary imperative that has involved feminist critics in a massive attempt to reform "a thousand years of Western culture."

I myself began to experience this revisionary imperative a few years after my interview with that harassed chairman, and at first my revisionary activities seemed minor enough. My nine-year-old daughter was reading *Little Women* and loving it so much that I reread it along with her. A few months later we read/reread *Jane Eyre* and *Wuthering Heights*. Rereadings led to reinterpretations, and my revisionary impulse became so strong that I was delighted when Susan Gubar, a colleague who was also revising her ideas about these books, agreed to team-teach a course in literature by women with me.

Revisionary as we felt, though—and we were both by now reading and rereading key feminist texts—my colleague and I were not entirely prepared for the new view of literary history our classroom reinterpretations revealed. We'd believed, I guess, that women and men participate equally in a noble republic of the spirit and that both sexes are equal inheritors of "a thousand years of Western culture." Rereading literature by both women and men, however, we learned that though the pressures and oppressions of gender may be as invisible as air, they're also as inescapable as air; and, like the weight of air, they imperceptibly shape the forms and motions of our lives. Assumptions about the sexes, we saw, are entangled with some of the most fundamental assumptions Western culture makes about the very nature of culture—that "culture" is male, for example, and "nature" female—and we decided that at least until the nineteenth century, even apparently abstract definitions of literary genres were deeply influenced by psychosocial notions about gender.[4] Again and again, moreover, as we explored such sexual poetics, we encountered definitions of cultural authority and creativity that excluded women, definitions based on the notion that (in the words of Gerard Manley Hopkins) "the male quality is the creative gift."[5] The treasures of Western culture, it began to seem, were the patrimony of male writers, or, to put it another way, Western culture itself was a grand ancestral property that educated men had inherited from their intellectual forefathers, while their female relatives, like characters in a Jane Austen novel, were relegated to modest dower houses on the edge of the estate.

This distinction between male patrimony, on the one hand, and female penury, on the other, can be seen of course in countless self-defining texts by male and female writers. But perhaps quotations from two volcano poems, besides being particularly pertinent right here and now, following the recent eruption of Mount St. Helens, will begin to illustrate both my meaning and my final subtitle. As you may recall, Wallace Stevens' "A Postcard from the Volcano" employs very much the same metaphor of the world as ancestral property that I have just used. Imagining his own and his cohort's extinction by the symbolic Mount St. Helens that annihilates every generation, Stevens prophesies also the imaginings of his heirs, "children picking up [his] bones" who will never entirely comprehend his passions. But these uncomprehending children will inherit a cosmic mansion that has been in some deep way transformed by his language, his literary authority, his power: "We knew for long the mansion's look," he notes, "And what we said of it became // A part of what it is . . . ," adding that when he is gone "Children . . . will say of the mansion that it seems / As if he that lived there left behind / A spirit storming in blank walls."

Emily Dickinson, who wrote many more volcano poems than Stevens did (a point to which I'll return later), had quite a different attitude toward both the mansion of the cosmos and her own Vesuvian presence:

> *On my volcano grows the Grass*
> *A meditative spot*
> *An acre for a Bird to choose*
> *Would be the General thought*
>
> *How red the Fire rocks below*
> *How insecure the sod*
> *Did I disclose*
> *Would populate with awe my solitude.*[6]

For Dickinson, the gulf between appearance and reality is bleaker, blacker, and more unbridgeable than the one Stevens records. Trained and defined as a lady, she is conscious that she herself seems to be a sort of decorous (and marginal) landscape, "a meditative spot" on the edge of the patriarchal estate, a quiet "acre for a Bird to choose." What is unimaginable is her volcanic (and powerful) interiority: the fierce fire, the insecure sod, and the awesomely quaking rock that not only enforce but create her "solitude." Moreover, it is that solitude, so different from Stevens' authoritative wistfulness, which in turn both determines and defines her alienation. Alone, unknown, and unimaginable, she is other and possibly awful to everyone, even to herself.

Reading many texts like these two volcano poems and trying to understand their implications for a sexual poetics (as I have tried to do here in an abbreviated way), I began to have a different vision—literally a re-vision—of "a thousand years of Western culture," that grand procession from *Die Meistersinger.* Those grave scholars, impassioned poets, and thought-worn philosophers were all male; the cosmos was their hereditary home, their ancestral mansion, as it was Stevens', and thus they were the apprentices as well as the lords and masters who marched across Wagner's glittering stage, while the beautiful stately ladies of my vision, like Wagner's Eva, were quite conscious of being their goals, their prizes, the objects of their desire. And if, like the voice that was great within Wallace Stevens or like Wagner's master singers, the men had the power of speech, the women, like Emily Dickinson, knew that they had, or were supposed to have, the graceful obligation of silence.

But what of the women who refused to be silent or who (again, like Dickinson) could not manage an enduring silence? My colleague and I realized that, more than most other participants in a thousand years of Western culture, these women had been forgotten, misunderstood, or misinterpreted. Yet it was they who inspired Virginia Woolf's remark that "towards the end of the eighteenth century a change came about which, if I were rewriting history, I should describe more fully, and think of greater importance than the Crusades or the Wars of the Roses. The middle-class woman began to write."[7]

Significantly, as my colleague and I reread the literature of these women, we saw that what they wrote may have seemed docile enough— may have seemed, indeed, "A meditative spot, / An acre for a Bird to choose"—but that, like Dickinson's work, it was often covertly subversive, even volcanic, and almost always profoundly revisionary. In fact, we came to understand that the revisionary imperative we had experienced was itself both an essential part of the female literary tradition we were attempting to recover and a crucial antidote to the female cultural alienation we were trying to overcome. Thus, as we have argued elsewhere, women writers have frequently responded to sociocultural constraints by creating symbolic narratives that express their common feelings of constriction, exclusion, dispossession.[8]

In these narratives, madwomen like Bertha Mason Rochester function as doubles through whom sane ladies like Jane Eyre (and Charlotte Brontë) can act out fantastic dreams of escape, or volcanic landscapes serve as metaphors through which apparently decorous spinsters like Emily Dickinson can image the eruption of anger into language. But in creating such symbolic narratives these literary women were revising the worldview they had inherited from a society that said women mattered less than men did, a society that thought women barely belonged in the great parade of culture, a society that defined women as at best marginal and silent tenants of the cosmic mansion and at worst guilty interlopers in that house.

Replacing heroes with heroines, these writers insisted, like Jane Eyre, that "women feel just as men feel . . . they suffer from too rigid a constraint . . . precisely as men would suffer." Revising the story of Western culture, they looked at an ordinary woman—a shopgirl, for instance—and declared, with Virginia Woolf, that "I would as soon have her true history as the hundred and fiftieth life of Napoleon or seventieth study of Keats and his use of Miltonic inversion which old Professor Z and his like are now inditing."[9] Creating new accounts of the Creation, they asked, with the eighteenth-century poet Anne Finch, Countess of Winchilsea, "How are we fall'n? fall'n by mistaken rules? / And Education's, more than Nature's fools . . . ?"[10] In other words, over and over again these women writers asked, as we feminist critics did and do, what has caused the cultural alienation—the silence, the marginality, the secondary status—of women.

But of course, to ask and to try to give revisionary answers to such questions about literary women is also to ask and answer questions about literary men, questions about the dynamics of male-female relations in the world of letters, questions about the nexus of genre and gender, questions about the secret intersections of sexuality and textuality. That these questions address long-standing problems and long-established texts is undeniable, and it is equally undeniable that, as I've been insisting, literary women have asked and answered them for centuries. I would also argue, though, that until quite recently such literary questions and answers have been as prudently disguised, as decorously encoded, as all the symbolic and revisionary narratives the female imagination has produced. What may most distinguish the new literary movement called feminist criticism, however, is precisely its effort to bring to consciousness such ancient, half-conscious questions about textuality and sexuality. Indeed, if I were to try to tell you very succinctly what feminist criticism, as a way of thinking about literary texts, wants philosophically (which, as you may recall, was to be my first topic), I would tell you that at its most ambitious it wants to decode and demystify all the disguised questions and answers that have always shadowed the connections between textuality and sexuality, genre and gender, psychosexual identity and cultural authority.

Obviously, or so it seems to me, such an enterprise is profoundly exciting. The impulse to revise our understanding of Western literary history and culture is, after all, energizing (and here I understate the case); as a well-known (male) medievalist remarked to me not long ago, "everything has to be done again," and at the very least our awareness of such a revisionary imperative makes us feminist critics feel needed. Moreover, the questions about sexuality and textuality we have lately decoded or brought to consciousness seem equally invigorating, for all touch on issues that are almost bracingly ontological. What, for instance, could be more fundamental, more a matter of ultimate realities, than an exploration of the relationships between sexual self-definition and literary authority, or an examination of the hidden psychosexual meanings of writing itself, the quintessentially cultural activity that distinguishes us not only from animals but also from one another?

Sadly, however—and here I move into my second essay—many of our male colleagues and students (and a few of our female ones) seem indifferent to the crucial questions that concern us feminist critics; worse, some even seem rather scornful of the excitement our enterprise has generated. Of course, I don't want to generalize too drastically; like every feminist critic, I must confess that some of my best friends are men, for I have a number of male colleagues who not only support and encourage my work (like the medievalist I quoted before) but engage in what I would call feminist criticism themselves. Yet it is nevertheless true—and I imagine I hardly need to document this assertion—that even the word "feminist" often evokes masculinist snickers or worse. Even if we aren't seen as wanting to "throw out a thousand years of Western culture," we are perceived as self-indulgent, trendy, frivolous, polemical, or marginal. Indeed, where Bloomians, Derrideans, Marxists, or Freudians sometimes encounter the rage with which people respond to ideas that seem genuinely threatening (because truly important), we often meet with the kind of scorn people reserve for notions they find boring or irritating (because merely trivial).

In an essay that appeared last year in a special issue of the *ADE Bulletin,* Carolyn G. Heilbrun puts this point so woefully well that I think I can do no better than quote her here: "I, thirty years girl and woman in the field of English studies," she writes, "wonder anew that among all the changes of 'the life and thought of our age,' only the feminist approach has been scorned, ignored, fled from, at best reluctantly embraced . . . Deconstruction, semiology, Derrida, Foucault may question the very meaning of meaning as we have learned it, but feminism may not do so."[11] And of course Heilbrun is by and large perfectly correct. Countless new journals of feminist thought have sprung up in the last decade—*Feminist Studies, Women's Studies, Signs, Frontiers, Chrysalis, Michigan Papers in Women's Studies, Women and Literature,* and so forth—most of which regularly publish interesting and useful feminist criticism of literature from classical antiquity to the present. In addition, the pages of more general literary/intellectual periodicals, ranging from *PMLA* to *Partisan Review,* from *Critical Inquiry* to *Contemporary Literature,* have begun to include essays in feminist literary criticism with fair regularity. Even the annual MLA convention, as I'm sure most of you have observed, has lately devoted what seems to be at least a fifth of its sessions to feminist literary issues. Yet within most English departments, as Heilbrun suggests, business goes on pretty much as usual, as if the intellectual transformation recorded in so many journals and meetings simply had not happened. Or, rather, business goes on with the usual ferment over the new ideas of newly interesting men—Derrida, Foucault, Lacan, for instance—just as if no significant feminist transformations had taken place.

More specifically, I would elaborate on Heilbrun's statement by noting that what amounts to the massive rejection (or perhaps more accurately the denial) of feminist criticism has taken three separate but related forms: simple indifference, apparently supportive tokenism, and outright hostility. The first—indifference—is by far the commonest and in some ways the most vexing form of rejection. As every feminist critic knows, many—indeed, most—of our male colleagues (and a few of our female ones) don't come to our talks, don't read our essays and books, don't in fact concede that we exist as thinkers, teachers, and writers who are part of a significant intellectual movement. Of course a number of these nonlisteners and nonreaders are probably infamous types we'd all, alas, recognize: people who rarely go anywhere except to the supermarket or the faculty club and whose most common out-of-class reading is *TV Guide*. I'm sure, too, that some apparently indifferent souls are really overworked administrators kept late at their desks by affirmative action forms and budgetary crises, persons whose indifference is more a matter of appearance than reality. Nevertheless, of those who stay away, those who neither read nor listen, those who claim to be ignorant, and those who claim to be bored—it seems to me that at least forty or fifty percent are in some sense denying or rejecting the whole enterprise of feminist criticism, and doing so for reasons that at first seem quite inexplicable.

The second form of rejection, which I've called "apparently supportive tokenism," is almost, though not quite, as vexing as simple indifference. Unlike the indifferent nonreader, the tokenist does concede the existence of feminist criticism and even, so it seems at first, the importance of this new literary approach. The tokenist occasionally reads or approvingly quotes an article by a feminist critic and quite genuinely believes that, in Lillian Robinson's words, "every good department should stock one" such creature.[12] But really—and this is why tokenists are tokenists—these apparently supportive colleagues only support feminist criticism because it is "in," it is popular, it is trendy. In fact, however, they cannot distinguish between one feminist and another, or even between one woman and another. An editor of a very well-known anthology, for instance, told me that, yes, he'd just added some poems by an eighteenth-century literary woman to his book; but when I asked him which eighteenth-century literary woman he'd used, he couldn't remember her name. She was a woman, period: a nameless token of trendiness.

In the same way, the tokenist believes that feminist courses should be offered because they bring up enrollments, like classes in sci-fi, film, ecology and lit, or the detective novel. But he doesn't differentiate among them because they aren't, of course, serious, like courses in Great Books from Plato to Pynchon. The tokenist's point of view is best expressed in the almost liturgical academic credo J. Hillis Miller offered at one of last year's ADE seminars:

> *I believe in the established canon of English and American literature and in the validity of the concept of privileged texts. I think it is more important to read Spenser, Shakespeare, or Milton than to read Borges in translation, or even, to say the truth, to read Virginia Woolf.*[13]

Note here that the Serious (indeed, the "privileged"!) Literary Canon is the traditional masculinist one—Spenser, Shakespeare, Milton, not, for example, Shakespeare, Milton, Jane Austen, or Shakespeare, Wordsworth, George Eliot—while the interesting otherness of a feminist writer like Virginia Woolf is equated with what Miller evidently perceives as the spurious brilliance of a trendy foreigner: "Borges *in translation* [my emphasis]."

The third form of rejection suffered by feminist criticism is outright hostility, and of course it is tautological even to name this. Nevertheless, as I'm sure you all know, it exists: if the indifferent person never heard of feminist criticism and the tokenist thinks every department should stock one feminist critic, the hostile man or woman is obviously the person who demands, "What need one?" Lately—and this is not a tautological point—our male colleagues are increasingly reluctant to express such hostility (though a few female colleagues seem to feel "privileged" to do so). Hostility does linger in some benighted places, however, and gets expressed in all kinds of sadly or comically misogynistic ways. In one department, for instance, the measured, elegant, and theoretical work of an accomplished young critic was dismissed as "the last war whoop of feminism." In another, members of a search committee rejected almost every feminist critic who applied for a job in Victorian literature (and three quarters of the female applicants for the job were feminist critics) with the wonderfully ambiguous phrase "fem. dupe." (Consciously, they meant that because these women defined themselves as feminists their credentials must inevitably duplicate those of the one feminist critic who already taught in that department. In other words, "What need two?" Unconsciously—well, I wouldn't venture to articulate what they meant unconsciously by "fem. dupe.")

In any case, though this form of rejection is distressing (and sometimes costly) for feminist critics, it is certainly clearer and thus less puzzling (and therefore less irksome) than indifference or tokenism. But of course all these modes of rejection are in some sense both bewildering and painful. Metaphorically speaking, they define those of us who do this kind of work as what the Victorians used to call "redundant women"—women who, said the social critic W. R. Greg, "in place of completing, sweetening, and embellishing the existence of others are compelled to lead an independent and incomplete existence of their own."[14] Defining us as "redundant," moreover, they devalue our work to students, discourage our admirers, dishearten our junior colleagues, and force us into destructive competition with one another for a few token jobs.

Why? To return to my quotation from Carolyn Heilbrun, why is it that "among all the changes of the life and thought of our age, only the feminist approach has been scorned, ignored, fled from, at best reluctantly embraced"? I want to be very fair, so I'll concede that a few feminist critics may be at least in part to blame. Some of the early work in the field, and to a lesser extent some work still being done, has been naïve. Some feminist critics, for example, have confused the political with the polemical; quite natural feelings of frustration and anger at injustice have got italicized into shrieks. Other feminist critics, confusing desire with reality, have made what psychologists call "positive role models" out of personages in literary texts or movements who were probably anything but positive. Still other feminist critics have confused fiction with reality and taxed imaginary beings with *not* being "positive role models."

But these failings are minor and I suspect each is associated with the intellectual excitement, the revisionary passion, and the undissociated sensibility that are the unique strengths of feminist criticism. Indeed, since feminist criticism does have such strengths, it seems disproportionately hostile to reject or deny its central ideas because of the naïveté of a few of its proponents. Recently, moreover, so much good work has appeared that it seems in another sense disproportionate to blame all feminist critics for the failings of a few. On the contrary, we feminist critics know what our revisionary passion can create because we have produced overviews of women's literature like Showalter's *A Literature of Their Own* and Moers' *Literary Women,* fine biographical studies like Wolff's *A Feast of Words* and Rose's *Woman of Letters,* anthologies like Bernikow's *The World Split Open,* and essay collections like Rich's *On Lies, Secrets and Silence.*

We know, too—and we wish more of our colleagues knew—that although lately almost everyone thinks literary studies are in the doldrums, the intellectual excitement generated by feminist criticism is especially able to regenerate literary studies. As you may recall, my second topic was to be "what feminist criticism wants from English departments"—in other words, what jobs and courses it imagines for its proponents. But that issue is inextricably related to yet another one of my subjects: what feminist criticism can do for English departments. Because, as Heilbrun also notes, feminist criticism does bring a unique vitality to both the classroom and the curriculum, I think we need, not token jobs and courses, not concessions to trendiness, but as many jobs and courses as the economy of literature will allow. Feminist revisions of traditional periodization and of the received literary canon, for example, suggest that there is far more to learn and to teach than we ourselves were ever taught. At the same time, feminist connections between the personal and the political, the theoretical and the practical, renew those bonds of feeling and thought that T. S. Eliot, that paradigmatic patriarchal critic, regarded as irrevocably severed. In fact, the feminist classroom, as anybody who has entered one will tell you, is the home of *un*dissociated sensibilities and thus—do I dare to say it?—a volcanically energetic place. But (of course) it is or should be productively volcanic, for the competent teacher of, say, literature by women must learn to harness or channel the powers of Vesuvius.

Finally, though all feminist approaches to literature are, as I have already argued, in some sense revisionary, our approaches to literature are also as various as those of our most scornfully masculinist colleagues: we are Marxists, Freudians, deconstructionists, Yale rhetoricians, and Harvard historians. Thus we can contribute to jobs and courses in all the ways that all such theorists can. At the same time, however, the revisionary imperative we have in common gives us also a common interest not just in the social, rhetorical, or psychological strategies of writing but in the meaning of writing as a psychosexual act, a matter I have already called "bracingly ontological." It would seem, therefore, that only the most artifically depressed economy could define us as "redundant." Why, then—why, for the ritual third time around—why doesn't everybody think our work is as necessary as we think it is? Here, at last, I move into my third "essay": "Feminist Mysteries: Male Critics and Feminist Criticism"—or perhaps it would be more accurate to say "masculinist mysteries," since it is the behavior of both male and female masculinists that has been puzzling me. In any case, a mystery is a mystery is a mystery, and I want briefly, as I conclude my exposition of what feminist critics want, to explore the associated mystery of what masculinist critics don't want, and why.

Putting aside the possibility that feminist criticism really is boring and trivial, a possibility I am not only unwilling to discuss but am constitutionally unable to consider, I suppose I should begin my investigation of these feminist/masculinist mysteries by speculating that many of our colleagues may really find us alarming, or at least unnerving. Precisely that passionately undissociated sensibility which gives volcanic energy to the feminist classroom may appear quite threatening. After all, those who have long been silent, those who have not revealed "how red the fire rocks below" their decorously meditative surfaces, would seem to be the Vesuvian creatures most likely to erupt into murderous rage. This is a point deeply understood by Emily Dickinson, to whose volcano poems I did promise I would return. In a fairly early piece, Dickinson observes that once volcanoes stop being acres for birds to choose, one discovers that

> *those old-phlegmatic mountains*
> *Usually so still*
>
> *Bear within—appalling Ordnance,*
> *Fire, and smoke, and gun,*

> *Taking villages for breakfast,*
> *And appalling Men—*

In another poem she elaborates on this vision, noting in particular what we might only half frivolously define as the deadly critical vocabulary of the volcano; she speaks of the

> *Solemn—Torrid—Symbol—*
> *The lips that never lie*
> *Whose hissing corals part and shut—*
> *And Cities ooze away—*[15]

Yet, though some of our colleagues may flatter us feminist critics by seeing us as solemn symbols, we are surely not very torrid, and though we may write about madwomen, we are rarely madwomen ourselves. As for appalling ordnance and villages for breakfast, we may perhaps fantasize such possibilities but—especially in this time of lowered enrollments, a time when women have actually lost rather than gained ground in the academy—our ordnance tends to be muted and our diet abstemious. The feminist mysteries whose rituals we enact in lecture rooms and learned journals, moreover, are certainly not death to look upon (though a classicist friend did suggest to me that some men might hesitate to come to our talks on feminist theory for fear of finding themselves in the position of Mnesilochus and Euripides in Aristophanes' *The Poet and the Women,* the play in which male interlopers at the Athenian women's festival called the Thesmophoria become the prisoners of a set of furious females, helpless hostages in the battle of the sexes). Nor does it seem likely that our feminist critical speech, powerful as I consider it, is so powerful that when we open our truthful mouths, "cities ooze away." After all, no cities of the mind seem to have oozed away lately, though some mental sidewalks may have been covered with a few inches of ash.

Or is it possible that cities, civilizations, literary styles, and subjects have begun to ooze away? Though I think feminist criticism is the very opposite of destructive—indeed, I think it is reconstructive rather than deconstructive—I want for a moment to meditate on the possibility that many of our colleagues ignore our work because its very existence is somehow a sign of profound changes that have recently shaken Western culture in general and English departments in particular, changes whose implications they do not want to acknowledge. Metaphorically speaking, perhaps whole intellectual villages and cities have disappeared, settlements that once seemed the strongholds of a thousand years of Western culture. In the largest sense, of course, I am referring to the democratization of society that has profoundly transformed most Western cultural institutions, including schools and universities, since the beginning of the nineteenth century. In this sense, too, I am thinking of the accelerated democratization of education that has particularly transformed English departments since the late fifties, giving us (among other phenomena) open enrollment, the sixties, enormous classes followed by tiny classes, extra sections of remedial English, generational squabbles on the faculty, and a whole new literary canon, including not just the works of Borges in translation and the novels of Virginia Woolf but also science fiction, films, women's literature, African-American literature, Latino literature, Asian-American literature, Native American literature, and more, much more.

More specifically, however, I am thinking of the often disregarded but volcanic eruption of women into the public realm of literary and political culture, as opposed to the private, semiliterate domestic world most women inhabited until the early or middle nineteenth century. As the director of the United States Census Bureau pointed out not long ago, this explosive transformation of women's lives was especially marked in the 1970s, the decade during which most feminist critics became feminist critics: "Women changed their attitudes dramatically over the decade," he observes, and "the effects can be seen in almost every aspect of society." But of course these theatrical-seeming changes had begun quite some time ago, with a feminist movement whose events and effects have been massively and I think deliberately forgotten until recently. More important, I would argue that the turn-of-the-century feminist movement was until recently forgotten for the same reason that feminist criticism has been, in Heilbrun's words, "scorned, ignored, fled from": it has been forgotten because it is central to most aspects of all our lives—central, crucial, and volcanically influential.[16]

To be quite plain, I am saying that we live the way we live now, and think the way we think now, because what was once a wholly masculinist patriarchal culture has begun—fragmentarily, haltingly, sometimes even convulsively, but, I suspect, irreversibly—to evolve into a masculinist-feminist culture, a culture whose styles and structures will no longer be patriarchal in the old way, even if they remain patrilineal. I am saying as well, therefore, that the way we read and write now, the way we imagine literary texts and traditions now, must inevitably and irrevocably change under the pressure of the sociocultural changes we are experiencing. And I am saying, finally, that it may be unnerving or even enervating to confront such changes, especially for those to whom they bring a diminution of authority (and of course I mean men), but also for those to whom they bring an accession of responsibility (and here of course I mean women).

Lest I seem entirely solipsistic in suggesting that changes in male-female relations must and will significantly transform our relation to literary studies, let me remind you that a number of quite respectable, unimpeachably masculine (and perhaps even masculinist) literary critics have made very similar assertions. Harold Bloom, for instance, declares in *A Map of Misreading* that "the first true break with literary continuity will be brought about in generations to come, if the burgeoning religion of Liberated Woman spreads from its clusters of enthusiasts to dominate the West. Homer will cease to be the inevitable precursor, and the rhetoric and forms of our literature then may break at last from tradition."[17] Bloom, you will note, speaks prophetically, using the future tense. But what if he too is simply evading his own secret recognition that this transformation of Western literary tradition has already begun?

Certainly so astute a literary historian as Walter Ong does believe it has begun. As I'm sure you will also recall, Ong tells us in his lectures on *The Presence of the Word* that the late eighteenth- and early nineteenth-century "movement to give formal schooling to girls was associated with the growing together of the academic and bourgeois worlds, and . . . helped wear down on several fronts" classical traditions that included the disputatious (and masculinist) art of the polemic, which had been central to academic life, as well as the specialized (and masculinist) use of "language teaching"—specifically the teaching of Latin and Greek— "as a male initiation procedure."[18] Psychoanalytically oriented critics of *écriture* like Derrida and Irwin would perhaps influence us to observe that much of the old masculinist energy of oral culture may have been projected into sexualized fantasies about the relation of the phallic pen to "the virgin page."[19] But Ong's vision of the female invasion of history is surely supported by the Derridean perception of the very nature of writing, which, once women were taught it, allowed a detachment, an anonymity, that in the long run had to be liberating, even transformative.

If I may return to Virginia Woolf one last time, I should say that it was no doubt her understanding of the transformative nature of writing that made her dwell so dramatically on that crucial moment in history, that moment "of greater importance than the Crusades or the War of the Roses [when] the middle-class woman began to write." In fact, I would argue that we feminist critics are still dwelling on and in that moment, still coming to terms with and through it. I believe that our terms, however—and here I arrive at my long-awaited peroration—must eventually be yours and, indeed, everybody's, for as Ong and Bloom and others have also perceived, we are still living in that moment of cultural transformation, even if we aren't dwelling on it.

In fact, what feminist critics most want from English departments is the chance to define the terms to which we are coming as we dwell with the volcanic changes we have experienced. What English departments should want from feminist critics are rigorous and responsible revisions of ourselves, our texts, our traditions. Such re-visions should function in two ways: as new visions or understandings of our literary lives and as new versions or transformations of those lives. Both approaches should suggest a possibility that I think unifies all three of my essays but that few people have taken seriously since the Romantic period: the possibility that through literary study we can renew our lives.

—1980

THE EDUCATION
OF HENRIETTA ADAMS

lthough Henrietta Adams was still a virgin by the time she reached
the twelfth grade, she was really a dynamo of a girl—shockingly
eager to read, surprisingly enthusiastic about learning. In fact, although
like many twelfth graders she knew little about what she wanted in life
and knew even less of what she knew, she was a keenly intelligent teenager for whom (despite her profound unconsciousness of many serious
questions) the aims and methods of literary study were a matter of deep
concern.

Hen, as she was called by most friends and many relatives, had been
adopted at the age of three months by a branch of the great American
Adams family (her father was a grandson of one of Henry Adams' brothers), so that, at least through nurture if not by nature, she was inevitably fitted for education—and particularly for literary education—in
the highest sense. To be sure, no one knew exactly what Hen's true origins were: she was slim, dark, and curly-haired: perhaps, therefore, her
adoptive parents proudly speculated, she was originally Italian, Jewish,
Latina, even maybe part Asian or part African. And no doubt this primordial mystery contributed to Hen's vague feeling of alienation from
her adoptive parents and siblings. Where great-great-uncle Henry had
sardonically reported his boyish sense that "a President was a matter of
course in every respectable family; he had two in his own," Hen—who

sometimes imagined herself as descended from a long line of adamantly dark and exotic unwed mothers—could not suppose that she had ever even been related (at least by blood) to a city councilwoman (although at times she had dreams that someday her family would at least produce a vice president).[1] Nevertheless, for most of her young life Henrietta Adams found that her education had brought her (as her adoptive great-great-uncle's had ostensibly brought him) in touch with much of the best that contemporary Western culture had to offer.

In the late sixties, when Hen was only six, her parents had moved from New England to Northern California, where her father worked as a computer programmer in a large high-tech firm (rumor has it that he was the dynamic force behind WordStar) and her mother had a job as a guidance counselor in a highly rated public high school (rumor has it that she facilitated a number of unusually imaginative, if comparatively virginal, encounter groups). The almost utopian American education Hen received at her flexible and progressive high school (the very school where her mother counseled freshmen and sophomores) would seem to have been peerless. Starting with a so-called "competency" model, some of Hen's teachers had assigned her carefully articulated tasks in grammar and reading, many of them coordinated with computers programmed by her dad, so that by the time she took the PSAT in the eleventh grade she was able to achieve a verbal score in the 700s—no mean achievement for a slim, dark, curly-haired sixteen-year-old of uncertain origins. Better still, working with a "process" model, a number of Hen's teachers had encouraged her to "get in touch with herself" in journals and rap sessions, even in the encounter groups established by her mom, so that by the time she graduated from high school Hen knew exactly "who she was," and she thought she knew what she was, as they say in California, "comfortable with."

Best of all, a few of Hen's teachers, using a "heritage" model, had introduced her to the Great Books of our culture, urging her, in the words of one educator, to "submit" herself to her literary heritage, specifically to "the rules and resources and established truths that constitute a culture standing beyond and over the self and containing criteria for showing wherein we fail."[2] Thus, by the time she was seventeen Hen had read such major texts as Sophocles' *Oedipus Rex,* some plays by Shakespeare, Hawthorne's *The Scarlet Letter,* Dickens' *Great Expectations,* Twain's *Huckleberry Finn,* Henry James' *The Turn of the Screw,* Sherwood Anderson's *Winesburg, Ohio,* F. Scott Fitzgerald's *The Great Gatsby,* Faulkner's "The Bear," some of Hemingway's Nick Adams stories, T. S. Eliot's "The Love Song of J. Alfred Prufrock," Tennessee Williams' *A Streetcar Named Desire,* Arthur Miller's *The Crucible,* and "The Lottery" by Shirley Jackson. She had had, in other words, a fine education, one that ought to have inspired her to seek further advances in her literary studies.

Why, then, did Hen experience an odd sensation of uneasiness every time she opened a book? She had, after all, learned to "submit" herself to the "established truths" so clearly stated by the texts she read. As Oedipus, she had interrogated, and yet acquiesced in, the fatality that causes a man to kill his father and marry his mother; as Pip, she had learned never to trust a fatal femme like Estella Havisham but rather to lower her expectations and make her own way in the world; as Huck Finn, she had lit out for the territories, escaping both the false gentility and the constricting domesticity of a slave-owning society ruled by fussy ladies like Aunt Polly; as J. Alfred Prufrock, she had worried about "the overwhelming question" toward which flighty women who "come and go / Talking of Michelangelo" might paradoxically lead her; as Nick Carraway, she had admired the Faustian intensity of Jay Gatsby and deplored the selfish aplomb of Daisy Buchanan. She had indeed, as the major educator says, learned "wherein we fail." Why, then—this may seem to some of us a foolish and tendentious question, but then most of us are not seventeen—why, then, did Hen feel anxious about literary study? Why had she, halfway through her freshman year, virtually decided either to follow in her father's footsteps and take up computer science or to trail her mother and apprentice herself as a radical psychotherapist?

It was not until, some years later, Hen studied the works of her illustrious great-great-uncle that she began to understand how interestingly her educational experiences had paralleled his. Recalling his early literary studies, you may remember, Hen's adoptive forebear wrote that "as far as happiness went, the happiest hours of the boy's education were passed in summer lying on a musty heap of Congressional Documents in the old farm-house at Quincy, reading *Quentin Durward, Ivanhoe,* and *The Talisman,* and raiding the garden at intervals for peaches and pears. On the whole he learned most then."[3]

In a well-received senior essay on her own education, Hen paraphrased Uncle Henry's lines: "As far as happiness went, the happiest hours of the girl's education were passed in summer lying on a heap of shiny computer magazines in the family room of the California split-level, reading *Little Women, Jane Eyre,* and *The Bell Jar,* and raiding the refrigerator now and then for diet sodas. On the whole she learned most then."

For Hen, as she discovered when she took a Women's Studies course in the second half of her freshman year, had become what Judith Fetterley calls a "resisting reader"; indeed, though she had always tried hard to "submit" herself to the "established truths" of the texts she studied in school, she had already begun half consciously "reading as a woman," to use Jonathan Culler's phrase. Yet even while she "identified against herself," as Fetterley would put it, dutifully adopting the traditionally male-centered perspective on experience recommended by her "heritage" teachers, Hen was looking "for grandmothers" the way Elizabeth Barrett Browning had more than a century earlier. She liked to write poetry, and sometimes she even thought she might attempt a novel someday; yet, although, in the words of Virginia Woolf, we "think back through our mothers if we are women" (at least we do sometimes), Hen's high school curriculum had offered her hardly any works by women, except, interestingly enough, "The Lottery," with its allegory of female sacrifice.

True, one of Hen's friends had actually studied Toni Morrison's *Sula* in a junior American literature class taught by an English teacher who was also a local black activist, and Hen had eagerly borrowed and read the novel; not only was it by and about a woman, it was by and about a black woman—and Hen, remember, sometimes speculated that she had had a black grandmother in her lineage. But then, she wondered what to do about *Sula* if, for example, she were asked a question pertaining to it on the College Boards. To what tradition or traditions did the book belong? How did *Sula* "fit in" with *Oedipus Rex* and *The Cru-*

cible and the Nick Adams stories and "The Love Song of J. Alfred Prufrock"? Suppose she had to write a compare-and-contrast essay about
such a novel. Although she had learned from her "competency" teachers how to organize paragraphs and bend sentences to her will, from her
"process" teachers how to let her prose flow in confessional analyses of
her dynamic though virginal sex life, and from her "heritage" teachers
what truths were usually articulated by Great Books, Hen was not just
bewitched but also bewildered by *Sula*.

It was lucky for Hen, therefore, that she took that Women's Studies course, for there, besides discovering that her uneasiness had arisen
because she was a "resisting reader," she learned that the books she'd so
happily read while lying on a pile of computer magazines in the California family room were actually part of a literary tradition that most of
her high school teachers didn't seem to know about. To be sure, many
of her college teachers also appeared to disregard, dismiss, or even dislike this tradition—yet, unlike swallows and summers, one or two teachers can make an education, and in her Women's Studies professor, Ms.
Charlene P. Gilman, Hen found a mentor who introduced her to a range
of works by and about women—Anne Bradstreet and Anne Finch, Elizabeth Barrett Browning and Christina Rossetti, Harriet Beecher Stowe
and Zora Neale Hurston, Willa Cather and Virginia Woolf, H. D. and
Gwendolyn Brooks—and who helped her to see how these works fit in
with the books by Alcott, Charlotte Brontë, Plath, and Morrison that she
had learned to love on her own. Professor Gilman even told Hen and
her other students that there was a branch of literary study called feminist criticism, whose proponents (Virginia Woolf, Ellen Moers, Patricia
Meyer Spacks, Carolyn Heilbrun, Elaine Showalter, Annette Kolodny,
Margaret Homans, Susan Gubar, and many others) had written extensively about this tradition.

By the time she had finished her junior year, then, Henrietta Adams
had become an adept if youthful practitioner of what Elaine Showalter calls "gynocriticism"—the analysis of the ways in which women not
only read as women but write as women. Yet how, Hen asked herself as
she boarded the plane home to California for a summer vacation of vol-
unteer work in a community women's center that her mother had just

helped found, how does this female tradition relate to the predominantly male tradition that, she now saw, she had studied in high school and in many of her college classes? Are there really two separate but equal literary traditions, Hen wondered (for she was, as we have seen, of an inquiring mind, and she could not let hard questions drop). What would a serious historian have to say about all this? she asked herself. And of course at this juncture—since the traditions of the Adams family were as powerful as its individual talents—nothing was more natural for her than to turn to the writings of her illustrious adoptive ancestor.

Hen had never read the works of her great-great-uncle Henry with any care—she had been too busy trying to find mothers to think back through—yet, because she had been inculcated with such respect for his name and fame, she was not surprised to find that he had strong and persuasive views on precisely the questions that now engaged her. In fact, it seemed to Hen that her uncle Henry had somehow planned his work with her in mind. Hadn't he said in the preface to *Mont Saint Michel and Chartres* that "the following pages . . . are written for nieces"? To be sure, he himself had confessed that he had an eighteenth-century sensibility—yet he associated the eighteenth century not only with his grandfather John Quincy Adams but also with his "Louis Seize" grandmother Louisa Catherine Johnson Adams, who, no less than her mother-in-law, "the venerable Abigail," was a woman from whom, he eventually decided, came "some of those doubts and self-questionings, those hesitations, those rebellions against law and discipline, which marked more than one of her descendants." Such doubts and self-questionings, moreover, had led him—as they were to lead the seventeen-year-old Hen—to a position of considerable skepticism toward education, in fact to a belief that "the chief wonder of education is that it does not ruin everybody concerned in it, teachers and taught." But, again as with his great-grandniece, Adams' skepticism had fostered in him a paradoxical desire for more and better education because "he regarded himself as the only person for whom his education had value, and he wanted the whole of it."[4]

Perhaps most important from Henrietta's point of view, however, was that in seeking the whole of his education her uncle Henry had focused his attention on just the holes she had perceived in her own high school curriculum. For when he decided that the Middle Ages were dominated, church and state, by the majestic figure of the Virgin Mother and by the two other queens—Eleanor and Isolde—who were her earthly surrogates, Uncle Henry had asked crucial questions about Western civilization that were curiously similar to her own: "Why did the gentle and gracious Virgin Mother so exasperate the Pilgrim Father? Why was the Woman struck out of the Church and ignored in the State?" Indeed, Uncle Henry had exclaimed, "if a Unity exists, in which and towards which all energies centre, it must explain and include Duality, Diversity, Infinity,—Sex!" Elsewhere, too, as if formulating Hen's own ambitions, he had written that "the proper study of mankind is woman," adding that "the study of history is useful to the historian by teaching him his ignorance of women; and the mass of this ignorance crushes one who is familiar enough with what are called historical sources to realise how few women have ever been known."[5]

But if Uncle Henry had felt this way, Hen now decided, perhaps he would have advised her to fill in the blanks of the literary history she'd been taught in high school (and in most of her college classes) with some of the material she had discovered while learning the "gynocriticism" practiced in her Women's Studies courses. Then her literary studies would truly reflect the "Duality" and "Diversity" Uncle Henry had extolled. For could she not show that he himself had inherited his skeptical sensibility not only from John Quincy Adams and Louisa Johnson Adams but also from Louisa Johnson Adams' seventeenth- and eighteenth-century foremothers, women ranging from the Americans Anne Bradstreet and Abigail Adams to the Englishwomen Margaret Cavendish and Anne Finch? After all, Hen reflected, these women— obscure though some may have been and forgotten though most were— had participated in the thought of their times as vigorously as their male contemporaries had. Naturally, their literary modes and manners were often quite different from the literary modes and manners of men, but perhaps examining that difference could teach her (as it might have taught Uncle Henry and other historians) a good deal. For though Uncle Henry—no doubt precisely because of the "ignorance of women" that he deplored in historians—believed that "excepting one or two like Madame de Sevigny, no woman has pictured herself," these women had pictured themselves and pictured men, too. Interestingly, moreover, a number of them, along with many of their descendants, had, in picturing themselves, depicted doubts about education not unlike Uncle Henry's: Hen's own ancestor (and Uncle Henry's great-grandmother) Abigail Adams had confided that "I regret the trifling, narrow, contracted education of the females of my own country," while in England Anne Finch had complained that women were "Education's more than Nature's fools," and female writers from Mary Wollstonecraft to Virginia Woolf had taken up their cry, with Woolf in addition expressing doubts about the traditional male historians' vision of woman ("a worm winged like an eagle, the spirit of life and beauty in the kitchen chopping up suet") that strikingly echoed Uncle Henry's.[6]

More interestingly still, thought Hen, the religion of the Pilgrim Fathers whose misogynistic severity Henry Adams so disliked had long been complemented by a theology of the Mother Goddess quite comparable to his own: as early as the fourteenth century, not long after the medieval men her uncle admired had articulated their admiration for the figure of the Virgin, whom he enthusiastically called "Christ the Mother," the English mystic Julian of Norwich had meditated on the attributes of "God the Mother"; in the seventeenth century, the Philadelphian preacher Jane Lead had had glowing visions of Sophia, God's Holy Virgin Wisdom; in the nineteenth century, Florence Nightingale had written that "perhaps the next Christ will be a female Christ." The female energy Uncle Henry had feared would be forgotten or dissipated had not disappeared. Finally, too, though Uncle Henry had worried that "the American woman of the nineteenth century will live only as the man saw her,"[7] Hen noted that a number of nineteenth-century women now at last lived in their own rights (and writings), and not just classic notables like Emily Dickinson, Harriet Beecher Stowe, and Louisa May Alcott; in the last few years—or so Professor Gilman had told her—the works of many significant American women writers had been recovered and reprinted by diligent and devoted scholars. Hen mentally reviewed only a few names: the black Shaker visionary Rebecca Cox Jackson, the sardonically Gothic New England writer Elizabeth Drew Stoddard, the black novelist Harriet E. Wilson, and the feminist-regionalist Kate Chopin. How would Uncle Henry's sense of history have been altered if he had known and read the works of these women?

But perhaps, speculated Henrietta, her uncle's vision of the past had been transformed by a woman. She had, of course, heard family legends about the life and death of Uncle Henry's wife, the brilliant but suicidal Clover Hooper Adams, and it occurred to her that although her great-great-aunt Clover was never mentioned in *The Education of Henry Adams*—Uncle Henry had in fact burned countless letters and diaries after she killed herself in 1885, and he rarely mentioned her in conversation—Clover Adams might have somehow been the force behind her husband's belief that "the proper study of mankind is woman." Had not Henry James remarked that his friend Henry Adams "wrote the story of his own life—as if he were telling it with her values, from her point of view"? Indeed, James had decided that "the ultimate judgment of *The Education of Henry Adams* is hers." Just recently, too, Gilman had reminded Hen that several scholars had written books about Clover Adams that explored the effect of her mind on her husband's; could Aunt Clover have been what Hen's theoretically minded teacher Jacqueline Nacal might call "the repressed center of Henry Adams's text(s)"? In that case, perhaps Uncle Henry was narrating his life so that he would live as she saw him, for, as one Women's Studies scholar put it, "Clover may have had more impact on people's ideas than any other Adams woman, with the possible exception of Abigail." Yet until lately, most people seemed to have forgotten that she was real—and really influential. "Ellen I'm not real" Clover had exclaimed during her final months of suicidal depression. "Oh make me real—you are all of you real!" Maybe, thought Hen, she could now help participate in the project of making Aunt Clover "real"—if not in a psychological sense (for Aunt Clover's life had long since failed her, and the reasons for that failure were still mysterious)—at least in a historical one.[8]

Henrietta sighed and set down her Diet Coke. It was the end of the summer, and she was still in the California family room, lying on the same old pile of computer magazines, though now they were frayed and shabby rather than shiny. Reading Uncle Henry and thinking about Aunt Clover had been surprisingly useful, she reflected, and now she knew what to do. After another year of college—during which she was, as we know, to write an exemplary senior thesis about her own education—she would go to graduate school for a few years, and then—and then: she would become a high school teacher. True, the pay was bad, but maybe such jobs would be considered more valuable in the next decade, and in any case she thought she might have something to contribute to the secondary school literary curriculum, something that students might carry over into their college literary studies, something that, she believed (rather grandiosely), would "justify her existence." Even more grandiosely, perhaps, she quoted Uncle Henry to herself—"Duality, Diversity, Infinity,—Sex!" Yes, she would teach *Oedipus Rex* and *The Scarlet Letter* and *The Crucible* and "The Love Song of J. Alfred Prufrock"; but she would also teach *The Awakening, Sula, A Room of One's Own,* the poems of H. D., and the visions of Rebecca Cox Jackson—and maybe she would talk, too, about *The Education of Henry Adams* and the life of Clover Adams, saying how these texts and lives worked together, what new complexities they proposed.

Of course, Hen knew she belonged to an elite. She had been adopted by a privileged family, and perhaps it had been partly a privilege that she had learned to "identify against herself" as she was instructed by, respectively, her "competency" teachers, her "process" teachers, and her "heritage" teachers (for now she could use many sophisticated tools to deconstruct and reconstruct what she had been taught). Yet she also knew that many of her less privileged friends—male and female, black and white—had been as uneasy about the aims and methods of their literary studies as she'd been about hers. Maybe what she taught would help them like both writing and reading better than they now did (for if you like to read, you generally do like to write, too). Maybe if they found the diverse intellectual ancestors she had found—female as well as male, black as well as white—they wouldn't feel quite so orphaned, so nervously adopted by traditions that seemed to ignore their individual talents. And yet—Henrietta frowned—what if students (and teachers, too) were troubled by diversity. What if her male students were bored or even threatened by *Jane Eyre* and her female students refused to read anything else? Could it be that society's gender arrangements marked people's lives and minds so deeply that any significant entrance of women into cultural history might elicit male backlash and female anxiety? Perhaps she herself would undertake her utopian pedagogical project but then her successors at the school where she taught would throw out her syllabi and change all the reading lists back to what they had been before she began to teach.

Exhausted by these meditations, yawning, stretching, Henrietta suddenly found herself feeling rather old, although, as we know, she was actually not yet twenty-one. Worse still, she was momentarily overwhelmed by a peculiar sensation of unreality. Was she real, she wondered, as if half consciously echoing her great-great-aunt Clover, or was she in fact fictional? If she was fictional, had she perhaps inhabited countless other stories besides this parable "The Education of Henrietta Adams" in which she was now (quite inexplicably) living? Such doubts are not often admitted into texts by authors, but as anyone who has played a part in someone else's story will agree, they are not infrequently felt by literary characters, especially by those who, like Henrietta, are inclined to skepticism about the world.

Now, as her feelings of age, of unreality, and of déjà vu intensified, Hen began hazily to remember other purposes she had served, other (vastly superior) tales in which she might have dwelt—all fantasies, all by women. She might have been called Mary Carmichael in one, she thought, and she would there have been a writer who broke the "sequence—the expected order" of traditional narratives while inventing a "woman's sentence." (That, she suspected, was a fantasy about a room or rooms that somehow symbolized female freedom.) In another, earlier story—something about a woman's country, a "her land"?—she might have been a wise woman ruler, a "land mother" who helped govern a just and loving female society. Even earlier—perhaps it was in the late Middle Ages?—she might have helped build a "City of Ladies" where women were restored to a revised history quite like the one Uncle Henry had (centuries later) recommended. But—and now Hen was overcome by a dreadful weariness—if she had lived through all those stories, why had she been revised and resurrected in yet another fantasy? Would there be no end to the number of female authors who dreamed her up, always with a different name and role yet always with the same hope?

Sighing, Henrietta glanced one last time at Uncle Henry's book. "New women," he proclaimed on page 1126, "had been created since 1840; all were to show their meaning before 1940." She paused a moment, brooding. Perhaps, then, if Uncle Henry, himself undeniably real, could make such a statement, she herself was real. Was her own mother one of these new women? Was she herself such a woman? In that case, both were real, although maybe neither had yet shown her meaning, despite encounter groups and 700s on the PSATs. And certainly—Hen brightened, thinking of the latest news—Geraldine Ferraro was real, and maybe really a distant relative. Henrietta rose. She shut *The Education of Henry Adams.* It was August 1984, and it was time to pack, time to believe in her own reality so that she could go back to school and show her meaning. Hers, she supposed, was not a significance Uncle Henry had altogether understood, but it would most likely change the meaning of the history he had tried to understand, and Henrietta was determined to show somebody what that meaning was.

—1985

A TARANTELLA OF THEORY

Hélène Cixous' and Catherine Clément's *Newly Born Woman*

Somewhere every culture has an imaginary zone for what it excludes, and it is that zone we must try to remember today.

—CATHERINE CLÉMENT

Everyone knows that a place exists which is not economically or politically indebted to all the vileness and compromise. That is not obliged to reproduce the system. That is writing. If there is a somewhere else that can escape the infernal repetition, it lies in that direction, where it writes itself, where it dreams, where it invents new worlds.

—HÉLÈNE CIXOUS

When "The Repressed" of their culture and their society come back, it is an explosive return, which is absolutely shattering, staggering, overturning, with a force never let loose before.

—HÉLÈNE CIXOUS

There is a voice crying in the wilderness, Catherine Clément and Hélène Cixous say—the voice of a body dancing, laughing, shrieking, crying. Whose is it? It is, they say, the voice of a woman, newborn and yet archaic, a voice of milk and blood, a voice silenced but savage.

For almost a decade now, Americans, especially American feminist readers, have heard from and of this voice. The first issue of *Signs: Journal of Women in Culture and Society* presented Cixous' by now classic (wo)manifesto, "The Laugh of the Medusa," and later, in *Signs* and in *New French Feminisms* (edited by Elaine Marks and Isabelle de Courtivron) as well as in other publications, we had the chance to become better acquainted with the ferocious soprano that issues from Paris's "psych et po" and other feminist/theoretical groups. But those of us who are, as the current vocabulary would have it, monolingual "anglophones" have had few opportunities to confront the global structures produced by such influential thinkers as Clément and Cixous. We take our pleasures where we can: in American or English journals and anthologies, or in hard-to-translate volumes smuggled home from Parisian discount bookstores like FNAC, or from hungry, intermittent visits to the Librairie des femmes, with its ironic location on the rue des Saints-Pères.

Now, though, we can meet the "newly born woman"—the ancient/ innocent/fluent/powerful/impossible woman—as she is, or as Clément and Cixous have envisioned her. What will we, products of a culture perhaps stodgier than France's, think of her thieving and flying, her utopian body, her desirous fantasizing and guilty shuddering? Everything about her—as most anglophone readers will no doubt feel—is intense, indeed hyperbolic. She is born of Flaubert and Baudelaire, of Rimbaud and Apollinaire, as well as (Clément and Cixous tell us) of the *Malleus Maleficarum,* Freud, Gênet, Kleist, Hoffmann, Shakespeare, and Aeschylus. Yet is she not in some sense the final figure of our own daydreams and nightmares (or even, in fact, our nightmères)? Is she not the one who erupts at, and disrupts, the edge of female consciousness, the liminal zone between sleeping and waking?

For an American feminist—at least for this American feminist—reading *The Newly Born Woman* is like going to sleep in one world and waking in another—going to sleep in a realm of facts, which one must labor to theorize, and waking in a domain of theory, which one must strive to (f)actualize. By turns dolorous and ecstatic, this extended, collaborative meditation forces us to confront what an old movie once called "monsters from the id," even as it asks us to surrender ourselves to visions of the mysteries controlled by the mistresses of our imaginations. On the surface, though, its structure is comparatively simple. In Part 1, "The Guilty One," Catherine Clément provides an analysis—a superbly sophisticated one—of "images of women," specifically images of the sorceress and the hysteric, as exemplary female figures. In Part 2, "Sorties: Out and Out: Attacks/Ways Out/Forays," Hélène Cixous elaborates brilliant imaginings of liberation, as well as some by now well-known theories of the phallocratic, patriarchal "hierarchization" that has led to the need for liberation. Finally, in Part 3, "Exchange," Clément and Cixous engage in an evidently unpremeditated dialogue that clearly illuminates the differences and similarities in their thinking. Throughout, however, their mutual focus is on the sometimes oppressive, sometimes privileged madness fostered by marginalization, on the wilderness out of which silenced women must finally find ways to cry, shriek, scream, and dance in impassioned dances of desire.

To dance: at the heart of *The Newly Born Woman* is the story of a southern Italian ritual, the tarantella. Early in the book, as she discusses the rebellious "celebrations" with which repressed (female) subjects have responded to their subjugation by patriarchal hierarchies, Clément tells a tale of women in the Mezzogiorno who can be cured of imaginary spider bites only by doing a ceremonial dance, which sometimes lasts for twenty-four hours. A village orchestra plays; a woman/patient dances—dances in a ferocious "festival of metamorphosis"—which subversively, sardonically, with a "tragic happiness," expresses her passionate rage, her raging passion. At the end of the episode, she transcends "the divine bite" and "leave[s] risk behind . . . to settle down again under a roof, in a house, in the family circle of kinship and marriage . . . the men's world." But she has had her interlude of orgasmic freedom.[1]

In some sense, this structure of the hellish/heavenly tarantella governs the shape of *The Newly Born Woman*. In the "Exchange," Clément explains to Cixous that there is a "difference between our discourses. Yours is a writing halfway between theory and fiction. Whereas my discourse is, or I would like it to be, more demonstrative and discursive, following the most traditional method of rhetorical demonstration." But in being "demonstrative and discursive," in revealing how Freud and Breuer (like Kramer and Sprenger, the authors of the *Malleus Maleficarum* [*The Witches' Hammer*]) reiterated and reinscribed conventional sociocultural judgments, Clément herself inflicts, yet again, the ghostly bite of the tarantula—the invisible yet powerful insect of patriarchal lore, lure, and law. In fact, she defines the theory of tarantellas, the cultural causality that would not only justify but explain the need for mad dances. And Cixous, then, whose writing is "halfway between theory and fiction," does the dance, the tarantella of theory necessitated by the hideously potent yet phantasmic incision. Combining autobiography and philosophy, literary analysis and utopian speculation, she transforms herself into the woman whose shrieks and steps mark her as "pure desire, frenzied desire, immediately outside all law."[2]

"Much Madness is divinest Sense," wrote Emily Dickinson in 1862, and in the same year she praised the "Divine Insanity" inspired in her by Elizabeth Barrett Browning's "Tomes of solid Witchcraft." Although she later conceded that "Witchcraft was hung, in History," this poet who defined her own life as a "Loaded Gun" was intuiting the argument about the sorceress and the hysteric, the witch and the madwoman, that Catherine Clément would make more than a century later. For even if witchcraft was "hung, in History," Dickinson triumphantly declared, it persists in the "ordinary" life—indeed, in the flesh—of the woman artist, the perceiving woman: "History and I / Find all the Witchcraft that we need / Around us, every Day—." Simultaneously drawing on and critiquing Michelet and Freud, Clément might almost be glossing these lines from nineteenth-century America. "The sorceress," she writes, "who in the end is able to dream Nature and therefore conceive it, incarnates the reinscription of the traces of paganism that triumphant Christianity repressed. The hysteric, who lives with her body in the past, who transforms it into a theater for forgotten scenes, bears witness to a lost childhood that survives in suffering." Yet the roles of both these figures are, she rightly observes, "ambiguous, antiestablishment, and conservative at the same time." Like the fervor that impels the tarantella, the misrule that governs witchcraft and the rebellious body/language that manifests hysteria are culturally stylized channels into which excess demonically flows—excess desire, excess rage; excess creative energy—only to be annihilated by the society that drove it in such directions. The tarantella dancer lapses into fatigued acquiescence; the sorceress is hanged—or burned, quartered, exorcized—leaving only "mythical traces," and the hysteric "ends up inuring others to her symptoms, and the family closes around her again, whether she is curable or incurable."

It makes sense, then, that Freud confided to Fliess in 1897 that he saw connections between his "hysterical" patients and the possessed, diabolical women described in the fifteenth-century *Malleus Maleficarum,* which became a standard handbook for witch-hunters and inquisitors. The illness or "anomaly" of womanhood in a culture governed by the invisible but many-legged tarantula of patriarchal law takes multiple forms, but its one energy derives from the singular return of the repressed. Dora, with her complicated resentment against her father and Mr. K., her complex attachment to Mrs. K., and her odd indifference toward her mother, is simply a little witch. Speaking in tongues, hallucinating, gagging, accusing Breuer of illicit paternity, Anna O. is another witchy woman. And Dickinson, too—becoming a gun or a volcano, "hysterically" possessed by a nameless "master" and uttering (for him) a deadly vocabulary—isn't she a bit like a witch? Even as she transforms herself into an "it" ("Why make it doubt, it hurts it so"), "it" cries in her: seeking refuge in writing, she finds a place where, as Cixous says, "it writes itself . . . it dreams . . . it invents new worlds."

Of course, to represent the historical range and variety of female experience chiefly in terms of such extreme figures as the sorceress and the hysteric may seem, on the one hand, hyperbolic and, on the other hand, reductive. Dora's situation was a special one, after all: how many young girls have become goods to be traded by their fathers to the husbands of their fathers' mistresses? As for Anna O., the illness that led to her intense encounter with Breuer was followed by a long and productive career as a social worker, and Emily Dickinson (my own addition to this cast of characters) carried on sometimes enigmatic yet always brilliant correspondences with such men as Samuel Bowles and Thomas Wentworth Higginson, despite her theatrical self-representations as a gun or a volcano. Reasonable as these caveats may seem, however, the paradigms of sorceress and hysteric become increasingly convincing when one contextualizes them with contemporary anthropological theory about—to use the scholar Gayle Rubin's phrase—"sex-gender systems."

Clément herself invokes Lévi-Strauss's hypothesis that "the elementary structures of kinship" are based on an exchange of women as well as his complementary notion that "women's periods, their uncontrolled flow, too close to nature and therefore threatening," paradoxically function as "the stabilizing element through which runs the split between nature and culture: simultaneously the rule and the unruly." But American readers will also find the postulates in *The Newly Born Woman* illuminated by Sherry Ortner's well-known article "Is Female to Male as Nature Is to Culture?" Drawing on Simone de Beauvoir and Mary Douglas as well as Lévi-Strauss, Ortner argues that although women's production of signs aligns them with (human) society, their reproductive functions identify them with the (animal) body, so they are universally perceived "as being closer to nature than [are] men." Thus, the female role represents "something intermediate between culture and nature, lower on the scale of transcendence than man." Such a position "on the continuous periphery of culture's clearing," she explains, would "account easily for both the subversive feminine symbols (witches, evil eye, menstrual pollution, castrating mothers) and the feminine symbols of transcendence (mother goddesses, merciful dispensers of salvation . . .)."[3]

If Ortner is right—and though her thesis has lately been critiqued by some feminist anthropologists, it has not really been refuted—the roles of the sorceress and the hysteric would indeed become exemplary tropes for the female condition. Since the etymological root of the word "hysteria" is the Greek *hyster,* or womb, the hysteric is, after all, the creature whose wandering, even wondering, womb manifests the distinctively female bonding, or bondage, of mind and body, the inescapable female connection between creation and procreation, the destiny that is inexorably determined by anatomy. And the sorceress—the witch, the wise woman, destroyer and preserver of culture—is she not the midwife, the intermediary between life and death, the go-between whose occult yet necessary labors deliver souls and bodies across frightening boundaries? As Clément tellingly notes, the hysteric weeps but the sorceress does not. In fact, like Kundry, the demonic seductress of Wagner's *Parsifal* who is condemned to a despairing immortality for having mocked Christ on his way to Calvary, the witch laughs at the solemnities of sacrifice that constitute culture. For the hysteric, pathos is the price of carnality; for the sorceress, irony is the privilege of marginality.

Yet, ruled by the womb, the *hyster,* isn't the sorceress/midwife also, like the womb itself, the vessel of a medicinal magic that can kill or cure, a magic whose power must therefore be contained by confinement to what the anthropologists Shirley Ardener and Edwin Ardener have described as a "wild zone" on the edge of culture? Given these points, it is no wonder that Clément, following Freud, succinctly affirms that "the hysteric is the remembrance of the sorceress."

It is not surprising, either, that Clément should meditate on the family romance that the father of psychoanalysis derived from his own meditations on the father-daughter incest reported by his hysterical patients. Tracing Freud's progress toward a theory of infantile sexuality, she shows how the daughter, who charges seduction, herself becomes defined as a seductress and how the plot of seduction and betrayal is further displaced as the history of the nuclear family, enmeshed in cultural codes, turns into a romance of accusation and counteraccusation in which guilt finally settles on the silenced figure who unites sorceress and hysteric in one body—the witchy, bitchy mother. And again American readers can contextualize her narrative with the poems of Emily Dickinson, whose sardonic prayers to "Papa above!" simultaneously seduce and betray the father even while her ecstatic invocations of "Strong Madonnas" attempt to resurrect and rehabilitate the lost mother.

Concluding her section of *The Newly Born Woman,* Clément tries, as Cixous will, to find ways out—sorties. Like her collaborator's, and like many other women's, her imaginative journeys across the frontier of prohibition are utopian, voyages out into a no place that must be a no man's and no woman's land. Specifically, she envisions this acultural no where in terms of a radical bisexuality through which sorceress and hysteric may be enabled to transcend the limits of a destiny that has historically liminalized their desire. For bisexuality, with its fluid pluralization of the erotic, its refusal to be imprisoned in fixity, "is coming out of the show, it is the end of a circus where too many women are crushed to death." The emblem of a "*jeune naissance*, [a] new young birth," it promises us that "they are no more, neither sorceress nor hysteric; and if someone dresses up as one it is an impersonation." In fact, confesses Clément, though "I have dearly loved them," these two monitory and mythic women "no longer exist," and the newborn woman, transcending the heresies of history and the history of hysteria, must fly/flee into a new heaven and a new earth of her own invention.

A new heaven and a new earth: this is the apocalyptic vision that energizes Hélène Cixous' brilliant and mystical tarantella of theory. Reviewing the "hierarchical oppositions" ("Culture/Nature, Day/Night, Father/Mother, Head/Heart, Form/Matter, Man/Woman"), through which Western philosophical thought has always organized the world, she excavates the assumptions that have oppressed and repressed female consciousness, alienating woman from the "dark continent" of her own bodily self and channeling female desire into the flights of the sorceress and the fugues of the hysteric. The "way out" of such a system, she declares, is through an escape that is also an attack: woman must challenge "phallo-logocentric" authority through an exploration of the continent of female pleasure, which is neither dark nor lacking, despite the admonitions and anxieties of patriarchal tradition. Out of such a repossession and reaffirmation of her own deepest being, woman may "come" to writing, constructing an erotic aesthetic rooted in a bisexuality that is not a "fantasy of a complete being which replaces the fear of castration . . . a fantasy of unity" but rather—as Clément suggested—a delight in difference, in multiplicity, in continuous awareness of "the other" within the self.

Some American as well as some French feminists have objected with varying degrees of intensity to the biological essentialism that sometimes seems to be implicit in Cixous' concepts of *féminité* or *écriture féminine*, yet as readers of *The Newly Born Woman* will discover, she herself repudiates the notion of persistent and consistent sexual essences. Noting that "there is 'destiny' no more than there is 'nature' or 'essence' as such," she remarks that "it is impossible to predict what will become of sexual difference—in another time" because "men and women are caught up in a web of age-old cultural determinations that are almost unanalyzable in their complexity. One can no more speak of 'woman' than of 'man' without being trapped within an ideological theater where the proliferation of representations, images, reflections . . . invalidate in advance any conceptualization." Her notion of *écriture féminine* is thus a fundamentally political strategy, designed to redress the wrongs of culture through a revalidation of the rights of nature.

American readers are bound to find that such a strategy, along with many of the dreams and dreads that Cixous articulates in the autobiographical opening of "Sorties," has English equivalents in the writings of such contemporary theorists as Susan Griffin in *Woman and Nature: The Roaring Inside Her* and Mary Daly in *Gyn/Ecology*—writers who also have attempted to reverse the hierarchies of mind/body that have repressed the female by identifying *mater* and matter, woman and (passive or dangerous) nature. Indeed, even the witty and rational Virginia Woolf may be seen as a crucial feminist precursor of Cixous (and Clément): what is Orlando if not an elegantly elaborated fantasy of bi- (or pluri-) sexual liberation—creative "hysteria" unleashed from the *hyster* and dedicated at last to "the other history" which Cixous has called for?

To be sure, recent Anglo-American feminists, heiresses of Wollstonecraft and Woolf, Barrett Browning and Gilman, often seem to begin projects of liberation from more moderately empirical positions than the one Cixous here articulates. Documentation is important to us, and we don't as a rule define our history as primarily "hystery"—or mystery. Yet, if we turn again to Dickinson, we can see that the fevers and fervors of enforced marginalization and compensatory witchcraft, of what she called "races nurtured in the dark," have been crucial to us too. Cixous' sardonically shuddering view of woman as having been "night to his day . . . Black to his white. Shut out of his system's space . . . The repressed that ensures the system's functioning" is by no means alien to our consciousness. And of course her story of a girlhood as a dispossessed female Algerian French Jew is one with which almost any immigrant—Jewish-, African-, Hispanic-, Italian-, Polish-American— woman can identify. In fact, even if we were, like Dickinson, WASPs, Yankee princesses, couldn't we at least sympathize? That the so-called Myth of Amherst, pacing her father's turreted homestead in her white dress, didn't need either the Algerian revolution or the Vietnam War, either the Paris barricades or the New York ghettos, to say "Good Morning—Midnight / I'm coming home," only makes Cixous' point more clear. As culture has constructed her, "woman" is "the dark continent" to which woman must return.

But returning, a sorceress and a hysteric—that is, a displaced person —Everywoman must inevitably find that she has no home, no *where*. Central to Cixous' thinking, and to Clément's, this sense of metaphysical alienation, symbolized by geographical dispossession, has also been important in the Anglo-American feminist tradition. Indeed, Cixous' reiteration of points made earlier in England and America seems almost uncanny. "I can never say the word *patrie*, 'fatherland,'" she confesses at one point, "even if it is provided with an 'anti,'" adding later that "I, revolt, rages, where am I to stand? What is my place if I am a woman? I look for myself throughout the centuries and don't see myself anywhere." Her words echo those of Virginia Woolf in the twentieth century ("As a woman, I have no country. As a woman I want no country") and those of Elizabeth Barrett Browning in the nineteenth century ("I look everywhere for grandmothers and find none"). We too have been seeking the other country as well as "the other history" for hundreds of years now. "Hysterics," intermittently mad (Woolf) or addicted to opium (Barrett Browning), our ancestresses were also sorceresses who transmitted to us what Dickinson, speaking of Barrett Browning, called "Tomes of solid Witchcraft" in which they too, though not so explicitly, fantasized about a new heaven and a new earth.[4]

If there is any aspect of Cixous' thought that has been and may continue to be problematic for Americans—as it has been for some French women—it is probably the metaphorical system through which her fantasies are transmitted, specifically the complex conceit represented by the now widely used phrase "writing the body." In France, the Questions Féministes group has argued that "there is no such thing as a direct relation to the body" because everyone's experience of sexuality is constructed by the conventions of her or his culture. Thus they go on to ask whether "this language of the body, this cry-language, is . . . enough to fight oppression." Or, as Christine Fauré puts it, "How could this changeless body be the source of a new destiny?" Similarly, the American critic Ann Rosalind Jones has conceded that "women's physiology has important meanings for women in various cultures, and it is essential for us to express those meanings rather than submit to male definitions—that is, appropriations—of our sexuality. But," she adds, "the female body hardly seems the best site to launch an attack on the forces that have alienated us from what our sexuality might become. For if we argue for an innate, precultural femininity, where does that position (though in content it obviously diverges from masculinist dogma) leave us in relation to earlier theories about women's 'nature'?"[5]

Empirical and skeptical, victims as well as beneficiaries of a *Playboy* society in which the erotic is a commodity and "coming" is de rigueur for everybody, some women on both sides of the Atlantic will inevitably wonder whether the jouissance implicit in what Cixous calls "coming to writing" is really liberating, even if—as Betsy Wing's valuable glossary reminds us—the currently popular French concept of *jouissance* implies a virtually metaphysical fulfillment of desire that goes far beyond any satisfaction that could be imagined by Hugh Hefner and his minions. Didn't D. H. Lawrence—in *Lady Chatterley's Lover* and elsewhere— begin to outline something oddly comparable to Cixous' creed of woman before she did? Describing the cosmic mystery of Connie's *jouissance,* this often misogynistic English novelist defines an "orgasm" whose implications, paradoxically enough, appear to anticipate the fusion of the erotic, the mystical, and the political that sometimes seems to characterize Cixous' thought on this subject, for Connie's coming to sexuality is also a coming to selfhood and coming away from the historically hegemonic Western "nerve-brain" consciousness that would subordinate body to mind, blood to brain, passion to reason. "She was like the sea," Lawrence enthuses about Connie's metamorphosis, "dark waves rising and heaving . . . the billows of her rolled away to some shore, uncovering her," and later he exults that "her whole self quivered unconscious and alive, like plasm." Similarly, defining the pleasure of the woman writer, Cixous proclaims that "her libido is cosmic . . . [She is] spacious singing Flesh . . . Her rising: is not erection. But diffusion. Not the shaft. The vessel." The questions raised by such curious parallels—like the issues raised by Questions Féministes, by Fauré, and by Jones—must be confronted as Cixous' dazzling tarantella of theory explodes on the page before us.[6]

Yet maybe the page itself is the answer to the questions, the page that the woman writer wishes to fill with her desire and that Lawrence, split between Romantic rebellion and patriarchal patronizing, fills for Connie Chatterley. In the past, surely—despite the struggles of "sorceresses" and "hysterics" like Barrett Browning, Dickinson, and Woolf—the pen/penis has been the privileged marker that was thought to leave the most significant traces on the apparent vacancy of nature, the blank spaces that had to be filled to "make" history. Thus women's words, traditionally relegated to margins, are inevitably the signs of the repressed, enigmatic hieroglyphs of an absence violently striving to become a presence. We in America may not want—as Cixous sometimes seems to tell us we should—to write in milk or blood; we may not always feel it necessary to overturn "mind" by valorizing "body" (because we may think our minds as distinctive, desirous, and desirable as our bodies), but we must agree with her passionate assertion that "a feminine text cannot not be more than subversive: if it writes itself it is in volcanic heaving of the old 'real' property crust."

Nor can we fail to join in Cixous' and Clément's dream of a transformed language/literature. We have been instructed by the prayers and prophecies not only of Dickinson and Woolf but also of H. D., Gertrude Stein, and Adrienne Rich, among others, so that we too have long yearned for what H. D. called "the unwritten volume of the new," for what Stein defined as a writing in the midst of which "there is merriment," for what Rich has more recently described (by negation) as "a book of myths in which our names do not appear." For us, too, the country of writing ought to be a no where into which we can fly in a tarantella of rage and desire, a place beyond "vileness and compromise" where the part of ourselves that longs to be free, to be an "it" uncontaminated by angel or witch (or by sorceress or hysteric) can write itself, can dream, can invent new worlds.

We too imagine drawing on the strength of nature (whatever that is—and we have to find out). We too fantasize transcending the censorings and censurings of culture (whatever they are—and we need to know). In a poem written more than a decade before *La Jeune Née* was published, Sylvia Plath spoke of this desire in a similar vision of liberation: "I step to you from the black car of Lethe / Pure as a baby." And a century earlier, Emily Dickinson dreamed of dancing "like a bomb abroad," a female/male/indefinable soul. We must be displaced to be re-placed, said Plath and Dickinson with Clément and Cixous. We must fly away to be regenerated. To be innocent as the healthiest processes of nature. To be immune to the hierarchical "principles" of culture. To be newborn.

—1986

REFLECTIONS ON A (FEMINIST) DISCOURSE OF DISCOURSE, OR, LOOK, MA, I'M TALKING!

If, in a synchronic analysis of the processes of signification through which the (female) subject is constituted, we problematize the intertextual (en)genderings of the signifier, will we foreground the possibility that language itself is always already phallologocentric? In other words, can women talk like women?

My mother would be astounded by the first formulation of this question; she might begin to understand the second one. And these two points "foreground" (you'll pardon the expression) a problem (or perhaps, to be slightly higher-brow, a "problematic") that seems to have something to do with the state of the language today. As those of us who are women, feminists, and academics begin increasingly to "deploy" an exclusionary "discourse of theory," what happens to our "status" in a political movement that has long celebrated sisterhood—and motherhood and daughterhood—as both powerful and empowering? If we believe, as some of us do, that we *are* speaking subjects (even if "intertextually" constructed by an elaborate system of "linguistic fields"), to whom do we speak, for whom do we speak, and in what words do we say our say?

In the history of feminism that is now somewhat deprecatingly called "the Anglo-American tradition," women have always tried to write and talk so that lots of other women could understand and be moved by their sentences. The unspoken assumption was clearly that "the Movement," so called, should be moving. From Mary Wollstone-craft's impassioned meditations on the rights and wrongs of woman-hood to Margaret Fuller's discussion of "the Great Law Suit" between the sexes, Sojourner Truth's forthright "Ain't I a Woman?," Elizabeth Cady Stanton's sardonic comments on the Bible, and Charlotte Perkins Gilman's frank put-downs of the private home, our tradition has been one of plain speaking. And of course such plain speech persists in the lives and works of a number of otherwise very different contemporary feminists—for instance, Betty Friedan and Andrea Dworkin, Germaine Greer and Gloria Steinem. Yet in the academy, just as (or perhaps because) feminist criticism has come into its own, those of us who spend much of our time, in the words of Mary Ellmann, "thinking about women," are being engulfed in a clamorous tide of "discourses." What do such discourses mean, how might they evaporate meaning, and what might be their consequences for feminism?

Complaining about language—even, to use a newer phrase, putting certain kinds of language "in question"—is, of course, always risky. On the one hand, if you protest vulgarisms or slang, you appear to be a prude. On the other hand, if you dislike specialized or difficult terminology, you seem to be a know-nothing. For Second Wave feminists like me, long inured to the sloganeering that inevitably goes with any mass enterprise—"up from the pedestal," "sisterhood is powerful," "off our backs"—the first issue isn't usually either a problem or a problematic. If the political is the personal, so is it also the accessible, the linguistically succinct. But that in itself makes the second issue a real one. Is there any way in which we can reject or revise the language of high theory without being anti-intellectual?

To be sure, such a question might be asked by male as well as female academics, especially literary critics. In the last decades, the old "New Criticism" has been replaced by an array of other "isms"—structuralism, deconstructionism, Marxism, new historicism—each of which comes *tout ensemble* with its own rarefied "discourse" (or, to put the matter less kindly, its own jargon). And the proliferation of such language has been a godsend for many literary critics, who feel marginal in a culture that by and large scorns poems and novels while revering the arcane knowledge secreted in the technical vocabularies of astrophysics and computer science, brain surgery and market analysis. Privileging and foregrounding, historicizing and defamiliarizing, putting texts *sous rature* or at least in question, manipulating signifier and signified, decontextualizing and interrogating material conditions, the professor of literature is no longer a mere reader, historian, and interpreter. He is both a technician with access to esoteric speech and a kind of philosopher king who lords it over those bodies of language that used to be called "authors." Remember the old joking definition of the literary critic as the guy who cleans up after the authorial elephant? Well, ever since interpretation has been replaced by theory and ordinary language by "discourse," there's no more mopping up after the elephant. The elephant is in fact dead. Long live the erstwhile cleaning man, who marches today at the head of the parade, all decked out in royal robes.

Obviously the strategies of self-certification that can turn cleaners into kings are, and no doubt should be, as available to academic women who do feminist criticism as they are to their male counterparts. But what if such strategies cut us off from many of the readers we need to reach? More, what if adopting the terminology of high theory subtly causes us—in a phrase of Judith Fetterley's—to "identify against ourselves"? That is, what if (to hazard another metaphor) the Empress's new clothes prove merely to be the Emperor's glad rags? It is arguable, after all, that the Emperor can afford to wear odd garments, especially if he only wants to talk to other kings and courtiers, but the feminist Empress presumably wants to make points with ordinary people.

Some current feminist thinkers would claim, however, that the points which most need to be made can *only* be made through the complex discourse of theory. Alice Jardine, herself the author of a difficult and ambitious book entitled *Gynesis*, has summarized this position in wonderfully straightforward language:

> *Roughly speaking*, "Anything worth saying can be said simply and clearly" *is our Anglo-American motto par excellence, while much of*

continental and especially French philosophy and criticism over the past twenty-five years has unveiled the presuppositions of that "simple clarity" with admirable lucidity. To choose an attitude toward interpretation—and therefore toward language—these days is to choose more than just an attitude: it is to choose a politics *of reading, it is to choose an* ethics *of reading, whose risks and stakes for feminism are what interest me.*[1]

In Jardine's formulation, clear and simple language is itself always already contaminated—polluted (though she does not say so here) by a patriarchal context and by a set of unspoken (and therefore primordially powerful) assumptions about origin and authority. And I suspect she would add, in response to any query of mine about "admirable lucidity," that whether or not continental theorists have unveiled such a context and such presuppositions with what most American readers would consider "lucidity," their enterprise has been crucial.

Significantly, Jardine's comment on "our Anglo-American motto" was made at the beginning of an important essay on the Bulgarian-French critic Julia Kristeva, whose *Revolution in Poetic Language* she sees as offering, through "semanalysis," "a non-Cartesian theory of the subject, not dependent on the ideology of language only as a transparent communication system, but as reverberated through the Freudian and Lacanian unconscious." Arguing that Kristeva's "vocabulary was refined and signed" in that work, Jardine exulted that *Revolution* showed us "how semanalyzing poetic language could help us to shed our stubborn Cartesian and Humanist skins—and begin to look beyond the so-called 'message' or 'ethic' of a text to its form, its networks of phantasies; to a sentence's rhythm, articulation, and its style—how it could help us to understand how those elements *are* the message, bound up in a conceptuality that we cannot hope to change only at the level of the utterance."[2]

And no doubt Jardine is right, accurate in her appraisal of the importance and impact that *Revolution in Poetic Language* has had, and right, or at least appealing, in her passionate desire for a way in which women might shed the "stubborn Cartesian and Humanist skins" we have inherited from centuries of patriarchal philosophy. Yet here is part of a passage in which Kristeva (in translation, to be fair) defines "the semiotized body" as "a place of permanent scission," and explains one of her key ideas:

> We view the subject in language as decentering the transcendental ego, cutting through it, and opening it up to a dialectic in which its syntactic and categorical understanding is merely the liminary moment of the process, which is itself always acted upon by the relation to the other dominanted [sic] by the death drive and its productive reiteration of the "signifier."[3]

What hidebound skins, one wonders, have been shed here—and by what exposed nerves have they been replaced?

To continue being fair: Kristeva is a traditional theorist, a European intellectual who has never, to my knowledge, sought to speak to "the people" or apologized for her participation in the empyrean *Tel Quel* group. Yet even while her descriptive work has been hailed—in the name of linguistic liberation—by a number of American feminists, it has also been (no matter what her own intentions are) closely allied with the *pre*scriptions, rather than *de*scriptions, of such Parisian colleagues as Luce Irigaray and Hélène Cixous. These last two figures, in particular, are the prophetesses of a *parler femme* or an *écriture féminine* in which woman might erotically "come to language" (as Cixous puts it). They are, in other words, the sibyls of a female speech that might be fluid, fluent, multiple, multifarious, and joyful (*jouissant*) in its overturning of the old, rigid, patriarchal "binaries" or "hierarchies." And here is one of Irigaray's celebratory meditations on such language, from her energetically subversive and sophisticated *Speculum*. It is a meditation, as readers will realize, in which—through such stylistic devices as hyphens, slashes, and parentheses as well as through impassioned metaphors—the French theorist practices what she preaches, "disconcerting" language in order to repudiate what she sees as the constraints and coercions of "univocal utterance."

> The (re)productive power of the mother, the sex of the woman, are both at stake in the proliferation of systems, those houses of ill fame

for the subject, of fetish-words, sign-objects whose certified truths seek to palliate the risk that values may be recast into/by the other. But no clear univocal utterance can, in fact, pay off this mortgage since all are already trapped in the same credit structure. *All can be recuperated when issued by the signifying order in place.* It is still better to speak only in riddles, allusions, hints, parables. Even if asked to clarify a few points. Even if people plead that they just don't understand. *After all, they never have understood. So why not double the misprision to the limits of exasperation? Until the ear tunes into another music, the voice starts to sing again, the very gaze stops squinting over the signs of auto-representation, and (re)production no longer inevitably amounts to the same and returns to the same forms, with minor variations.*

This disconcerting of language, though anarchic in its deeds of title, nonetheless demands patient exactitude.[4]

I quote this passage at such length not only because it is exuberant and anarchic but also because it is prose poetry that is self-consciously aware of the risks it (or its "author") takes through a commitment to "riddles, hints, parables," self-consciously aware of danger, with its weary concession that people may "plead that they just don't understand." But what if people really do plead that they don't understand? What if my mother, and my daughters, and my sisters in "the Movement," *don't* understand? What if they say, *a multiple and anarchic language can't change my life as a woman: it won't pass the ERA, it won't get me a job or an abortion—or child care—and it won't even really help me in graduate school, though it may very well sell books for the "avant-garde."*

Aha: the avant-garde! The avant-garde has "always already" been alienated from "ordinary people," so why shouldn't we feminists "go with the flow"—to descend from the theoretical to the colloquial? No one would pretend, in any case, that literary criticism has anything to do with regular "life." Or would they? I guess, for some of us, in the wake of a major election year, this looks like a serious question. It looks (in our country) as though we ought to wonder whether we should put our energies into an interrogation of clear and simple language or into an effort to *use* clear and simple language, with all its flaws, to change the world (whatever that is).

And speaking of the world, hasn't David Lodge's classically parodic *Small World* already hinted at how, in our solemnity, we revisionary feminist theorists might inadvertently, or advertently, align ourselves with those whose philosophical verities we protest? Readers will perhaps recall that at the end of Lodge's brilliant *commedia dell'Accademia* his erstwhile heroine gives an MLA paper whose excesses seem, at certain points, to exceed even those of the onetime followers of the authorial elephant. "Jacques Derrida has coined the term 'Invagination,'" proclaims Angelica Pabst, a beautiful theorist of "romance," "to describe the complex relationship between inside and outside in discursive practices. What we think of as the meaning or 'inside' of a text is in fact nothing more than its externality folded in to create a pocket which is both secret and therefore desired and at the same time empty and therefore impossible to possess." But although Angelica discusses Barthes, "climax," "deferred satisfaction," and textual "orgasm" from a determinedly feminist perspective, denouncing Barthes as "overly masculine," "no one . . . in the audience" except for Lodge's naïve hero, Persse, seems "to find anything remarkable or disturbing about her presentation." In the *opera buffa* of our profession, the feminist critic can too often, it seems, become a comedienne whose "letter C" (to recall Stevens) evokes little more than, on the one hand, Co-optation, and on the other hand, Cacophony.[5]

I do write here as someone who has argued elsewhere that we women *can* write as women without performing very many linguistic acrobatics. In the final chapter of our recent *The War of the Words*, Susan Gubar and I insisted that language—ordinary language—is ours, if for no other reason than that mothers teach daughters how to talk, even when their efforts are mediated, à la Lacan, by patriarchal structures.[6] But the urgency I feel at this moment actually transcends my own theoretical position. At a conference my collaborator and I attended recently, someone punningly suggested to Susan that feminism now occupies a "dying berth" in the academy because it has been so marginalized in "mainstream" culture. We've lost the ERA, George H. W. Bush has won the election, who knows what will happen in the Supreme Court, and the so-called gender gap didn't do us a bit of good. In humanities departments on university campuses, as I noted earlier, arcane and eso-teric vocabularies—those that sound like the language of astrophysics or brain surgery—will always trump clear and simple speech because they will always function to foster self-certification for the marginalized few, who necessarily must define themselves (ourselves) as the fortunate few, the happy few. And given (what one hopes is merely) a temporary fal-tering of the feminist movement, it may seem to some that such lexical moves are the only ones that might keep us, albeit hermetically, alive.

Yet when Virginia Woolf called for a "woman's sentence," and when she rejoiced that her fictive Mary Carmichael, one of the imaginary her-oines of *A Room of One's Own*, had broken "the sequence" of received narrative as well as of patriarchal language, she surely did not think we should be indifferent if people "plead that they just don't understand." In 1974, in an interview that has since been widely reprinted, Julia Kristeva remarked that "in women's writing, language seems to be seen from a foreign land; is it seen from the point of view of an asymbolic, spas-tic body? Virginia Woolf describes suspended states, subtle sensations, and, above all, colors—green, blue—but she does not dissect language as Joyce does. Estranged from language, women are visionaries, danc-ers who suffer as they speak."[7] Throughout *A Room of One's Own*, how-ever, Woolf speaks to, for, and about women: this famous text of hers, in fact, began as "two papers read to the Arts Society at Newnham and the Odtaa at Girton in October 1928."

Always aware of her audience, and of an urgent need to move them, Woolf writes not as an "asymbolic, spastic body" but with an impera-tive lucidity that seeks to facilitate change. Her prose, in fact, takes for granted the idea that women want to be comprehended by other women, that it would be a bad thing if her listeners and readers said "they just don't understand." Of her radiantly mythic Judith Shakespeare, for example, she argues that "she lives; for great poets do not die . . . they need only the opportunity to walk among us in the flesh. This opportu-nity, as I think, it is now coming within your power to give her. For my belief is that if we live another century or so . . . then the opportunity will come and the dead poet who was Shakespeare's sister will put on the body which she has so often laid down."[8]

Woolf's romance of a woman writer's linguistic resurrection, then, is really a fierce and hortatory dialogue with an audience which, in her view, *must* understand. And she does not suffer as she speaks; she would suffer if she could not speak. Indeed, were Woolf to "put on the body" that she "laid down" in 1941, she might well wonder what hope there can be for Judith Shakespeare—and for our mothers, sisters, and daughters—if, in our desperate desire to transform a "man's world," we simply buy into some of the equally desperate commodities—the discourses and dialectics, the indeterminacies and idiolects—of that world.

—1990

Part II

READING AND

REREADING

WOMEN'S WRITING

"MY NAME IS DARKNESS"

The Poetry of Self-Definition

"Something hangs in back of me," wrote Denise Levertov in "The Wings," a poem published in the middle sixties. "I can't see it, can't move it. // I know it's black, / a hump on my back . . . black // inimical power." A few years later, in 1972, Anne Sexton published a poem called "The Ambition Bird" that made a similar point:

> *I would like a simple life*
> *yet all night I am laying*
> *poems away in a long box.*
> ....
> *All night dark wings*
> *flopping in my heart.*
> *Each an ambition bird.*

Both poets, whether consciously or not, seem to have been echoing the terrified and yet triumphantly self-defining metaphors of Sylvia Plath's "Stings":

> *I stand in a column*
>
> *Of winged, unmiraculous women,*
> ....

but I
Have a self to recover, a queen.
Is she dead, is she sleeping?
Where has she been,
With her lion-red body, her wings of glass?

Now she is flying
More terrible than she ever was . . .

And all three women—Plath, Levertov, Sexton—are writing in a vein of self-definition that has also been worked by other recent women poets as diverse as Adrienne Rich, Diane Wakoski, Muriel Rukeyser, Ruth Stone, Gwendolyn Brooks, Erica Jong, Audre Lorde, and Margaret Atwood. In fact, I'd like to speculate here that the self-defining confessional genre, with its persistent assertions of identity and its emphasis on a central mythology of the self, may be (at least for our own time) a distinctively female poetic mode.

"Confessional" poetry has, of course, been generally associated with a number of contemporary male poets, most notably Berryman, Lowell, and Snodgrass. A tradition of such writing, moreover, can easily be traced back through such male mythologists of the self as Whitman and Yeats to Wordsworth and Byron, those Romantic patriarchs whose self-examinations and self-dramatizations probably fathered not only the poetry of what Keats called the egotistical sublime but also the more recent ironic mode we might call the egotistical ridiculous. Most male poets, however, have been able to move beyond the self-deprecations and self-assertions of confessional writing to larger, more objectively formulated appraisals of God, humanity, society. Writers like Bly and Snyder, though they, too, are descendants of Whitman and Wordsworth, cannot by any stretch of the vocabulary be called confessional. Such obviously confessional male poets as Lowell and Berryman write verse in which (as M. L. Rosenthal's definition of confessional poetry puts it) "the private life of the poet himself . . . often becomes a major theme." Yet they manage to be "at once private and public, lyrical and rhetorical" (as Rosenthal also notes) because the personal crisis of the male poet "is felt at the same time as a symbolic embodiment of national and cultural crisis." Thus, just as the growth of Wordsworth's mind stands for the growth of all self-fulfilling human minds, so "the 'myth' that Lowell creates is that of an America . . . whose history and present predicament are embodied in those of his own family and epitomized in his own psychological experience."[1]

The male confessional poet, in other words, even while romantically exploring his own psyche, observes himself as a representative specimen with a sort of scientific exactitude. Alienated, he's nevertheless an ironic sociologist of his own alienation because he considers his analytic perspective on himself a civilized, normative point of view. Lowell, describing his own mental illness with desperate intensity, is still able to write with detachment in "Man and Wife" about the "hackneyed speech" and "homicidal eye" of "the kingdom of the mad," and, recalling an impassioned past, to describe his younger self with surgical precision as "boiled and shy / and poker-faced." Like other modern male *poètes maudits,* in short, he has a cool faith in his own ability to classify his own exemplary sufferings, a curious, calm confidence that even in madness he is in some sense at the intellectual center of things. Can it be (at least in part) that because he's a man, he can readily picture himself as Everyman?

Certainly, by contrast, the female confessional poet seems to feel no such paradoxical ease with her own anxieties. Even when she observes herself with amused irony, as Plath does in "Lady Lazarus" ("What a trash / To annihilate each decade . . . It's the theatrical // Comeback in broad day . . . That knocks me out"), she enacts as well as dissects her suffering, her rage, her anxiety:

> *Herr God, Herr Lucifer*
> *Beware*
> *Beware.*
>
> *Out of the ash*
> *I rise with my red hair*
> *And I eat men like air.*

The detached irony of a Lowell or a Berryman—the irony possible for a self-assured, normative sensibility—is totally unavailable to her, unavailable because even at her most objective she feels eccentric, not representative; peripheral, not central. More, she struggles with her suffering, grapples with it in bewilderment, writing what Plath (who is again paradigmatic here) called "sweating, heaving poems," because she cannot easily classify either herself or her problem. To define her suffering would be to define her identity, and such self-definition is her goal, rather than her starting point.

The male confessional poet—Lowell, Berryman, Yeats—writes in the certainty that he is the inheritor of major traditions, the grandson of history, whose very anxieties, as Harold Bloom has noted, are defined by the ambiguities of the past that has shaped him as it shaped his fathers.[2] The female poet, however, even when she is not consciously confessional like Plath or Sexton, writes in the hope of discovering or defining a self, a certainty, a tradition. Striving for self-knowledge, she experiments with different propositions about her own nature, never cool or comfortable enough to be (like her male counterparts) an ironic sociologist; always, instead, a desperate Galileo, a passionate empiricist who sees herself founding a new science rather than extending the techniques and discoveries of an old one. It is for this reason, I believe, that otherwise radically different poets like Plath, Sexton, Rich, Wakoski, and Levertov all write verse characterized by such recurrent self-defining statements—hypotheses, really—as the following:

> "I am your opus, / I am your valuable."
> "I am a nun now . . ."
> "I am not a nurse . . . I am not a smile."
> "I am dark-suited and still, a member of the party."
> "I am the arrow, / The dew that flies / Suicidal . . ."
> "I am a miner."
> "I am a letter in this slot . . ."
> "I / Am a pure acetylene / Virgin."
> "I think I may well be a Jew." "I am not a Caesar."
> "I am the magician's girl."

"I am no source of honey."

"I am no drudge . . ."

"O God, I am not like you . . ."[3]

"I am a tree gypsy: you can't shake me out of your branches."

"Here I am . . . a strange combination of images."

"I am like the guerrilla fighter / who must sleep with one eye / open for
     attack."

"I am blue, / I am blue as a blues singer, / I am blue in the face . . ."

"My body dries out / and becomes a bone sceptre . . ."

"I am the sword with / the starry hilt."

"I am ringless, ringless . . ."

"I am a blackbird."

"I am / also a ruler of the sun, I am the woman whose hair lights up a
     dark room, whose words are matches . . ."

"I am solitary, I like the owls I never see . . ."[4]

"I'm . . . a naked man fleeing / across the roofs . . ."

"I am a galactic cloud . . . / I am an instrument in the shape of a
     woman . . ."

"I am a woman in the prime of life, with certain powers . . ."

"I am the androgyne / I am the living mind you fail to describe . . ."

"I am she: I am he / Whose drowned face sleeps with open eyes . . ."

"I am an American woman, / my body a hollow ship . . . / I am not the
     wheatfield / nor the virgin forest."[5]

"Everyone in me is a bird, / I am beating all my wings."

"I am no different from Emily Goering."

"I am a watercolor. / I wash off."

"I'm Ethan Frome's wife. I'll move when I'm able."

"I am no longer the suicide / with her raft and paddle."

"I am not an idler, / am I?"

"Yes! I am still the criminal . . ."

"I have become a tree, / I have become a vase . . ."

"I am an ocean-going vessel . . ."

"I am a small handful . . ."

"I am not immortal. Faustus and I are the also-ran."[6]

"The moon is a sow / . . . and I a pig and a poet."

"Am I a pier, / half-in, half-out of the water?"
"I am faithful to / ebb and flow . . . / I hold steady / in the black sky . . .
/ There is no savor / more sweet, more salt / than to be glad to be /
what, woman, / and who, myself / I am, a shadow / that grows longer
as the sun / moves, drawn out / on a thread of wonder."[7]

Though they were taken out of context, you probably recognized many of these lines. In order of appearance, they were by Plath, Wakoski, Rich, Sexton, and Levertov. But they might all have been by one, anxiously experimental, modern Everywoman, so strikingly similar are they in structure and intention. Considering and discarding different metaphors, different propositions of identity, each of these five writers seems to be straining to formulate an ontology of selfhood, some irreducible and essential truth about her own nature. While the male poet, even at his most wretched and alienated, can at least solace himself with his open or secret creativity, his mythmaking power, the female poet must come to terms with the fact that as a female she is that which is mythologized, the incarnation of otherness (to use Beauvoir's terminology) and hence the object of anthologies full of male metaphors. Many of her hypotheses about herself are therefore in one way or another replies to prevalent definitions of her femininity, replies expressing either her distress at the disparity between male myths about her and her own sense of herself, or else her triumphant repudiation of those myths. Men tell her that she is a muse. Yet she knows that she is not a muse, she *has* a muse (and what is its sex?). Men tell her she is the "angel in the house," yet she doesn't *feel* angelic, and wonders, therefore, if she is a devil, a witch, an animal, a criminal. Men tell her that she is Molly Bloom, Mother Earth, Ishtar, a fertility goddess, a *thing* whose periodicity expresses the divine order (or is it the disorder?) of seasons, skies, stars. They tell her, echoing Archibald MacLeish's definition of a poem, that she should not mean but be. Yet meanings delight her, along with seemings, games, plays, costumes, and ideas of order, as they delight male poets. But perhaps, she speculates, her rage for order is mistaken, presumptuous?

"Alas!" complained Anne Finch, Countess of Winchilsea, in the late seventeenth century,

> a woman that attempts the pen,
> Such an intruder on the rights of men,
> Such a presumptuous Creature, is esteem'd,
> The fault, can by no vertue be redeem'd.
> They tell us we mistake our sex and way;
> Good breeding, fassion, dancing, dressing, play
> Are the accomplishments we shou'd desire;
> To write, or read, or think, or to enquire
> Wou'd cloud our beauty, and exaust our time,
> And interrupt the Conquests of our prime;
> Whilst the dull mannage, of a servile house
> Is held by some, our outmost art, and use.

Given these disadvantages, she admonished herself to "Be caution'd then . . . and still retir'd . . . / Conscious of wants, still with contracted wing, / To some few freinds [sic], and to thy sorrows sing . . ."[8] Nevertheless, this modest poetess of "Spleen" and sorrow, contending against a sense of her own contracted wing, pioneered a poetic mode for other women, a mode of reticence conquered by assertion and self-examination, a mode of self-definition *within* and *against* the context of prevailing male definitions of women.

Today, doubting her likeness to crops and fields, the woman poet asks herself, with Adrienne Rich, "Has Nature shown / her household books to you, daughter-in-law, / that her sons never saw?" and, refusing to be "a woman in the shape of a monster," she defines herself instead as "an instrument in the shape / of a woman trying to translate pulsations / into images for the relief of the body / and the reconstruction of the mind." With Esther Greenwood in *The Bell Jar* she denies that she is the passive "place an arrow shoots off from" and proposes, rather, to "shoot off in all directions" herself, to be as active and full of intentions as "the colored arrows from a Fourth of July rocket." Yet all the while, limited and defined by others, enclosed in cells of history, she perceives that she is supposed to be living quietly in her kitchen, adhering, as Plath wrathfully wrote, "to rules, to rules, to rules." And so she wonders if she is, after all, a monster like Spenser's Duessa. "A thinking woman sleeps with monsters," notes Adrienne Rich, "The beak that grips her, she becomes." And Plath asks, "What am I / That these late mouths"—the dissenting mouths of her mind—"cry open . . . ?"[9]

What am I? Who am I? What shall I call myself? Another aspect of the woman poet's struggle toward self-definition is her search for a name. Significantly, the problems and possibilities of naming recur throughout the poetry of such writers as Plath, Rich, Sexton, Levertov, and Wakoski. Perhaps even more significantly, however, where the male confessional poet uses the real names of real people to authenticate his ironic sociology, the self-defining female poet uses names as symbolic motifs, as mythic ideas. Robert Lowell, for instance, entitles one of his books *For Lizzie and Harriet,* and confesses that "hand on glass / and heart in mouth [I] / outdrank the Rahvs in the heat / of Greenwich Village . . ." while Dewitt Snodgrass sardonically insists that "Snodgrass is walking through the universe." But Levertov gives herself a generic name, reconciling herself with deep serenity to "what, woman, / and who, myself, / I am." And Plath, trapped in the identity crisis Levertov appears to have transcended, relinquishes her name, symbolic of a mistaken identity, with intense relief: "I am nobody; I have nothing to do with explosions. / I have given my name and my day-clothes up to the nurses . . ."[10]

Even Sexton, who seems at first to be playing with her name as Snodgrass toys with his, invents an imaginary Christopher to go with the reality of Anne and sets the two names in the context of a series of psalms outlining a private myth of origins: "For Anne and Christopher were born in my head as I howled at the grave of the roses . . ." Adrienne Rich goes further still, defining herself as a participant in a mysterious universal reality—"The Stranger," "the androgyne"—and noting, therefore, that "the letters of my name are written under the lids / of the newborn child." Finally, Diane Wakoski, perhaps the most obsessed with names of all these poets, mythologizes one aspect of herself by emphasizing the various implications of her name: "If you know my name, / you know

Diane comes across diamond in the word book," she writes in "The Diamond Merchant," "crossing my life . . . leaving me incomplete . . ." Elsewhere she adds: "There is / an ancient priestess / whose tears make the spiderlilies grow. / She knows my name is darkness." And she reveals a crucial tension between her name and her real identity: "Feeling the loneliness / of my cold name, I live in a secret place, / behind a carved door. / My house is a diamond and my life / is unspoken."[11]

This tension between the woman's name and the reality it may not after all represent suggests, however, a central problem that shadows all the attempts at self-definition made by the female poets discussed here. For as she struggles to define herself, to reconcile male myths about her with her own sense of herself, to find some connection between the name the world has given her and the secret name she has given herself, the woman poet inevitably postulates that perhaps she has not one but two (or more) selves, making her task of self-definition bewilderingly complex. The first of these selves is usually public and social, defined by circumstance and by the names the world calls her—daughter, wife, mother, Miss, Mrs., Mademoiselle—a self that seems, in the context of the poet's cultural conditioning, to be "her natural" personality (in the sense of being both physiologically inevitable and morally proper or appropriate). The female poet's second self, however, is associated with her secret name, her rebellious longings, her rage against imposed definitions, her creative passions, her anxiety, and—yes—her art. And it is this doppelgänger of a second self which, shadowing the woman's uneasiness with male myths of femininity, gives energy as well as complexity to her struggle toward self-definition.

For if the first self is public, rational, social, and therefore seems somehow "natural," this dark, other, second self is private, irrational, antisocial, and therefore—in the best Romantic tradition—associated with the supernatural. Denise Levertov's poem "In Mind" outlines the dichotomy between the two selves better than any prose analysis could. Noting that the poet's mind contains two radically opposite (but implicitly complementary) selves, Levertov describes the first of these as "a woman / of innocence," a woman who is "unadorned" but sweet-smelling and "fair-featured." She wears

a utopian smock or shift, her hair
is light brown and smooth, and she

is kind and very clean without
ostentation—
                        but she has
no imagination.

Shadowing this kindly public woman, however, the poet imagines a

turbulent moon-ridden girl

or old woman, or both,
dressed in opals and rags, feathers

and torn taffeta,
who knows strange songs—

but she is not kind.[12]

Innumerable male writers have also, of course, spoken in ways similar to this of doubles and otherness, imagining second, supernatural selves ranging from good wizards like Superman to bad alter egos like Mr. Hyde. But the exploration of inner alterity is only one of many modes of self-analysis available to the modern male confessional poet, whereas all the women whose poetry I've discussed here seem to share a real obsession with the second, supernatural self. "The Other" and "Again and Again and Again" are just two of many poems by Sexton that deal with this phenomenon of otherness. In the first, interestingly, she describes her supernatural self—her "other"—as masculine, an early avatar, I suppose, of Christopher, the imaginary twin she associates (in *The Death Notebooks*) with the mad eighteenth-century poet Christopher Smart:

Under my bowels, yellow with smoke,
it waits.

Under my eyes, those milk bunnies,
it waits.
It is waiting.
It is waiting.
Mr. Doppelgänger. My brother. My spouse.
Mr. Doppelgänger. My enemy. My lover.

Like Levertov's second self, Sexton's is unkind and therefore unfeminine, aggressive, masculine. My "other," she writes, "swallows Lysol."

When the child is soothed and resting on the breast
....
My other beats a tin drum in my heart.
....
It cries and cries and cries
until I put on a painted mask
and leer at Jesus in His passion.
Then it giggles.
It is a thumbscrew.
Its hatred makes it clairvoyant.
I can only sign over everything,
the house, the dog, the ladders, the jewels,
the soul, the family tree, the mailbox.

Then I can sleep.

Maybe.[13]

Inhabited by such rage, it is no wonder that the woman poet often struggles, with a kind of feverish panic, to define herself, frantically clearing away the debris of alternative selves like "old whore petticoats"— to quote Sylvia Plath—in the hope of reattaining the blazing chastity, the unviolated singleness, of a "pure acetylene / Virgin." For, inhabiting her, the second self is a cry that keeps her awake—to go on quoting Plath—flapping out nightly and "looking, with its hooks, for something to love." Yet she can define it no more precisely, can define instead only her own pain, her fear of its otherness. "I am terrified by this dark thing / That sleeps in me . . . ," Plath continues in "Elm." "All day I feel its soft, feathery turnings, its malignity." In "Again and Again and Again" Sexton notes: "I have a black look I do not / like. It is a mask I try on. /. . . its frog / sits on my lips and defecates." Even Adrienne Rich, usually affirmative in her definition of a second, supernatural self, acknowledges the awful anxiety associated with such experiences of interior otherness: "A pair of eyes imprisoned for years inside my skull / is burning its way outward, the headaches are terrible." Diane Wakoski, who writes of wanting "to smash through the fortified walls of myself / with a sledge," describes, in heavily sexual terms, "the anger of my own hair, / which is long / and wants to tie knots, / strangle, avenge this face of mine . . ." Inhabited by this cry of fury, these self-assertive, witch-dark wings that flap inside so many women poets, she feels a sort of supernatural electricity "dripping" from her "like cream" and perceives the whole world as transformed, seething with magical dangerous blue phenomena: "blue trains rush by in my sleep. / Blue herons fly overhead . . . / Blue liquid pours down my poisoned throat and blue veins / rip open my breast. Blue daggers tip / and are juggled in my palms. / Blue death lives in my fingernails." "The Eye altering alters all," as Blake observed so long ago, and the woman poet who defines herself as possessor of (or possessed by) a deadly second self inevitably begins to imagine that she's lost in a universe of death.[14]

Where is the way out of such a universe? What kind of self-definition is possible to someone who feels herself imprisoned there, her back humped with black inimical power, black wings flapping in her heart?— to go back to the poems with which I began these speculations. One answer, the one Sylvia Plath most often chooses, is for the woman poet to completely reject the "natural" self—the public, outer self of roles and names—and instead to identify entirely with her supernatural self. "Mrs. Hughes," for instance, is clearly one of Plath's old whore petticoats, as are "Otto Plath's daughter" and "the guest managing editor of *Mademoiselle*." Her real self, she insists, is "no drudge" but a queen, unleashed and flying, more terrible than she ever was. Yet here the terror is not a cause of anxiety but a sign of life and triumph. Become celestial like Rich's woman-as-galactic-cloud, healing the wounds of self-division, Plath's supernatural self appears at last as a "red / Scar in the sky, red comet," flying "Over the engine that killed her— / The mausoleum, the wax house" of the dying "natural" self. Denise Levertov, on the other hand, opts in "The Wings" for a very different solution to the problem of her black inimical power, speculating that she may have *two* wings, two second selves, both equally supernatural but "one / feathered in soot, the other // . . . pale / flare-pinions." "Well—" she asks, repudiating the rage of Plath's terrible flying scar, "Could I go / on one wing, // the white one?"[15] Perhaps, she implies, the second self is not witch, devil, animal, but in the best, Blakean sense, goddess, angel, spirit.

But, of course, to go on only one wing is a compromise, an admission of defeat and fragmentation akin to Anne Finch's sorrowful presentation of her "contracted wing." And Adrienne Rich, determined "to save the skein" of "this trailing knitted thing, this cloth of darkness, / this woman's garment" of enigmatic selfhood, refuses to compromise. Like both Plath and Levertov, however, she identifies primarily with a supernatural self, a self flying "lonely and level" as "a plane . . . / on its radio beam, aiming / across the Rockies."[16] But unlike Plath in "Stings" or Levertov in "The Wings," she's untroubled by questions about the morality of this second self. Neither black nor white, neither terrible nor blessed, it exists, Rich suggests, because it has to, for the sake of the survival of all women. Thus, the second pair of eyes, which gave the poet headaches in the 1968 "Ghazals," reappears later in "From the Prison House" as a single, healthy, visionary third eye that is impervious to pain, pure, objective, an instrument of accurate perception:

> *Underneath my lids another eye has opened*
> *it looks nakedly*
> *at the light*
>
> *that soaks in from the world of pain*
> *even when I sleep*

....

> *This eye*
> *is not for weeping*
> *its vision must be unblurred*
> *though tears are on my face*
>
> *its intent is clarity*
> *it must forget*
> *nothing.*

Despite this affirmation of the justice and inevitability of her visionary anger, it's plain that Rich, too, sees herself as fragmented. Displacing her poetic vision onto a supernatural third eye and leaving the eyes of her outer, natural self merely for weeping, she implicitly concedes—at least in this poem—the difficulty of achieving a wholeness, a single, entirely adequate self-definition. And to be honest, very few women poets, from Anne Finch to the present, have in fact managed a definitive statement of self-assertion, a complete self-definition. Yet I hope that these preliminary speculations have at least partly recorded what I think women poets themselves have fully recorded: a difficult process of self-discovery that is in full progress, moving all women continually forward toward what D. H. Lawrence (for whom the problem was considerably simpler) called "self-accomplishment."[17]

Like Lawrence, W. B. Yeats was an heir of the Romantic movement's egotistical sublime, so it was natural for him to imagine a woman singing, "'I am I, am I; / The greater grows my light / The further that I fly,'" and to note, "All creation shivers / With that sweet cry." But soon, perhaps, such self-assertive imaginings will be equally natural for women poets. Already Muriel Rukeyser, in one of her most famous passages, has envisioned a radiant union of inner and outer selves, a first jubilant joining of the fragments into a true creative whole: "No more masks! No more mythologies! / Now, for the first time, the god lifts his hand, / the fragments join in me with their own music."[18] And Denise Levertov, transcending her divided self of black and white wings, has proclaimed: "There is no savor / more sweet, more salt / than to be glad to be / what, woman, / and who, myself, / I am . . ." As for the hump of black inimical power on her back, the burden of her wings, that other self can be assimilated, she suggests, into a force that nourishes her wholeness:

> *If I bear burdens*
> *they begin to be remembered*
> *as gifts, goods, a basket*
>
> *of bread that hurts*
> *my shoulders but closes me*
>
> *in fragrance. I can eat as I go.*

—1977

"A FINE, WHITE FLYING MYTH"

The Life/Work of Sylvia Plath

Though I never met Sylvia Plath, I can honestly say that I have known her most of my life. To begin with, when I was twelve or thirteen I read an extraordinary story of hers in the "By Our Readers" columns of *Seventeen*. It was called "Den of Lions," and though the plot was fairly conventional, something about the piece affected me in inexplicable, almost "mythic" ways—ways in which I wouldn't have thought I could be affected by a *Seventeen*-reader's story. For one thing, I was faintly sickened by the narrator's oddly intense vision of her experience, an evening spent at a bar with a suave young man and some of his friends. "Is that a real flower, Marcia?" asks one of the men in the story, "with [an] oily smile . . . He had her cornered," thinks Marcia, the protagonist. "No matter what she thought to say, it would be meat for the sacrifice. 'Yes,' she said . . . 'It's real, it's basic' . . . Basic. The word had been what they wanted. *Toss a slab of raw meat to the lions.* Let them nose it, paw it, gulp it down, and maybe you'll have a chance to climb a tree out of their reach in the meantime."[1]

Could the world really be like this, I wondered. *Was* it like this? How had selves of blood and meat been admitted into the glossily sanitized pages of *Seventeen*? How could anyone so close to my own age have imagined such selves? "Sylvia enjoys being seventeen—'it's the *best* age'" was an editorial comment I found next to another of her contributions. But did she?

Plath next surfaced, of course, as a guest editor of *Mademoiselle* and as winner of that magazine's college fiction contest—the literary young woman's equivalent of being crowned Miss America. And when I myself became a guest editor, four years after she did, I found myself assigned to the same staff editor she had worked for. Now our likenesses, our common problems, as well as our divergences, began to clarify. What I had unconsciously responded to in "Den of Lions," what had made me uneasy about it, was probably that it was a story of female initiation, an account of how one girl learns to see herself as intelligent meat—victim and manipulator of men, costumes, drinks, cigarettes—flesh and artifice together. But what I much more consciously knew about the *Mademoiselle* experience was that for me, as for Sylvia and all the other guest editors, it was a kind of initiation ritual, a dramatic induction into that glittery Women's House of fashion and domesticity outside whose windows most of us had spent much of our lives, noses pressed to the glass, yearning to get in, like—to echo Yeats—Keats outside the candy shop of the world.

As *The Bell Jar* suggests, we guest editors were on the whole nice, ambitious young women from colleges all over the country. Some of us were interested in fashion, art, and design. But most had won the contest by writing stories or poems or think pieces about our "Silent Generation," intellectual work that might in other circumstances produce a place on the dean's list or a Phi Beta Kappa key—an entrance into the spacious male world of work. Instead, because all of us were ambivalent about ourselves, cashmere sweater collectors as well as collectors of good grades, we had entered the house of female work, a house, despite all our earlier peering through windows, astonishingly different from what we'd expected.

The magazine offices were pastel, intricately feminine, full of clicking spiky heels. One could almost believe that at midnight they mopped the floors with Chanel No. 5. And almost all the editors and secretaries and assistant editors were "career gals," who, as soon as we arrived, began giving us tokens of what we were and where we were, tokens quite unlike those we had become accustomed to at school. Instead of tests or books or grades, for instance, they gave us *clothes.* We sat around in a room that looked like a seminar room, and they wheeled in great racks of college-girl blouses and skirts. Into these we had to fit ourselves, like Cinderella squeezing into the glass slipper. Woe unto you if the blouse doesn't fit, was the message. If the skirt doesn't fit, wear it anyway—at least for the photographer. Later they gave us new hairdos; makeup cases, as in *The Bell Jar*; sheets and bedspreads; dances on starlit rooftops; and more, much more. On those long, hot June afternoons we sat around in our pastel air-conditioned seminar room discussing these objects and events as if they were newly discovered Platonic dialogues.

For of course the whole experience of *Mademoiselle* was curiously metaphorical: events occurred, as in a witty fiction, that seemed always to have a meaning beyond themselves. The poisoning in Plath's year, for example, really happened. Yet that doesn't diminish its symbolic significance in *The Bell Jar*. The fashionable menus of Madison Avenue (*Mad Ave* for short) were figuratively as well as literally indigestible. And naturally such unexpected tokens of femininity took their toll among the guest editors. Some couldn't bear to go near the "official" residential hotel (which for good reason Plath calls the Amazon). Others became *hysterical,* portentous word, at work or after work. Esther Greenwood, perhaps like Plath herself, throws away her New York clothes, no doubt including all the free "collegiate" outfits.

To complicate things further, for me and for Plath, there was the woman Plath calls Jay Cee, the editor with whom we worked every day. Jay Cee was the only woman at the magazine who was not a stereotypical "career gal." Instead, she was a serious, unfashionable, professional woman. But in those ruffly, stylish corridors she seemed somehow desexed, disturbing, like a warning of what might happen to you if you threw away the clothes and entered the nunnery of art. And, like the bald "Disquieting Muses" in an early poem of Plath's, the "dismal-headed / Godmothers" who "stand their vigil in gowns of stone," she constantly forced us to confront ourselves and, additionally, the abyss into which we seemed to be falling. "What are you going to do next?" she would ask. "What are your plans for the future? Have you attempted to publish?

Have you thought about a career?" She was efficient; she was kind; she was perfect; yet she seemed, in some mysterious way, terrible.

The next I heard of Sylvia Plath was in the early sixties. She was publishing careful, elegantly crafted poems in places like *The Atlantic* and *The New Yorker,* poems that bore out Robert Lowell's later remarks about her "checks and courtesies," her "maddening docility."[2] Then one day a friend who worked at *The New Yorker* called to say, "Imagine, Sylvia Plath is dead." And three days later "Poppies in July," "Edge," "Contusion," and "Kindness" appeared in the *Times Literary Supplement.* Astonishingly undocile poems. Poems of despair and death. Poems with their heads in ovens (although the rumor was at first that Plath had died of the flu or pneumonia). Finally the violence seeped in, as if leaking from the poems into the life, or, rather, the death. She had been killed, had killed herself, had murdered her children, a modern Medea. And at last it was really told, the story everyone knows already, and the outlines of history began to thicken to myth. All of us who had read her traced our own journey in hers: from the flashy Women's House of *Mademoiselle* to the dull oven of Madame, from college to villanelles to babies to the scary skeletons of poems we began to study, now, as if they were sacred writ. The Plath Myth, whatever it meant or means, had been launched like a queen bee on its dangerous flight through everybody's psyche.

The Plath Myth: Is there anything legitimate about such a phrase? Is there really, in other words, an identifiable set of forces which nudge the lives and works of women like Plath into certain apparently mythical (or "archetypal") patterns? In answer, and in justification both of my imagery and of my use of personal material that might otherwise seem irrelevant, I want to suggest that the whole story I have told so far conforms in its outlines to a mythological way of structuring female experience that has been useful to many women writers since the nineteenth century. In Plath's case the shape of the myth is discernible both in her work and in the life that necessitated that work. In addition, the ways in which as woman and as writer she diverges from the common pattern are as interesting as those ways in which she conforms to it; perhaps, indeed, they will prove more valuable for women writers in the future.

The poet Robert Bly has recently been writing and speaking about the connection between the female psyche and what I am calling the mythological mode. He argues, for instance, that the fairy tale was distinctively a female form, a womanly way of coming to terms with reality, the old matriarchy's disguised but powerful resistance against the encroachments of the patriarchy. While I don't intend, here, to explore all the implications of this assertion, it is obviously related to what I am saying. Women writers, especially when they're writing *as women,* have tended to rely on plots and patterns that suggest the obsessive patterns of myths and fairy tales. For instance, what Ellen Moers has called "Female Gothic" is a characteristically mythological genre: it draws heavily upon unconscious imagery, apparently archetypal events, fairy-tale plots, and so forth.[3] And, to use Frank Kermode's distinction between myth and fiction, it implies not an "as if" way of seeing the world but a deep faith in its own structures, structures which, to refer briefly to Lévi-Strauss' theory of myth, offer psychic solutions to serious social, economic, and sexual-emotional problems. (Male writers, especially since the Romantic period, have also of course worked in this mode, but not with such evident single-mindedness. And male "confessional" poets like Lowell and Berryman seem quite able to organize their experience into serious metaphors without it.)

An important question then arises: *Why* do so many women writers characteristically work the mythological vein? Some critics might account for the phenomenon—following Bachofen, Neumann, and others—with what I regard as a rather sentimental and certainly stereotypical explanation. The dark, intuitive, Molly Bloomish female unconscious, they would say, just naturally generates images of archetypal power and intensity.

But it seems to me that a simpler, more sensible explanation might also be possible. Women as a rule, even sophisticated women writers, haven't until quite recently been brought to think of themselves as conscious subjects in the world. Deprived of education, votes, jobs, and property rights, they have also, even more significantly, been deprived of

their own selfhood. "What shall I do to gratify myself—to be admired—
or to vary the tenor of my existence? are not the questions which a
woman of right feelings asks on first awaking to the avocations of the
day," Mrs. Sarah Stickney Ellis admonished the women of England in
1844. Instead, that energetic duenna of Victorian girls, the Ann Landers
of her age, formulated an ideal of ladylike unselfishness—or, better, *self-
lessness.* "Woman . . . is but a meager item in the catalogue of humanity,"
she reminded her readers, unless she forgets her "minute disquietudes,
her weakness, her sensibility"—in short, unless she forgets her self.[4] So
many important men (like Rousseau, Ruskin, and Freud) also expressed
this idea that it is no wonder women haven't been able to admit the complex problem of their own subjectivity—either to themselves or others.
Rather, they have disguised the stories of their own psychic growth, even
from themselves, in a multitude of extravagant, apparently irrelevant
forms and images.

For instance, when Charlotte Brontë undertook to write what is
essentially a *Bildungsroman,* the story of one young woman's develop-
ment to maturity, she couldn't write the serious, straightforward, neo-
Miltonic account of the "growth of a poet's mind" that Wordsworth
produced. A female version of such a narrative would be unprecedented.
She couldn't really even use the kind of domestic symbolism Joyce and
Lawrence employed, though attention to domestic detail was said by
George Henry Lewes to be a special feminine talent.[5] Instead, she had
to sublimate, disguise, mythologize her *rite de passage,* especially in *Jane
Eyre* (though also to a lesser extent in *Villette*). This was partly, no doubt,
for good commercial reasons. Female Gothic sells, sells now, still, as it
sold then. But the main reason, neither inherent nor commercial, was
psychosocial. Though Brontë, like many other women, could not think
her own inner growth important enough to describe in naturalistic
detail, the story itself is of course important: it is herstory and forces its
way out despite the "checks and courtesies" that have folded themselves
around her mind, forces its way out in a more conventionally "interesting" and "acceptable" disguise. Thus, in Jane Austen's novels the dramatis
personae of drawing-room comedy apparently replace the Wordswor-
thian egotistical sublime, while in the works of Mary Shelley and the

Brontës the most intimate conflicts of the self with the self, consciously inadmissible, are objectified in exotic psychodramas—the self splitting, doubling, mythologizing itself until it hardly seems any longer to have an existence within itself. Finally, with Emily Dickinson, dressed in white, addressing unread riddles to the world; or Virginia Woolf, laden with stones, merging with the waters of that dull canal the river Ouse; or Sylvia Plath, head in a mythic oven, we see the woman writer herself enacting the psychodrama in life as she had in art, becoming—as Charles Newman says of Sylvia Plath—the "myth of herself."[6]

So, I would argue, the Plath Myth began with an initiation rite described in the pages of *Seventeen,* and continued with the induction into the fashionable world of *Mademoiselle* that is examined in *The Bell Jar,* and with the publication of doggedly symmetrical poems, and the marriage in a foreign country, and the births of two babies, to the final flight of *Ariel* and the denouement in the oven and all the rest. And it was of compelling interest to Plath's female readers because, like the stories told by Charlotte Brontë and Mary Shelley, it was figuratively if not literally the same old story. Disguised, perhaps, but the same. And our own.

But what *was* the story exactly, what were its hidden lineaments, what was its message? I can best begin to answer this multiple question with references to a few good critics of Plath's work. Her husband, the poet Ted Hughes, commented shortly after her death that "the opposition of a prickly, fastidious defence and an imminent volcano is, one way or another, an element in all her early poems." And the words "prickly" and "fastidious" recall Robert Lowell's remark about "the checks and courtesies" of her "laborious shyness," her "maddening docility." George Stade, in the best single essay I know about Plath's work, relates these statements about fastidiousness and docility versus volcanic intensity to the middle-period poem "In Plaster," a piece in which the speaker complains that she has been trapped in a tidy but murderous replica of herself, a plaster cast. "I shall never get out of this!" she exclaims. "There are two of me now: / This new absolutely white person and the old yellow one." "The persona speaking out of any given poem by Sylvia Plath, then," writes Stade,

may be either sulphurous old yellow, or the plaster saint, or a conscious-
ness that sometimes contains these two and sometimes lies stretched
between them . . . The outer shell of consciousness may be completely or
dimly aware of the presence within: it may feel itself a puppet jerked by
strings receding into an interior distance where a familiar demon sits, in
possession, or it may try to locate the menace outside of itself . . .[7]

Plaster, the outer shell, fastidious defense, checks and courtesies, docility: all these elements clearly fit together in some way. Yet the movement of "In Plaster," as Stade notes, is *out* of the tidiness of plaster, away from the smug perfection of the carved saint, just as the movement of, say, *The Bell Jar* is out of the stale enclosure of the bell jar into a more spacious if dangerous life. And similarly the great poems of *Ariel* often catapult their protagonist or their speaker out of a stultifying enclosure into the violent freedom of the sky. "Now she is flying," Plath writes in "Stings," perhaps the best of the beekeeping poems,

> *More terrible than she ever was, red*
> *Scar in the sky, red comet*
> *Over the engine that killed her—*
> *The mausoleum, the wax house.*

And in the title poem of the collection, the one that describes the poet's runaway ride on the horse Ariel, she insists that "I / Am the arrow, / The dew that flies / Suicidal, at one with the drive / Into the red eye, the cauldron of morning." In *The Bell Jar* Plath informs us that Mrs. Willard, the mother of Esther Greenwood's repellent boyfriend Buddy, believes that "What a man is is an arrow into the future and what a woman is is the place the arrow shoots off from." But, says Esther, "the last thing I wanted was . . . to be the place an arrow shoots off from. I wanted . . . to shoot off in all directions myself, like the colored arrows from a Fourth of July rocket."[8]

Being enclosed—in plaster, in a bell jar, a cellar, or a wax house— and then being liberated from an enclosure by a maddened or suicidal or "hairy and ugly" avatar of the self is, I would contend, at the heart of the myth we piece together from Plath's poetry, fiction, and life, just as it is at the heart of much other important writing by nineteenth- and twentieth-century women. The story told is invariably a story of being trapped, by society or by the self as an agent of society, and then somehow escaping or trying to escape.

At the beginning of *Jane Eyre*, for instance, Jane is locked into a room—the red-room, interestingly, where Mr. Reed, the only "father" she has ever had, "breathed his last": in other words, a kind of patriarchal death chamber, for in this room Mrs. Reed still keeps "divers parchments, her jewel-casket, and a miniature of her dead husband" in a secret drawer in the wardrobe. Panicky, the child stares into a "great looking-glass" where her own image looms toward her, alien and disturbing. "All looked colder and darker in that visionary hollow than in reality," the grown-up narrator explains.[9] But a mirror, after all, is a sort of box, in which ideas or images of the self are also stored, like "divers parchments." Mirrors, says Sylvia Plath in a poem called "The Courage of Shutting Up," "are terrible rooms / In which a torture goes on one can only watch." So Jane is doubly enclosed, first in the red-room, then in the mirror. Later, of course, it is the first Mrs. Rochester, the raging madwoman, who is closely locked in an attic room, while Jane is apparently free to roam Thornfield at her pleasure. Yet both Jane and the madwoman, it becomes clear, have to escape, whether from actual or metaphorical confinement, Jane by madly fleeing Thornfield after learning of the madwoman's existence, and the madwoman by burning down her prison and killing herself in the process, just as if, curiously, she were an agent not only of her own desires but of Jane's.

Similarly, when we first encounter Sylvia Plath in the macabre contemporary *Bildungsroman* we might as well call *Sylvia Plath*, she is figuratively and later even literally locked into a patriarchal death chamber. "You do not do," she writes at the beginning of "Daddy," in perhaps her most famous lines, "you do not do / Any more, black shoe / In which I have lived like a foot / For thirty years, poor and white, / Barely daring to breathe or achoo." And then, significantly, "Daddy, I have had to kill you." The enclosure—the confinement—began early, we learn. Though her childhood was free and Edenic, with the vast expanse of ocean before her (as she tells us in the essay "Ocean 1212-W") when she was nine, "my father died, we moved inland"—moved away from space and playfulness and possibility, moved (if she had not already done so) into the black shoe. "Whereupon," she concludes, "those first nine years of my life sealed themselves off like a ship in a bottle—beautiful, inaccessible, obsolete, a fine, white flying myth."[10] And this is an important but slightly misleading statement, for it was she who was sealed into the bottle, and what she longed for was the lost dream of her own wings. Because, having moved inland, she had moved also into a plaster cast of herself, into a mirror image alien as the image that frightens Jane in the red-room or the stylish mirrors of the pages of *Mademoiselle,* into the bell jar, into the cellar where she curled like a doped fetus, into the mausoleum, the wax house.

In this state, she wrote, "the wingy myths won't tug at us anymore," in a poem in *The Colossus.* And then, in poem after poem, she tried to puzzle out the cause of her confinement. "O what has come over us, my sister . . . What keyhole have we slipped through, what door has shut?" she asked in "The Babysitters," a piece addressed to a contemporary. "This mizzle fits me like a sad jacket. How did we make it up to your attic . . . Lady, what am I doing / With a lung full of dust and a tongue of wood . . . ?" she complained in "Leaving Early," a poem written to another woman. "Soon each white lady will be boarded up / Against the cracking climate," she wrote in "Private Ground." And yet again, in a poem called "Dark House," she declared, "This is a dark house, very big. / . . . It has so many cellars, / Such eelish delvings . . . / I must make more maps." For her central problem had become, as it became Jane Eyre's (or Charlotte Brontë's), how to get out. How to reactivate the myth of a flight so white, so pure, as to be a rebirth into the imagined liberty of childhood?

Both Jane and Charlotte Brontë got out, as I suggested, through the mediating madness of the woman in the attic, Jane's enraged, crazed double, who burned down the imprisoning house and with it the confining structures of the past. Mary Shelley, costumed as Frankenstein, got out by creating a monster who conveniently burned down domestic cottages and killed friends, children, the whole complex of family relationships.

Emily Dickinson, who saw her life as "shaven / And fitted to a frame," got out by persuading herself that "The soul has moments of Escape— / When bursting all the doors— / She dances like a Bomb, abroad."[11] Especially in *Ariel*, but also in other works, Plath gets out by (1) killing daddy (who is, after all, indistinguishable from the house or shoe in which she has lived) and (2) flying away disguised as a queen bee (in "Stings"), a bear (in the story "The Fifty-ninth Bear"), superman (in the story "The Wishing Box"), a train (in "Getting There" and other poems), an acetylene virgin (in "Fever 103°"), a horse (in "Ariel" and other poems), a risen corpse (in "Lady Lazarus"), an arrow (in "Ariel," *The Bell Jar*, and "The Other"), or a baby (in too many poems to mention).

Of these liberating images or doubles for the self, almost all except the metaphor of the baby are as violent and threatening as Dickinson's bomb, Shelley's monster, or Brontë's madwoman. "I think I am going up. / I think I may rise— / The beads of hot metal fly, and I, love, I / Am a pure acetylene / Virgin," Plath declares in "Fever 103°," ascending "(My selves dissolving, old whore petticoats) / —to Paradise." But not a very pleasant paradise, for this ascent is "the upflight of the murderess into a heaven that loves her," to quote from "The Bee Meeting," and rage strengthens her wings, rips her from the plaster of her old whore life. As the bridegroom, the "Lord of the mirrors," approaches, the infuriated speaker of "Purdah," trapped at his side—"the agonized / Side of green Adam" from which she was born—threatens that "at his next step / I shall unloose . . . From the small jewelled / Doll he guards like a heart . . . / The lioness, / The shriek in the bath, / The cloak of holes." "Herr God, Herr Lucifer, / Beware / Beware," cries Lady Lazarus. "Out of the ash I rise with my red hair / And I eat men like air." "If I've killed one man, I've killed two—" Plath confesses in "Daddy." "The villagers never liked you. / They are dancing and stamping on you." And in "The Fifty-ninth Bear," a tale in which a couple traveling across the western United States on vacation have bet on the number of bears they'll encounter, a great hairy ugly bear lumbers out of the wilderness—and it is the fifty-ninth bear, the wife's bear, for she has chosen the number fifty-nine. First it mauls the woman's silly sun hat, symbol of her whorish domesticity; then it violently attacks the husband, who, *"as from a rapidly receding planet*" (italics mine), hears his wife's wild cry, "whether of terror or triumph he could not tell." But we can tell. We know Sadie, the wife, is dancing like a bomb abroad, like Emily Dickinson or like "Sivvy" Plath herself. We know we are witnessing "the upflight of the murderess into a heaven that loves her."[12]

Flying, journeying, "getting there," she shrieks her triumph: "The train is dragging itself, it is screaming— / An animal / Insane for the destination / . . . The carriages rock, they are cradles. / And I, stepping from this skin / Of old bandages, boredoms, old faces / Step to you from the black car of Lethe, / Pure as a baby." *Pure as a baby!* Skiing suicidally away from "numb, brown, inconsequential" Buddy, Esther Greenwood in *The Bell Jar* plummets down "through year after year of doubleness and smiles and compromise" toward "the pebble at the bottom of the well, the white sweet baby cradled in its mother's belly." *Sweet as a baby!*

How do we reconcile this tender new avatar with the hairy bear, the ferocious virgin, the violent and dangerous Lady Lazarus? That Sylvia Plath wanted to be reborn into the liberty of her own distant childhood—wanted once more to be "running along the hot white beaches" with her father—is certainly true.[13] Yet at the same time her father represented the leathery house from which she wished to escape. And the baby images in her poems often seem to have more to do with her own babies than with her own babyhood. In fact, critics often puzzle over the great creative release childbirth and maternity apparently triggered for Plath. That she loved her children is indisputable, but does not seem any more immediately relevant to an understanding of the self-as-escaping baby than her longing for her own childhood. Yes, the baby is a blessing, a new beginning—"You're . . . Right, like a well-done sum," says Plath to her child in the poem "You're." Indeed, for the doting mother the baby is even (as in "Nick and the Candlestick") "the one / Solid the spaces lean on, envious . . . ," analogous to the redeeming Holy Child, "the baby in the barn." But what have these blessings to do with the monster-mother's liberation? Doesn't the baby, on the contrary, anchor her more firmly into the attic, the dark house, the barn?

The answer to this last question is, I think, *no*, though with some qualifications. In fact, for Plath the baby is often a mediating and comparatively healthy image of freedom (which is just another important reason why the Plath Myth has been of such compelling interest to women), and this is because in her view the fertile mother is a queen bee, an analogue for the fertile and liberated poet, the opposite of that dead drone in the wax house who was the sterile, egotistical mistress of darkness and daddy.

We can best understand this polarity by looking first at some poems that deal specifically with sterility, nullity, *perfection*. "Perfection is terrible, it cannot have children," Plath wrote in "The Munich Mannequins." "Cold as snow breath, it tamps the womb / Where the yew trees blow like hydras, / . . . Unloosing their moons, month after month, to no purpose. / The blood flood is the flood of love / The absolute sacrifice. / It means: no more idols but . . . me and you." Snow, menstrual blood, egotism, childlessness, the moon, and, later in the poem, the (significantly) *bald* mannequins themselves, like "orange lollies on silver sticks"—all together these constitute a major cluster of images which appears and reappears throughout *Ariel* and the other books. Women like the frightening godmother Jay Cee seemed to be are what they equal for me, and I'm sure what they equaled for Plath. "My head ached," says Esther Greenwood at one point in *The Bell Jar*. "Why did I attract these weird old women? There was the famous poet and Philomena Guinea and Jay Cee . . . and they all wanted to adopt me in some way, and . . . have me resemble them." Bald, figuratively speaking, as "the disquieting muses" of Plath's poem and de Chirico's painting, these emblems of renunciation were Plath's—and perhaps every academically talented girl's—earliest "traveling companions." They counseled A's, docility, working for *Mademoiselle*, surrendering sexuality for "perfection," using daddy's old red-leather thesaurus to write poems, and living courteously in daddy's shoe, not like a thumbtack, irascible and piercing, but like a poor white foot, barely daring to breathe or achoo.

But "two girls there are," wrote Plath in "Two Sisters of Persephone"; "within the house / One sits; the other, without. / Daylong a duet of shade and light / Plays between these." The girl within the house, Jay Cee's girl, "in her dark wainscotted room . . . works problems on /

A mathematical machine," and "at this barren enterprise / Rat-shrewd go her squint eyes." The other girl, however, "burns open to sun's blade ... Freely becomes sun's bride ... Grows quick with seed" and, "Grass-couched in her labor's pride, / She bears a king." Or, we might add, a queen.

The first girl, like the "childless woman" of another poem, sees her "landscape" as "a hand with no lines," her sexuality as "a tree with nowhere to go." The second girl, on the other hand, producing a golden child, produces flight from the folds of her own body, self-transcendence, the dangerous yet triumphant otherness of poetry. For, as Simone de Beauvoir acutely observes in *The Second Sex*, the pregnant woman has the extraordinary experience of being both subject and object at the same time. Even while she is absorbed in her own subjectivity and isolation, she is intensely aware of being an object—a house—for another subject, another being which has its own entirely independent life. Vitality lives in her *and* within her: an ultimate expression of the Shelley-Brontë-Dickinson metaphors of enclosure, doubleness, and escape. "Ordinarily," Beauvoir remarks, "life is but a condition of existence; in gestation it appears as creative ... [The pregnant woman] is no longer an object subservient to a subject [a man, a mother, daddy, Jay Cee]; she is no longer a subject afflicted with the anxiety that accompanies liberty; she is one with that equivocal reality: life. Her body is at last her own, since it exists for the child who belongs to her."[14]

That this liberating sense of oneness with life was precisely Plath's attitude toward childbirth and maternity is clear from "Three Women," a verse play on the subject in which the voice of the First Woman, the healthily golden and achieving mother, is obviously the poet's own, or at least the voice for which the poet strives. Repudiating yet again the "horrors," the "slighted godmothers" (like the bald muses) "with their hearts that tick and tick, with their satchels of instruments," this speaker resolves to "be a wall and a roof, protecting ... a sky and a hill of good." For, she exclaims, "a power is growing in me, an old tenacity. / I am breaking apart like the world ... / I am used. I am drummed into use." Though this passage may sound as if it is about escaping or about writing poetry, it is really about having a baby. And when the child appears later on, he appears in flight—like the escaping virgin, the arrow, or the lioness—a "blue, furious boy, / Shiny and strange, as if he had hurtled from a star . . . ," who flies "into the room, a shriek at his heel." And again Plath stresses the likeness of babies, poems, and miraculous escapes: "I see them," she says of babies, "showering like stars on to the world . . . These pure small images . . . Their footsoles are untouched. They are walkers of air." Living babies, in other words, are escaping shrieks—as poems are; pure small images—as poems are; walkers of air—as poems are: all ways for the self to transcend itself.

Conversely, Plath speaks of dead poems, the poems of jeweled symmetry that would please the disquieting muses, as being like stillborn babies, an analogy which goes back to the male tradition that defines the offspring of "lady poets" as abortions, stillbirths, dead babies. "These poems do not live," she writes in "Stillborn." ". . . it's a sad diagnosis . . . they are dead, and their mother near dead with distraction." It becomes clear that certain nineteenth- and twentieth-century women, confronting *confinement* (in both senses of the word) simply translated the traditional baby-poem metaphor quite literally into their own experience of their lives and bodies. "I, the miserable and abandoned, am an *abortion,* to be spurned . . . ," said Mary Shelley's monster—and he was, for he escaped from confinement to no positive end. I "step to you from the black car of Lethe / Pure as a baby," cried Plath—meaning, my poems, escaping from the morgue of my body, do that. And "I was in a boundary of wool and painted boards . . . ," wrote Anne Sexton. But "we swallow magic and we *deliver* Anne." For the poet, finally, can be delivered from her own confining self through the metaphor of birth.[15]

Can be, but need not necessarily be. And here we get to the qualifications I mentioned earlier. For while, as Beauvoir pointed out, the processes of gestation link the pregnant woman with life even as they imply new ways of self-transcendence, they are also frightening, dangerous, and uncontrollable. The body works mysteriously, to its own ends, its product veiled like death in unknowable interior darkness. Just as the poet cannot always direct the flow of images but instead finds herself surprised by shocking connections made entirely without the help or approval of the ego, so the mother realizes, as Beauvoir notes, that "it is beyond her power to influence what in the end will be the true nature of this being who is developing in her womb . . . she is [at times] in dread of giving birth to a defective or a monster." (In other words, in Plath's case, to the ugly bear or the acetylene virgin she both fears and desires to be.) Moreover, to the extent that pregnancy depersonalizes the woman, freeing her from her own ego and instead enslaving her to the species, it draws her backward into her own past (the germ plasm she shelters belongs to her parents and ancestors as well as to her) and at the same time catapults her forward into her own future (the germ plasm she shelters will belong to her children and their survivors as well as to her). "Caught up in the great cycle of the species, she affirms life in the teeth of time and death," says Beauvoir. "In this she glimpses immortality; but in her flesh she feels the truth of Hegel's words: 'the birth of children is the death of parents.'"[16] To Plath, this network backward and forward was clearly of immense importance. For, if having babies (and writing poems) was a way of escaping from the dark house of daddy's shoe, it was also, paradoxically, a frightening reencounter with daddy: daddy alive, and daddy dead.

Nowhere is that re-vision of daddy more strikingly expressed than in the beekeeping sequence in *Ariel*. Otto Plath was a distinguished entomologist, the author of many papers on insect life, including (significantly) one on "A Muscid Larva of the San Francisco Bay Region Which Sucks the Blood of Nestling Birds." But his most important work was a book called *Bumblebees and Their Ways,* an extraordinarily genial account of the lives of bee colonies, which describes in passing the meadows, the nest boxes, the abandoned cellars inhabited by bumblebees, and the "delicious honey" they make, but concentrates mostly on the sometimes sinister but always charismatic power and fertility of the queens. The induction of the colony into the bee box, stings, wintering, "the upflight of the murderess into a heaven that loves her"—all these are described at length by Otto Plath, and his daughter must have read his descriptions with intense attention. Her father's red-leather thesaurus, we're told, was always with her. Why not also *Bumblebees and Their Ways*? Considering all this, and considering also the points made by Beauvoir, it's almost too fictionally neat to be true that Plath told an interviewer after the birth of her son Nicholas that "our local midwife has taught me to keep bees."[17] Yet it is true.

Plath's beekeeping, at least as it is represented in the *Ariel* sequence, appears to have been a way of coming to terms with her own female position in the cycle of the species. When the colony is put into the box by "the villagers," *she* is put into "a fashionable white straw Italian hat" (the sort of hat the fifty-ninth bear tears up, the sort of hat they would have given us at *Mademoiselle*) and led "to the shorn grove, the circle of hives." Here she can only imagine the "upflight" of the deadly queen— for she (both the queen and the poet), the poem implies, has been put into a box along with the rest of the colony. "Whose is that long white box in the grove, what have they accomplished, why am I cold," she asks. But the question is merely rhetorical, for the box is hers, hers and (we learn in the next poem) perhaps her baby's. "I would say it was the coffin of a midget," she decides there, "or a square baby / Were there not such a din in it." And the rest of the piece expresses the double, interrelated anxieties of poetry and pregnancy: "The box is locked, it is dangerous . . . I have to live with it . . . I can't keep away from it . . . I have simply ordered a box of maniacs . . . They can be sent back. / They can die, I need feed them nothing. I am the owner . . . ," culminating in a hopeful resolution: "The box is only temporary."

But when the box is opened, in the third poem, the bees escape like furious wishes, attacking "the great scapegoat," the father whose "efforts" were "a rain / Tugging the world to fruit." And here, most hopefully, the poet, mother of bees and babies, tries to dissociate herself from the self-annihilating stings her box has produced. "*They* thought death was worth it, but I / Have a self to recover, a queen." And "Now she is flying / More terrible than she ever was, red / Scar in the sky, red comet / Over the engine that killed her— / The mausoleum, the waxhouse."

Alas, her flight is terrible because it is not only an escape, it is a death trip. Released from confinement, the fertile and queenly poet must nevertheless catapult back into her dead past, forward into her dead future, like Esther Greenwood, plummeting toward the "white sweet baby cradled in its mother's belly," which is, after all, likened to a dead inanimate thing, a still "pebble." "I / Am the arrow, / The dew that flies / Suicidal, at one with the drive / Into the red / Eye, the cauldron of morning," Plath had cried in the poem "Ariel." But just as the fertile poet's re-vision of daddy is killing, so the suicidal cauldron of morning is both an image of rebirth and a place where one is cooked; and the red solar eye, certainly in Freudian terms, is the eye of the father, the patriarchal superego which destroys and devours with a single glance.

A profound and inescapable irony of many literary women's works and lives is that in her flight from the coffin of herself the woman-writer or the character who is her surrogate is often consumed by the Heraclitean fires of change that propel her forward. Charlotte Brontë's madwoman burns up Rochester's house *and* herself; Mary Shelley's monster plans a funeral pyre to extinguish himself entirely, soul and all; Emily Dickinson's bomb of the spirit will surely explode any minute; and Sylvia Plath, dissolving into the cauldron of morning, "is lost," as she says in the poem "Witch-Burning," "lost in the robes of all this brightness." One may be renewed like a baby in the warm womb of the mythic oven, but the oven is also Auschwitz, Dachau, a place where one is baked like a gingerbread body back into the plaster cast of oneself.

For this reason, it is the paradox of Plath's life (perhaps of any woman's life) and of the Plath Myth that even as she longs for the freedom of flight, she fears the risks of freedom—the simultaneous reactivation and disintegration of the past it implies. "What I love is / The piston in motion," Plath says in the poem "Years," then adds ambiguously, "My soul *dies* before it." "And you, great Stasis," she continues, "What is so great in that!" Yet at the same time she is drawn to the sea, "that great abeyance"—to the pool of Stasis where the hair of the father spreads in tides like unraveled seaweed. "Father," she had complained in an early poem, "this thick air is murderous . . . I would breathe water." And elsewhere, "Stone, stone, ferry me down there," she begged: ferry me into the pit, the oven, the sea of stasis, the bottom of the pool where (as she says in "Words") "fixed stars govern a life" and (as she declares in "Edge") "the woman is *perfected*," her children—her independent adulthood—"folded back into her body," "the illusion of a Greek necessity" flowing in "the scrolls of her toga; her bare feet . . . saying, we have come so far, it is over."

What is the way out of this dilemma? How does a woman reconcile the exigencies of the species—her desire for stasis, her sense of her ancestry, her devotion to the house in which she has lived—with the urgencies of her own self? I don't know the answer. For Sylvia Plath, as for many other women, there was apparently, in real life, no way out. But there was a way out in art. And to honor Sylvia Plath, to honor the achievement of her poems as well as their place in my own life, I want to stress the positive significance of her art and its optimistically feminine redefinition of traditions that have so far been primarily masculine.

Women and Romantic poets are, after all, alike in certain interesting respects. "Not I, not I, but the wind that blows through me," cried D. H. Lawrence, echoing Wordsworth, Shelley, and a whole Norton Anthology full of others. "A fine wind is blowing the new direction of time." So, to Plath, when she was working at her best it must have seemed that, as she tells us in *Ariel*, "some god got hold" of her; the recesses of body and mind worked their own will, independent of the observing consciousness (which was itself by turns pleased, amused, disgusted, and terrified); cells of thought buzzed and multiplied like bees swarming, or wintering, quiescent; and the babies arrived, Ted Hughes tells us, easily, Frieda, the first, "at exactly sunrise, on the first day of April, the day [Sylvia] regularly marked as the first day of Spring." And so also, and also at sunrise, in (Plath herself noted) "that still blue almost eternal hour before . . . the glassy music of the milkman," the "cool morning hours" when Otto Plath wrote that it was best to work and the bees were least "pugnacious," the poems began to arrive, with the strenuous ease of babies, as if the same musing double, the lion-red queen bee Robert Bly would call the "ecstatic mother," had liberated them and herself from some Pandora's box. And like the babies, the poems had, now, a squalling imperfection. Where the lines of the earlier "stillborn" works had been stonily symmetrical, jeweled, chiseled, the lines of these later works are long and short, irregular as gasping breath, deliberately imperfect, not because of an impulse to self-indulgence or a failure of control, but because of a conscious decision that "perfection is terrible, it cannot have children."[18]

"The poets I delight in are possessed by their poems as by the rhythms of their own breathing. Their finest poems seem born all of a piece, not put together by hands," Plath wrote toward the end of her life.[19] The description applies to her own late poems: possessed of the imperfections of breath, they are nevertheless "born all of a piece," alive, viable, self-sufficient. Out of the wax house of *Mademoiselle,* out of the mausoleum of the woman's body, out of the plaster of the past, these poems fly, pure and new as babies. Fly, redeemed—even if their mother was not—into the cauldron of morning.

—1978

THE WAYWARD NUN
BENEATH THE HILL

Emily Dickinson and the Mysteries of Womanhood

Young Mabel Loomis Todd had been living for two months in Amherst, Massachusetts, where her husband David had just been appointed director of the Amherst College Observatory, when on November 6, 1881, she wrote her parents an enthusiastic letter about one of the town's most fascinating citizens:

I must tell you about the character of Amherst. It is a lady whom the people call the Myth. She is a sister of Mr. Dickinson, & seems to be the climax of all the family oddity. She has not been outside of her own house in fifteen years, except once to see a new church, when she crept out at night, & viewed it by moonlight. No one who calls upon her mother & sister ever sees her, but she allows little children once in a great while, & one at a time, to come in, when she gives them cake or candy, or some nicety, for she is very fond of little ones. But more often she lets down the sweetmeat by a string, out of a window, to them. She dresses wholly in white, & her mind is said to be perfectly wonderful. She writes finely, but no one ever sees her. Her sister, who was at Mrs. Dickinson's party, invited me to come & sing to her mother sometime

. . . People tell me the myth *will hear every note—she will be near, but unseen . . . Isn't that like a book? So interesting?*

By now that letter has become almost as famous as the Mythic Miss Dickinson herself, largely because it seems to have contributed to a process of mystification and fictionalization that surrounded one of America's greatest writers with what Thomas Wentworth Higginson once called a "fiery mist."[1]

Higginson himself also, of course, contributed to this process that transformed a reclusive poet-cook into a New England Nun of Love-and-Art. More than a decade before Mabel Todd recorded the rumors she had heard about "the rare mysterious Emily," he visited his self-styled "Scholar" in her Amherst home, and though his notes on the meeting are not as Gothic as the stories Mrs. Todd reported to her parents, they add both fire and mist to the mythic portrait, with their description of how there was "a step like a pattering child's in entry" and "a little plain woman . . . in a very plain & exquisitely clean white pique . . . came to me with two day lilies, which she put in a sort of childlike way into my hand & said, 'These are my introduction' in a soft frightened breathless child-like voice . . ." Interestingly enough, moreover, even the "little plain woman's" most prosaic remarks seemed to enhance the evolving Myth with just the dash of paradox needed to give a glimmer of irony to the dramatic halo around her: "She makes all the bread," Higginson observed, "for her father only likes hers & says, '& people must have puddings,' this *very* dreamily, as if they were comets—so she makes them."[2]

After her death, in fact, a number of Dickinson's admirers liked to dwell on that ineffable glimmer of irony. "Even though her mind might be occupied with 'all mysteries and all knowledge,' including meteors and comets, her hands were often busy in most humble household ways," wrote her cousin Helen Knight Wyman in a 1905 article for the *Boston Cooking-School Magazine* on "Emily Dickinson as Cook and Poetess." She "wrote indefatigably, as some women cook or knit," added R. P. Blackmur in 1937. As the Myth grew and glowed, drama, domesticity, and Dickinson seem to have become inseparable. It is no wonder, then—given this unlikely, often absurdly literary image of an obsessively childlike, Gothic yet domestic spinster—that recent readers of Dickinson's verse have struggled to deconstruct the "Myth of Amherst" and discover instead the aesthetic technician, the intellectual, and the visionary, whose lineaments would seem to have been blurred or obliterated in the "fiery mist" generated not by the poet herself but by her friends and admirers.[3]

I want to argue here, however, that though their fictionalizations may sometimes have been crude or melodramatic, Mabel Loomis Todd, Thomas Wentworth Higginson, and many others were not in fact projecting their own fantasies onto the comparatively neutral (if enigmatic) figure of Emily Dickinson. Rather, as I will suggest, all of these observers were responding to a process of self-mythologizing that led Dickinson herself to use the materials of daily reality, and most especially the details of domesticity, as if they were not facts but metaphors, in order to re-create herself-and-her-life as a single, emblematic text, and often, indeed, as a sort of religious text—the ironic hagiography, say, of a New England nun. More specifically, I want to suggest that Dickinson structured this life/text around a series of "mysteries" that were distinctively female, deliberately exploring and exploiting the characteristics, even the constraints, of nineteenth-century womanhood so as to transform and transcend them.

Finally, I want to argue that such a provisional and analytic acceptance of the Dickinson Myth may serve the reality of Dickinson's art better than the contemptuous rejection of legend that has lately become fashionable. For by deciphering rather than deconstructing the intricate text of this poet's life, we may come closer to understanding the methods and materials of her actual, literary texts. Throughout this essay, therefore, I will try to "read" biographical mysteries, and I will use the word "mystery" in almost all the current as well as a few of the archaic senses given by the *OED*. These include "a religious truth known only from divine revelation"; "a mystical presence"; a "religious . . . rite, especially a sacramental rite of the Christian religion"; "an incident in the life of [Christ] regarded . . . as having a mystical significance"; "a hidden or secret thing . . . a riddle or enigma"; "a 'secret' or highly technical operation in a trade or art"; a secret rite; a "miracle-play"; "a service, occupation; office, ministry"; "a handicraft, craft, art, trade, profession, or calling"; and finally "a kind of plum cake." All of these senses of "mystery"—even, or perhaps especially, the plum cake—have some application to both the Myth and the mythmaking of Emily Dickinson.

For like her Romantic precursor John Keats, one of the poets to whom she turned most often for sustenance, Dickinson understood that a "life of any worth is a continual allegory." Thus she ambitiously undertook to live (and to create) "a life like the scriptures, figurative—which [some] people can no more make out than they can the hebrew Bible." Such a life, as Keats observed, need not be theatrical; one might be both public and melodramatic without achieving true significance. "Lord Byron cuts a figure—but he is not figurative—," Keats commented wryly, and Dickinson would have seen such a remark as offering her permission to dramatize the private "trivia" of domesticity, rather than public turmoil, permission even to conflate puddings and comets. For again, like Keats, she would have perceived the essential reciprocity of the life/text and the literary text. About Shakespeare, for instance, Keats famously observed that he "led a life of Allegory: his works are the comments on it." But as I hope to show, the same striking statement can be made about the mysteries Dickinson enacted and allegorized.[4]

Dickinson's impulse to enact mysteries can be traced back almost to her childhood. Two episodes from her year at Mount Holyoke, for instance, seem to have signaled what was on the way. The first is one Mabel Todd claimed to have heard about from the poet's sister Vinnie. The seventeen-year-old Emily, wrote Mrs. Todd, "was never floored. When the Euclid examination came and she had never studied it, she went to the blackboard and gave such a glib exposition of imaginary figures that the dazed teacher passed her with the highest mark." The second episode is more famous and has been widely discussed, even by biographers and critics who dislike the "Myth of Amherst." Throughout Dickinson's time at Mount Holyoke, the school was in the throes of an evangelical revival eagerly encouraged by Mary Lyon, the school's founder and principal. According to Clara Newman Turner, there was an occasion when "Miss Lyon . . . asked all those who wanted to be Christians to rise. The wording of the request was not such as Emily could honestly accede to and she remained seated—the only one who did not rise."[5]

In these two episodes, we can discern the seeds of personal and religious mysteries that Dickinson was to develop and dramatize throughout both her life/text and her literary texts. Moreover, these two episodes suggest that we can reduce the major Dickinsonian mysteries to two categories: mystery as puzzle (secret, riddle, enigma, or blackboard battle with imaginary figures), and mystery as miracle (mystic transformation, inexplicable sacrament, or private parallel to traditional Christian professions of faith). If we bear these two categories in mind as we meditate on Dickinson's "life as Allegory," we find that, on the one hand, at the center of this poet's self-mythologizing mystery-as-puzzle we confront a kind of absence or blank, the enigmatic wound that many biographers have treated as if it were the subject of a romantic detective novel called *The Mystery of the Missing Lover*. At the center of the Dickinson mystery-as-miracle, on the other hand, we encounter a presence or power, the *"White Heat"* of Dickinson's art, whose story we might label *The Mystery of the Muse*. Yet these two mysteries—we might also call them the mysteries of Life and Art—are of course connected. For, even more than most other writers, Emily Dickinson the poet mysteriously transformed the pain associated with the puzzle at the center of her life into the miracle of her art; through that transformation, indeed, she became the "Myth of Amherst."

To speak of puzzles and miracles, however—or even to speak of all the finely distinguished definitions of "mystery" the *OED* offers—is still to speak in generalities. When one becomes more specific, however, the puzzle of Dickinson's life is, at least on the surface, vulgarly and easily defined: Who *was* "he"? Or "she"? Were there several? And was it because of "him" or "her" (or "them") that this brilliant woman more or less completely withdrew from the world? When she declared, at the age of thirty-eight, that "I do not cross my Father's ground to any House or town,"[6] was she secretly anticipating "his" return? By now, a century and a half since Emily Dickinson was born, it seems fairly certain that we will never know "his" (or "their") identity. But that the "Myth of Amherst" spent part of her poetic lifetime nurturing romantic feelings about someone, whether real or imaginary, is quite certain: we know, for instance, from her so-called "Master" letters and from the later letters to Judge Lord, that this puzzling poet was a dazzling writer of love letters, better than Charlotte Brontë and at least as good as John Keats. In addition, she produced a series of elegant and often sensual verses memorializing romance, real or imaginary—poems that range from the suave and courtly "The Daisy follows soft the Sun—" to the subtly voluptuous "Wild Nights—Wild Nights!"

It is clear, too, that Dickinson's relationship with her real or imaginary lover (or lovers) gave her "great pain" that must have had something to do with her renunciation of him and/or the world. Her heartbroken and heartbreaking "Master" letters suggest this, and impassioned poems like "Why make it doubt—it hurts it so—" and "My life closed twice before its close—" would be hard to understand otherwise. "Why make it doubt," for instance, is obviously tormented and almost certainly autobiographical, describing the suffering "it" as

> *So sick—to guess—*
> *So strong—to know—*
> *So brave—upon its little Bed*
> *To tell the very last They said*
> *Unto Itself—and smile—And shake—*
> *For that dear—distant—dangerous—Sake*
> *But—the Instead—the Pinching fear*
> *That Something—it did do—or dare*
> *Offend the Vision—and it flee—*
> *And They no more remember me—*
> *Nor ever turn to tell me why—*
> *Oh, Master, This is Misery*

Mysteriously, the poet/speaker transforms herself here into a mere lump of pain, but the identity of the Master whose favor she begs is more mysterious. Still, even the stumblings and hesitations, the advances and retreats in this work authenticate the torment it expresses. Gasping and elliptical, it seems like a speech spun out of delirium; reading it, we become witnesses to a crisis in love's fever, watchers by the sickbed of romance.

It is difficult, though, to ignore the curiously theatrical language evoked by Dickinson's odd combination of speech and silence, frankness and mystery. In the sentence before last I used the words *seems, fever, romance*. These words do, of course, refer to states of being that are somehow "true," but their truth is more likely the truth of art, of metaphor, than the truth of "reality." As we watch this puzzling enactment of "a woman's life," we may begin to feel rather like a dazed audience watching a brilliant schoolgirl solve entirely imaginary problems in geometry. Significantly, indeed, the more vivid the mystery-as-puzzle of Dickinson's life becomes, the more it melts into the mystery-as-miracle of Dickinson's art. For if the mysteries of this poet's life are often riddles of absence or silence, then the mysteries of her art are marvels of transformation, what she once called "conversion of the mind" in which we see a great performer turning defeat into triumph like a magician changing water into wine.[7]

Dickinson wrote a number of verses that not only enact but also describe and analyze such marvelous transformations. In these works, her Master/lover has stopped being an ordinary man—if he ever was one—and becomes a miraculous and sacramental being, on at least one occasion a god in the garden of love, and, more frequently, a muse in the heaven of invention. In "There came a day at Summer's Full / Entirely for me," for example, the speaker's lover is a "Sealed Church" with whom she is "Permitted to commune" on this one transfigured occasion. When the two part, she declares that "Each bound the Other's Crucifix— / We gave no other Bond—:" but that, she adds, is "Sufficient troth, that we shall rise— / Deposed—at length, the Grave— / To that new Marriage, / Justified—through Calvaries of Love—." Most striking here is Dickinson's deft fusion of the language of love with the vocabulary of Christianity, a poetic gesture that goes back at least to the medieval romance—for instance to the "Cave of Love" inhabited by Tristan and Isolde—but that this self-mythologizing New England nun makes distinctively her own. For as she transforms her real or imaginary lover/Master into a suffering god of love and herself into his "Empress of Calvary," Dickinson performs a complementary conversion. Defining her-self and her lover as "Sealed churches" and their erotic communion as a sacrament, she converts the Christianity she had begun to reject as a seventeen-year-old Mount Holyoke student into a complex theology of secular love.

In "I have a King, who does not speak—" and "My Life had stood—a Loaded Gun—" she performs equally skillful but slightly different acts of poetic prestidigitation, converting the mysterious figure she romanti-cizes from a lover into a male muse. Significantly, moreover, though the male muse in both these poems is given an impressive title—in one he is a King, in the other a Master—he is strangely passive and silent in both works; indeed, it is his passivity and silence that apparently empower the poet's triumphant speech. The enigmatic "King who does not speak," for instance, enables Dickinson, like a modern priestess of Delphi, to "peep" at night, "thro' a dream" into "parlors shut by day."

> *And if I do—* [she declares] *when morning comes—*
> *It is as if a hundred drums*
> *Did round my pillow roll,*
> *And shouts fill all my Childish sky,*
> *And Bells keep saying "Victory"*
> *From steeples in my soul!*

Similarly, when the poet imagines herself as a "Loaded Gun" she arranges for her owner and Master to carry her into "Sovereign Woods" where "everytime I speak for Him— / The Mountains straight reply—"

> *And do I smile* [she adds ironically], *such cordial light*
> *Upon the Valley glow—*
> *It is as a Vesuvian face*
> *Had let its pleasure through—*

Plainly, no matter what Dickinson meant by the famous riddle that ends this mysterious work, the central mystery-as-miracle the poem records is the woman writer's appropriation of her Master/owner's power.[8]

Though he has identified her, seized her, carried her away, it is finally she who, in a kind of prototypical role reversal, guards him with her deadly energy. "None stir the second time—" she boasts, "On whom I lay a yellow Eye— / Or an emphatic Thumb."

The mysteries of Dickinson's art accomplished some transformations of experience, however, that were even more remarkable than those recorded in "I have a King" and "My Life had stood." There, the poet had made the Master/lover who evidently humbled her into a figure who paradoxically strengthened her. But in other poems, she converted "great pain" itself—the humiliating vicissitudes of romance, for instance, along with all the other terrors of her life—into an extraordinary source of energy. "A *Wounded* Deer—leaps highest," she insists quite early in her poetic career, and in the same poem she also points out the power of "The *Smitten* Rock that gushes! / The *trampled* Steel that springs!"—eerie transformations of anguish into energy. A year or two later (1861), in one of her many mortuary poems, she exclaims that the sight of death is "so appalling—it exhilarates— / So over Horror, it half Captivates—." Brooding by someone's deathbed, she remarks that here "Terror's free— / Gay, Ghastly, Holiday"—an even eerier transformation of agony into energy. In a number of poems about volcanoes, moreover, she speculates

> *If the stillness is Volcanic*
> *In the human face*
> *When upon a pain Titanic*
> *Features keep their place—*

and wonders

> *If at length the smouldering anguish*
> *Will not overcome—*
> *And the palpitating Vineyard*
> *In the dust be thrown?*[9]

Finally, in a poem that is both searingly sincere and a triumph of irony, Dickinson describes the way she herself has been transformed through the sufferings of love into a paradoxical being, an *Empress* of *Calvary,* a Queen of Pain.

> *Title divine—is mine!*
> *The Wife—without the Sign!*
> *Acute Degree—conferred on me*
> *Empress of Calvary!*

Surely this poem's central image is almost the apotheosis of anguish converted into energy, what Dickinson elsewhere called the "ecstasy of death." Transforming the puzzles of life into the paradoxes of art, the poet/speaker is on a kind of "Gay, Ghastly, Holiday," reminding us that she is the same woman who once told Thomas Wentworth Higginson that "I had a terror . . . I could tell to none—and so I sing, as the Boy does by the Burying Ground—because I am afraid—."[10]

It is significant, however, that the "Gay, Ghastly, Holiday" into which Dickinson so often converts her "great pain" is not a weekend in "Domingo" or a passage to India. On the contrary, though she characterizes herself as an Empress of Calvary, this poet is always scrupulously careful to explain that she "never saw a moor . . . never saw the sea." Her muse-like "King who does not speak" maintains his inspiring silence in a *parlor,* after all, and even the Master who owns the "Loaded Gun" of her art sleeps on an "Eider-Duck's / Deep Pillow" that sounds as homely as any bedding nineteenth-century New England had to offer. Dickinson loved exotic place-names—admiring, for instance, the "mail from Tunis" that the hummingbird brought to the bushes on her father's ground—but nevertheless the news of those distances came to her at home, in her parlor, her kitchen, her garden. For her,

> *Eden is that old-fashioned House*
> *We dwell in every day*
> *Without suspecting our abode*
> *Until we drive away.*

Moreover, as Adrienne Rich has reminded us in one of the best recent essays on Emily Dickinson's cloistered art, Dickinson felt that although

> *Volcanoes be in Sicily*
> *And South America . . .*
> *Volcanoes nearer here*
> *A Lava step at any time*
> *Am I inclined to climb*
> *A Crater I may contemplate*
> *Vesuvius at Home.*

For as a mistress of the mysteries of transformation, Dickinson was not just an extravagant miracle-worker, an Empress of Calvary; she was a magician of the ordinary, and hers was a Myth of *Amherst,* a Myth, that is, of the daily and the domestic, a Myth of what could be seen "New Englandly." In this commitment to dailiness, moreover, even more than in her conversions of an unidentified figure into a muse and agony into energy, she defines and enacts distinctive mysteries of womanhood that have great importance not only for her own art but also for the female poetic tradition of which she is a grandmother.[11]

Many male poets, of course, have also performed miracles of literary transformation. Some, for instance, have metamorphosed beloved women into muses (one thinks of Keats' "La Belle Dame sans Merci"). Others have transformed agony into energy (Donne's Holy Sonnets). Still others have even converted the ordinary into the emblematic, the secular or domestic into the sacred (Wordsworth, Stevens, George Herbert). What is notable about Dickinson, however, is (first) that in poems and letters she performs all these kinds of transformations, sometimes simultaneously, and (second) that the images into which she transforms ideas and events are so often uniquely "female"; that is, they are associated with women's literature and women depicted in literature, or else they are associated with woman's life and woman's place. Specifically, the womanly mysteries-as-miracles of Emily Dickinson's life/text fall into five major groups: the mystery of romance (a woman's literary genre); the mystery of renunciation (a woman's duty); the mystery of domesticity (a woman's sphere); the mystery of nature (figuratively speaking, a woman's analog or likeness); and the mystery of *woman's* nature.

As we have already seen, the first two of these groups include poems in which Dickinson describes and discusses her transformations of her mysterious Master into an empowering muse as well as her conversion of agony into energy—both metamorphoses accomplished with the aid of imagery drawn from "Female Gothic" novels like *Jane Eyre* and *Wuthering Heights* or with the help of ideas drawn from the works of a woman artist of renunciation like George Eliot. With astonishing frequency, however, this poet's transformative processes are facilitated not just by literary models but by non-literary female activities. More often than not, indeed, she negotiates the difficult passage from life to art through the transformation of objects and images drawn from her "ordinary" daily domestic experience. In fact, she uses such objects not only as key symbols in an elaborate mythology of the household, but also as props in her poetry's parallel mysteries of romance and renunciation.

No doubt the most striking and ubiquitous of Dickinson's domestic symbols is her white dress. As I have argued elsewhere, that extraordinary costume is in one sense a kind of ghostly blank, an empty page on which in invisible ink this theatrical poet quite consciously wrote a letter to the world that never wrote to her.[12] But to begin with, of course, Dickinson's radiantly symbolic garment was "just" a dress, an "ordinary" "everyday" item of clothing not unlike the morning dresses many Victorian young ladies wore. At the Dickinson Homestead in Amherst, indeed, it is still possible to see a white cotton dress said to have been the poet's. Enshrouded in a very prosaic and very modern plastic bag, its carefully protected tucks and ruffles remind the viewer that such a costume would have had to be maintained—laundered, ironed, mended—with intense dedication. And Dickinson was as conscious of that requirement as her descendants are, not only conscious that her white dress made special demands on her life but conscious that the idea of her dress made special demands on her art. In a fairly early poem she confessed this most dramatically.

> *A solemn thing—it was—I said—*
> *A woman—white—to be*

And wear—if God should count me fit—
Her blameless mystery—

A hallowed thing—to drop a life
Into the purple well
Too plummetless—that it return—
Eternity—until— . . .

And then—the size of this "small" life
The Sages—call it small
Swelled—like Horizons—in my vest
And I sneered—softly—"small"!

Though it is in some ways obscure—what exactly is "the purple well," for instance?—this poem is particularly clear about one point: Dickinson's white dress is the emblem of a "blameless *mystery*," a kind of miraculous transformation that rejoices and empowers her. Dropping her life into that puzzling purple well, she renounces triviality and ordinariness in order to "wear"—that is, to *enact*—solemnity, dedication, vocation. In return, she will receive an indefinable bliss associated with the transformative power of "Eternity." But—and this is just as important—even as she dedicates her self and her life to becoming "a woman—white," she realizes the intrinsic significance of that self and life. "The Sages—call it small—": to conventionally "wise" men her female works and days may seem tiny, trivial; but as she meditates upon her own transformative powers, she feels this apparently "small" life swell "like Horizons—in my vest—" and, sneering "softly— 'small'!," she utters the arrogance to which, as an artist of the ordinary, she has a right.

If the mysteries of romance and renunciation Dickinson enacted in life and recorded in her poetry both parallel and complement the mystery of domesticity she also explored, all three quasi-religious concerns are particularly well served by her transformation of an ordinary white dress into the solemn habit of a New England nun. Apparently (or so she often hints) some event connected with the secret drama of her relationship with a muse-like Master (or a masterful Muse) affected her so deeply that it forced the very idea of whiteness across the shadow line that usually separates the metaphorical from the literal. Most people, after all, are capable of imagining themselves in what Dickinson calls "uniforms of snow." Even most poets, however, don't make the passage from the mental pretense implied in the metaphorical to the physical pretense of a theatrical enactment. Yet this is the extraordinary passage Dickinson did make. What she affirms as "Mine—by the Right of the White Election!" therefore, suggests not only that she transformed her life into art more readily than most other writers but also that, more than most, she used her "small" life itself as an instrument of her great art: even the most ordinary materials of her life, that is, became a set of encoded gestures meant both to supply imagery for, *and* to supplement, the encoded statements of her verse.

In one of her most famous self-explanations, Dickinson once assured Higginson that "When I state myself, as the Representative of the Verse—it does not mean me—but a supposed person."[13] The remark may seem a reasonable confession to those who have grown accustomed to New Critical theories about the "extinction" of personality in poetry, but if one meditates long enough on the central mysteries of this artist's "life of Allegory," it is impossible not to conclude that even in making such an apparently straightforward remark she was performing one of her most cunning acts of transformation. For after all, the point her white dress most definitively makes is that she herself, the "real" Emily Dickinson, was as much a "supposed person" as the so-called "Representative of the Verse." Clad in her white costume, she was, in literal fact, the "Myth of Amherst," and this precisely because she was the mystery—both the puzzle and the miracle—of Amherst.

Into what sort of extraordinary "supposed person" did this transfiguration of a white dress convert her, however? As I have suggested elsewhere, Dickinson as a "woman—white" was a relative of Wilkie Collins' notorious *Woman in White,* of many a Gothic ghost and pallid nun, of Elizabeth Barrett Browning's Aurora Leigh (who wears a "clean white morning gown"), of the redeemed spirits in the biblical Book of Revelation (who go in shining white raiment), and of Hawthorne's "Snow

Maiden" (who wears, of course, a "uniform of snow").[14] In addition, as Mabel Todd noticed, she is related to Charles Dickens' Miss Havisham (who flaunts a tattered, decades-old wedding dress to assert, as Dickinson also did, that she is "the Wife without the Sign").[15] Like Hawthorne's Hester Prynne, moreover, the "Myth of Amherst" uses an item of apparel to signify both tribulation and redemption, while like Melville's Moby-Dick she embodies the contradictory mystery of her identity in a color that is no color, a color that is an absence of color. At the same time, however, the line that probably tells us most about the allegorical (rather than allusive) "meaning" of her white dress is the one that promises the least: "Big my secret but it's *bandaged.*"

In a poem that begins, enigmatically, "Rearrange a 'Wife's' affection!" and that is evidently devoted to some of the more painful (and melodramatic) aspects of Dickinson's romance, this sentence tells us simply that the speaker's secret is a bandaged *wound*, but we cannot doubt that the mysterious hurt is bandaged in white—bandaged, that is, in this poet's central metaphor for aesthetic redemption born of pain, bandaged in myth born of mystery—and therefore, as she also tells us, "It will never get away." Earlier in the poem, however, though Dickinson does not actually tell us her "secret," she gives us a useful clue about its function in her life. The work begins by describing the constancy of anguish that sustains this wounding hidden love.

> *Rearrange a "Wife's" affection!*
> *When they dislocate my Brain!*
> *Amputate my freckled Bosom!*
> *Make me bearded like a man! . . .*
>
> *Love that never leaped its socket—*
> *Trust entrenched in narrow pain*
> *Constancy thro' fire—awarded*
> *Anguish—bare of anodyne!*

In particular, however, the poet insists that her secret incurable "anguish" is a

Burden—borne so far triumphant
None suspect me of the crown,
For I wear the "Thorns" till Sunset
Then—my Diadem put on.

A crown of thorns converted into a glittering diadem: without presuming to speculate about the "facts" Dickinson may or may not be describing through this secularized crucifixion imagery, it is possible to see that her fictionalizing of those "facts" tells us something crucial about the transformative energy her white dress represents. For as the garment of a mythic or supposed person who is the Empress of Calvary, that dress is once again a paradoxical image of agony transformed into energy; in itself, in fact, it is a paradoxical, even an oxymoronic, costume—as oxymoronic as the "fiery mist" with which Higginson complained that she surrounded herself. Through this artful bandage, this cloth that both shrouds and staunches, conceals and reveals, the mysterious poet of transformation converts absence into presence, silence into speech, in the same way that Christ, through *his* mysteries, converted thorns into jewels, bread and wine into flesh and blood, death into life.

At first, of course, it may seem that in her dependency on Christian imagery, as in her allusions to male-created female characters from Hester Prynne to Miss Havisham, Dickinson was enacting and examining traditional masculine mysteries rather than distinctively feminine ones. Not only is her Christianity notably heterodox, however; the real white dress on which she founded her drama of supposition was significantly different from the white garments she would have encountered in most male-authored sources. For the white dresses imagined by the nineteenth-century male writers who seem to have been most interesting to Dickinson are invariably exotic or supernatural. Wilkie Collins' woman in white is a madwoman attired in the uniform of her derangement. Hawthorne's snow maiden is an eerily romantic being dressed for a fairy tale. Dickens' Miss Havisham wears a gown designed for a most unusual occasion—a wedding that has been indefinitely postponed. Even Melville's metaphysical whale is a freak of nature who represents the freakishness of Nature. Only a female-created character, Elizabeth Barrett Browning's Aurora Leigh, wears an *ordinary* dress—a "clean white morning gown" transformed by art into an extraordinary costume.[16]

But of course, like Aurora, another "supposed person" whose life as a woman was inseparable from her defiantly female poetry, Emily Dickinson wore such a dress, an ordinary dress made extraordinary by neither circumference nor circumstance but only by the white heat of her creative energy. And indeed, she tells us in one of her most direct poems, this transformation of the ordinary into the extraordinary is a bewitching female art she actually learned from Elizabeth Barrett Browning.

> *I think I was enchanted*
> *When first a sombre Girl—*
> *I read that Foreign Lady—*
> *The Dark—felt beautiful—*

she begins, describing her first encounter with Barrett Browning's "witchcraft." Then she goes on to list a series of witty transformations through which the common became the uncommon, the daily the divine.

> *The Bees—became as Butterflies*
> *The Butterflies—as Swans*
> *Approached—and spurned the narrow grass—*
> *And just the meanest Tunes*
>
> *That Nature murmured to herself*
> *To keep herself in Cheer—*
> *I took for Giants—practising*
> *Titanic Opera—*
>
> *The Days—to Mighty Metres stept*
> *The Homeliest—adorned*
> *As if unto a Jubilee*
> *'Twere suddenly confirmed— . . .*

It is not insignificant, surely, that these metamorphoses, like so many others Dickinson explores in her life/text, not only depend upon the patriarchal Christian mysteries of transformation, they parody and subvert them. For ultimately, Dickinson's symbolic use of her white dress in life and art is only one example of what is not only a striking mythology of domesticity but also an extraordinary theology of the ordinary, the homely, the domestic, a theology that constitutes a uniquely female version of the philosophy Thomas Carlyle called "natural supernaturalism."[17] Like many of her male contemporaries, including Carlyle himself, this woman who had even as a schoolgirl rejected Christianity grew up doubting traditional Christian pieties. But where Carlyle substituted a belief in the grandest sacraments of nature for his lost faith in the established Church, Dickinson celebrated mysteries that such Victorian sages would have thought "smaller"—the sacraments of the household, the hearth, the garden. And where in his famous *Sartor Resartus* (The Tailor Retailored) Carlyle saw all the natural world as the metaphorical clothing of a mysterious God's cosmic energy, Dickinson in both life and art transformed her own clothing into a metaphor for the energy that moved her own, female mysteries. Thus, although she never yielded to Miss Lyon's evangelical fervor, although she was never born again as a "hopeful" Christian, this skeptical poet was converted, and by a woman teacher, to a religion that parodied and paralled patriarchal Christianity.

An alternate version of the last stanza of Dickinson's tribute to Barrett Browning tells us that when she first "read that Foreign Lady"

> *The Days—to Mighty Metres stept—*
> *The Homeliest—adorned*
> *As if unto a* Sacrament
> *'Twere suddenly confirmed—*

and then the poet goes on to explain her own transformation further:

> *I could not have defined the change—*
> *Conversion of the Mind*

Like Sanctifying in the Soul
Is witnessed—not explained—

Learning from Barrett Browning how to see the sacramental radiance of the ordinary world around her—the "small" world of the household and the garden—this onetime dissenter seems to have been born again as a "wayward nun" dedicated to celebrations that her father and her minister might find mysterious indeed. " 'Twas a Divine Insanity—" she goes on to say, describing her introduction to Barrett Browning, and adds that she means to keep herself "mad" (since such madness is of course "divinest sense"): if she should once again feel the "Danger to be Sane," she would turn for "Antidote" to "Tomes of solid Witchcraft." For converted to this new religion, she finds that the life the "Sages" called "small" really has "swelled like Horizons" in her breast, and her days, transformed by "Magic," are stepping to "Mighty Metres."

In fact, I would argue that once she had learned the female mysteries of "solid Witchcraft" from Elizabeth Barrett Browning's powerful example, Emily Dickinson became a "wayward nun" who regularly spoke—in life as well as in art—through an elaborate code of domestic objects, a language of flowers and glasses of wine, of pieces of cake and bread and pudding—and of a white dress, a point her Amherst neighbors intuited quite early. If we return to Mabel Todd's description of the "Myth of Amherst," moreover, we can see, now, that Mrs. Todd's observations emphasize not only the mystery and magic but even the *textuality* of the behavior that characterized Dickinson's "life of Allegory." Indeed, beginning with two observations that subtly contradict each other ("She dresses wholly in white . . . but no one *ever* sees her"), the fascinated Mrs. Todd goes on to report gestures that sound more like those of a goddess or a priestess than those of a New England spinster. "Her sister . . . invited me to come & sing . . . & if the performance pleases her, a servant will enter with wine for me, or a flower . . . but just probably the token of approval will not come then, but a few days after, some dainty present will appear for me at twilight. People tell me that the *myth* will hear every note—she will be near, but unseen . . . *Isn't that like a book?*" (italics mine). That the "myth" will be near but unseen recalls the schoolgirl working her magic on imaginary figures, transforming an ordinary blackboard into a setting for epic prestidigitation. But the code of wine and flowers or wine and cake suggests the rituals of a strange yet oddly familiar religion. Put together, moreover, these puzzles and miracles that haunted even the more prosaic souls of Amherst are indeed "like a book." In fact, they are part of the book of poems that a supposed person named Emily Dickinson actually wrote.

It should not be surprising, of course, that a woman poet transformed the minutiae of her life into the mysteries of her art. That is, after all, what countless male poets do, though with very different material. More to the point, celebrations of domesticity streamed from the pens of almost all of the female novelists and poets who were Dickinson's contemporaries, as Nina Baym shows in her study of nineteenth-century American "woman's fiction." Even more than most of these writers, moreover—many of whom were tough, independent professionals and some of whom seem to have propagandized for domesticity without transforming its details into significant metaphors or myths—Dickinson was actually immersed in the transformative mysteries of the household. As one of her relatives explained a few years after her death, "Emily Dickinson was a past mistress in the art of cookery and housekeeping. She made the desserts for the household dinners; delicious confections and bread, and when engaged in these duties had her table and pastry board under a window that faced the lawn, whereon she ever had pencil and paper to jot down any pretty thought that came to her, and from which she evolved verses, later."[18] In fact, a number of Dickinson's poems were written on the backs of recipes, for the mysteries of the kitchen, the view from the kitchen window, and the mysteries of art seem to have been almost inseparable for this writer who confined herself absolutely to the intricate interior of the "Homestead" that was ostensibly her "Father's" but which, through both striking and subtle metamorphoses, she made her own.

I should immediately note, however, that I am not arguing here for a return to the image of Emily Dickinson best represented by John Crowe Ransom's 1956 description of her as "a little home-keeping person" whose life was "a humdrum affair of little distinction."[19] Such a vision of the "Myth of Amherst," or of any other woman poet, implies that the very substance of most female lives is so trivial, so "humdrum," that it could not possibly inspire or energize great art. On the contrary, I am suggesting that for Dickinson the private life of the household was as charged with potential meaning as the public life of politics and philosophy. Or perhaps it was charged with potentially greater meaning. For this ironic "little home-keeping person" placed herself quite consciously in a great tradition of women writers who have scorned patriarchal male definitions of what is important in history and what is not important.

Near the beginning of that tradition, we hear Jane Austen's Catherine Morland speaking in *Northanger Abbey*:

> *History, real solemn history, I cannot be interested in . . . I read it a little as a duty; but it tells me nothing that does not either vex or weary me. The quarrels of popes and kings, with wars or pestilences in every page; the men all so good for-nothing, and hardly any women at all, it is very tiresome . . .*

At the modern end of the tradition, we hear the voice of Virginia Woolf:

> *When one has read no history for a time the sad-coloured volumes are really surprising. That so much energy should have been wasted in the effort to believe in something spectral fills one with pity. Wars and Ministries and legislation—unexampled prosperity and unbridled corruption tumbling the nation headlong to decay—what a strange delusion it all is!—invented presumably by gentlemen in tall hats . . . who wished to dignify mankind. Our point of view they ignore entirely: we have never felt the pressure of a single law; our passions and despairs have nothing to do with trade; our virtues and vices flourish under all Governments impartially.*

And in between we hear the characteristically compressed comment of Emily Dickinson: "'George Washington was the Father of his Country'—'George Who?' That sums all Politics to me—."[20]

Like Austen, who claimed that hers was an art of the miniature, an art that engraved domestic details on a "little bit (two Inches wide) of Ivory," Dickinson created out of what the "Sages" might call "small" details a mystery play that questioned the very concept of size. Like Woolf, whose Mrs. Dalloway and Mrs. Ramsay transform the "humdrum" acts of party-giving, stew-making, knitting, and sewing into rich aesthetic rituals, Dickinson invented a religion of domesticity, a mystery cult in which she herself was a kind of blasphemously female "Word made Flesh" and the servings of cake and wine she sent to chosen friends were sacramental offerings. But even more than Austen or Woolf, the self-consciously female "Myth of Amherst" had a vision of what Muriel Rukeyser has called a "world split open"—a world transformed through the transformation of vision itself. In this, interestingly, she was a prototypical modernist-surrealist as well as a prototypical modern woman poet who followed her great mother Elizabeth Barrett Browning in creating a new way of seeing for all the poetic daughters who have come after her. Another anecdote recounted by one of Dickinson's bemused relatives will help illustrate the kind of distinctively female, protomodernist surrealism that marked this writer's transformed and transformative vision of domestic details. The poet's "little nephew [Ned]," wrote her cousin Clara Newman Turner in 1900,

> boylike had a way of leaving anything superfluous to his immediate needs at Grandma's. After one of these little "Sins of Omission," over came his high-top rubber boots, standing erect and spotless on a silver tray, their tops running over with Emily's flowers. At another time the little overcoat was returned with each velvet pocket pinned down, and a card with "Come in" on one, and "Knock" on the other. The "Come in" proved to be raisins; the "Knock," cracked nuts.[21]

Besides telling us, again, about Dickinson's wit and charm, this story tells us something about her ability to see ("New Englandly," of course) through the ordinariness of things to the seeds of the extraordinary, the roots of difference concealed behind appearance. For if boots can hold flowers and pockets can hide raisins, then it is no wonder that the flesh may be a word and words may be "esoteric sips / Of the communion Wine"—sacramental signals of mysterious power and energy. It is no wonder, either, that such power is not to be found by questing through distances but instead is lodged "at home," in an ordinary bedroom; no wonder that the priestess of this power once took her niece up to that room and, mimicking locking herself in, "thumb and forefinger closed on an imaginary key," said "with a quick turn of her wrist, 'It's just a turn—and freedom, Matty!'"[22] Going *in* to the ordinary, *in* to the seed, *in* to the flower in the boot, *in* to the flesh in the word and the word in the wine was the central maneuver of all Dickinson's mysteries of transformation, a point that should help explain not only the sometimes puzzling imagery of her life/text but also her sometimes puzzling dislocations of language.

Such dislocations, after all, are really other kinds of transformations, and they come about because as she enters and splits open the commonplace Dickinson also necessarily cracks open ordinary usages, revising and reinventing the vocabulary she has inherited from a society that does not share her piercing visions. "They shut me up in Prose," Dickinson tells us punningly,

> *As when a little Girl*
> *They put me in the Closet—*
> *Because they liked me "still"—*

But "Still!" she boasts, "Could themself have peeped—"

> *And seen my Brain—go round*
> *They might as wise have lodged a Bird*
> *For Treason—in the Pound—*
>
> *Himself has but to will*
> *And easy as a Star*
> *Abolish his Captivity*
> *And laugh—No more have I—*

To this wayward nun, as to all winged things, walls and fences pose no problems: she frets not at the convent walls of language because she knows she can leap over them anytime she pleases, or perhaps, more accurately, she can transform them into windows whenever she wants. A number of phrases from the poems quoted in these pages exemplify such linguistic metamorphoses, for example, "the Instead—the Pinching fear," and even "They shut me up in Prose." Such transformations of vocabulary abolish the "Captivity" implicit in ordinary usage, and—importantly—they do this by expanding, rather than annihilating, meaning.[23]

Ultimately, moreover, such expansions of meaning, together with the transformations of vision that energized them, must have led Dickinson from an exploration and enactment of the mysteries of domesticity to related celebrations of the mysteries of nature and of woman's nature. This priestess of the daily, after all, continually meditated upon the extraordinary possibilities implicit in the ordinary flowerings of the natural world. In her "real" life as the "Myth of Amherst," she created a conservatory and a herbarium; in the supposed life of her poetry, she saw through surfaces to the "white foot" of the lily, to the "mystic green" where "Nicodemus' Mystery / Receives its annual reply," to the time of "Ecstasy—and Dell," and to the time when "the Landscape listens." In one of her most astonishing visions of transformation, too, she recorded the moment when "the Eggs fly off in Music / From the Maple Keep." For hers was a world of processes in which everything was always turning into everything else, a world in which her own, and Nature's, "cocoon" continually tightened, and colors "teased," and, awakening into metamorphosis, she struggled to take "the clue Divine."[24]

That this vision of nature-in-process, together with her transformative visions of domesticity, eventually brought Dickinson back to a complementary vision of the mystical powers in woman's nature seems inevitable. It is in the female human body, after all, that the primary transformations of human nature happen: egg and sperm into embryo, embryo into baby, blood into milk. (And it is the female bird who produces and nurtures those musical eggs.) As anthropologists observe, moreover, and as a poet of domesticity like Dickinson knew perfectly well, it is women who perform the primary transformations of culture: raw into cooked, clay into pot, reed into basket, fiber into thread, thread into cloth, cloth into dress, lawless baby into law-abiding child. And it is because of such natural and cultural transformations, Erich Neumann tells us, that the Great Mother was worshipped throughout the matriarchal ages he postulates.[25]

Though Dickinson may not have consciously worshiped such a goddess, some glimmering consciousness of that deity's powers must always have been with her, presiding over *all* of the mysteries she served. Two poems tell us this, the poem from which I take my title and one other. Both are quite clearly matriarchal prayers, but they emphasize different aspects of Dickinson's distinctively female answer to traditional Christianity. In the first, she tells us quite frankly both whom she worships and who she is:

> *Sweet Mountains—Ye tell Me no lie—*
> *Never deny Me—Never fly . . .*
>
> *My Strong Madonnas—Cherish still—*
> *The Wayward Nun—beneath the Hill—*
> *Whose service—is to You—*
> *Her latest Worship—When the Day*
> *Fades from the Firmament away*
> *To lift Her Brows on you—*

In the second, interestingly enough, Dickinson tells us what she will not tell us—as if to remind us that her mysteries are both miracles and puzzles. What she worships, she declares, is "Only a Shrine, but Mine"—and then she continues in an enigmatic prayer:

> *Madonna dim, to whom all Feet may come,*
> *Regard a Nun—*
> *Thou knowest every Woe—*
> *Needless to tell thee—so—*

But can'st thou do
The Grace next to it—heal?
That looks a harder skill to us—
Still—just as easy, if it be thy Will
To thee—Grant me—
Thou knowest, though, so Why tell thee?

With this last poem, of course, we come full circle back to where we began; we confront once more the mystery of absence, the gap that haunts Dickinson's own account of her life, as well as everybody else's story of it. Now, however, we may be able to see how richly and powerfully this wayward nun transformed that apparent emptiness into a fullness, how the hollow rubber boot bloomed with flowers and the flowers had white feet and the silent eggs suddenly began to sing. Now, too, it may be clear that most of the *OED*'s senses of the word "mystery" have some application to this artist's "life of Allegory." Certainly her fivefold transformations—of romance, renunciation, domesticity, nature, and woman's nature—tell us truths about her own religion while hinting at paradoxical enigmas and riddles; certainly, too, her poetic "witchcraft" involves both esoteric and ordinary arts—the secrets of the poet as well as the skills of the housewife. As she mythologizes herself, moreover, she even transforms her own life into a kind of "miracle play," a mysterious existence in which, as the Empress of Calvary, she enacts mysteries that parallel those that marked the life of Christ. And didn't she, finally, speak to her communicants both literally and figuratively through "a kind of plum cake"? Sending her famous black cake to her friend Nellie Sweetser in 1883, she wrote, "Your sweet beneficence of Bulbs I return as Flowers, with a bit of the swarthy Cake baked only in Domingo."[26] But of course by "Domingo" she meant her own kitchen, where her mysteries of culinary and literary transformation took place side by side.

—1983

JANE EYRE AND THE SECRETS
OF FURIOUS LOVEMAKING

Wild Nights—Wild Nights!
Were I with thee
Wild Nights should be
Our luxury! . . .

Rowing in Eden—
Ah, the Sea!
Might I but moor—Tonight—
In Thee!

—EMILY DICKINSON

In the spring of 1975, I found myself, rather to my own surprise and for the first time, theorizing about a novel. To be sure, I'd produced fiction myself, including not only a few published short stories but also a vaguely experimental novel, the typescript of which was still rather hopelessly circulating among New York editors. But in the professional life as teacher and critic on which I had fairly recently embarked, I really considered myself a "poetry person." I'd been writing poems since I was a child and had studied mostly poetry—especially Romantic and modernist verse but the theory of the genre, too—in college and graduate school. My dissertation was on the poetry of D. H. Lawrence, and after I'd expanded, "booked," and in 1973 published it, I planned an intensive study of "death as metaphor" in nineteenth- and twentieth-century

160

poetry. As a product of sixties radicalism, moreover, I'd sworn only to write, on the one hand, Meaningful Books and, on the other hand, literary journalism (Meaningful Reviews and Significant "Think Pieces"), and never, never to start grinding out academic hack articles like what Henry James once called "an old sausage mill." But now I was writing what would ordinarily be defined as an article, though I thought of it as an essay ultimately destined to become part of a book. And that article was about the novel *Jane Eyre*.

What had intervened to change my supposedly well-laid plans? Lots of intangibles, no doubt, but the proximate causes, so far as I could see, were, first, my youngest child, and second, the women's movement. When she was eight or nine, my daughter Susanna had begun devouring nineteenth-century novels, especially such female-authored standards as *Little Women, Jane Eyre,* and *Wuthering Heights.* (My other two children read voraciously too, but had different literary tastes.) Nostalgically—for the books Susanna read were the ones I myself had loved best when I was growing up—I reread along with her, and as we discussed the books we often tried to explain to each other our feelings about episodes or settings each of us found particularly compelling. Susanna especially loved what she called "the wonderful tea" featuring seed cake and sympathy with which stately Miss Temple nourishes Jane and Helen amidst the desolation of Lowood. I was drawn over and over again to the sanctuary in the attic where, "wild and savage and free" as the young Cathy in *Wuthering Heights,* obstreperous Jo pens her blood-and-thunder Gothics, far from the pieties of superegoistic Marmee and long before meeting censorious Professor Bhaer. And, too, as I'd been when as a teenager I read *Jane Eyre* for the second time, I was delighted by the illicit glamour of the romance between Charlotte Brontë's "poor, plain, little" governess and her brooding master. When the so-called Second Wave of feminism crested in the seventies, I was more than ready—was indeed desperately eager—to understand the manifold ways in which not only is the personal the political (as the famous movement motto had it) but the literary is, or can be, both the personal *and* the political.

That we bring ourselves to what we read—that, as Emerson put it, our "giant" goes with us wherever we go—is hardly a new insight. In an era of cultural studies, new historicism, and gender theory, such a notion seems self-evident. Yet for those of us raised on the austere dicta of the New Criticism (Beware the extra-textual! Never look an author in the intentions! One ambiguity is worth a thousand histories!), it was profoundly exhilarating to find myself, as I had in the fall of 1974 at Indiana University, team-teaching what I sensed was a largely undiscovered literary tradition in the context of a history—the history of *women*—that I'd never myself been taught. In response to departmental needs, Susan Gubar and I were that term offering a course we called "The Madwoman in the Attic," so in my daily professional life I frequently found myself reflecting with considerable intellectual passion on books that in my personal life I'd lately been exploring far more naïvely. For indeed, though in some part of myself I must have understood even then that no reading is altogether innocent, the readings I'd begun doing with my nine-year-old daughter felt both innocent and sentimental, if only because they were not only outside my disciplinary "field," but they were also rereadings and rememberings, hence, recapturings, of experiences I'd had when I myself was at least a more innocent reader.

And a more innocent moviegoer! For surely my memories of such classics as *Jane Eyre, Little Women,* and *Wuthering Heights* were colored not just by my almost kinetic recollections of the fat gold armchair in Queens where, romantic and dreamy, I'd curled up to read them but also by the Hollywood versions of these books I'd seen in my growing-up years, versions that amounted to a series of pop-culture exegeses of the nineteenth-century novel. If Jo was always already a tomboy played by Katharine Hepburn, Heathcliff was perpetually Laurence Olivier, stalking apart in a fit of Byronic "joyless reverie," while Rochester was inevitably an even more Byronically glowering Orson Welles. That Jane and Cathy were more dubiously identified with, on the one hand, the timid prettiness of Joan Fontaine and, on the other hand, the come-hither elegance of Merle Oberon testifies to a tension between page and screen that would prove productive for feminism—for weren't Fontaine and Oberon just the kinds of socially sanctioned female figures the Brontë heroines were struggling *not* to become? I didn't quite realize this when

I first began my researches into books and movies past, but it would become clear soon enough, as I gained sophistication in the new field of Women's Studies.

What I *did* realize was that there was a commonality among these (and other) female-authored novels—as well as, very differently, among their film redactions—that went beyond the Gothic elements about which Jo March writes and among which Jane and Cathy live. In my first critical efforts at defining this commonality, I saw it as a shared discomfort with *houses* that issued in repeated and, to me, quite charismatic acts of defiance by all the heroines. Jo flees to the attic in order to escape the moralizings of the parlor, where she is obliged to act like a "little woman." Jane suffocates in the red-room where Aunt Reed imprisons her, then grows up to pace the battlements at Thornfield, brooding on social injustice. Cathy oscillates discontentedly between the oppressive squalor of Wuthering Heights and the bourgeois constraints of Thrushcross Grange. Soon the women's movement would provide me with a vocabulary through which to define these "patriarchal strictures and structures" that fostered what Matthew Arnold, writing of Charlotte Brontë, called "hunger, rebellion and rage" in so many of the heroines (and novels and authors) my daughter and I admired. But my uncertainty about the issues at hand was probably reflected in the first title I proposed to give the class Susan and I were planning for the fall of 1974: "Upstairs, Downstairs," after the popular television series.

That I was rather taken aback when Susan quite reasonably objected to my title as not only vulgar but misleading shows, I think, how much I had to learn about the subject we were soon going to teach. Yet the replacement on which we quickly settled—"The Madwoman in the Attic"—was, from my point of view anyway, merely a more precise formulation of the argument I wanted to make about neighboring fictional spaces inhabited by turbulent spirits. Thus, when Susan and I decided that the course to which we'd given that name had been so illuminating, indeed so intellectually transformative for both of us that we had to write a book based on what we'd been learning as well as teaching, it fell to me to write an article (out of which we'd develop a chapter) through which the madwoman of Thornfield Hall resonantly wanders, with her mystery breaking out "now in fire and now in blood, at the deadest hours of night." And inevitably, of course, my article was both infused with and shaped by the extraordinary feminist excitement of the season in the mid-seventies that had inspired me to abandon my sixties snobbery about "articles," along with my bias toward poetry rather than fiction. Bliss was it in that spring to be alive, but to be embarking on a feminist analysis of one of the greatest and most influential novels in the female literary tradition was very heaven!

My analysis was a product of its historical moment, and so it obviously emphasized just those aspects of *Jane Eyre* that dramatized issues to which we in the women's movement had begun to awaken with special passion in those years: the "hunger, rebellion and rage" fostered in both Charlotte Brontë and her heroines by a coercive cultural architecture; the subversive strategies through which author and characters alike sought to undermine the structures of oppression; and the egalitarian sexual as well as social relationships toward which the novel strove. That Brontë's earliest readers had themselves been struck by these elements in her work seemed to me evident not only from Arnold's well-known phrase but also from other remarks made by nineteenth-century reviewers. Not surprisingly, I was particularly fond of Elizabeth Rigby's 1848 assertion that "*Jane Eyre* is throughout the personification of an unregenerate and undisciplined spirit," of Anne Mozley's 1853 comment that the book seemed to have been written by "an alien . . . from society [who was] amenable to none of its laws," and of Margaret Oliphant's 1855 observation that "the most alarming revolution of modern times has followed the invasion of *Jane Eyre*."[1]

There were, however, a few Victorian responses to which I paid less attention. I don't think, for instance, that I quite knew what to make of the clause that preceded Mrs. Oliphant's description of the "alarming revolution" that ensued after "the invasion of *Jane Eyre*": "Ten years ago we professed an orthodox system of novel-making. Our lovers were humble and devoted." And still less was I certain how to treat her further description of the book's distinguishing characteristic as its portrayal of "furious lovemaking"—a kind of lovemaking that she thought constituted "a wild declaration of the 'Rights of Woman' in a new aspect." To be frank, seventies feminism was uneasy in the presence of the erotic, torn between Erica Jong's notorious celebration of the "zipless fuck" and Kate Millett's not unrelated claim that "there is no remedy to sexual politics in marriage." Commenting on the writings of two contemporaries she much admired, Sylvia Plath and Diane Wakoski, Adrienne Rich noted in her influential "When We Dead Awaken" that "in the work of both . . . [the] charisma of Man seems to come purely from his power over [woman] and his control of the world by force, not from anything fertile or life-giving in him," and this because of "the oppressive nature of male/female relations." Within a decade, Andrea Dworkin would declare that (hetero)sexual intercourse virtually by nature entails a tyrannical master/slave relationship between male and female, with the man "communicating to her cell by cell her own inferior status . . . shoving it into her, over and over . . . until she gives up and gives in— which is called *surrender* in the male lexicon." And such a diagnosis of desire would seem to have been a logical outcome of Plath's embittered "Every woman adores a Fascist, / The boot in the face, the brute / Brute heart of a brute like you."[2]

"*Furious* lovemaking" in *Jane Eyre*? Well, the oxymoronic phrase could be at least in part understood if one factored in the ferocity with which the novel urged "the 'Rights of Woman' in a new aspect." But from the born-again perspective of seventies feminism, that new aspect had more to do with Jane's declarations of independence *from* Rochester than with expressions of erotic feeling *for* him. To be sure, I saw Jane's story as ending with a vision of egalitarian marriage that was a consummation devoutly to be wished, if only a utopian one. But how were we to understand the complex, at times tyrannical or even sadistic "lovemaking" that led to a fantasy of such bliss? When in moments of what sociologists call "introspection" I analyzed my own earlier responses to the relationship between Jane and her "master," I had to admit to myself that in my teens I'd wanted more than anything for her to run off with him to the south of France, or even indeed to the moon, where at one point he had playfully promised to bring her to "a cave in one of the white valleys among the volcano-tops." And why, after all, shouldn't politically astute readers wish that she and her lover had at least eloped, if not to the moon, to France? Such real-life literary heroines as George Sand and George Eliot had done as much! Why did feminist critics, of all people, have to accept the marriage-or-death imperatives built into what Nancy Miller called "the heroine's text"?

In those days, however, there seemed to be no middle ground between the banal rhetoric of the pulp novelist who declared that "*Jane Eyre* is one of the most passionate of romantic novels" because "it throbs with the sensuality of a woman's growing love for a man; there is the deep longing of the lonely heart in its every line" and Adrienne Rich's stern insistence that "we believe in the erotic and intellectual sympathy of [Jane and Rochester's] marriage because it has been prepared by [Jane's] refusal to accept it under circumstances which were mythic, romantic or sexually oppressive." Indeed, to many of us the "deep longing" of a woman's "lonely heart" for the "brute / Brute heart of a brute like" a man appeared to be a radical weakness—a neurotic flaw—in the otherwise talented and politically correct Charlotte Brontë. Hadn't such feverish yearnings for the love of a (bad) Byronic hero left her vulnerable to Thackeray's rude ruminations on the "poor little woman of genius! The fiery little eager brave tremulous homely-faced creature! I can read a great deal of her life as I fancy in her book, and see that rather than have fame, rather than any other earthly good or mayhap heavenly one she wants some Tomkins or another to love and be in love with."[3]

Rich's classic (and still brilliant) essay on *Jane Eyre* is entitled "The Temptations of a Motherless Woman," and it focuses on the moment, not long after Rochester's seductive plea to Jane that she flee with him to France, when the maternal moon rose to reveal a "white human form" gazing at the tormented governess and gloriously admonishing, "'My daughter, flee temptation!'" Brontë herself had had to flee temptation (though she had done so with considerable ambivalence) when she left Brussels and her adored Monsieur Heger. And as a feminist critic in the seventies, I knew that I too had to flee temptation. I had to rigorously repress my own desire for Jane and Rochester's "furious lovemaking" to reach a romantic—and more specifically a sexual—climax and undertake instead a weary journey across the moors to a political position where, along with Charlotte Brontë and Adrienne Rich, I could rejoice in our heroine's new life as "a village schoolmistress, free and honest, in a breezy mountain nook in the healthy heart of England."

Still, wasn't there an element of bad faith in this reading? If as Judith Fetterley so persuasively argued, we women readers had long been acculturated to identify against ourselves when we perceived the world (and in particular our own gender) from a patriarchal, male perspective, weren't we identifying against ourselves in another way when we refused to acknowledge the rebellious sexual passion driving Jane's assertion to Rochester that "if God had gifted me with some beauty and much wealth, I should have made it as hard for you to leave me, as it is now for me to leave you"? Though we might quite properly scorn the clichés of those who saw the novel as primarily a romance that "throbs with sensuality" and a book that "only the lonely" could have written, oughtn't we to have conceded that something about the "furious lovemaking" in the book was what made it ragingly popular in the first place? Or at least that the "'Rights of Woman' in a new aspect" had as much to do with something about the lovemaking as did the more obviously feminist striving toward equality?

Since Brontë first published her bestseller in 1847, there have been at least forty dramas (several of them musicals), nine television versions, and ten movies based on the book, most of them focused on the complexities of its "lovemaking." And when the writer herself was told of the first of these adaptations, a play staged in London just a few months after the novel's appearance, her instant reaction was to wonder "what . . . would they make of Rochester?" and then to fear that what "they [would] make of *Jane Eyre*" would be "something very pert and very affected." Clearly she sensed the charisma of the interactions between her hero and her heroine, and she may have sensed, too, that along with Jane's feminist insubordination, her sexual aggressiveness—the indecorous demeanor with which she confesses her feelings to Rochester while rebuking what she considers his indifference ("Do you think I am an automaton?—a machine without feelings?")—might be represented as "pert" or even "affected" in a setting where the personalities of the characters had been "woefully exaggerated and painfully vulgarized by the actors and actresses." What (in another context) one feminist critic rather dismissively called "romantic thralldom" may have been Brontë's problem in her frustrated relationship with Heger, but her fantasy of fulfillment liberated Jane into erotic as well as linguistic assertion. For this reason, the novel in which this "poor, plain, little" governess unabashedly tells her story very likely seemed scandalous to its earliest readers not just because its narrator was uppity and "pert" but also—perhaps more importantly—because she was uppity and frankly desirous.[4]

Let me make it quite plain that I don't in any way want to repudiate earlier claims I've made about *Jane Eyre*. Rather, I want to elaborate, complicate, and enrich them by speculating that the perpetual fascination of this novel arises at least in part from its ambivalent obsession with "furious lovemaking," that is, from its impassioned analyses of the multiple dramas of sexuality. Like so many other (yes) romance writers, Charlotte Brontë created a heroine who wants to learn what love is and how to find it, just as she herself did. Unlike most of her predecessors, though, Brontë was unusually explicit in placing that protagonist amid dysfunctional families, perverse partnerships, and abusive caretakers. Unlike most of her predecessors, too, she endowed her main characters—hero as well as heroine—with overwhelmingly powerful passions that aren't always rational and often can't be articulated in ordinary language. This sense of unspeakable depth or fiery interiority imbues both Rochester and Jane with a kind of mystery that has always been charismatic to readers. But it was almost certainly the startling, even shocking intensity with which Jane publicly expresses unladylike eroticism as well as indecorous social resentment that struck so many Victorians as revolutionary. Here, therefore, Mary Oliphant's association of Brontë's book with Mary Wollstonecraft's *A Vindication of the Rights of Woman* "in a new aspect" was not just accurate but perhaps unnervingly so. For even while Jane formulates a traditional feminist creed when she argues that "women feel just as men feel; they need exercise for their faculties, and a field for their efforts as much as their brothers do . . . and it is narrow-minded in their more privileged fellow-creatures to say that they ought to confine themselves to making puddings and knitting stockings," her narrative dramatizes a "furious" yearning not just for political equality but for equality of desire.

That *Jane Eyre* introduced audiences to the "wild declarations" and egalitarian strivings of an unprecedentedly passionate heroine certainly explains why the novel has always had a special appeal for women, who tend to identify—and want to identify—with this compelling narrator's powerful voice. For the same reason, the work has often elicited different, at times less enthusiastic, responses from male readers, with some dismissing Jane as priggish (for refusing to succumb to her desires) and others disparaging her ferocity (in articulating those desires). Yet of course Brontë's novel broods as intently on the mysteries of male sexuality as it does on those of female eroticism, transcribing the fantasies of both sexes with uncanny clarity and (for its period) astonishing candor. To men as well as women, in other words, *Jane Eyre* tells a shifting, almost phantasmagoric series of stories about the perils and possibilities of sexual passion. For indeed, as Elaine Showalter observed some years ago, a "strain of intense female sexual fantasy and eroticism runs through [even] the first four chapters of the novel and contributes to their extraordinary and thrilling immediacy."[5]

To be sure, Brontë was working with plots familiar to many of her readers, who would have known, among other significant precursors, the Cinderella story Samuel Richardson told in *Pamela* and the Bluebeard tale of Ann Radcliffe's *Mysteries of Udolpho*. But the author's genius in *Jane Eyre* consisted in the fervor with which she defamiliarized such received plots by putting them together in a new way. In fact, as a number of comparatively traditional analyses have long since suggested, it's possible to summarize this novel's narrative with a *National Enquirer* headline: CINDERELLA MEETS BLUEBEARD! More particularly, a "poor, obscure, plain and little" but notably rebellious stepchild/orphan becomes the servant of a princely master, falls in love with him, and desires him intensely, even while finding herself used and abused by him. In fact, this not very acquiescent Cinderella sees her Prince Charming turn into Bluebeard, the jailor (and murderer) of wives, while she herself simultaneously toys with fantasies of seducing him and rebels against his sway by struggling to subvert his power. Brontë's book thus asks a number of crucial questions. For example, what if instead of wielding her broom Cinderella rages against (and amidst) the cinders? And what if Prince Charming is not just a charming aristocrat but a Bluebeard who elicits passionate desire in Cinderella? And at the same time, what if Bluebeard feels he has exonerating reasons for locking up his sexual past? Can, or *should,* a Cinderella like this one live happily ever after with such a Bluebeard?

To say that *Jane Eyre* "is" Cinderella and that Rochester "is" Bluebeard is of course to imply that they embody ideas of the feminine and the masculine in a particularly resonant way: an impoverished and orphaned dependent in a hostile household, Cinderella is, after all, condemned to a life of humiliating servitude from which she can only hope to escape through the intervention of an imperious man, and significantly, in the old tale, she finally achieves release through diminution. The ancient plot stresses not just her modesty (and the modesty of her needs) but also her physical daintiness—notably the tininess of her feet compared to those of her arrogant stepsisters, both of whom are literally as well as figuratively swollen with pride and ambition. As for Bluebeard, in the old tale he is depicted as a mysteriously predatory, dark ("blue"), even swarthy figure whose beard signifies an animal physicality frighteningly associated with his femicidal erotic past, and, more particularly, with the bloody chamber in the attic where he keeps the ghastly relics of past sexual conquests.

From one of the perspectives of the Victorian culture whose myths and anxieties Charlotte Brontë so eerily transcribed in *Jane Eyre,* then, to embody the feminine in Cinderella is to call attention to the physical, financial, and emotional deprivation—in a sense, the diminution—endured by married as well as single women in a society where the "second sex" was politically, economically, legally, and erotically disempowered, a culture in which, according to the famous if apocryphal advice Victoria is said to have given one of her daughters, on her wedding night a good woman was supposed to "close her eyes and think of England!" Similarly, to embody the masculine in Bluebeard is to call attention not just to the public power but also to the often fatal private knowledge of sexuality attributed to men in a society that often claimed men were beasts—insisting that, as one of the post-Darwinian heroines of Gilbert and Sullivan's *Princess Ida* put it, "a man is only a monkey shaved." And perhaps, in fact, because such images of the feminine and the masculine were both so pervasive and so troublesome for Brontë and her contemporaries, there is a sense in which all the female characters in the novel can be seen as variations on the theme of Cinderella, with special emphasis on the problem fleshly desire poses for that heroine, while all the men can be considered variations on the theme of Bluebeard's sexuality.

In this reading, then, the styles of what we now call "the feminine" available to *Jane Eyre* are variously represented in the stories told about a range of other female characters. The possibilities these subplots explore extend from extreme resignation to equally extreme rebelliousness, from suicidal self-abnegation to murderous passion.[6] The angelic Helen Burns, for instance, is a kind of Cinderella who was abandoned, in effect "orphaned," when her father remarried. But her solution to what we might call the Cinderella problem deviates radically from the fairy-tale ending. Opting for absolute repudiation of desire in the physical realm of the present, Helen consumes her own body (dying, indeed, of "consumption") for the sake of a spiritual afterlife. Similarly, though in a twist on the Cinderella plot that more closely evokes the traditional story, Miss Temple manages to escape the hardships of her job at Lowood through marriage to a Prince Charming. Yet her self-abnegation requires a rigidity that virtually turns her body to marble: by implication, indeed, she is repressing desire as well as rage when, in one famous scene, her mouth closes "as if it would have required a sculptor's chisel to open it."

But there is yet another, even more disturbing mode of "the feminine" Jane encounters on her desirous pilgrimage, and it is quite literally embodied in the slavish flirtatiousness that characterizes little Adèle (Rochester's ward), as well as the hardheaded quid pro quo eroticism of the child's mother Céline (Rochester's French mistress), and even the practiced charm of Blanche Ingram (his supposed fiancée). As Jane clearly sees, each of these characters is eager to overcome her sexual helplessness in a male-dominated society by selling herself to the highest bidder. Prancing and flouncing like a living doll, Adèle is plainly in training for the career of polished coquetry that in different ways shapes the destinies of Céline and Blanche, since if Céline openly prostitutes herself, Blanche is perfectly willing to sell herself on the marriage market. To Jane, who vehemently declares that "I am a free human being with an independent will," all these modes of sexual slavery represent a degradation far more radical than the self-abnegation of the consumptive and the self-repression of the governess.

But if, taken together, many of these minor characters demonstrate to Jane the problems Cinderella faces in a male world, the "eccentric murmurs" our heroine hears echoing in her mind and in the corridors of her Bluebeard's chambers—the "low, slow ha! ha!" she herself associates with Grace Poole, but which Brontë also connects with Jane's own self-defined "restlessness"—suggest that, whatever form it takes, female desire may breed dissatisfaction, resentment, and even madness. I have argued elsewhere that the intensity of this Cinderella's own anger at the inequalities she has had to face throughout her life is ultimately embodied in the source of the "eccentric murmurs" and "low, slow ha! ha!" that haunt the third story of her master's mansion, for Rochester's mad wife, Bertha Mason Rochester, might be said to represent a kind of "third story" about Jane-as-Cinderella, a tale in which, instead of practicing unearthly renunciation or gaining earthly reward, the hapless heroine gives way to rage. Specifically, as I've also argued, Jane's own incendiary "hunger, rebellion and rage" are theatrically enacted by Bertha when the madwoman sets Rochester's bed on fire, when she attacks her own brother like a vampire, when she rips up Jane's bridal veil, and finally, most dramatically, when she torches the central symbol of Rochester's power, his ancestral mansion.[7]

At the same time, however, even while Bertha enacts Jane's rebellious rage at servitude, she may also be said to dramatize the sexual "hunger" all of the women in this novel either repress (in the hope of spiritual reward) or pervert (for financial gain)—sexual hunger that (as Showalter also noted in the seventies) some Victorian physicians thought could drive a woman to madness. The beautiful but dissolute daughter of a "Creole" (probably French and Spanish) mother, Bertha is most likely of European descent, although her upbringing in the hot West Indies has led to a tradition of critical speculations that she is racially mixed.[8] Whether or not this is the case, she certainly appears to be "other" than Brontë's small, pale, outwardly austere and self-controlled heroine. Rochester himself describes her as a "fine woman, in the style of Blanche Ingram: tall, dark, and majestic" at the time of their first meeting, and like Blanche, she is a woman who has willingly offered herself as a sexual trophy on the marriage market.

Unlike any of the Englishwomen we encounter in *Jane Eyre,* however, Bertha is the product of a symbolic as well as literal tropic in which desire flourishes, or so Rochester claims. After marriage, he tells Jane, "her vices sprang up fast and rank . . . and what giant propensities [she had]!" Although his language is guarded (he is after all talking to a supposedly pure English virgin), Victorian readers would certainly have been able to decode what Rochester is saying when he describes such "giant propensities" as causing his wife to be "at once intemperate and unchaste," noting that her nature was "gross, impure, depraved," and adding that "her excesses had prematurely developed the germs of insanity." Even if she is not, in his phrase, "a professed harlot," Rochester is explaining to Jane that Bertha's virtually nymphomaniac abandonment to excesses of desire—to the heat of lust—has "sullied [his] name" and "outraged [his] honor," while driving *her* to madness.

Significantly, too, the "third story" of Bertha's desire-driven madness has both masculinized and, as it were, *animalized* her (a not-so-surprising phenomenon in a culture professing that "men are beasts"). Thus, when Jane, Rochester, and the other members of the interrupted wedding party finally view the madwoman in the attic at Thornfield, she is described as a sort of beastly "it": "at the farther end of the room, a figure ran backwards and forwards. What *it* was, whether beast or human being, one could not, at first sight tell: *it* grovelled, seemingly, on all fours; *it* snatched and growled like some strange wild animal: but *it* was covered with clothing, and a quantity of dark, grizzled hair, wild as a mane, hid *its* head and face" (emphasis added). A minute later, as Rochester strives to subdue her, she is revealed as "a big woman, in stature almost equalling her husband, and corpulent besides," who shows "virile force in the contest" while the contest itself, taking place "amidst the fiercest

yells and the most convulsive plunges," is cast in terms that simultaneously evoke mud wrestling and sexual intercourse.

Considered as a scene of instruction, this episode—with its overtones of what Mrs. Oliphant called "furious lovemaking"—would seem
at the very least darkly monitory to a Cinderella who experiences herself
as utterly enthralled by her Bluebeard. Shortly before the disrupted marriage, after all, Jane had struggled to check not only Rochester's desires
but her own. In one of the novel's more explicit love scenes, the heroine's "master"—now her fiancé—sits down at the piano and sings melt-
ingly to her, but she quails when he "rose and came towards me, and I
saw his face all kindled, and his full falcon-eye flashing, and tenderness
and passion in every lineament." My "task," she goes on to explain, "was
not an easy one; often I would rather have pleased than teased him," for
"[m]y future husband was becoming to me my whole world; and more
than the world . . . He stood between me and every thought of religion
. . . I could not, in those days, see God for his creature: of whom I had
made an idol." Sunk in the abyss of desire, this apparently decorous and
dainty Cinderella may well be in danger of yielding to the same "giant
propensities" that (as we will soon learn) turned her Bluebeard's first
bride into a beast monstrously swollen or bloated ("corpulent"!) with
intemperate sensuality. For from one Victorian perspective, the pious
position that would seem to have been official dogma, it's not just rage
and rebellion, but sexual hunger that threatens to leave a woman gibbering the "eccentric murmurs" and "low, slow ha! ha!" of an animal
imprisoned in an attic. At the same time, however, from a less officially
pious point of view, it may have been, even pre-Freud, *unsatisfied* sexual
hunger that could turn a lady into a tiger (or, as *Jane Eyre* later puts it, a
"clothed hyena").

I return to, and meditate on, "official" and less official positions
because I want to claim, following Mrs. Oliphant's insight into the charisma of this novel's "furious lovemaking," that in her role as Jane's as well
as Bertha's author and alter ego Charlotte Brontë was far more ambivalent toward female sexual hunger than has usually been conceded.
Elaine Showalter's influential analysis of Bertha's sexuality, for example,
depends heavily on Dr. William Acton's notion (articulated in his 1857

textbook on the "reproductive organs") that strong sexual appetite in women might lead to "moral insanity," to "nymphomania [as] a form of insanity." But more recent commentators—beginning most notably with Peter Gay—have significantly complicated our picture of Victorian attitudes toward the erotic, allowing us a more nuanced understanding of the "giant propensities" of desire that drive Jane as well as Bertha toward "furious lovemaking." In his incisive *The Education of the Senses,* Gay devotes a chapter to the sexually charged diaries of Mabel Loomis Todd, a woman only a generation or two away from the Brontës who was not only the mistress of Emily Dickinson's brother, Austin, but also one of the (notoriously insensitive) editors of Dickinson's poetry. Noting Todd's frequently and fervently expressed delight in the erotic, he argues that her experience was exemplary rather than exceptional—a joy in the kinds of "Wild Nights—Wild Nights!" of sexual "Rowing in Eden" for which Dickinson herself also expressed a passionate, if more obliquely formulated, desire. Indeed, Gay observes, by the 1880s the Scottish gynecologist J. Matthews Duncan was insisting that "desire and pleasure ... may be ... *furious,* overpowering, without bringing the female into the class of maniacs" (emphasis added), while Elizabeth Cady Stanton (with a candor rather like *Jane Eyre*'s) was announcing, "I have come to the conclusion that the first great work to be accomplished for women is to revolutionize the dogma that sex is a crime."[9]

Thus, yes, on the one hand, Jane herself—along with Charlotte Brontë, Dr. Acton, and Mrs. Oliphant—would second Rochester's contention that in imprisoning the snatching, growling, and groveling Bertha, Thornfield guards a heart of darkness no proper virgin should confront. Stanton had not yet, after all, revolutionized "the dogma that sex is a crime." "This girl," declares Rochester to the bemused Reverend Wood (who would have married the pair but now cannot) "knew no more than you ... of the *disgusting secret*" (emphasis added) in the attic. But on the other hand, like Stanton herself, Jane knows all too well the intricacies of that secret. Defining herself as "an ardent expectant woman," she has to battle the desire that mounts in her even as she exerts her will to renounce Rochester. Just as "the clothed hyena [that was Bertha] rose up, and stood tall on its hind-feet" before falling on Rochester in what he feared would be "the sole conjugal embrace I am ever to know," so Jane responds to her master's seductive pleas by considering herself "insane—quite insane, with my veins running fire, and my heart beating faster than I can count its throbs." Her project throughout the novel, indeed, won't be (as most critics have thought) to eradicate but to accommodate and decriminalize this fiery and desirous animal self that marks her as a most unusual Cinderella: the mate rather than the prey of Bluebeard.

In the light of recent work on Victorian sexuality, what makes this point especially important is that after all, from Bluebeard's point of view the problem of the conjugal embrace—that is, how, when, where, and with whom desire should be satisfied—was also difficult to resolve. Was a "disgusting secret" about masculinity imprisoned in the virtually official sexual double standard of the age? If so, Rochester's story implies that it was not easy for men themselves to come to terms with the erotic "beastliness" that could easily drive a woman mad, despite the fact that an animal nature was supposedly part and parcel of their own sexual structure. Thus, just as Brontë rings changes on a number of Cinderella stories in order to investigate the life possibilities available to Jane, she offers virtuoso variations on the theme of Bluebeard to represent the life options available to Rochester. In particular, through the subplots she spins around a range of minor and major male characters, she comments on the choices made by the man Jane calls her "master" and specifically about what it would mean either to give in to beastliness or to try conquering it altogether. Unlike as the wealthy owner of Thornfield and the supposedly poor plain governess who tends his ward may seem, in fact, Brontë suggests that Jane and Rochester face comparable dilemmas. Just as Jane seems to have been forced toward either extreme resignation or equally extreme rebelliousness, Rochester appears to be confronted with the alternatives of masochistic self-abnegation or sadistic passion, even though the mystery of male sexuality inevitably plays itself out differently from that of female sexuality.

To be sure, at least the first of the beastly men Jane encounters as she moves toward adulthood is in fact the virulently anti-erotic clergyman Brocklehurst, whose wolfish countenance—"What a face he had . . . ! what a great nose! and what a mouth! And what large, prominent teeth!"—demonstrates "the horror! The horror!" of repression, even while (or perhaps especially because) this sanctimonious villain does act like a Bluebeard when in a grotesque parody of Christianity he punishes the bodies of the girls at Lowood with the ostensible goal of saving their souls, in the process murdering a number of them en masse. But an even more obviously beastly male character appears earlier in the book. Brontë depicts young Master John Reed as virtually a paradigm of the Victorian bad boy, wallowing in gluttony, sadism, and a host of other deadly sins. Even at fourteen, the boy Jane reviles as a murderer, a slave driver, and a Roman emperor "gorged himself habitually at table, which made him bilious, and gave him a dim and bleared eye and flabby cheeks." And after he has left Gateshead, we learn that he has become so degraded that even his mother, herself Jane's wicked stepmother, dreams that she sees "him laid out with a great wound in his throat, or with a swollen and blackened face."

At the same time, however, Mrs. Reed's dreams of the most depraved and vicious of *Jane Eyre*'s male characters seem curiously to evoke an opposite extreme. As Susan Gubar has cogently observed, the suicidally submissive Richard Mason, Bertha Mason Rochester's ingenuous brother, is laid out at the center of the narrative with a great wound in his throat and a "corpse-like face." In a sense, then, if Brocklehurst and Master Reed demonstrate exactly how unattractive the role of Bluebeard is, the feminized Mason appears more like one of the fairy-tale villain's bloody victims. After having gone to visit the attic's inhabitant, Mason—who looks pale and feeble, "like a child" and a sickly one at that—moans over the "trickling gore" that flows from a hideous bite on his shoulder, reduced to whimpering terror of the sister who "sucked the blood: she said she'd drain my heart." Can it be that some men are so horrified by the aggressiveness implicit in the equation of masculinity with bestiality that they attempt to repress even their own instincts of self-defense? Are some so distressed by their own animal potential to wound that they would rather be wounded? Or does Mason represent a male anxiety about being drained of vital masculine fluids?[10]

St. John Rivers, one of the most complex characters in the book, suggests that Brontë may have been toying with the last of these three alternatives. Rather than become a bestial Bluebeard or one of his drained emasculated victims, Rivers renounces desire altogether, at great cost and pain to himself. Admitting that he loves Rosamond Oliver "wildly—with all the intensity . . . of a first passion," he scorns this rapture as "a mere fever of the flesh," incommensurate with the "convulsion of the soul" that convinces him to dedicate his life to missionary work in India. Yet when he attempts to coerce Jane into a loveless marriage that would, as she herself insists, "kill" her, it becomes clear that even the most apparently renunciatory of men may incarnate the femicidal threat symbolized by Bluebeard. Describing her "ecclesiastical cousin's . . . experiment kiss[es]" as "marble kisses or ice kisses," Jane defines each as "a seal affixed to my fetters" and fears that as St. John implores her to marry him an "iron shroud" is contracting round her, especially because as his wife she would have to "endure all the forms of love (which I doubt not he would scrupulously observe)" though "the spirit" would be "quite absent."

But if the consequences of male sexual repression are represented by the "cold cumbrous column" into which the river of St. John Rivers' passion has frozen, the problems of unchecked male eroticism are most vividly dramatized in this novel by its ur-Bluebeard, Edward Rochester himself, for just as the mystery of female sexual hunger is incarnated in Bertha Mason Rochester, the mystery of male sexuality resides in her tormented husband. But while Bertha's lustful madness masculinizes her, Rochester's response to it feminizes (that is, disempowers) him in curious ways, or at least threatens to. Indeed, it is arguable that if in this Victorian psychodrama unfeminine sexual hungers may leave a woman gibbering like a corpulent animal in an attic, such inappropriate and unwomanly appetites are equally dangerous to men, reducing even a powerful "master" to a terrifying awareness that unless he asserts mastery over the female animal she may tear him apart. Does Bluebeard murder his wives because he fears that their inordinate desires might unman him? Do the possibilities of female sexuality imperil male passion? Although Rochester effectively represses whatever explicitly bloodthirsty impulses he may have, his confessions to Jane, after the wrestling scene in which his wife displays "virile force," emphasize his dread of feminization on several counts.

To begin with, as a second son who could not inherit property in a patrilineal culture where wealth passes automatically to the firstborn male, Rochester believes himself to have been used by his father and brother as a tool to enable *them* to gain a fortune. Like Blanche Ingram, indeed, Rochester himself was commodified on the marriage market: his father (like Blanche's mother) arranged for him to be "provided for by a wealthy marriage" that would also profit his relatives. Just as painfully, during the charade of his courtship in the West Indies, he was tricked by *Bertha's* family (who kept secret his bride's five-year seniority as well as her mother's madness) because they wished to secure a man "of a good race." Like Queen Victoria's daughter, Rochester was supposed to sacrifice his youthful body to this marriage of convenience, and, if necessary, on his wedding night he was supposed to "close his eyes and think of England." At the same time, to further complicate the matter, the language with which he describes his earliest responses to Bertha reveals that her eroticism had at first "stimulated," "excited," and "besotted" him, even turning him into a "gross, grovelling, mole-eyed blockhead." The symbolically foreign and beastly, "impure, depraved" nature he associates with his madly sexual wife remains "a part of me," he admits. That after consigning Bertha to Thornfield's attic he has indulged in erotic adventures with a series of foreign (and thus metaphorically alien and beastly) mistresses lends substance to this confession. What, Brontë seems to wonder, if female desire is simultaneously debilitating and contagious (to men), even while it is maddening (to women)?

In one sense, then, through its portrayal of "furious lovemaking" and its meditation on the dangers of desire, *Jane Eyre* investigates the problem that even a closely guarded wish for such lovemaking posed to both sexes in Victorian society. From this perspective, the secret in the attic is not simply Brontë's rebellion and rage against the subordination of women, but also her intuition that the social enforcement of such subordination was grounded in widespread fears of yearnings that, if not properly controlled, could turn into insatiable and deadly sexual hungers. Certainly, the novelist's Bluebeard is as frightened of beastly Bertha as is her Cinderella: if the madwoman at Thornfield instills in Jane a dread that she will turn into a groveling, intemperate harlot besotted with desires of "giant propensities" for her "master," she also evokes in Rochester an anxiety that either his own virility will be found wanting in a sexual contest or that he will be turned into an instrumental "block-head" who is himself subordinated to—destined merely to service!—a growling, snatching wild animal. In another sense, however, *Jane Eyre*'s (and Jane Eyre's) preoccupation with "furious lovemaking" represents an unusually candid rejection of Victorian moral constraints. Indeed, it is arguable that an implicit repudiation of sexual double standards was a major source of the novel's power, for ultimately Brontë allowed her heroine to acknowledge, accommodate, and articulate her own as well as her mate's "giant propensities" without becoming either a clothed hyena or a sacrificial lamb.

Throughout the novel, indeed, Jane's gaze turns voraciously, even at times voyeuristically, toward Rochester, as she catalogs his bodily parts and properties in what amounts to a series of female-authored *blazons*. His "broad and jetty eyebrows, his square forehead, made squarer by the horizontal sweep of his black hair . . . his decisive nose . . . his full nostrils, denoting, I thought, choler; his grim mouth, chin, and jaw" and "his great dark eyes" all receive her close scrutiny, along with his "unusual breadth of chest, disproportionate almost to his length of limb," the "unconscious pride in his port" and his hand that is "a rounded, supple member, with smooth fingers, symmetrically turned" and "a broad ring flash[ing] on the little finger." When he confides to her what from any conventional Victorian perspective are the sexual improprieties in his past, she "hear[s] him talk with relish . . . never startled or troubled by one noxious allusion." Indeed, she explains, "my bodily health improved; I *gathered flesh and strength*" (emphasis added) while his face becomes "the object I best liked to see." Growing ever less ethereal, more physical, she becomes ever more easily intimate with him, so much so that after she wakes him from his burning bed in chapter 15, she rather boldly remains in his presence while he gets "into some dry garments," then huddles in his cloak for half the night in his smoky chamber while he goes to deal with "Grace Poole." And that at first he himself explicitly associates the ostensibly pale, pure governess with the ungovernable elements of fire and water that have engulfed him in his sleep—first inflaming, then flooding—surely has erotic resonance. "'In the name of all the elves in Christendom, is that *Jane Eyre*?' he demand[s], 'What have you done with me, witch, sorceress?'" Nor is the significance of this interaction lost on Jane, who delightedly records the "strange energy . . . in his voice, strange fire in his look," then repairs to her bed, trying to "resist delirium" and "warn passion" though she is too "feverish to rest."

Interestingly, while many of us seventies feminists concentrated on Jane's "wild declaration of the 'Rights of Woman'" in their old aspect, Brontë bestows on the ice-encrusted St. John Rivers the same awareness of her sexual intensity that informed Mrs. Oliphant's identification of the "alarming revolution" fostered by the novel's commitment to a "new aspect" of the "'Rights of Woman'" that would condone a female desire for "furious lovemaking." Though Jane never confesses to St. John her fear that "as his wife . . . [she would be] forced to keep the fire of my nature continually low, to compel it to burn inwardly and never utter a cry, though the imprisoned flame consumed vital after vital," he nevertheless intuits her ineradicable passion. "I know where your heart turns and to what it clings," he declares, adding censoriously, "The interest you cherish is lawless and unconsecrated. Long since you ought to have crushed it: now you should blush to allude to it. You think of Mr. Rochester?" But indeed, Jane doesn't merely "think" of Mr. Rochester. Rather, in a moment of mystically orgasmic passion she virtually brings him into being. As St. John prays over her, reading (tellingly) from the Book of Revelation inscribed by his namesake—a sacred text in which female sexuality, figured as the Whore of Babylon, is banished to the desert so that a new heaven and new earth can be constituted from the blood of the lamb—the "May moon shin[es] in through the uncurtained window," as powerfully as the July moon had shone on the night at Thornfield when a glorious maternal figure bade Jane to "flee [from] temptation." Now, however, the same moon silently advises the heroine to flee *to* temptation, in a moment whose erotic charge is unmistakable:

All the house was still; for I believe all, except St John and myself, were now retired to rest. The one candle was dying out: the room was full of moonlight. My heart beat fast and thick: I heard its throb. Suddenly it stood still to an inexpressible feeling that thrilled it through, and passed at once to my head and extremities. The feeling was not like an electric shock, but it was quite as sharp, as strange, as startling: it acted on my senses as if their utmost activity hitherto had been but torpor, from which they were now summoned, and forced to wake. They rose expectant: eye and ear waited while the flesh quivered on my bones.

In fact, what Jane discovers through this climax of impassioned epiphany is that the paradise for which she longs is not St. John's heaven of spiritual transcendence but rather an earthly paradise of physical fulfilment. And it is at this instant, of course, that she hears her "master's" voice and declares that she is "coming" to him. Her saintly—and sanctimonious—cousin had prayed "for those whom the temptations of the world and the flesh were luring from the narrow path," had "claimed the boon of a brand snatched from the burning." But although she had briefly seen "death's gates opening, show[ing] eternity beyond," and toyed with the notion that since "safety and bliss [were] there, all here might be sacrificed in a second," she now, definitively, chooses "the burning" of her own desire for gratification "here" rather than "there": "My powers were in play and in force," she declares, explaining that she now willingly "fell on my knees; and prayed in *my way—a different way to St John's, but effective in its fashion*" (emphasis added).

That this "way" of prayer is defiantly different must have been, again, as clear to Mrs. Oliphant as it had been to St. John Rivers himself, for Brontë's heroine was quite frankly replacing a Christian theology of renunciation with a more hedonistic theology of love. Importantly, she does not know at this point that Rochester has been freed to marry her by Bertha's death. Instead, she determines to return to him with a lucid consciousness of the "temptation" he constitutes. The "spirit, I trust, is willing, but the flesh, I see, is weak," comments the cousin whose "iron shroud" of morality she has experienced as a deadly—a "killing"— superego, but the ambiguity of her response to his warning hints that a deep skepticism toward received morality is driving her back toward the "furious lovemaking" she had only temporarily rejected: "'My spirit,' I answered mentally, 'is willing to do what is right; and my flesh, I hope, is strong enough to accomplish the will of Heaven, *when once that will is known to me*'" (emphasis added).

To be sure, those of us who know the story realize, as Jane does not, that the will of Heaven is for her to fulfill her desire within the bounds of lawful matrimony—but there is surely a sense in which that will (indistinguishable from the will of the narrative, after all) has chosen to reward her precisely for the acquiescence in temptation that under-lies her challenge to the clerical custom St. John so frostily incarnates. Thus while there is no doubt justice in Adrienne Rich's claim that "we believe in the erotic and intellectual sympathy of [Jane and Rochester's] marriage because it has been prepared by [Jane's] refusal to accept it under circumstances which were mythic, romantic, or sexually oppres-sive," that assertion must be qualified by a recognition of the powerful Romanticism (with a capital *R*) that shapes not just Jane's but Brontë's refusal of circumstances that are drearily quotidian, anti-romantic, or morally oppressive. In a proud denial of St. John's insulting insistence that she is "formed for labor, not for love," Jane chooses—and wins—a destiny of *love's* labors.

As seventies feminism (rightly) saw it, of course, given the inequal-ity of the sexes in nineteenth-century England if not in Brontë's imagi-nation, the Bluebeard in Rochester had in some sense to be diminished, even mutilated, in order for the Cinderella in Jane to become whole. And the redeemed pair had to retreat into a world outside history so as to construct a personal story of fulfilled desire. Yet if the Rochester of Fern-dean appears at first to be a "sightless Samson" who is "desperate and brooding" as "some wronged and fettered wild beast," Jane's yearning gaze discerns in him still the physical properties that had first aroused her desire, and once more she lingeringly catalogs them. "His form was of the same strong and stalwart contour as ever: his port was still erect, his hair was still raven black," she tells us, confessing that she longs to "drop a kiss on that brow of rock, and on those lips so sternly sealed beneath it."

There can be no question, then, that what Jane calls the "pleasure in my services" both she and Rochester experience in their utopian woodland is a pleasure in physical as well as spiritual intimacy, erotic as well as intellectual communion. "Ever more absolutely bone of [Rochester's] bone and flesh of his flesh," Jane has reconstructed herself as literally part of her husband's body—"his right hand"—in a postlapsarian Eden where she is also the "apple of his eye," and he is her audience, fit though few. In the meantime, St. John Rivers—the quintessentially anti-erotic Bluebeard of self-denial—has been banished from an England where wild nights are now not the torment but the luxury of Jane and Rochester. It is no doubt to emphasize this point that the novel ends with an otherwise puzzling focus on the unmarried missionary's anticipation of death in faraway India ("My Master . . . has forewarned me. Daily He announces more distinctly, 'Surely I come quickly!' and hourly I more eagerly respond, 'Amen; even so, come, Lord Jesus!' "). With the exorcism of both the id-like Bertha and the superegoistic St. John from the plot, repression can be repressed, sacrifice sacrificed. Jane has come to Rochester, and St. John is coming to God.

That Jane and Rochester have built their bower of bliss in a "nowhere" kind of place, however, has generic as well as theological significance, reminding us yet again that despite the richly observed texture of, say, the Lowood episode, *Jane Eyre* is more a romance in the mode of such diversely Gothic descendants as *The Turn of the Screw*, *Rebecca*, and *Wide Sargasso Sea* than it is a "realistic" novel in the mode of *The Mill on the Floss* or *Middlemarch*. In a sense, Rochester has brought "Mademoiselle" to the "cave in one of the white valleys" of the moon where he had fantasized to Adèle that he would bring his bride—or at least he has lured her to the *Minnegrotte*, the sacramental Cave of Love where Tristan and Isolde consummate their love in the medieval romance. For it's arguable, indeed, that *Jane Eyre*'s "furious lovemaking" participates as much in the mystical Romanticism of Wagner's nineteenth-century re-visioning of the Tristan plot as it does in the genres of fairy tale, Gothic, and feminist polemic. Hard as it is to imagine a happy ending to the adulterous affair of Wagner's tortured lovers (could Isolde ever have said, "Reader, I married him"?), the merging Jane and Rochester achieve at Ferndean, as they become bone of each other's bone and flesh of each other's flesh, recalls the desire of "Tristan *und* Isolde" to eradicate the *und* and become "TristanIsolde" or, better, *"nicht mehr Isolde! / nicht mehr Tristan! / Ohne Nennen, / ohne Trennen."*[11]

Of course, if I return in conclusion to the comparisons of *Jane Eyre*–the-novel and *Jane Eyre*–the-movie I attempted earlier in this re-visionary enterprise, I'd certainly have to concede that none of the many screen translations of Brontë's novel are especially Wagnerian. On the contrary, the two best-known versions—the 1944 film directed by Robert Stevenson and the recent (1996) film directed by Franco Zeffirelli—generally speaking "read" the book as a paperback romance that "throbs with the sensuality of a woman's growing love for a man" because "there is the deep longing of the lonely heart in its every line." The proposal scene in the Zeffirelli movie is particularly banal. True, it offers erotic intensity. Indeed, the soulful kiss with which Charlotte Gainsbourg rewards the avowals of William Hurt was classed as one of the "ten best movie kisses of the year" in a 1996 film roundup. But, neither "furious" nor Romantically mystical, the lovers' embraces are determinedly healthy in a "sensitive" postmodern sort of way, as if Jane and Rochester had separately been taking lessons from Dr. Ruth. And even the madwoman in this film seems trendily sedated, less like "some strange wild animal" than a doped-up housewife in a neatly starched nightgown from a *Victoria's Secret* catalog.

Rather more appropriately, the proposal scene in the 1944 movie does feature a kind of operatic melodrama, with Jane (Joan Fontaine) cringing before a swaggeringly Byronic Rochester (Orson Welles) and the pair's confessions of love punctuated by Welles' wildly glittering eyes and counterpointed by a howling wind that suggests the onset of tempestuous desires, as well as a ferocious streak of lightning that cleaves the novel's infamous "great horse-chestnut" in one fell swoop. But there's hardly any "wild declaration of the 'Rights of Woman'" in either an old or a "new aspect" here, much less the sort of "furious lovemaking" that would have shocked Victorian audiences. What I think must have impressed me as a teenager, however, was the voyeuristic fixity of Jane's gaze at Rochester, a gaze that (as current film theory would have it) gave

Joan Fontaine's otherwise incorrectly timid Jane a compelling epistemo-logical authority.[12] Equally impressive to me, also, must have been the extraordinarily powerful moment when, as if to convey the dangers presented by the "furious lovemaking" that might constitute an "alarming revolution," Stevenson's film positions us—its viewers—in the shadows with the unseen, howling madwoman, while Welles and Fontaine stand in a lighted doorway as if confronting the forces of (sexual) darkness only tentatively contained in the attic. In a brilliant stroke, Stevenson exploits a cinematic reticence comparable to Brontë's narrative secrecy: we never see the madwoman as Jane and Rochester see her; instead, we see the lovers as she—raging with pain and desire—sees them. Finally, perhaps, that fierce gaze of darkness is what Jane and Rochester, similarly riddled by desire, assimilate into themselves. And perhaps, too, their defiant acceptance of such darkness makes the "wild nights" of their Romanticism so compelling to me that once again, to my own surprise, here I am, theorizing about the novel in which they star.

—1998

THE KEY TO HAPPINESS

On Frances Hodgson Burnett's *The Secret Garden*

A plain and lonely little girl; a rambling mansion in the Yorkshire wilds; a closemouthed housekeeper; a kindly chambermaid; a brooding, Byronic, reclusive master; mysterious keys and corridors; strange noises in the night: Frances Hodgson Burnett's children's classic begins as a brilliant riff on Charlotte Brontë's *Jane Eyre*, the pioneering grown-up romance that made a mark on countless subsequent novels. Unlike such other Brontë derivatives as Daphne du Maurier's *Rebecca*, however, Burnett's riveting tale is a *Jane Eyre* with not one but two secrets—and a *Jane Eyre* that also borrows liberally from a work by one of Charlotte's sisters. For Emily Brontë's powerfully poetic novel of Yorkshire, *Wuthering Heights*, must surely have helped supply *The Secret Garden* with crucial elements of plot and setting, including a wild landscape where the wind is always "wuthering" over the moors, and two poor little rich children who are (at first) at least as quarrelsome as Edgar and Isabella Linton, the spoiled heirs of Thrushcross Grange.

But of course Frances Hodgson Burnett was writing a book for youngsters, even though the product of her labor has influenced and inspired quite a few grown-ups. Thus *The Secret Garden* is a work that might have been composed by one of the Brontës in an uncharacteristically optimistic mood. To begin with, the novel is bracingly leavened with lessons in "good Magic" as well as references to the kinds of happy fairy tales, joyous myths, and sprightly nursery rhymes that the often dour Brontës tended to revise from bleak perspectives. At the same time, more realistically, it's a book that the authors of *Jane Eyre* and *Wuthering Heights* mightn't have written unless they'd been born a century later than they were. For Charlotte and Emily Brontë, to be wounded in the spirit—as Rochester and Heathcliff are—was an almost hopelessly Byronic plight. Rochester survives the mayhem inflicted by his mad first wife, yes, but he survives maimed, with a useless arm and temporarily damaged vision. And Heathcliff is literally destroyed by his desperate passion for Cathy, the estranged beloved of his childhood. Burnett's initially unhappy protagonists, however, turn out merely to be damaged or sick— that is, "neurotic" in the modern, Freudian sense—and therefore repairable or indeed, as we'd now put it, *curable.*

To be sure, Burnett was neither by temperament nor by training a writer likely to experiment with the bleak, the ironic, the aesthetically innovative. On the contrary, she was from the start of her career resolutely commercial. Although Frances Hodgson (later Burnett) was born in 1849 into the comfortable household of a prosperous Manchester merchant, her father died when she was four and his widow and children were fairly soon reduced to what the Victorians used to call "straitened circumstances." Eventually young Frances' mother brought the family to live in genteel poverty with an uncle in Tennessee, where the teenage author-to-be began scheming to raise extra money with her pen. Always literarily inclined, as a schoolgirl Frances Hodgson had often related long, elaborately embroidered romantic stories to her classmates during sewing sessions that were aptly termed "Embroidery Afternoons." In these tales, she later remembered, "penitent lovers were always forgiven, rash ones were reconciled, wickedness was always punished, offended relatives always relented . . . opportune fortunes were left invariably at opportune moments."[1] Clearly, in other words, the young storyteller's tales were eminently *marketable* stories—and at a precociously early age their author shrewdly set out to sell them.

Indeed, the writer was just fifteen when, as she reported in her memoir *The One I Knew Best of All,* she drafted a remarkably firm letter to the editor of a major women's magazine: "SIR: I enclose stamps for the return of the accompanying MS., 'Miss Desborough's Difficulties,' if you do not find it suitable for publication in your magazine. My object is remuneration. Yours Respectfully, F. Hodgson." And within a relatively short time an actual "Editor" (the capitalization is Burnett's) had in fact accepted not one but two tales by the young writer, who then (as she was later to put it) "crossed the delicate, impalpable dividing line" between childhood and adulthood, or perhaps, more accurately, between amateur romancing-for-fun and professional, well-paid authorship.[2] For if her principal object was, as she'd confessed, "remuneration," she more than achieved it, quickly embarking on a lucrative career in which she earned for herself and her family an "opportune fortune" at an "opportune moment."

Burnett's first (and still perhaps most famous) bestseller for children was the widely adored sentimental tale *Little Lord Fauntleroy* (1886), which—with its satisfying dramatization of a wicked old earl's conversion to convivial kindness through the agency of angelic, golden-ringleted little Cedric Errol and the equally angelic widowed mother he invariably calls "Dearest"—appealed to just about every aspect of the late Victorian sensibility on both sides of the Atlantic. Translated into more than a dozen languages, *Fauntleroy* was such a sensation that, as one Burnett scholar notes, by 1893 it "appeared in more American libraries than any book except *Ben Hur,* and [its] popularity spawned a variety of related products such as Fauntleroy toys, playing cards, writing paper, chocolate, and the notorious dark velvet suits with lace collars, emphasized in Reginald Birch's illustrations for the book."[3]

In the theater, too, *Fauntleroy* (like many of Burnett's subsequent efforts) met with an astonishing success—and a success that emphasizes its author's business acumen. For when one E. V. Seebohm pirated the book for the London stage, she promptly countered with a play she titled *The Real Little Lord Fauntleroy,* earning far more positive reviews than the Seebohm version. Shrewd as ever, Burnett had kept the child hero she called her "dear little boy" for her own profit while authoring a drama so poignant that it was said to have set the octogenarian Oliver Wendell

Holmes and a group of his friends to "crying like babies." Although she was later in her life to define herself as "The Romantick Lady" and a kind of "Fairy Grandmother" of children's literature who consistently "tried to write more happiness into the world," she was never too "romantick," ethereal, or grandmotherly to confront the rough-and-tumble of commercial competition.[4]

By the time Burnett conceived the plot of *Little Lord Fauntleroy*, she had already won herself such a reputation in the literary marketplace that she made major contributions to the support of the husband—Dr. Swann Burnett—whom she'd married in 1873, and the two sons—Lionel and Vivian—born to the couple in 1874 and 1875. And if she drew on her maternal experiences in crafting her fiction, with adorable little Vivian the model for Cedric Errol and consumptive Lionel (who died at fifteen) memorialized as Colin Craven in *The Secret Garden,* the realism underlying the "romantick" portraits only made her work even more compelling to readers. When she was in her thirties Burnett was widely reviewed as a "woman of genius" while her publisher proudly called her the "Coming Woman" in literature. And when in 1900, two years after she divorced Swann Burnett, she married her "business and stage manager Stephen Townsend," a man ten years her junior with whom she'd evidently had a long affair, the union made headlines, with one New York paper trumpeting news of the "AMAZING [and presumably scandalous] MARRIAGE OF . . . AMERICA'S GREAT WOMAN NOVELIST TO HER PRIVATE SECRETARY."[5]

Burnett's marriage to Townsend broke up rather quickly, and the novelist apparently confided to a friend that she had been "forced and blackguarded and blackmailed" into this union, perhaps because Townsend threatened to reveal more information about their relationship than she wanted known to the proper Victorian public which so idolized her "dear little" Lord Fauntleroy. But the chicanery she may have encountered from her second husband seems to have left its victim unfazed and unjaded, for she continued to produce romantically optimistic books in which "wickedness was always punished, offended relatives always relented," and "opportune fortunes were left invariably at opportune moments." And eventually the royalties from these works made possible, first, her lease of Maytham Hall, a spacious country house in Kent, and, later, her ownership of "an Italianate villa" in Plandome, Long Island, which was her primary home until her death in 1924.[6]

Tellingly, the gardens of these residences were crucially important to Burnett. At Maytham Hall, according to one biographer, she became "a passionate gardener," and spent lyrical hours writing "in her favorite rose garden" dressed all in white. And in Plandome she produced what was clearly for her a philosophically significant final book. Drafted during her last illness and published posthumously, *In the Garden* (1925) is an extended essay in which the dying Frances Hodgson Burnett meticulously recounted the quotidian details of gardening as she traced the seasonal cycles of planting, blooming, and harvesting. "Every one in the world really wants a garden" and "can have one," even "if it is only two yards wide," she fervently declared here, insisting that "As long as one has a garden one has a future; and as long as one has a future one is alive."[7]

The seeds of *In the Garden* had surely been planted in the second decade of the twentieth century when Burnett began composing *The Secret Garden* (1911), probably her richest and most marvelous romance of childhood. Here, whether or not she consciously intended to do so, she revised and reworked the key elements of *Jane Eyre* and *Wuthering Heights* mentioned earlier, lacing them with upbeat fantasy and evocative fairy-tale motifs to construct an inspired and inspiring story of two forlorn ten-year-olds gradually healing into wholeness, and a grieving widower learning the lesson of survival through their example. *The Secret Garden* begins with parental deaths and the traumatic sorrow of orphaned or neglected children, but it ends in a rebirth of what William Blake called "Infant Joy" manifested through what yet another poet, T. S. Eliot, described as the "the hidden laughter / Of children in the foliage" who are "Quick now, here, now, always"—the happy laughter of formerly sick, unhappy children now so newly strengthened that they believe they can "live for ever—and ever—and ever!"[8]

Stiff, plain, disagreeable little Mary Lennox, the *Secret Garden*'s heroine, is the first neglected orphan whose rehabilitation Burnett's classic novel records. Born in India and raised not by her colonial administrator father or her indifferent, pleasure-loving mother but by their native servants, Mary is quite literally abandoned in an empty house when her unloving parents and her *ayah* die in a cholera epidemic and the other servants flee in terror of the disease. Not surprisingly, considering that her parents had "never talked to her about anything in particular" and barely divulged her existence to others in the English colony, Mary is almost an automaton when the book begins: a loveless girl with "a queer, unresponsive little face" and many other "unhappy disagreeable ways" who has "always been ill in one way or another." When she's at first sent to live with an English missionary family in India, she's so unpleasant that the children of the household tauntingly label her "Mistress Mary Quite Contrary." And when she's shipped back to England to live with Mr. Archibald Craven, the widower of her father's sister, she's "a very small, odd little black figure" who only knows how to relate to others with awkward silence or by ordering them around "in her imperious little Indian way."

Clearly Mary doesn't understand what "home" in any sense of the word might mean. The parental residence in which she was attended by unloving servants and ignored by selfish parents could hardly be considered "home-like." Nor is the land of her birth (India) her "home"land. Yet when the missionary's children tell her that she is to be "sent home" (to England), she blankly responds, "Where is home?" Given her parents' coldness and distance, the notion of a native land or "home"land— a *father*land or *mother* country—is at least as alien to her as India is. But even when Mary arrives in England the place where she finds herself doesn't seem at all like a home. For Misselthwaite Manor, the grief-stricken Archibald Craven's ancestral mansion, proves to be a great grim mournful fortress of a house "with a hundred rooms nearly all shut up" and a house surrounded by a moor that sour Mrs. Medlock, the housekeeper in charge of Mary, defines as "miles and miles and miles of wild land that nothing grows on but heather and gorse and broom, nothing lives on but wild ponies and sheep . . . a wild, dreary enough place to my mind."

How is a child to survive in such a hostile environment and with such an unpromising history? This is the first problem Mary and her creator confront in *The Secret Garden,* and the first agent of change appears on the first morning of the "disagreeable" little girl's stay at Misselthwaite. Martha, the merry young housemaid who has been assigned to Mary as a kind of nurse, begins the process of cheerfully toughening her young charge when she refuses to "salaam" as the servants had in India and expresses honest bewilderment at the imperious orphan's inability to dress herself ("Why doesn't tha' put on tha' own shoes?") and picky appetite ("Tha' doesn't want thy porridge!"). More important, though, this "untrained Yorkshire rustic" heralds metamorphoses far more radical than improvements in manners and appetite as she names for Mary the characters (Dickon, Mother Sowerby) and settings (the Secret Garden, the moor) that will eventually transform the "contrary" child into a laughing healthy Mary as merry as Martha herself.

Just as important, it's on the first morning of her first day at Misselthwaite that, inspired by Martha's stories, Mary begins to search for the mysterious garden that's been locked for ten years because "Mr. Craven had it shut when his wife died so sudden . . . He locked th' door an' dug a hole and buried th' key." As she travels the winding paths on the grounds of Misselthwaite Manor, she passes through a series of green doors, and after she opens the first she encounters a magical-seeming robin who is eventually to become a sort of spirit guide, leading her to the locked garden. And, too, as she wanders the maze of paths, she meets the aged gardener Ben Weatherstaff, who will also function as what folklorists call a "helper figure," facilitating her blossoming relationship with the robin by modeling a way of speaking to the bird in his broad Yorkshire dialect: "Where has tha' been, tha' cheeky little beggar? . . . I've not seen thee before today. Has tha' begun tha' courtin' this early in th' season? Tha'rt too for'art?"

When the winsome robin gives Mary "a queer feeling in her heart, because he was so pretty and cheerful and seemed so like a person," her true regeneration begins. As the "queer feeling in her heart" increases and the old gardener remarks that this particular robin "was a knowin' one an' he knew he was lonely," she confides her own heart's truth to the bird: *"I'm lonely"* (emphasis added), and she begins to chat with the creature, who warbles back so responsively that Ben remarks "he's made up his mind to make friends with thee" while complimenting her on speaking to the robin "as nice an' human as if tha' was a real child instead of a sharp old woman. Tha' said it almost like Dickon talks to his wild things on the moor." To speak to other living things with respect rather than contempt, to *honor* all life, Ben's comment implies (and Dickon's example will reveal), is to be a healthy human being for whom the world is a home rather than a colony.

In chapter 7 of *The Secret Garden*—the chapter tellingly entitled "The Key of the Garden"—it becomes clear not only that the garden is a kind of double for Mary, a symbolic representation of her nearly dead (shutdown, locked-up) emotional self, but also that the key to the garden's revival, as to the revival of the self, is *liking* others. When Ben Weatherstaff tells the child more about the garden, where things are "stirring down below in the dark," she muses on the connection between a place and a person: "Ten years [is] a long time," she thinks, contemplating the locked garden, and she knows this because *"she had been born ten years ago"* (emphasis added). The Secret Garden of Misselthwaite Manor, it begins to seem, is straight out of the "Sleeping Beauty." For Mary "had read of secret gardens" in fairy tales where "Sometimes people went to sleep . . . for a hundred years" and this one, though only slumbrous for ten years, seems analogous.

Young Mary, though, is waking up, for as Burnett in her role of narrator tells us, "She had no intention of going to sleep, and, in fact, she was becoming wider awake every day which passed at Misselthwaite. She was beginning to like to be out of doors; she no longer hated the wind, but enjoyed it." Indeed, at this point the reinvigorated Mary sometimes startles Ben Weatherstaff "by seeming to start up beside him as if she sprang out of the earth," so that when she makes a crucial admission to him— "I—I want to play that—that I have a garden of my own" because "there is nothing for me to do. I have nothing—and no one"—she can see that he's "actually a little sorry for her." Significantly, therefore, just as Mary realizes this, she comes lovingly close to the robin in what is plainly for her a moment of unprecedented happiness: "Oh! to think that he should actually let her come as near to him as that! . . . She was so happy that she scarcely dared to breathe." And thus it's at this figuratively "key" moment that, watching the robin search for a worm, she finds the literal key to the garden—"an old key" that has "been buried a long time."

Mary's further encounters and adventures at Misselthwaite complete and confirm the processes of renewal that began with her search for the "sleeping" secret garden that represents her nearly lost, long locked-up, and unhappily "contrary" self. Wandering on rainy days through Misselthwaite Manor with its "hundred mysteriously closed rooms," the once indifferent child becomes wakeful, curious, and begins to explore origins. "In India she had always been too hot and languid and weak to care much about anything, but in this place she was beginning to care and to want to do new things. Already she felt less 'contrary,' though she did not know why." Mother Sowerby, the almost mythically nurturing earth-mother figure who is the parent of a dozen children—among them Martha and Dickon—sends this newly lively Mary a skipping rope via Martha and, no longer quite contrary, the child actually says "thank you" to Martha. So now, at last, Mother Sowerby's gift brings Mary to the secret garden, for as this newly perky little girl skips around the paths, she finds the door and opens it with the key to which the robin had pointed.

How Mary brings the garden, and herself, back to blooming and fruitful life is an important part of the rest of Burnett's richly resonant romance. But how, as she renews the garden that is a surrogate self, she also revives and revitalizes her *other* double, the sickly ten-year-old cousin—Colin Craven—who has been in his way as abandoned and neglected as she has, forms another crucial part of this restorative story. And if such helpers as Martha, the robin, Ben Weatherstaff, and Mother Sowerby function as therapeutic guardians who guide the two lost children back to home and health, Mother Sowerby's eldest son Dickon acts as a kind of pastoral spirit of the garden, teaching the cousins about the lure and lore of nature as he works with them to revive native plants that still remain "wick"—alive or "quick"—despite a decade of neglect.

Before Dickon appears on Burnett's pages, both Ben and Martha prophesy his presence. Says Ben, "Everybody knows him. Dickon's wanderin' about everywhere. Th' very blackberries an' heatherbells knows him. I warrant th' foxes shows him where their cubs lies an' th' skylarks doesn't hide their nests from him." And when Mary finally meets this twelve-year-old who's at least as adept a magician as her totemic robin, it becomes obvious that he's a Pan or an Orpheus who "charms" animals (as Mary thinks) the way "the natives charm snakes in India," for he's

> sitting under a tree, with his back against it, playing on a rough wooden pipe . . . And on the trunk of the tree he leaned against, a brown squirrel was clinging . . . and from behind a bush near by a cock pheasant was delicately stretching his neck to peep out, and quite near him two rabbits sitting up and sniffing . . . it appeared as if they were all drawing near to watch him and listen to the strange low, little, call his pipe seemed to make.

Nor does the Orphic Dickon fail to charm Mary herself. Almost immediately she feels able to confide in him and tell him about her personal secret of the secret garden—though she soon begins to cry at the thought that he might betray her trust. Because he's indeed a nature spirit, however, Dickon quickly reassures her, and does so with a curiously significant simile. Mary will be, he promises, as safe in her secret garden as the *missel thrush in its nest.*

A "missel thrush," says that great nineteenth-century catalog of ornithology *Bewick's Book of British Birds*—a tome young Jane Eyre is perusing at the beginning of Charlotte Brontë's novel about her—is a bird native to Europe that "continues in England the whole year, and frequently has two broods." Its "nest is made of moss, leaves, &c. lined with dry grass, and strengthened on the outside with small twigs."[9] And Mary? As a "missel thrush in [her] nest," Mistress Mary Quite Contrary has found a place in which and to which she belongs, and in which, therefore, she can't be "contrary." If India was an alien land, a place among whose colonized, oppressed, and therefore servile people she "had always felt hot and too languid to care much about anything," she's finally arrived in what might be a home, a landscape where "the fresh wind from the moor had begun to blow the cobwebs out of her young brain and to waken her up a little."

Here in *Missel*thwaite—the native place of the "missel thrush" who is Mistress Mary (no longer quite contrary)—the "wutherin'" of the wind makes a "hollow, shuddering sort of roar" in the midst of which she hears the voice of her cousin Colin, a child's crying to which she is now able to answer with sympathy. And here too she can finally respond to the "broad Yorkshire" in which Dickon, Mary, and Mother Sowerby speak, and respond with cadences that show she's begun to learn her "mother" tongue. Urging Colin to join her in the secret garden and to speak the dialect that's native to both of them, she cries, "I canna' talk as graidely as Dickon an' Martha can, but tha' sees I can shape a bit. Doesn't tha' understand a bit o' Yorkshire when tha' hears it? An' tha' a Yorkshire lad thysel' bred an' born!" Language, too, in Burnett's romance of the secret garden that is the heart's home, evokes precisely the belonging for which these two dispossessed children have been longing.

"Mistress Mary, quite contrary, / How does your garden grow?" The missionary children in India had used this old nursery rhyme as a weapon against sad, disagreeable little Mary Lennox. But by the end of Burnett's novel the revitalized child's garden does indeed grow "With silver bells and cockle shells, / And *mari*golds all in a row." For through the intervention of Orphic Dickon and generously nurturing Mother Sowerby and merry Martha and even needy cousin Colin, Mistress Mary has found a patch of earth that is her own, in which she can plant the seeds of selfhood without the servile acquiescence of colonized people but instead with the ready responsiveness of those to whom she herself has given love and trust.

That Burnett's story of this literally and figuratively orphaned girl's regeneration may have given rise to such fascinating offshoots as D. H. Lawrence's *Lady Chatterley's Lover* (in which a Panlike gamekeeper who is a sort of "animal charmer" rescues a sorrowful heroine) and T. S. Eliot's "Burnt Norton" (in which the laughter of children hidden in a garden is "Quick now, here, now, always") shouldn't astonish us.[10] For as Dickon tells Mary and Colin, when spring comes to the moor where the missel thrush makes her home, nature is always "workin' an' hummin' an' scratchin' an' pipin' an' nest-buildin' *an' breathin' out scenes*" (emphasis added) because the world's "all fair begun again." Or to turn to what might well be Burnett's own comment on this novel of renewal and its literary seedlings, "As long as one has a garden one has a future; and as long as one has a future one is alive."

—2003

"DARE YOU SEE A SOUL AT THE WHITE HEAT?"

Thoughts on a "Little Home-keeping Person"

i: Dickinson in the Kitchen

She's a cliché, right? Bent over the stove, weighing, measuring, stirring, portioning out the sweet and bitter, the sour and salty: she's John Crowe Ransom's notorious "little home-keeping person"—one who wrote poems, added Ransom's contemporary R. P. Blackmur, as "indefatigably as some women cook or knit." She's a cliché and even a sexist cliché, for who would want to align herself with men who saw this great artist's life as "a humdrum affair of little distinction" in which "the cultural predicament of her time drove her to poetry instead of anti-macassars."

And yet—and yet, *my* Emily Dickinson has always inhabited a kitchen, though not perhaps a very ordinary one. We know, don't we?, that she very likely kept a basket of language handy—snippets of sentences, odd usages, off rhymes—as she brooded over batter and butter. We know that she probably salted phrases while snipping herbs, sweetened quatrains and quarts of cream at the same time. Look, there she is, between the stove and the window, in a white dress unsullied by anyone's sauciness, suddenly flashing toward us a knowledgeable gaze from eyes "the color of the sherry the guest leaves in the glass."

When I've put Emily Dickinson with all her magical selves—
"Emily, Emilie, Brother Emily, Uncle Emily"—into a poem, she's always
been in or near a kitchen. My first poem about her, "Emily's Bread,"
virtually dictated itself long ago when I learned that she'd judged a
bread-baking contest; there I imagined her as the inhabitant of a sort of
culinary prison:

> *Inside the prize-winning blue-ribbon loaf of bread,*
> *there is Emily, dressed in white,*
> *veiled in unspeakable words,*
> *not yet writing letters to the world.*
>
> *No, now she is the bride of yeast,*
> *the wife of the dark of the oven,*
> *the alchemist of flour, poetess of butter,*
> *stirring like a new metaphor in every bubble*
>
> *as the loaf begins to grow.*

But the next of my Dickinson poems presented me with a very different version and vision of Dickinson in the kitchen, one that enthralled
but mystified me. I was fascinated at that time by Dickinson's genius at
metamorphosis—her fluid and fluent selves that were brother, uncle,
cousin, male, female, and always compelling. I adored her boastfulness,
what she called "Uncle Emily's ardor for the lie" and followed with the
swaggering claim that "my flowers are near and foreign, and I have but
to cross the floor to stand in the Spice Isles." Most of all I was hooked
on her recipe for "black cake"—a recipe that begins, if you recall, "Take
a milk pail" and ends with a cake so massive one imagines that the citizens of Amherst may well have all gathered to consume it as part of some
lyrical ceremony on the village green. She herself, remember, defined it
as "the swarthy Cake baked only in Domingo . . ." although, as I always
believed, Domingo was really her own kitchen.

My poem "The Emily Dickinson Black Cake Walk" meditated therefore on Dickinson's kitchen as (Santo) Domingo, the ancient capital of

spice—earliest European settlement in the New World—out of which emerged a darkly nutritive sweetness for which I longed because it was in some sense flesh of Dickinson's own poetic flesh. In fact, this poem became a prayer for aesthetic manna, an invocation of transformation:

> Black cake, black Uncle Emily cake,
> I tunnel among your grains of darkness
> fierce as a mouse: your riches
> are all my purpose, your currants and death's eye raisins
> wrinkling and thickening blackness,
> and the single almond of light she buried
> somewhere under layers of shadow. . . .
>
> One day I too will be Uncle Sandra:
> iambic and terse. I'll hobble the tough sidewalks,
> the alleys that moan go on, go on.
> O when I reach those late-night streets,
> when acorns and twigs
> litter my path like sentences
> the oaks no longer choose to say,
>
> I want that cake in my wallet.
> I want to nibble as I hobble.
> I want to smile and nibble
> that infinite black cake,
>   and lean
> on Uncle Emily's salt-white
> ice-bright sugar cane.[1]

To me, this poem says that the poet/cook is a magician, her kitchen centered on the dangers and desires of the oven in which quotidian reality miraculously reshapes itself to emerge in loaves of solace sufficient to the appetites of all who hunger for the strength they provide.

But what an oven, then, this poet's was! And what a kitchen enclosed that stove over which she bent! As always, she herself described it best, better than any other poet or critic could dream of portraying it—and her description, characteristically, was infused with braggadocio: "Dare you see a Soul *at the White Heat?* / Then crouch within the door—" This poem only pretends to be about a blacksmith and a forge, or so I tell myself as I muse on Dickinson's kitchen. The fabulous *"White Heat"* is really the volcanic intensity of the oven in which—like some anti-self of the witch in the tale of Hansel and Gretel—this "little home-keeping person" baked cakes that turned into poems that turned into sustenance for herself, her "sister Sue," and all the rest of us.

ii: The White Heat Casts Its Shadows

Yes, but.

But what if the *"White Heat"* darkened, what if its smoke blackened the walls of the oven? Then what of the "sustenance" I've so ecstatically described? Would it shrivel to cinders, would it be bitter to the tongue and harsh in the mouth? The Dickinson I've encountered more recently, and whose bleak flames have surely, in some way, cast flickering shadows on my own poems, is still a shamanistic visionary, a sorceress of a cook and therefore mistress of transformations. Yet though her metamorphoses are still quite often grounded in manipulations of the domestic quotidian, that quotidian sometimes verges on the nihilistic rather than the nourishing.

This is the Dickinson whose views of dying and death, grief and its performance as mourning, I encountered as I investigated the elegiac while working on my book *Death's Door: Modern Dying and the Ways We Grieve.* It was this Dickinson, I found—perhaps especially this "little home-keeping person"—who transmuted the Victorian sentimentality of, say, Mrs. Lydia Sigourney, the "Sweet Singer of Hartford," into skeptical, proto-modern dramas of loss. For where Sigourney's mortuary verses in *The Weeping Willow* (1847), one of her twenty best-selling volumes, were dedicated to her patron "Daniel Wadsworth, Esq.," whom she sententiously described as "the Friend of All Who Mourn," the antithetical Dickinson mostly offered cold comfort to real or imagined readers. Rather, from the vantage of kitchen or parlor, she continually cast a keen eye on her town and its customs as the *"White Heat"* of her sensibility incinerated consolation.

This Dickinson is the poet who likes "a look of Agony / Because I know it's true," because, that is, she knows from long acquaintance with the "death *watch*" as it was practiced among those who saw, as she did, "New Englandly," how and why "Agony" is "true":

> Men do not sham Convulsion,
> Nor simulate, a Throe—
>
> The Eyes glaze once—and that is Death—
> Impossible to feign
> The Beads upon the Forehead
> By homely Anguish strung.

And this is the Dickinson who, literally or figuratively peering through the windows of the house behind whose walls she hid herself, reduced ethereal visions of death's aftermath to ashes with just a few terse notations:

> There's been a Death, in the Opposite House,
> As lately as Today—
> I know it, by the numb look
> Such Houses have—alway—
>
> The Neighbors rustle in and out—
> The Doctor—drives away—
> A Window opens like a Pod—
> Abrupt—mechanically—
>
> Somebody flings a Mattress out—
> The Children hurry by—
> They wonder if it died on that—
> I used to—when a Boy—

The Minister—goes stiffly in—
As if the House were His—
And He owned all the Mourners—now—
And little Boys—besides—

And then the Milliner—and the Man
Of the Appalling Trade—
To take the measure of the House—

There'll be that Dark Parade—

Of Tassels—and of Coaches—soon— . . .

Processed in the furnace of a mind at the *"White Heat,"* how absolutely the details of bereavement turn weird, turn ashen, turn fateful. First there's the "numbness" that goes with (as Dickinson puts it elsewhere) the "letting go." Then there's the terrible window that opens eerily—but *"mechanically"* as a seedpod so that an anonymous "Somebody" can fling a mattress out. And if a soiled mattress is the seed the "Pod" delivers, what does *that* tell us of the expired soul?

Then there are the children, all scared *boys,* including the poet her/himself, who wonder at the remarkably transformed *its* demise. Then arrives the stiff and vaunting "Minister"—more a minister and administrator of death than of redemption—who "owns" the whole unnerved and unnerving company now, although he'll be followed shortly by the punningly described "Man / Of the Appalling Trade—" who comes inexorably to take the mortal and moral "measure of the House": can the coffin pass through doorways? What size were the mind and body of the *it* who died, anyway?

But Dickinson's searing vision was capable of even more ashen imaginings. In "There's been a Death, in the Opposite House" she looks at death from the outside in, as it were, but in poems inflamed by scarier narratives she inspects her own mortality from the inside out, calibrating the ways and means through which the oven or furnace of the self must chill from the furious intelligence of *"White Heat"* to the rigor and austerity of marble. In "Because I could not stop for Death" she figures Death, that "Minister" of stiffness, as a courtly suitor come a-calling, then prophesies how she will freeze in his embrace—"For only Gossamer, my Gown— / My Tippet—only Tulle—"—as even the almighty sun abandons her to the terror of a journey "toward Eternity."

But in a more literal imagining of the experience confronted by the dying *it* at the center of the circle of death watchers, she fiercely dramatized that scene in "I heard a Fly buzz when I died," a poem whose syntax and narrative seem so straightforward that the piece is frequently taught to schoolchildren, but whose enigmatic preoccupation with a "mere" fly makes it as hard to decipher as it is to forget:

> *I heard a Fly buzz—when I died—*
> *The stillness in the Room*
> *Was like the Stillness in the Air—*
> *Between the Heaves of Storm—*
>
> *The Eyes around—had wrung them dry—*
> *And Breaths were gathering firm*
> *For that last Onset—when the King*
> *Be witnessed—in the Room—*
>
> *I willed my Keepsakes—Signed away*
> *What portion of me be*
> *Assignable—and then it was*
> *There interposed a Fly—*
>
> *With Blue—uncertain stumbling Buzz—*
> *Between the light—and me—. . .*

Here's a classic nineteenth-century death watch, with the *agon* of mortality played out in a domestic setting, the sufferer surrounded by family and friends who have at this point composed themselves in preparation for the inevitable, while the speaker has made her last wishes known (willed "Keepsakes," "Signed away" the properties of her material self) so that all are reverently awaiting the arrival of "the King."

But who is this "King"—and what does the uncertain, stumbling, buzzing interposition of a "Fly" have to do with him? Ordinarily, in the religious culture out of which Dickinson's poems arose we'd associate such a majestic personage with God. And in this setting it would certainly make sense to believe that the poet has imagined God regally arriving to scoop up and judge the soul as it passes through the veil that separates this world from what the nineteenth century often called "the other side." Moreover, if the "King" is God, then "witnessing" his presence in the room would be a ceremonial act of piety, since the word "witness" is itself an evangelical term.

That Dickinson disliked evangelism, however—and had actually as a girl rejected evangelical proseletyzings at her school—suggests that the word "witnessed" is itself ambiguous. For such a skeptical thinker, Christian "witnessing" was problematic, especially when the coming of physical death was about to be *clinically* witnessed during the death watch. If we read the poem literally, then, the "King" in fact equals death "himself," who is, in this interpretation, the king or ruler of life, the rigorous minister-in-charge. Yet when the "King"—whether God the Father or King/Father Death—is expected to appear, the speaker instead encounters a "Fly."

Can the "Fly" then *equal* the "King"? If so, does the Fly-as-King signify *God* the King or *Death* the King—or both (which would add up to a dark image of God)? And if the Fly isn't identical with the King but is just "His" herald, what then? Can this cryptic insect's "Blue— uncertain stumbling Buzz" be a metaphor for the speaker's struggling last breaths—her death "rattle"? "And then / I could not see to see": or is the Fly itself a symbol of the "Blue—uncertain stumbling" soul as, expiring, it escapes from the body, leaving the eyes of the flesh—in the poem's last line—unable to "see [physically how] to see [spiritually]"? And how did the poet strengthen herself here to transcribe (with fierce accuracy) the deathbed truth that the sense of hearing, as nurses often explain to relatives of the dying, is "the last to go"? (Even when you can't "see to see" you can hear, say, a fly's buzzing.)

There are so many ways to read this disturbing poem that its plot line comes with blurred ambiguities from the furnace of the poet's mind. But we can see that when Dickinson identifies in fantasy with the dying object of the death watch, she herself watches, with terrified irony, the juxtaposition of King and Fly as the eyes of the dying, like the windows in the poem, "fail": life stumbles away into an indeterminate blindness while the speaker—the poet herself?—imagines becoming the insentient *it* of whom she so often speaks.[2]

How did Dickinson's artfully frightening self-reifications influence me as a poet? Confronting radical bereavement as I had to some years ago, I think I learned from her to reimagine myself as an "it"—an abandoned *thing* teetering on the lip of the world. Here's a poem in which I presented myself that way.

Objet Trouvé

Something put me in this place where I am
and I am not I:

and there's a yellow light, a great light
bearing down on me, a wheel of heat,

and black and white in subtle turns,
the print of cryptic characters—

the Times, *the* News*—around me,*
and a clot of sticky stuff that clamps me to a space

I never thought would happen,
where enormous lines

cross, cling, and hold me still—
and still I'm drifting, drifting out of

what you call a picture, out of your collage,
And hanging here in silence

while the watchers gawk,
I wriggle out of the bloody glue,

and move,
and gather speed.

Outside the design it's blue,
it's green and blue.

There's wild iris in a meadow, the toss of a sea
that's nobody's museum.

Faster and faster, I'm tearing out of the frame.
If you tell me who I am,

if you tell me my name,
I'll imagine you back.

I might even try to love you
if you tell me what I'm flying into.[3]

Yet even here, I now realize, I couldn't go the whole dread distance with Dickinson. I wanted to fly into love, couldn't let the windows close, couldn't look hard at the ashes.

I still wanted—how much I wanted!—to mimic the triumphs with which the "Myth of Amherst" rewarded herself as she baked the great cake of life in her kitchen, wanted to be "Uncle Sandra" as she was "Uncle Emily." And I still dreamed of leaning on the glittering sugar cane that she shaped in the white heat of her oven, even when she grieved, even when she shuddered.

—2008

Part III

MOTHER RITES:
MATERNITY, MATRIARCHY,
CREATIVITY

FROM *PATRIA* TO *MATRIA*

Elizabeth Barrett Browning's *Risorgimento*

Then Lady Reason . . . said, "Get up, daughter! Without waiting any longer, let us go to the Field of Letters. There the City of Ladies will be founded on a flat and fertile plain . . ."
    —CHRISTINE DE PIZAN, *THE BOOK OF THE CITY OF LADIES*

Our lives are Swiss—
So still—so Cool
Till some odd afternoon
The Alps neglect their Curtains
And we look farther on!

Italy stands the other side!
While like a guard between—
The solemn Alps
The siren Alps
Forever intervene!
                    —EMILY DICKINSON

Our insight into this early, pre-Oedipus phase in the little girl's development comes to us as a surprise, comparable in another field with the discovery of the Minoan-Mycenaean civilization behind that of Greece.
                    —SIGMUND FREUD, "FEMALE SEXUALITY"

211

And now I come, my Italy,
My own hills! Are you 'ware of me, my hills,
How I burn toward you? do you feel to-night
The urgency and yearning of my soul,
As sleeping mothers feel the sucking babe
And smile?

                                    —*AURORA LEIGH*[1]

When in 1860 Elizabeth Barrett Browning published *Poems before Congress,* a frankly political collection of verses that was the culmination of her long commitment to Italy's arduous struggle for reunification, English critics excoriated her as unfeminine, even insane. "To bless and not to curse is woman's function," wrote one reviewer, "and if Mrs. Browning, in her calmer moments, will but contrast the spirit which has prompted her to such melancholy aberrations with that which animated Florence Nightingale, she can hardly fail to derive a profitable lesson for the future." Interestingly, however, the very first poem in the volume depicts Italy as a friendless, powerless, invalid woman, asking if it is ". . . true,—may it be spoken,—" that she is finally alive

. . . who has lain so still,
With a wound in her breast,
And a flower in her hand,
And a grave-stone under her head,
While every nation at will
Beside her has dared to stand,
And flout her with pity and scorn . . .

Creating an ostensibly "unfeminine" political polemic, Barrett Browning consciously or unconsciously seems to adopt the persona of a nurse at the bedside of an imperiled relative, almost as if she *were* a sort of literary-political Florence Nightingale. Putting aside all questions about the inherent femininity or unfemininity of political poetry, I will argue that this English expatriate's visions of *Italia Riunità* had more to do with both her femaleness and her feminism than is usually supposed. In fact, where so magisterial a reader as Henry James believed that Barrett Browning's commitment to "the cause of Italy" represented a letting down of "her inspiration and her poetic pitch," I believe instead that, as Flavia Alaya has also observed, Italy became for a complex of reasons both the embodiment of this woman poet's inspiration and the most vivid strain in her "poetic pitch."[2]

Specifically, I will suggest that through her involvement with the revolutionary struggle for political identity that marked Italy's famous *risorgimento*, Barrett Browning enacted and reenacted her own personal and artistic struggle for identity, a *risorgimento* that was, like Italy's, both an insurrection and a resurrection. In addition, I will suggest that, by using metaphors of the healing and making whole of a wounded woman/land to articulate both the reality and fantasy of her own female/ poetic revitalization, Barrett Browning figuratively located herself in a re-creative female poetic tradition that descends from Sappho and Christine de Pizan through the Brontës, Christina Rossetti, Margaret Fuller, and Emily Dickinson to Renée Vivien, Charlotte Perkins Gilman, H. D., and Adrienne Rich. Infusing supposedly asexual poetics with the dreams and desires of a distinctively sexual politics, these women imagined nothing less than the transformation of *patria* into *matria* and thus the *risorgimento* of the lost community of women that Rossetti called the "mother country"—the shadowy land, perhaps, that Freud identified with the mysterious "Minoan-Mycenaean civilization behind that of Greece." In resurrecting the *matria*, moreover, these women fantasized resurrecting and restoring both the *madre*, the forgotten impossible dead mother, and the *matrice*, the originary womb or matrix, the mother-matter whose very memory, says Freud, is "lost in a past so dim . . . so hard to resuscitate that it [seems to have] undergone some specially inexorable repression."[3]

Not surprisingly, then, Barrett Browning begins her covertly political 1857 *Künstlerroman, Aurora Leigh,* with a meditation on this lost mother, using imagery that dramatically foreshadows the figure with which the poet opens her overtly political *Poems before Congress.* Gazing at a portrait of her mother that was (significantly) painted after the woman's death, young Aurora sees the maternal image as embodying in turn all the patriarchal myths of femaleness—muse, Psyche, Medusa, Lamia; "Ghost, fiend, and angel, fairy, witch, and sprite." But most heart-rendingly she sees her as "Our Lady of the Passion, stabbed with swords / Where the Babe sucked": the only *maternal* image of the lost mother dissolves into the destroyed woman/country from *Poems before Congress,* "who has lain so still, / With a wound in her breast" while "every nation" has flouted her "with pity and scorn."[4]

Among eighteenth-, nineteenth-, and early twentieth-century English and American writers, tropes of Italy proliferated like flowers in Fiesole, so much so that the country, as its nationalist leaders feared, would seem to have had no reality except as a metaphor. As far back as the sixteenth but especially in the late eighteenth century, English romancers had exploited what Kenneth Churchill calls "the violence-incest-murder-prison paradigm of Gothic Italy." More seriously, from Gibbon to Byron and Shelley to John Ruskin, George Eliot, Henry James, Edith Wharton, and D. H. Lawrence, English-speaking poets and novelists read the sunny, ruin-haunted Italian landscape as a symbolic text, a hieroglyph, or, perhaps more accurately, a palimpsest of Western history, whose warring traces seemed to them to solidify in the stones of Venice and the bones of Rome. Shelley, for instance, reflecting in "Adonais" on the ancient city where Keats died seeking health, sees it both as "that high Capital, where kingly Death / Keeps his pale court in beauty and decay" and as "the Paradise, / The grave, the city, and the wilderness"— a place whose ruins, building on and contradicting one another, suggest the paradoxical simultaneity of the originary moment (paradise) and the fall from that moment (the grave), the invention of culture (the city) and the supervention of nature (the wilderness). In "St. Mark's Place," Samuel Rogers is less metaphysical, but he too elaborates a vision of Italy as text, asserting that "Not a stone / In the broad pavement, but to him who has / An eye, an ear for the Inanimate World, / Tells of past ages," and George Eliot develops a similar perception when she writes in *Middlemarch* of "the gigantic broken revelations" of Rome. Finally, emphasizing the dialectic between culture and nature that, as Shelley also saw, underlies all such statements, Edith Wharton summarizes the point most simply: Italy, she writes, is "that sophisticated landscape where the face of nature seems moulded by the passions and imaginings of man."[5]

Interestingly, however, as post-Renaissance Italy sank ever further into physical decay and political disarray, lapsing inexorably away from the grandeur that was imperial Rome and the glory that was fourteenth-century Florence, both native and tourist poets increasingly began to depict "her" as a sort of fallen woman. In Byron's famous translation, for example, the seventeenth-century Florentine patriot Vincenzo da Filijaca imagines "Italia" as a helpless naked seductress, while Byron himself writes of Venice as "a sea Cybele" and Rome as the "Lone mother of dead Empires," "The Niobe of nations!" Similarly, Ruskin, who sees Venice as "the Paradise of cities," the positive of Shelley's more equivocal Rome, hints that "her" charm lies in her seductive femininity, and the expatriate novelist Ouida writes of her adopted city that "in Florence [the past is] like the gold from the sepulchres of the Aetruscan kings that shines on the breast of some fair living woman." The trope of Italy or of one of "her" city-states as a living, palpable, and often abandoned woman had become almost ubiquitous by the time Barrett Browning began to write her poems about the *risorgimento,* and of course it derived from a traditional grammatical convention that tends, at least in most Indo-European languages, to impute metaphorical femaleness to such diverse phenomena as countries, ships, and hurricanes. As applied to Italy, however, this metaphor of gender was often so intensely felt that, most notably for women writers, it frequently evolved from figure to fantasy, from speculation to hallucination. Thus Italy as art object "moulded by the passions and imaginings of man" becomes Italy as Galatea and, worse still, a Galatea seduced and betrayed by her creator, while Italy as destroyed motherland becomes Italy as wounded mother, Madonna of the Sorrows whose restored milk and honey might nourish errant children, and especially daughters, of all nations. Ultimately, then, such women writers as Christina Rossetti and Elizabeth Barrett Browning revise and revitalize the dead metaphor of gender that is their literary and linguistic inheritance, using it to transform Italy from a political state to a female state of mind, from a problematic country in Europe to the problem condition of femaleness.

Redeeming and redeemed by Italy, they imagine redeeming and being redeemed by themselves.[6]

More specifically, as artists like Rossetti and Barrett Browning (and Emily Dickinson after them) struggle to revive both the dead land of Italy and the dead metaphor of "her" femaleness, they explore five increasingly complex but always interrelated definitions of this lost, fragmented woman-country: (1) Italy as a nurturing mother—a land that feeds, (2) Italy as an impassioned sister—a land that feels, (3) Italy as a home of art—a land that creates, (4) Italy as a magic paradise—a land that transforms or integrates, and (5) Italy as a dead, denied, and denying woman—a land that has been rejected or is rejecting.

Christina Rossetti's ostensibly religious lyric "Mother Country" is the most visionary statement of the first definition, for in it this poet, who was (paradoxically enough) fully Italian only on her father's side, mourns her exclusion from a dreamlike, distinctively female Mediterranean queendom:

> Not mine own country
>> But dearer far to me?
> Yet mine own country,
>> If I may one day see
> Its spices and cedars
>> Its gold and ivory.

Glamorous, rich, and giving, such a maternal paradise is opposed to *this* (implicitly patriarchal) country, in which "All starve together, / All dwarfed and poor," and the metaphorical climates of the two locales strongly suggest that the luxurious mother country is Italy while the impoverished fatherland—"here"—is England. As if to support such an interpretation with matter-of-fact reportage, Elizabeth Barrett Browning writes countless letters from Pisa and Florence, praising the nurturing maternal land to which she has eloped with Robert Browning after her perilous escape from the gloomily patriarchal household at 50 Wimpole Street. Food, in particular, seems almost eerily ubiquitous. Barrett Browning never tires of describing great glowing oranges and luscious bunches of grapes; the Italian landscape itself appears largely edible, the scenery deliciously beautiful. As for "real" meals, they continually materialize at her table as if by magic. In Florence, she reports that "dinner, 'unordered,' comes through the streets and spreads itself on our table, as hot as if we had smelt cutlets hours before," while more generally, in another letter, she observes that "No little orphan on a house step but seems to inherit naturally his slice of watermelon and bunch of purple grapes."[7]

This land that feeds is also a land that feels. As both a mother country and, again in Rossetti's words, a "sister-land of Paradise," female Italy neither contains nor condones the superegoistic repressions that characterize patriarchal England. Literary visions of Italy had always emphasized the passion and sensuality of "her" people, but where Renaissance playwrights and Gothic romancers had dramatized the stagey strangeness of violent Italians, women writers like Barrett Browning, Rossetti, and later Dickinson wistfully set the natural emotiveness of this mother country against the icy artifice of the Victorian culture in which they had been brought up. Indeed, from Barrett Browning's Bianca in "Bianca among the Nightingales," who freely expresses her fiery rage at the cold Englishwoman who has stolen her lover away, to Rossetti's Enrica, who "chill[s]" Englishwomen with "her liberal glow" and "dwarf[s]" them "by her ampler scale," the women who represent Italy in women's writing increasingly seem like ennobled versions of Jane Eyre's Bertha Mason Rochester: large, heated, dark, passionate foreigners who are wholly at ease—even at one—with the Vesuvius of female sexual creativity Dickinson was later to find uneasily "at home" in her breast.

Together, in fact, such heroines as Barrett Browning's Bianca, her Laura Savio of "Mother and Poet," and Rossetti's Enrica seem almost to propose an ontology of female power as it might be if all girls were not, in Rossetti's words, "minted in the selfsame [English] mould." That most of these women are in one way or another associated with a violent uprising against the authoritarian rule of Austria and the patriarchal law of the pope, with Enrica (according to William Michael Rossetti) based on a woman who knew both Mazzini and Garibaldi, further cements their connection with Brontë's rebellious Bertha, but with a Bertha revised and transformed so that she, the alien, is free, and English Jane is trapped. As if to demonstrate this point, Christina Rossetti was "en route" to Italy ("Italy, Io Ti Saluto") when she imagined herself as "an 'immurata' sister" helplessly complaining that

> Men work and think, but women feel,
>   And so (for I'm a woman, I)
>   And so I should be glad to die,
>   And cease from impotence of zeal . . .

For, as Barrett Browning (and Charlotte Brontë) also knew, that "Italian" speech of feeling was only "half familiar" and almost wholly inaccessible to Englishwomen.

What made the inaccessibility of such speech especially poignant for poets like Rossetti and Barrett Browning, besides Italy's role as a feeding, feeling mother-sister, was "her" special status as the home, even the womb, of European art; this mother-sister became a muse whose shapes and sounds seemed to constitute a kind of primal aesthetic language from which no writer should allow herself to be separated. In Florence, Barrett Browning imagines that she is not only in a city that makes art, she is in a city that *is* art, so much so that, as in some Edenic dream, the solid real and the artful unreal merge uncannily: "The river rushes through the midst of its palaces like a crystal arrow, and it is hard to tell . . . whether those churches . . . and people walking, in the water or out of the water, are the real . . . people, and churches."[8] That the art of Florence is almost entirely male—Michelangelo's monuments of unaging intellect, Ghiberti's doors—appears oddly irrelevant, for living in Florence Barrett Browning begins to believe, if only briefly, that she might live in, even inherit, this art; insofar as art is Italy's and Italy might be her lost and reclaimed self, art itself might at last be her own.

In allowing herself such a dream, the author of *Aurora Leigh* was tacitly acknowledging the influence of a foremother she greatly admired, Madame de Staël, whose *Corinne, ou, l'Italie* was "an immortal book" that, said Barrett Browning, "deserves to be read three score and ten times—that is, once every year in the age of man." For not only is *Corinne,* in the words of Ellen Moers, "a guidebook to Italy," it is specifically a guidebook to an Italy that is the nurturing *matria* of a "woman of genius," the enchanting *improvisatrice* Corinne, whose brilliant career provided a paradigm of female artistry for count-less nineteenth-century literary women on both sides of the Atlantic. Like Aurora Leigh, Staël's poetic heroine is the daughter of an Italian mother and an English father, and, like Barrett Browning herself, she transforms the Italy dominated by relics of such great men as Michelangelo and Ghiberti into a land of free women, a female aesthetic utopia. Corinne herself, writes Staël, is *"l'image de notre belle Italie."* Triumphing as she improvises on the theme of Italy's glory, dances a dramatic tarantella, and translates *Romeo and Juliet* into *"sa langue maternelle,"* Corinne becomes not only a symbol of redemptive Italy but also a redemptive emblem of the power of symbolization itself, for, observes Staël, *"tout était langage pour elle."* No wonder, then, that Barrett Browning, *Corinne's* admirer, seems secretly to imagine an Italian heaven of invention whose speech constitutes a different, mystically potent language, a mother tongue: as if to balance Rossetti's remark that "our [English] tongue grew sweeter in [Enrica's] mouth," she writes wistfully of the way in which "the Tuscan musical / Vowels . . . round themselves as if they planned / Eternities of separate sweetness."[9]

Such a sense that even Italian speech encompasses "eternities of . . . sweetness" inevitably translates itself into a larger vision of Italy as earthly paradise, a vision that brings us back to the "green golden strand" of Rossetti's mother country and the vehement *"Italy"* of Dickinson's "Our lives are Swiss—." In this fourth incarnation, however, Italy is not just a nurturing mother country, she is a utopian motherland whose glamour transforms all who cross her borders, empowering women, enno-bling men, and—most significantly—annihilating national and sexual differences. Describing the hopeful celebration of Florentine freedom that miraculously took place on the Brownings' first wedding anniver-sary in 1847, Barrett Browning writes about a jubilant parade: "class after class" took part, and "then too, came the foreigners, there was a place for them." She notes that "the people were *embracing* for joy" and express-ing "the sort of gladness in which women may mingle and be glad too." In this setting, both sexes and all nationalities become part of the newer, higher nationality of Florence, so that expatriation turns, magically, into expatriotism. Less mystically and more amusingly, Virginia Woolf makes a similar point about Italy as utopia in *Flush,* her biography of the Brownings' dog. Arriving in Pisa, this pedigreed spaniel discovers that "though dogs abounded, there were no ranks; all—could it be possible?—were mongrels." At last inhabiting a classless society, he becomes "daily more and more democratic . . . All dogs were his brothers. He had no need of a chain in this new world."[10]

Finally, however, as Rossetti's "Mother Country," "Enrica," and "An 'Immurata' Sister" suggest, women writers from Barrett Browning to Dickinson are forced to admit that the nurturing, utopian, artful, feelingful, female land of Italy is not their own. Bred in what Barrett Browning and, after her, Rossetti call "the rigid North," such writers are forever spiritually if not physically excluded from "the sweet South," forever alienated from Italy's utopian redemption, if only by symbolic windows like those of Casa Guidi, which mark Barrett Browning's estrangement from Florence's moment of regeneration even while they allow the poet to view the spectacle of that rebirth. As the poets make this admission, maternal Italy, guarded by the intervention of the "solemn Alps" and "the bitter sea," lapses back into the negated and negating woman whose image opens both *Poems before Congress* and *Aurora Leigh.* Dead, she is denied and denying: as Aurora leaves for England, her mother country seems "Like one in anger drawing back her skirts / Which suppliants catch at," and Christina Rossetti, exclaiming "Farewell, land of love, Italy, / Sister-land of Paradise," summarizes in "En Route" the mingled regret and reproach with which these English daughters respond to the drastic loss such denial enforces:

> *Wherefore art thou strange, and not my mother?*
> *Thou hast stolen my heart and broken it:*
> *Would that I might call thy sons 'My brother,'*
> *Call thy daughters 'Sister sweet':*
> *Lying in thy lap, not in another,*
> *Dying at thy feet.*

For Rossetti, the despair these lines express becomes a characteristic gesture of resignation; the mother country is not to be found, not in this world at any rate, and so she immures herself in the convent of her soul, for "Why should I seek and never find / That something which I have not had?" For Barrett Browning, however, the struggle to revive and re-approach, rather than reproach, the lost mother country of Italy becomes the narrative project to which she devotes her two major long poems, *Casa Guidi Windows* (1851) and *Aurora Leigh.*[11]

Though explicitly (and successfully) a political poem that meditates on two carefully defined historical occasions, *Casa Guidi Windows* is also a preliminary working through of important psychological materials that had long haunted Barrett Browning; as such, it is a crucial preface to the poet's more frankly confessional *Aurora Leigh.* To be specific: even while Barrett Browning comments in part 1 on the exuberant 1847 demonstration with which the Italian and "foreign" citizens of Florence thanked Duke Leopold for granting them the right to form a militia, and even while she mourns in part 2 the temporary failure of the *risorgimento* when in 1849 the Austrians defeated the Italians at Novara, she tells a more covert story—the story of Italy's and her own seduction and betrayal by the brutality, indifference, and greed of patriarchal history. From this betrayal, this fall into the power of powers not her own, Italy/ Barrett Browning must regenerate herself, and she can only do this, the poet's metaphors imply, through a strategic deployment of female, especially maternal, energies. By delivering her children both to death (as soldiers) and life (as heirs), she can deliver herself into the community of nations where she belongs.

For Barrett Browning this plot had distinctively personal overtones. "After what broke [her] heart at Torquay"—the drowning of her beloved alter ego, "Bro"—she herself, as she later told her friend Mrs. Martin, had lived for years "on the outside of my own life . . . as completely dead to hope . . . as if I had my face against a grave . . ." Immuring herself in her room at 50 Wimpole Street, she had entrusted her future entirely to the will and whim of her notoriously tyrannical father, so much so that, as she also told Mrs. Martin, employing a strikingly political metaphor, "God knows . . . how utterly I had abdicated myself . . . Even my poetry . . . was a thing, on the outside of me . . . [a] desolate state it was, which I look back now to [as] one would look to one's graveclothes, if one had been clothed in them by mistake during a trance." Clearly, in some sense, the drowning of the younger brother who was Barrett Browning's only real reader in the family and for whose death she blamed herself, caused a self-alienation so deep that, like Emily Brontë's Catherine Earnshaw Linton mourning the absence of *her* male alter ego, Heathcliff, she felt the world turn to "a mighty stranger." Invalid and isolated, she herself became a figure like Italy in part 1 of *Casa Guidi Windows,* who

> *Long trammeled with the purple of her youth*
> *Against her age's ripe activity,*
> *Sits still upon her tombs, without death's ruth,*
> *But also without life's brave energy.*[12]

Yet just as the Italy of *Casa Guidi Windows,* part 1, trusts "fathers" like Leopold II and Pio Nono to deliver "her" from her living death, Barrett Browning expected her father to care enough to cure her illness; and just as Italy is duped by "her" faith in these patriarchs, Barrett Browning was deceived by her faith in her father, who refused to send her south (significantly, to Italy) for her health, so that she was "wounded to the bottom of my heart—cast off when I was ready to cling to him." But the plot thickens as the poet quickens, for, again, just as in Barrett Browning's own life a *risorgimento* came both from another younger brother figure—Robert Browning—and from the female deliverance of motherhood, so, in *Casa Guidi Windows,* promises of resurrection are offered wounded Italy both by the hope of a sturdy male leader who will "teach, lead, strike fire into the masses" and by the promise of "young children lifted high on parent souls," children whose innocence, fostered by maternal grace, may unfold "mighty meanings."[13]

Given the personal politics embedded in this story, it is no wonder that Barrett Browning prefaces the first edition of *Casa Guidi Windows* with an "advertisement" in which she takes especially intense "shame upon herself that she believed, like a woman, some royal oaths"; that in part 2 she reproaches herself for her "woman's fault / That ever [she] believed [Duke Leopold] was true"; and that she also asks "what woman or child will count [Pio Nono] true?" It is no wonder, either, that, in aligning herself with the revolutionary cause of Italy, Barrett Browning aligns herself against the strictures and structures of her fatherland, England, whose "close, stifling, corrupt system," like her imprisoning room in Wimpole Street, "gives no air nor scope for healthy . . . organization," a country for which "nothing will do . . . but a good revolution." As magisterial and patriarchal as Edward Moulton Barrett, England has "No help for women, sobbing out of sight / Because men made the laws" and "no tender utterance . . . For poor Italia, baffled by mischance." What is more remarkable in *Casa Guidi Windows*, however, and what more directly foreshadows the Italian dream of *Aurora Leigh* is the way in which Barrett Browning, dreaming behind the mediation of her windows, imagines Italy ultimately redeemed by the voices and visions of mothers and children: part 1 begins, after all, with "a little child . . . who not long had been / By mother's finger steadied on his feet," singing "*O bella libertà, O bella*," and part 2 ends with the poet's "own young Florentine, not two years old," her "blue-eyed prophet," transforming society with a clear, unmediated gaze not unlike Wordsworth's "eye among the blind." In between these epiphanies, Miriam the prophetess appears, clashing her "cymbals to surprise / The sun," and Garibaldi's wife outfaces "the whistling shot and hissing waves, / Until she [feels] her little babe unborn / Recoil within her."[14]

But what is finally perhaps most remarkable and, as Julia Markus points out, "most daring" about *Casa Guidi Windows* is the way in which, as Barrett Browning meditates on the plight of wounded "Italia," the poet finally presents herself, against the weight of all of the literary history she dutifully recounts throughout the work, as "the singer of the new day":

> And I, a singer also, from my youth,
> Prefer to sing with those who are awake,
> With birds, with babes, with men who will not fear
> The baptism of the holy morning dew . . .

. . . .
Than join those old thin voices with my new . . .

Crossing the Anglo-Italian frontier represented by Casa Guidi windows, Barrett Browning gains her strongest voice in Italy and regains, as we shall see, a vision of her strengthened self from and as Italy, for the female artistic triumph this passage describes points directly to the triumphant *risorgimento* of the woman poet that *Aurora Leigh* enacts.

As its title indicates, *Aurora Leigh* is a mythic narrative about "the baptism of the holy morning dew" Barrett Browning proposed to sing in *Casa Guidi Windows.* But before she and her heroine can achieve such a sacrament or become true singers of "the new day" and of the renewed *matria/matrice* that day implies, both must work through precisely the self-division that left "Italia" (in *Casa Guidi Windows*) and Barrett Browning (in Wimpole Street) living "on the outside" of their own lives. Significantly, therefore, the tale of the poet-heroine's *risorgimento,* which parallels the plot of the poet-author's own insurrection-resurrection, begins with a fragmentation of the self that is both symbolized and precipitated by a shattering of the nuclear family, a shattering that leads to a devastating analysis of that structure. Just as significantly, the story ends with a reconstitution of both self and family that provides a visionary new synthesis of the relationships among men, women, and children.

As if to emphasize the larger political issue involved in these emotional dissolutions and resolutions, the heroine's self and family are defined by two *paysages moralisés,* her mother country of Italy and her fatherland of England, between which (although at one point Aurora claims that "a poet's heart / Can swell to a pair of nationalities, / However ill-lodged in a woman's breast") she must ultimately choose. Both in its theatrical, sometimes hectically melodramatic, plot, then, and in its intensely symbolic settings, *Aurora Leigh* continually reminds us that it is not only a versified *Künstlerroman* which famously aims to specify the interaction between an artist and the particular "full-veined, heaving, double-breasted Age" that created her, it is also an "unscrupulously epic" allegory of a woman artist's journey from disease toward what Sylvia Plath once called "a country far away as health."[15]

Not surprisingly, given these geographical and dramatic imperatives, *Aurora Leigh* begins and ends in Italy, the lost redemptive land that must be redeemed in order for both poet-heroine and poet-author to achieve full selfhood. Here, in book 1, Aurora encounters and is symbolically rejected by her dead mother, "a Florentine / Whose rare blue eyes were shut from seeing me / When scarcely I was four years old," and here, even as she comes to terms with "a mother-want about the world," her father dies, leaving her suddenly awake "To full life and life's needs." While the mother seems irremediably gone, however, the father, "an austere Englishman," is quickly replaced by "A stranger with authority" who tears the child so abruptly from the land which has come to represent her mother that, watching "my Italy, / Drawn backward from the shuddering steamer-deck, / Like one in anger drawing back her skirts," she is uncertain whether the mother country has been rejected ("drawn back") or is rejecting ("drawing back").

This violent, neo-Wordsworthian fall into division from the mother and into "my father's England," home of alien language and orphanhood, is followed by a more subtle but equally violent fall into gender. Arriving in patriarchal England at the crucial age of thirteen, Aurora discovers that she is a *girl,* destined to be brought up in "A sort of cage-bird life" by a new and different "mother"—her "father's sister," who is her "mother's hater," for "Italy / Is one thing, England one"; inexorably parted, the two nations are irrevocable emblems of separation. Hence, as many feminist critics have pointed out, the girl is coerced into (at least on the surface) accepting a typical Victorian education in "femininity," reading "a score of books on womanhood / To prove, if women do not think at all, / They may teach thinking," learning "cross-stitch," and so forth. That she has "relations in the Unseen" and in Nature, which romantically persist and from which she draws "elemental nutriment and heat . . . as a babe sucks surely in the dark," and that she darkly remembers "My multitudinous mountains, sitting in / The magic circle, with the mutual touch / Electric . . . waiting for / Communion and commission"—another striking image of the mother's nurturing breasts—are the only signs that somewhere in the shadows of her own psyche her mother country endures, despite the pseudo-Oedipal wrenching she has undergone.

As Aurora grows into the fragmentation that seems to be (English) woman's lot, things go from bad to worse. Exiled from the undifferentiated unity of her mother country, the girl discovers that her parents have undergone an even more complicated set of metamorphoses than she at first realized, for not only has her true dead southern mother been replaced by a false and rigid northern stepmother—her "father's sister"—but her true dead father, after being supplanted by "a stranger with authority," has been replaced by a false and rigid northern stepfather, her cousin Romney Leigh, who, upon her father's death, has become the putative head of the family. To be sure, as Aurora's cousin, Romney has the potential for becoming a nurturing peer, an empowering "Bro" rather than a debilitating patriarch. But certainly, when the narrative begins, he is a symbolic father whose self-satisfied right and reason represent the masculine "head" that inexorably strives to humble the feminine "heart."

"I am not very fond of praising men by calling them *manly*; I hate and detest a masculine man," Barrett Browning told one correspondent, and clearly by "masculine" she did not mean "virile" but "authoritarian." Yet such (implicitly patriarchal) authoritarianism is exactly what characterizes Romney Leigh at the cousins' first meeting, for his, says Aurora, was "The stranger's touch that took my father's place / Yet dared seem soft," and she adds "A godlike nature his." That Aurora has evidently been destined to marry this man makes the point even more clearly. Drawn away from the natural lore and lure of the mother, she has been surrendered to what Lacan calls the law of the father, inscribed into a patrilineal kinship system where she is to be doubly named by the father, both as daughter-Leigh and as wife-Leigh, just as Elizabeth herself was originally named Elizabeth Barrett Barrett. That Romney refuses to read her poetry, claiming that her book has "witchcraft in it," clarifies the point still further. Her work is either "mere" or "magical" "woman's work" because she exists "as the complement / Of his sex merely," an (albeit precious) object of exchange in a network of marital transactions that must by definition deprive her not only of her autonomy but, more importantly, of her desire.[16]

Nevertheless, Aurora insists on continuing to transcribe the texts of her desire, poems whose energy is significantly associated with her inner life, her "relations in the Unseen," and her mother country. At the same time, because she has been exiled in her fatherland, she must inevitably write these works in her father tongue. Inevitably too, therefore, because she is struggling to find a place in traditions created by that masculine (and masculinist) language, she must study her father's books. Creeping through the patriarchal attic "Like some small nimble mouse between the ribs / Of a mastodon," she finds a room "Piled high with cases in my father's name" and "nibbles" fiercely but randomly at what amounts to a paradigmatic library of Western culture. Inevitably, too, however, this furtive self-education, which both parallels and subverts her aunt's effort to educate her in "femininity," leads to further self-division. She can and does reject both Romney's offer of marriage and the financial legacy he tries with magisterial generosity to bestow on her, but once she has internalized—nibbled, devoured—the texts that incarnate patriarchal history, she is helplessly implicated in that history, so that even her "own" poetry is tainted, fragmented, impure.

How, then, is Aurora to rectify and clarify both her art and her self? Barrett Browning's "unscrupulous" epic seeks to resolve this crucial issue, and, perhaps paradoxically, the author begins her curative task by examining the ways in which her other major characters are just as fragmented and self-alienated as her heroine. To start, for instance, she shows that, despite (or perhaps because of) his superegoistic calm, Romney too is self-divided. This "head of the family," she quickly suggests, is no more than a "head," abstractly and, as his abortive wedding to Marian Erle will prove, ineffectually espoused to "social theory." In fact, he is not just a false father because he has replaced Aurora's "true" father, he is a false father because, as Barrett Browning decided after her long imprisonment in Wimpole Street, all fathers are in some sense false. Indeed, the very idea of fatherhood, with its implications of social hierarchy and psychic fragmentation ("man with the head, woman with the heart"), is dangerously divisive, not only for women but for men. As a brother like her own "Bro," Romney might be able to "read" (and thus symbolically unite with) the texts of female desire that transcribe Aurora's otherness, but as a father he is irremediably blind to them. As a brother, moreover, he might more literally unite himself to the social as well as sexual others from whom his birth and breeding separate him, but as a father or "head," he is, again, hopelessly estranged from most members of the "body" politic.[17]

That Romney craves a union with both social and sexual others is, however, a sign that, like Aurora, he is half consciously struggling toward a psychic reunification which will constitute as much of a *risorgimento* for him as it will for her. His ill-fated and "mis-conceived" proposal to Aurora suggests his intuition of his own need, even while the fact that she "translates" him "ill" emphasizes the impossibility of communion or communication between them. In addition, his eagerness to go "hand in hand" with her among "the arena-heaps / Of headless bodies" till, through her "touch," the "formless, nameless trunk of every man / Shall seem to wear a head with hair you know, / And every woman catch your mother's face" implies that, at least metaphorically, he understands the self-division that afflicts both him and his cousin, even while Aurora's reply that since her mother's death she has not seen "So much love . . . / As answers even to make a marriage with / In this cold land of England" once again outlines the geography of "mother-want" in which both characters are situated. Similarly, his subsequent plan to "take [a] wife / Directly from the people" reveals once more his yearning to heal in his own person the wounds of the body politic, even while Aurora's recognition that his scheme is both artificial and divisive, "built up as walls are, brick by brick," predicts the project's failure. For Romney, who feels himself "fallen on days" when marriages can be likened to "galley-couplings," redemption must come not from the outward ceremony of marriage but from an inward metamorphosis that will transform him from (false) father to (true) brother, from (false) "god" to (true) groom.

Despite its misguided formulation, however, Romney's impulse to wed Marian Erle does begin the crucial process of metamorphosis, for this "daughter of the people," an "Erle" elf of nature rather than an "earl" of patriarchy, has a history that parallels his and Aurora's history of fragmentation at the same time that she is an essential part of the reunified family/being he and Aurora must become.[18] Ignored and emotionally abandoned by a drunken father who beat her and a bruised mother who tried to prostitute her to a local squire, this "outcast child . . . Learnt early to cry low, and walk alone." Her proletarian education in alienation offers a darkly parodic version of Aurora's bourgeois education in femininity. Reading the "wicked book" of patriarchal reality with the same fervor that inspired Aurora's studies of her father's patriarchal texts, Marian imagines a "skyey father and mother both in one" just as Aurora imagines inscribing her desire for her motherland in her father's tongue. Finally, too, the shriek of pain Marian utters when her mother tries to sell her to the squire—"God, free me from my mother . . . / These mothers are too dreadful"—echoes and amplifies Aurora's impassioned protest against the "Keeper's voice" of the stepmother-aunt, who tells her that she has been "promised" to her cousin Romney: "I must help myself / And am alone from henceforth." Repudiating the false mothers of patriarchal England, both these literally or figuratively orphaned daughters cry out, each in her own way, the intensity of the "mother-want" that will eventually unite them, along with Romney and with Marian's child, in the motherland of Italy, where each will become a nurturing mother country to the other.

When Marian and Aurora first meet, however, both are stranded in the alienating cityscape of nineteenth-century London, where each lives in an attic that seems to symbolize her isolation from world and self alike. Though Aurora has ostensibly become a successful poet, her ambition continually reminds her of her failure, since it constantly confronts her with fragmented verses whose "heart" is "Just an embryo's heart / Which never yet had beat," while Marian, though her "heart . . . swelled so big / It seemed to fill her body," lives up a "long, steep, narrow stair, 'twixt broken rail / And mildewed wall." Parts of a scattered self—the one heartless, the other too great-hearted—this pair of doubles must be unified like the distant and dissonant city-states of Italy, and ultimately, of course, the two are brought together by Romney's various though similar desires for them. To begin with, however, they are united by the visits of yet another potential wife of Romney's—Lady Waldemar—to their parallel attics.

Voluptuous and vicious, the figure of Lady Waldemar offers a further comment on nineteenth-century ideals of "femininity." In fact, as we shall see, she is the (false) wife/mother whose love the (false) father must reject if he is to convert himself into a (true) brother. At the same time, though, her beckoning sexuality both initiates and instigates the "plot" proper of *Aurora Leigh,* emblematizing a fall into heterosexual desire with which Aurora and Marian must variously struggle before they can become whole. Almost at once, Aurora perceives this fashionable aristocrat as a male-created, socially defined "lady"—"brilliant stuff, / And out of nature"—a perception Lady Waldemar's name reinforces with its reminiscences of generations of Danish kings. But even while Aurora defines her as "out of nature" in the sense that she is an antinatural being, a cultural artifact, this "fair fine" lady defines herself as being "out of nature" in the sense that she is *from* nature, nature's emissary. For, confessing that she has "caught" love "in the vulgar way," Lady Waldemar instructs the poet-heroine that "you eat of love, / And do as vile a thing as if you ate / Of garlic" since "love's coarse, nature's coarse." Two books later, when she reappears at a party Aurora attends, the very image of Lady Waldemar's body reiterates her "natural" sexuality. Gorgeously seductive, "the woman looked immortal," her bare breasts splitting her "amaranth velvet-bodice down / To the waist, or nearly, with the audacious press / Of full-breathed beauty."

As emblems of nurturing maternity, breasts have obsessed both author and heroine throughout *Aurora Leigh,* but this is the first time their erotic potential is (quite literally) revealed, and tellingly the revelation is associated with Aurora's growing sense of artistic and sexual isolation: "Must I work in vain, / Without the approbation of a man?"; with her confession of "hunger . . . for man's love"; and, most strikingly, with her feeling that her "loose long hair [has begun] to burn and creep, / Alive to the very ends, about my knees." Furthermore, Lady Waldemar's eroticism is associated with—indeed, causes—Marian's betrayal into sexuality, a betrayal that leads to both a "murder" and a rebirth, while Aurora's mingled fear of and fascination with Lady Waldemar's erotic presence finally drive the poet back to her motherland of Italy, where she is ultimately to be reunited with both Marian and Romney. In fact, what have often been seen as the awkward or melodramatic turns of plot through which Barrett Browning brings these three characters back together in a sort of Florentine paradise are really important dramatic strategies by which the author herself was trying to work out (and out of) the "problem" of female sexuality by first confronting the engendered world as it is and then reengendering and reconstituting it as it should be.

Trusting the duplicitous Lady Waldemar, who "wrapped" the girl in her arms and, ironically enough, let her "dream a moment how it feels / To have a real mother," Marian is treacherously brought to France by the servant of this false "mother," placed in a brothel where she is drugged and raped, and thereby sold into sexual slavery—a deed that, as Marian herself notes, was "only what my mother would have done." At the same time, Aurora—missing her "woodland sister, sweet maid Marian," and convinced that Romney is about to marry the "Lamia-woman," Lady Waldemar—finally decides to return to the Italy that she has long heard "crying through my life, / [with the] piercing silence of ecstatic graves." Not coincidentally, she plans to finance her trip by selling the "residue / Of my father's books," a crucial first step in what is to be a definitive renunciation of the power of the fatherland. Her journey to the mother country, however, is impelled as much by desire as by denial, for, in the passage I have used as an epigraph to this essay, she "burns" toward her "own hills" and imagines that they desirously reciprocate her "yearning . . . As sleeping mothers feel the sucking babe / And smile." Thus, when en route she encounters the lost Marian in a Paris flower market, she begins the process of reunification that will regenerate both these wounded daughters. For the "fallen" Marian, whose face haunts Aurora like the face of a "dead woman," has become a mother whose assertion of what J. J. Bachofen was later in the century to call "mother right"—"I claim my mother-dues / By law"—proposes an empowering alternative to "the law which now is paramount," the "common" patriarchal "law, by which the poor and weak / Are trodden underfoot by vicious men, / And loathed for ever after by the good." Becoming such a powerful figure, moreover, she has become a creative authority whose maternal eroticism speeds the two women toward the unfallen garden of female sexuality that they will plant in the richly flowering earth of Florence. There Marian's "unfathered" child will "not miss a . . . father," since he will have "two mothers," there Aurora will set Marian like a "saint" and "burn the lights of love" before her pure maternity, and there, in a revision of her own eroticism, Aurora will exorcise the haunting vision of what she now comes to see as Lady Waldemar's distorted (lamia-like) sexuality.

For when she returns to her motherland with Marian as her sister/self, Aurora returns transformed. No longer merely an aching outcast daughter crying her inchoate "mother-want," she has become herself, symbolically at least, a mother, since she is one of the "two mothers" of Marian's child. In addition, transformed into a hierophant of "sweet holy Marian," she has learned to devote herself to the specifically female theology of the Madonna, the Queen of Heaven whom the Florentine women worship and whose rituals facilitate Aurora's increasing self-knowledge. Finally, she has become a poet, an artist-heroine who can not only weep but word her desire, in a language that through her inter-action with Marian she has begun to make into a mother tongue. In fact, as she learns some weeks after her arrival in Florence, people in England have finally begun to "read" her. Her new book, writes her painter friend Vincent Carrington, "Is eloquent as if you were not dumb," and his fian-cée, who has Aurora's verses "by heart" more than she has her lover's words, has even insisted on having a portrait painted with "Your last book folded in her dimpled hands / Instead of my brown palette as I wished."

That Marian's child is "unfathered" contributes in yet another way to the regenerative maternity both women now experience, for, after all, the baby is only figuratively unfathered; literally, he was fathered by some nameless customer in a brothel. To call him "unfathered," therefore, is to stress the likeness of his mother, Marian, not only to the fallen woman Mary Magdalene but also to the blessed Virgin Mary, whose immac-ulate conception was the sign of a divine annunciation. That Barrett Browning surrounds Marian's maternity with the rhetoric of Mariolatry implies the theological force she wants to impute to this "maiden" moth-er's female energy. As opposed to the often sentimentally redemptive power ascribed to such Victorian "mothers' boys" as Gaetano (in Brown-ing's *The Ring and the Book*), Leonard (in Mrs. Gaskell's *Ruth*), or Paul Dombey (in Dickens' *Dombey and Son*), Marian's son has an austerely religious significance. Nameless but beautiful, he is hardly ever characterized as a real child might be. Rather, when Marian explains that, in her despair after her rape, "I lived for him, and so he lives, / And so I know, by this time, God lives too", the ambiguity of her language—does she believe that he is the "God" who "lives" or does his survival mean that "God lives"?—argues that he is in some sense a divine child, a baby god whose sacred birth attests to the divinity of his mother. Thus, even while she revises the story of the annunciation to question the brutality of a male God who uses women merely as vessels for his own ends, Barrett Browning suggests that the female creativity "holy" Marian and reverent Aurora share can transform the most heinous act of male sexual brutality, a rape, into a redemption. At the same time, by demonstrating the self-sufficient strength of Marian and Aurora's mutual maternity, she interrogates the idea that there is anything more than a momentary biological need for fathers or fatherhood.

It is noteworthy, then, that when she returns to Italy Aurora keeps reminding herself that she has returned to the land where her father is buried, the land of her mother's birth and her father's tomb, her "father's house / Without his presence." Though both her parents are buried near Florence, it is, curiously enough, evidence of only her father's disappearance that Aurora seeks and finds; when she revisits "the little mountain-house" where she had lived with him, she discovers that it has been effaced by female fertility symbols—"lingots of ripe Indian corn / In tessellated order and device / Of golden patterns"—so that "not a stone of wall" can be seen, and a black-eyed Tuscan girl sits plaiting straws in the doorway, as if forbidding entrance. While Aurora's mother lives on in the Italian motherland, her father is as irretrievably dead as Marian's child's father is nonexistent.

But how are both Aurora and Barrett Browning to deal with the wished-for but unnerving fate of the dead father? Freud famously argued that anxiety about the murder of this mythic figure ultimately constituted a social order in which "his" absent will was internalized as the superego that creates the law. Barrett Browning, however, as if responding in advance to Freud's hypothesis, implicitly suggests that man as father must be exorcised rather than internalized and that, in a *risorgimento* of matriarchal law, he must be replaced with man as brother or man as son. For, unlike such a precursor as Christine de Pizan (in *City of Ladies*) or such a descendant as Charlotte Perkins Gilman (in *Herland*), Aurora does not envision an all-female paradise. Rather, she longs for a mother country or "sisterland to Paradise" in which women *and* men can live together free of the rigid interventions and interdictions of the father.[19]

Thus, even when she and Marian and Marian's child have been securely established in "a house at Florence on the hill / Of Bellosguardo," from which, like goddesses surveying past and future, they can see sunrise and sunset, "morn and eve . . . magnified before us"—a scene that recalls Marian's "skyey father and mother both in one"—Aurora yearns obsessively for Romney. "Like a tune that runs / I' the head," the erotic longing for her cousin that was first signaled by the appearance of Lady Waldemar has made her, she admits at last, just what Lady Waldemar confessed herself—a "slave to nature." In addition, that longing reveals Aurora's radical sense of incompleteness, a feeling of self-division which suggests that, for Barrett Browning as for her heroine, a *matria* without men might become madly and maddeningly maenadic. As she sinks into a sort of sexual fever, Aurora notes that even her beloved Florence "seems to seethe / In this Medean boil-pot of the sun" and ruefully confesses that, in the absence of the consort whom she desires because his presence would complete the new configuration of humanity toward which she aspires, even her old "Tuscan pleasures" seem "worn and spoiled."

In endowing a woman named *Aurora Leigh* with such erotic feeling for a cousin whom she wishes to remake in the image of a brother, however, Barrett Browning must at least half consciously have understood that her wish to provide her protagonist with a fraternally understanding and erotically egalitarian lover might oblige her to risk retracing the outlines of the nineteenth century's most notorious brother-sister incest plot: Byron's affair with his half-sister, *Augusta Leigh*. Unlike such "realistically" depicted sister-brother pairs as Tom and Maggie Tulliver in *The Mill on the Floss*, but like Romney and Aurora, Byron and Augusta rarely met until they were young adults, when both couples discovered and resisted similar mutual attractions. To be sure, the socially illicit Byronic duo made a far weaker effort at resistance than Barrett Browning's socially "legitimate" pair of cousins. Nevertheless, what Leslie March-and says of Byron and Augusta is equally true of Romney and Aurora: "in their formative years they had escaped the rough familiarity of the brother-sister relationship," so that "consanguinity," with all the equality it might imply for peers of the same generation, was "balanced by the charm of strangeness." But Barrett Browning, who as a girl had dreamed of dressing in boy's clothes and running away to be Lord Byron's page, grew up to become, if not as censorious as her friend Carlyle was toward the hero of Missolonghi, at least ambivalent toward him. Even while insisting that her "tendency" was "not to cast off my old loves," she wrote that Byron's poems "discovered not a heart, but the wound of a heart; not humanity, but disease." In addition, she was close to both the "wronged" Lady Byron's friend Anna Jameson and to Harriet Beecher Stowe, the author of *Lady Byron Vindicated,* both of whom would have reminded her of the masculine exploitativeness involved in Byron's sexual exploits.[20]

Simultaneously inspired and exasperated by the Byron story, therefore, Barrett Browning had to rewrite it to gain strength from it. Thus the seductive and anti-poetic Augusta Leigh becomes the pure poet Aurora Leigh, and the morally corrupt but sexually devastating and romantically self-dramatizing Byron becomes the morally incorruptible but physically devastated and romantically diffident Romney. Furthermore, the sexual inequities implied by Byron's sordid secret affairs and by Romney's onetime authority as "head" of the Leigh family are eradicated both by Aurora's purity and by her recently achieved matriarchal strength. Newly defined "brother" and "sister" can unite, and even unite erotically, because the Byron episode has been reenacted on a "higher" plane, purged of social disorder and sexual disease.

The humbled Romney's arrival in Florence does, then, complete both the reconfiguration of the family and the regeneration of the motherland that poet-author and poet-heroine have undertaken. Blinded in a fire that recalls yet another famous nineteenth-century plot—the denouement of *Jane Eyre*—this former patriarch seems to have endured the same punishment Brontë's Bertha dealt Rochester, although in personality Romney is closer to Jane Eyre's austere cousin St. John Rivers than to that heroine's extravagant "master." Significantly, however, Barrett Browning who seems vigorously to have repressed her memory of the *Jane Eyre* episode, no doubt so she could more freely revise it—swerved from Brontë in having Romney's injury inflicted not by a mad wife but by a bad father: William Erle, the tramp and poacher who began his career of destructiveness by bruising and abusing his daughter Marian. Women do not need to destroy the fatherland, Barrett Browning implies by this revision, because it will self-destruct. Again, Barrett Browning swerves from Brontë in allowing her disinherited patriarch to rescue one item from the house of his fathers—a portrait of the lady from whom Aurora inherited her mouth and chin. A woman, she implies by this revision, may be an inheritor. In the end, therefore, as Romney describes "the great charred circle" where his ancestral mansion once stood with its "one stone stair, symbolic of my life, / Ascending, winding, leading up to nought," his saving of the picture suggests also that the power of the Leighs has not been destroyed but instead transferred to "a fairy bride from Italy," who has now become the true heir and "head" of the family.[21]

That Aurora has successfully become a "head" of the family, the figure both Romney's father, *Vane* Leigh, and Romney himself only vainly strove to be, is made clearest by her blinded cousin's revelation that he has at last really read and recognized her work. Seeing through and because of his blindness, like wounded father figures from Oedipus and Gloucester to Rochester, Romney receives and perceives Aurora's prophetic message—"in this last book, / You showed me something separate from yourself, / Beyond you, and I bore to take it in / And let it draw me"—and that message, "Presented by your voice and verse the way / To take them clearest," elevates her to the "dearest light of souls, / Which rul'st for evermore both day and night!" Finally too, therefore, he has become, as both "Bro" and Robert Browning were for Barrett Browning herself, a "purely" attentive brother-reader who can at last comprehend the revisionary mother tongue in which the woman poet speaks and writes. It is no coincidence, surely, that Barrett Browning has Aurora, who never before associated Romney with the ocean, envision her lost lover as arising from beneath the bitter waters that had engulfed her lost brother and standing before her like a "sea-king" while "the sound of waters" echoes in her ears.[22] Deciphering the texts of Aurora's desire, Romney has accomplished his own transformation into an ex-patriarch who entrusts himself and his sister-bride to the "one central Heart" of love that may ultimately unify all humanity by eradicating the hierarchies and inequities of patriarchy. At the same time, emigrating from the rigid north of the Leighs to the warm south ruled by his "Italy of women," he has become both an expatriate and an ex-patriot, a dweller in the new *matria* where, in a visionary role reversal, the empowered Aurora will "work for two" and he, her consort and cohort, "for two, shall love."

Romney's violent metamorphosis reminds us of Barrett Browning's implicit belief that, as in *Casa Guidi Windows* (where the poet advocates the self-sacrifice of Italian men), only the devastation of the fatherland can enable the *risorgimento* of the mother country.[23] Both Marian and Aurora too, however, have experienced violent metamorphoses, Marian literally, in the rape she describes as a "murder," and Aurora figuratively, in her passionate struggle to come to terms with the eroticism Lady Waldemar incarnates and with the murderous rage "the Lamia-woman" evokes. Now, though, after all this violence, these characters are brought together in a symbolically reunified family of brother/husband and sister/wife and mother and son. Is Aurora the dawn in which Marian and Romney can be reborn? Is Marian the womb that gives new life to Aurora's and Romney's light? Is Romney the lover who can read their new roles rightly in the "bittersweet" darkness of his visionary blindness? Is Marian's child the redemptive son whose coming signals a new day? There is certainly a temptation to define each member of this prophetic quartet allegorically. But even without stipulating meanings that the epic "unscrupulously" leaves in shadow, it is clear that in its final wholeness this newly holy family integrates what the writer called "Philosophical Thought" with what she called "Poetical Thought" and unifies both with the powerful dyad of mother and child, womb and womb fruit.[24] Eastering in Italy, moreover, these four redeemed beings begin to make possible the "new day" that their author imagined in, for, and through the country she chose as her *matria*. For among themselves they constitute—to go back to the qualities women writers have sought in Italy—a land that feels, that feeds, that makes art, and that unmakes hierarchies. In mythologizing them as she does, Barrett Browning sets against the exhaustion of belatedness that she thought afflicted contemporary (male) poets "who scorn to touch [our age] with a finger tip" a matriarchal future that she hoped would be sacramentally signaled by "the holy baptism of the morning dew."

In its ecstatic delineation of a female *risorgimento,* the redemption of Italy that Barrett Browning began to imagine in *Casa Guidi Windows* and fully figured in *Aurora Leigh* was both predictable and precarious. Given the long history of Italy as a literary topos, together with the country's personal association for this woman poet, it is not surprising that that embattled nation would come to incarnate both a mother's desire for *bella libertà* and a daughter's desire to resurrect the lost and wounded mother. Certainly Barrett Browning's American contemporary Margaret Fuller imagined the country in a similar way. "Italy has been glorious to me," she wrote Emerson in 1847, explaining that her expatriate experience had given her "the full benefit of [a] vision" of rebirth "into a state where my young life should not be prematurely taxed." In an 1848 dispatch to the *Tribune,* she added that in Rome "the sun and moon shine as if paradise were already re-established on earth. I go to one of the villas to dream it is so, beneath the pale light of the stars."[25]

Part of this visionary passion no doubt arose from Fuller's revitalizing and egalitarian romance with Angelo Ossoli, in whom, as one observer put it, she loved "an imagined possibility in the Italian character" much as Aurora, in loving Romney (and Elizabeth Barrett, in loving Robert Browning), loved "an imagined possibility" in the English character. At the same time, however, Fuller's dream of an Italian paradise was not just energized by her hope for a utopian future that the *risorgimento* might make possible; it was also shaped by her sense that behind Italy's "official" history of popes and patriarchs lay another history, the record of a utopian, and specifically matriarchal, past. Visiting "an Etrurian tomb" in 1847, she noted that "the effect . . . was beyond my expectations; in it were several female figures, very dignified and calm . . . [whose] expression . . . shows that the position of women in these states was noble." Later, passing through Bologna, she remarked that "a woman should love" that city "for there has the spark of intellect in woman been cherished with reverent care," and she made similar points about Milan, as well as, more generally, about the Italian "reverence to the Madonna and innumerable female saints, who, if like St. Teresa, they had intellect as well as piety, became counsellors no less than comforters to the spirit of men."[26]

But in particular Fuller's analysis of Etruscan tomb paintings, like the novelist Ouida's apparently casual likening of Florence's past to "gold from the sepulchres of the Aetruscan kings . . . on the breast of some fair living woman," should remind us that as early as the 1840s, in just the years when both Fuller and Barrett Browning were imagining the *risorgimento* of an Italian *matria,* the Swiss jurist J. J. Bachofen was visiting Etruscan tombs outside Rome, where his discovery of a painting depicting "three mystery eggs" led him to speculate that in "Dionysian religion . . . the supreme law governing the transient world as a *fatum* [is] inherent in feminine matter" and that "the phallic god striving toward the fertilization of matter" stands merely "as a son" to "the maternal womb." This speculation, published only two years after *Aurora Leigh* in Bachofen's 1859 *Essay on Mortuary Symbolism,* led in turn to the even more radical hypotheses of his *Mother Right* (1861), in which he presented the first strong argument that matriarchy was the primordial form of social organization.[27]

In visiting, studying, and "reading" Etruscan tombs (as Freud too would do some fifty years and D. H. Lawrence some eighty years later), Bachofen was in one sense "reading" the palimpsest of Italy the way travelers like Shelley, Rogers, and Ruskin did in the archaeological metaphors I quoted earlier. Unlike them, however, and like both Fuller and Barrett Browning, he was "reading" beyond or beneath the patriarchal history Western tourists had always expected to find among the ruins of Rome and the monuments of Florence and interpreting his reading as Freud did his reading of the "Minoan-Mycenaean" age. Thus Bachofen too was preparing at least his female audience to resurrect the old lineaments of what Barrett Browning called a "new, near Day" just as the newly matriarchal Aurora does at the end of Barrett Browning's epic when, in a re-visionary swerve from Shelley and Ruskin, Barrett Browning has her "read" an Italian sunrise for Romney in the language of Apocalypse: "Jasper first . . . And second, sapphire; third, chalcedony; / The rest in order:—last, an amethyst." Through such re-visionary readings, moreover, both writers (along with Fuller) were setting the scene for such a descendant as H. D.: her *Tribute to Freud* ends with a reading of Goethe's "Kennst du das Land," the German poet's vision of Italy as sister land to paradise, a vision that makes the American modernist think of "the *Ca d'Oro*, the Golden House on the Grand Canal in Venice . . . the *domus aurea* of the Laurentian litany." That it was Goethe who sought also to understand the *Ewige Weibliche* and whose injunction to "go down to the Mothers" deeply influenced Bachofen would have surely given extra richness to the regenerated Italy of his (and H. D.'s) "Land wo die Zitronen blühn . . ." Guarded by siren mountains and a bridge of clouds, as Emily Dickinson also believed, the regenerated *matria* of Italy stands "on the other side" of patriarchal history.[28]

Yet both Goethe's poem and H. D.'s *Tribute* end with Mignon's equivocal plea: "*O Vater, lass uns ziehn!*" For both the female poet and her German precursor, the journey to the magic land can only be accomplished with the guidance of the father. If he permits, the *matria* will be revealed; if not, the Alps and clouds, emblems of despair as well as desire, must, in Dickinson's words, "forever intervene." Similarly, Barrett Browning's visions of female regeneration are subtly qualified, for even while the plots and characters of *Aurora Leigh* and *Casa Guidi Windows* propose matriarchal apocalypses, the poet acknowledges that such consummations, though devoutly wished, require (in this world) male cooperation—Romney's abdication, the sacrifices of Italian men—and (in heaven) the grace of God the Father, who, with masculine wisdom, will build into "blank interstices" and "make all new."[29] By the time she wrote *Poems before Congress,* Barrett Browning's quasi-feminist vision had darkened even further. In just the poem whose image of Italy as an invalid woman echoes and illuminates Aurora's vision of her dead mother as "Our Lady of the Passion, stabbed with swords," the author imagines the redemption of her *matria* by, and only by, the grace of the French ruler Louis Napoleon, whose feats of male military bravery will make him "Emperor / Evermore." And, in fact, Italy's *risorgimento* was finally achieved only by the maneuvers of traditionally masculine "heroes" like Louis Napoleon, Mazzini, Garibaldi, Victor Emmanuel, Charles Albert, and—most of all—the Machiavellian statesman Cavour. Thus the specifically matriarchal *risorgimento* of *Aurora Leigh* is ultimately almost as momentary and provisional as the brief hopeful revelation of the "mercy Seat" behind the "Vail" that ends *Casa Guidi Windows.* For inevitably the reality of patriarchal history, with its successes and successions, obliterated Barrett Browning's implicit but impossible dream of a *matria.*[30]

Though Barrett Browning was disturbed by the unfavorable comparison one English reviewer made between her and Florence Nightingale, then, she might have sympathized with the view that unfairly stereotyped "lady with a lamp" expressed in a book the author of *Aurora Leigh* probably never read. As if commenting on the marriage of true minds Barrett Browning's epic envisions at its close, Nightingale argued in *Cassandra* (written in 1852 and privately printed in 1860) that "the true marriage—that noble union, by which a man and woman become together the one perfect being—probably does not exist at present upon earth." Indeed, this woman, whose Christian name—Florence—was intended to honor the very city in which Barrett Browning found a modicum of *bella libertà* and who hoped that the "next Christ" might be, like the redemptive Aurora, a "female Christ," used a specifically Italian metaphor to describe the enchained reality of nineteenth-century woman: "She is like the Archangel Michael as he stands upon Saint Angelo at Rome. She has an immense provision of wings . . . but when she tries to use them, she is petrified into stone."[31]

Perhaps, given the power and pressure of history, a woman who is "nobody in the somewhere of patriarchy" can only, as Susan Gubar has observed, be "somebody in the nowhere of utopia," for even a land like Italy, with all the metaphorical possibilities that give it strength as a matriarchal topos, is inextricably part of the larger topos of European time. As such, it is a text whose usefulness to women can be countered by masculinist rereadings that redeem it for both the father and the phallus. Even Bachofen, the theorist of matriarchy, was to argue that "mother right" must historically be transformed and transcended by "father right," and sixty years after Barrett Browning imagined Italy as a *matria,* D. H. Lawrence claimed the land as a metaphorical *patria,* asserting that "to the Italian the phallus is the symbol of individual creative immortality, to each man his own Godhead." Even the word *matria,* moreover, which I have used throughout this essay to describe the visionary country sought by women like Fuller, Rossetti, Barrett Browning, and Dickinson, is nonexistent. The real Italian word for "motherland" is *madrepatria,* a word whose literal meaning—"mother-fatherland"—preserves an inexorably patriarchal etymology. In Italian linguistic reality, there is no matriarchal equivalent to patriarchal power: one can only imagine such an antithetical power in the "nowhere" of a newly made vocabulary.[32]

It is no wonder, then, that Barrett Browning appointed Louis Napoleon "Emperor / Evermore" and that in the last poem she ever wrote, entitled "The North and the South," she came full circle back to Aurora's self-divided beginnings, admitting the dependence of the matriarchal south on the patriarchal language of the rigid north. While the north sighs for the skies of the south "that are softer and higher," the south sighs "For a poet's tongue of baptismal flame, / To call the tree or the flower by its name!"[33] Though she had enacted and examined a vision of female redemption far more radical than any Rossetti had allowed herself to explore, Barrett Browning would have conceded that, along with Rossetti, she was chained like Nightingale's angel to the rock of patriarchal Rome, and, along with Rossetti, she finally had to bid farewell to the Italy both had dreamed might be a sister land to paradise. As Christine de Pizan and Charlotte Perkins Gilman knew, in the world as it is, the City of Ladies can only be built on "the Field of Letters."

—1986

"LIFE'S EMPTY PACK"

Notes Toward a Literary Daughteronomy

No mother gave me birth. Therefore the father's claim
And male supremacy in all things . . .
. . . wins my whole heart's loyalty.

—ATHENE, IN AESCHYLUS, THE EUMENIDES

If underneath the water
You comb your golden hair
With a golden comb, my daughter,
Oh would that I were there!

—CHRISTINA ROSSETTI, "FATHER AND LOVER"

Sad and weary I go back to you, my cold father, my cold
mad father, my cold mad feary father . . . I rush, my only,
into your arms.

—ANNA LIVIA PLURABELLE, IN JAMES JOYCE, FINNEGANS WAKE

O father, all by yourself
You are pithy and historical as the Roman Forum.

—SYLVIA PLATH, "THE COLOSSUS"

For the first time all of us, men and women alike, can look back on nearly two centuries of powerful literary ancestresses. Aside from the specifically literary-historical implications of such a phenomenon—an issue that Susan Gubar and I have discussed elsewhere—what effects has this unprecedented situation had?[1] In particular, what paradigms of female sexuality have strong female precursors passed on to other women writers? These are questions I want to begin to address here—specifically, by exploring an aspect of female psychosexual development. A dark, indeed problematic, pattern emerges when we juxtapose the accounts of female maturation and obligation that are offered by theorists like Sigmund Freud and Claude Lévi-Strauss with the meaning that George Eliot's frequently studied *Silas Marner* may have had for the women who are in a sense that powerful literary mother's aesthetic daughters.

I choose Eliot as my paradigm of the female precursor because, as Virginia Woolf put it, she was "the first woman of the age," a thinker who became, in one historian's words, a "Man of Ideas," her official importance sanctioned by the biography Woolf's own father dutifully produced for the English Men of Letters Series. At the same time, however, I see Eliot as paradigmatic because her very power—the success that made her into what we call a "precursor"—evidently disquieted so many of her female contemporaries and descendants. As Elaine Showalter reminds us, "most nineteenth-century women novelists seem to have found [Eliot] a troubling and demoralizing competitor, one who had created an image of the woman artist they could never equal." "George Eliot *looks* awful. Her picture frightens me!" exclaims a character in Elizabeth Robins' novel *George Mandeville's Husband*.[2] Even Eliot's most fervent female admirers, moreover, express ambivalence toward her in the rhetoric through which they try to come to terms with her. Two of these notable Eliotian heiresses are Emily Dickinson and Edith Wharton. Both offer commentaries curiously haunted by ambiguities, and though these commentaries are ostensibly about the writer's life story, they provide a dramatic set of metaphors that can help us interpret the messages these literary daughters extracted from such an apparently "legendary" story as *Silas Marner*. In 1883, after having waited with great anxiety to receive a copy of the Eliot biography written by John Walter Cross, the novelist's husband in the last year of her life, Dickinson wrote a thank-you note to the Boston publisher Thomas Niles in which she succinctly mythologizes the career of her English precursor. "The Life of Marian Evans had much I never knew," she begins. "A Doom of Fruit without the Bloom, like the Niger Fig," and a poem follows this strange introduction.

> *Her Losses make our Gains ashamed—*
> *She bore Life's empty Pack*
> *As gallantly as if the East*
> *Were swinging at her Back.*
> *Life's empty Pack is heaviest,*
> *As every Porter knows—*
> *In vain to punish Honey—*
> *It only sweeter grows.*

"A Doom of Fruit without the Bloom." "Life's empty Pack." "In vain to punish Honey." These are striking but mysterious phrases. Where do they come from, and what do they mean?[3]

Several remarks by Wharton, though almost equally paradoxical, begin to provide some clarification. Reviewing Leslie Stephen's *English Men of Letters Series* volume on Eliot, Wharton writes that "unconsciously, perhaps, [the Victorian novelist] began to use her books as a vehicle of rehabilitation, a means, not of defending her own course, but of proclaiming, with increasing urgency and emphasis, her allegiance to the law she appeared to have violated." Earlier in her essay, Wharton offers a metaphorical, almost Dickinsonian statement of what she means by "the law": "The stern daughter of the voice of God," she writes, "stands ever at the side of *Romola* and Dorothea, of Lydgate and Maggie, and lifts even Mr. Farebrother and poor Gwendolyn to heights of momentary heroism."[4]

Putting statements like these together with Woolf's sense of Eliot's success and centrality, we can begin to see why the author of *Silas Marner* was both a paradigmatic and a problematic female precursor. Metaphorically speaking, such a conflation of reactions suggests that Eliot represents the conundrum of the empty pack which until recently has confronted every woman writer. Specifically, this conundrum is the riddle of daughterhood, a figurative empty pack with which—as it has seemed to many women artists—not just every powerful literary mother but every literal mother presents her daughter. For such artists, the terror of the female precursor is not that she is an emblem of power but, rather, that when she achieves her greatest strength, her power becomes self-subverting: in the moment of psychic transformation that is the moment of creativity, the literary mother, even more than the literal one, becomes the "stern daughter of the voice of God" who paradoxically proclaims her "allegiance to the law" she herself appears to have violated.

As such a preceptor, the literary mother necessarily speaks both of and for the father, reminding her female child that she is not and cannot be his inheritor: like her mother and like Eliot's Dorothea, the daughter must inexorably become a "foundress of nothing." For human culture, says the literary mother, is bound by rules which make it possible for a woman to speak but which oblige her to speak of her own powerlessness, since such rules might seem to constitute what Jacques Lacan calls the "Law of the Father," the law that means culture is by definition both patriarchal and phallocentric and must therefore transmit the empty pack of disinheritance to every daughter.[5] Not surprisingly, then, even while the literary daughter, like the literal one, desires the matrilineal legitimation incarnated in her precursor/mother, she fears her literary mother: the more fully the mother represents culture, the more inexorably she tells the daughter that she cannot have a mother because she has been signed with and assigned to the Law of the Father. Like Eliot, who aspired to be a "really cultured woman," this "culture-mother" uses her knowledge, as Eliot advised in her scornful essay "Silly Novels by Lady Novelists," "to form a right estimate of herself"—that is, to put herself (and, by implication, her daughters) in the "right" place.[6]

This speculation rests of course on syntheses of Freud and Lévi-Strauss that such psychoanalytic thinkers as Lacan and Juliet Mitchell have produced. Concentrating on the Oedipus complex, these writers have argued that every child enters the language-defined system of kinship exchange we call "culture" by learning that he or she cannot remain permanently in the state of nature signified by the embrace of the mother;

instead, the child must be assigned a social place denoted by the name (and the Law) of the Father, the potent symbol of human order who disrupts the blissful mother-child dyad. What this means for the boy—a temporary frustration of desire coupled with the promise of an ultimate accession to power—has been elaborately and famously explored by both Freud and Lacan (and also, in a different way, by Lévi-Strauss). What it means for the girl is much less clearly understood; hence, in meditating on the empty pack of daughterhood, I am necessarily improvising both literary and psychoanalytic theory. But my task will, I hope, be made possible by Eliot's status as paradigmatic female precursor, or symbolic culture-mother, and made plausible by the juxtaposition of one of Eliot's texts, *Silas Marner,* with what we might call a revisionary daughter-text, Wharton's *Summer.*

A definition of Eliot as renunciatory culture-mother may seem an odd preface to a discussion of *Silas Marner* since, of all her novels, this richly constructed work is the one in which the empty pack of daughterhood appears fullest, the honey of femininity most unpunished. I want to argue, however, that this "legendary tale," whose status as a schoolroom classic makes it almost as much a textbook as a novel, examines the relationship between woman's fate and the structure of society in order to explicate the meaning of the empty pack of daughterhood. More specifically, this story of an adoptive father, an orphan daughter, and a dead mother broods on events that are actually or symbolically situated on the margins or boundaries of society, where culture must enter into a dialectical struggle with nature, in order to show how the young female human animal is converted into the human daughter, wife, and mother. Finally, then, this fictionalized "daughteronomy" becomes a female myth of origin narrated by a severe literary mother who uses the vehicle of a half-allegorical family romance to urge acquiescence in the Law of the Father.

If *Silas Marner* is not obviously a story about the empty pack of daughterhood, it is plainly, of course, a "legendary tale" about a wanderer with a heavy yet empty pack. In fact, it is through the image of the packman that the story, in Eliot's own words, "came *across* my other plans by a sudden inspiration"—and, clearly, her vision of this burdened outsider is a re-vision of the Romantic wanderer who haunts the borders of society, seeking a local habitation and a name. I would argue further, though, that Eliot's depiction of *Silas Marner*'s alienation begins to explain Ruby Redinger's sense that the author of this "fluid and metamorphic" story "is" both Eppie, the redemptive daughter, and Silas, the redeemed father. For in examining the outcast weaver's marginality, this novelist of the "hidden life" examines also her own female disinheritance and marginality.[7]

Almost everything we learn about Silas and the tribe of pack-bearing wanderers he represents tends to reinforce our sense that he belongs in what anthropologists call a "liminal zone."[8] Pallid, undersized, alien-looking, he is one of the figures ordinary country folk see at the edges of time and place—"on the upland, dark against the early winter sunset," "far away among the lanes, or deep in the bosom of the hills." As a weaver, moreover, he is associated with those transformations that take place on the borders of culture—activities, notes his author, that seem to partake "of the nature of conjuring." Again, he is liminal because, both shortsighted and cataleptic, he cannot participate meaningfully in the social world. That he dwells on the edge of Raveloe, near the disused Stone-pits, and never strolls "into the village to drink a pint at [the local pub called] the Rainbow" further emphasizes his alienation, as does the story of his Job-like punishment when the casting of lots in Lantern Yard "convicted" him of a theft he had not committed. Finally, his obsessive hoarding, in which gold is drained of all economic signification, reduces the currency of society to absurdity, further emphasizing his alienation.

Considering all of these deprivations and denials of social meaning, it is no wonder that this wanderer's pack seems to be heavy with emptiness. Psychologically, moreover, it is no wonder that Eliot in some sense "is" the Silas whom we first encounter at the Stone-pits, if only because through him she examines the liminality Mary Anne Evans experienced in fact and Maggie Tulliver in fiction. Her own metaphors frequently remind us, furthermore, that just as he weaves textiles, she "weaves" texts—and at the time his story "thrust itself" into the loom

of her art, her texts were turning to gold as surely (and as problemati-
cally) as his textiles did. In addition, as the man without a place, Silas
carries with him the dispossession she herself had experienced as part
of the empty pack of daughterhood. Perhaps, indeed, it is because he
shares to some extent in what Sherry Ortner has seen as woman's liminal estate that Silas is often associated not only with the particulars of
Mary Anne Evans' femaleness but also with a number of socially defined
female characteristics, including a domestic expertise which causes him,
in the words of one Raveloer, to be "partly as handy as a woman."[9]

Paradoxically, however, it is his handily maternal rearing of Eppie
that redeems Silas as a man even while his transformation from outcast
to parent reflects a similar but more troubled metamorphosis that Mary
Anne Evans was herself undergoing at the time she wrote the novel.
Significantly, at the moment the plot of *Silas Marner* began to "unfold"
in her mind, George Eliot was becoming a "mother" to George Henry
Lewes' children. But where her ambiguous status as "mother" of "a great
boy of eighteen . . . as well as two other boys, almost as tall" isolated her
further from the society that had cast her out, Silas' status as father of
a golden-haired daughter definitively integrates him into a community
that had previously thought him diabolic.[10] His transformations of role
and rank, therefore, suggest at least one kind of redemption a fallen literary woman might want to imagine for herself: becoming a father.

Silas' redemptive fatherhood, which originates at Christmastime, is
prepared for by Eliot's long meditation on the weaver's relationship to his
gold, perhaps the most compelling passage of psychological analysis in
the novel and the one that most brilliantly propounds the terms of the
submerged metaphor that is to govern the book's dramatic action. For
the miser, as I noted earlier, what would ordinarily be a kind of language
that links members of society is empty of signification and therefore not
only meaningless but dead-ended. Halted, static, even regressive, the
currency does not flow: nothing goes out into the world, and therefore
nothing returns.[11] Silas' history is thus a history without a story because
it is without characters—without, that is, both persons and signifiers.
Yet its terror consists not merely in the absence of meaning but in the
presence of empty matter: the shining purposeless heaps of coins which

"had become too large for the iron pot to hold them." It is this mass of lifeless matter that must be imprinted with vital signification if the outcast weaver is to be resurrected and redeemed. And ultimately, indeed, Silas' transformation from fall to fatherhood is symbolized, in a kind of upside-down myth of Midas, by the metamorphosis of his meaningless gold into a living and meaningful child, a child whose Christmas coming marks her as symbolically divine but whose function as divine daughter rather than sacred son is to signify, rather than to replace, the power of her newly created father.

To make way for Eppie, who is his gold made meaningful, Silas must first, of course, be separated from his meaningless gold. What is surely most important about this loss, however, is that the absence of the gold forces the miser to confront the absence his gold represented. In addition, if we think of this blank, this empty pack, in relation to the Christmas myth for which Eliot is preparing us, we can see that Silas' dark night of the soul is the long dark night of the winter solstice, when dead matter must be kindled and dead flesh made Word if culture is to survive. That "the invisible wand of catalepsy" momentarily freezes the weaver in his open doorway on the crucial New Year's Eve that is to lead to his resurrection merely emphasizes this point. His posture is that of the helpless virgin who awaits annunciation "like a graven image . . . powerless to resist either the good or evil that might enter there."

Because it depends on drastic role reversals, however, Eliot's deliberate parody of the Christmas story suggests that she is half consciously using the basic outlines of a central culture myth to meditate not on the traditionally sanctified relationship of Holy Mother and Divine Son but on another, equally crucial, bond—that of Holy Father and Divine Daughter. In doing so, she clarifies for herself and for her readers the key differences between sonship and daughterhood. For when the divine child is a son he is, as the Christian story tells us, an active spiritual agent for his mother. To put the matter in a Freudian or Lacanian way, he is the "Phallus" for her, an image of sociocultural as well as sexual power.[12] But when the divine child is a daughter, or so the story of *Silas Marner* tells us, she is a treasure, a gift the father is given so that he can give it to others, thereby weaving himself into the texture of society. To put the matter in a Lévi-Straussian way, she is the currency whose exchange constitutes society, a point Eliot stunningly anticipated in her submerged metaphor of the girl who is not only as good as but better than gold because her very existence is a pot of gold not at the end but at the beginning of the Rainbow covenant between man and man.

This last allusion is, of course, a reference to the central notion of *The Elementary Structures of Kinship*, in which Lévi-Strauss argues that both the social order, which distinguishes culture from nature, and the incest taboo, which universally manifests the social order, are based upon the exchange of women. In this anthropological view, a daughter is a treasure whose potential passage from man to man insures psychological and social well-being: if the very structure of a patrilineage guarantees that ultimately, inexorably, a man's son will *take* his place and his name, it also promises that a daughter will never be such a usurper since she is an instrument—rather than an agent—of culture. In fact, because she is the father's wealth, his treasure, she is what he *has*, for better or worse.[13]

That Silas christens his Christmas child "Hephzibah" dramatizes this point even while it begins to weave him deeply into the common life of "Bible names" and knit him back into his own past. "Hephzibah," or "Eppie," was the name of both Silas' mother and his sister: in gaining a new Hephzibah, he has regained the treasure of all his female kin. Even more significantly, the name itself, drawn from Isaiah, refers to the title Zion will be given after the coming of the Messiah. Literally translated as "my delight is in her," "Hephzibah" magically signifies both a promised land and a redeemed land. Diffusely female, this delightful land incarnates the treasure that is possessed and exchanged by male citizens, and therefore it represents the culture that is created by the covenant between man and man as well as between God and man. A philological fact upon which Eliot herself once meditated enriches further such an association. According to an etymology given by the *Oxford English Dictionary* and based upon Grimm's law, the Anglo-Saxon word "daughter" can be traced back to the Indo-European root *dhugh*, meaning "to milk." Hence, this daughter named Hephzibah is not only milkmaid but milk-giver, she who nurtures as well as she who is nurtured—for, as defined by the Law and reinforced by the lexicon of the Father, a daughter is the promised land of milk and honey, the gift of wealth that God the Father gives to every human father.[14]

Most of these points are made quite explicit in the concern with weddings that permeates *Silas Marner,* a concern which surfaces in the famous conversation that happens to be taking place at the Rainbow Tavern just when Silas is discovering the loss of his gold. Old Mr. Macey, the parish clerk, is recounting the story of the Lammeter marriage, a ceremony in which the minister got his phrases oddly turned around. The tale asks the question, "Is't the meanin' or the words as makes folks fast i' wedlock?" and answers that "it's neither the meaning nor the words— it's the regester does it—that's the glue." But of course, as we learn by the end of *Silas Marner,* it is the very idea of the wedding itself, the having and giving of the daughter, that is the glue. For as Silas and Eppie, Aaron and Dollie parade through Raveloe on their way back to Silas' enlarged cottage after Eppie's marriage to Aaron, the harmony of the bridal party contrasts strikingly with our memory of Silas' former isolation. In marrying Aaron, Silas' daughter has married Silas—married him both to the world and to herself. What had been the "shrunken rivulet" of his love has flowed into a larger current and a dearer currency, a treasure he has given so that it can return to him. And it has returned: "O father," says Eppie, just as if she had married him, "What a pretty home ours is." Unlike that other Romantic wanderer, the Ancient Mariner, *Silas Marner* is a member of the wedding. But then, the Ancient Mariner never got the Christian Christmas gift of a daughter.[15]

How does the gift feel about herself, however? What does it mean to Eppie to mean all this for Silas? Certainly Eliot had long been concerned with the social significance and cultural possibilities of daughterhood. Both *The Mill on the Floss*—the novel that precedes *Silas Marner*—and *Romola*—the one that follows it—are elaborate examinations of the structural inadequacies of a daughter's estate. As for Mary Anne Evans, moreover, her real life had persistently confronted her with the problematic nature of daughterhood and its corollary condition, sisterhood. As biographers have shown, her feelings for her own father were ambivalent not only during his lifetime but throughout hers; yet his superegoistic legacy pervaded other relationships she formed. When she was in her early twenties, for instance, she became a dutiful disciple to the Casaubon-like Dr. Brabant, who "punningly baptized her *Deutera* because she was to be a second daughter to him." And even when she was a middle-aged woman, she remembered her older brother Isaac as a kind of miniature father, "a Like unlike, a Self that self restrains," observing wistfully that "were another childhood-world my share, / I would be born a little sister there." Since "Eppie" was the name of Silas' little sister, it seems likely that, in being "born" again to the mild weaver, Mary Anne Evans did in fiction if not in fact re-create herself as both daughter and little sister.[16]

Certainly Eppie's protestations of daughterly devotion suggest that she is in some sense a born-again daughter. "I should have no delight i' life any more if I was forced to go away from my father," she tells Nancy and Godfrey Cass. Like the Mary Anne Evans who became "Deutera," Eppie is not so much a second daughter as twice a daughter—a doubly daughterly daughter. As such a "Deutera," she is the golden girl whose being reiterates those cultural commandments Moses set forth for the second time in Deuteronomy. Thus, although scrupulous Nancy Lammeter Cass has often been seen as articulating Eliot's moral position on the key events of this novel, it is really the more impulsive Eppie who is the conscience of the book.

This becomes clearest when Nancy argues that "there's a duty you owe to your lawful father." Eppie's instant reply, with its counterclaim that "I can't feel as I've got any father but one," expresses a more accurate understanding of the idea of fatherhood. For in repudiating *Godfree* Cass, who is only by chance (*casus*) her natural father, and affirming *Silas Marner,* who is by choice her cultural father, Eppie rejects the lawless father in favor of the lawful one, indicating her clear awareness that fatherhood itself is both *a* social construct (or, in Stephen Dedalus' words, "a legal fiction") and *the* social construct that constructs society.[17] Having achieved and acted on this analysis, she is rewarded with a domestic happiness which seems to prove Dickinson's contention that it is "vain to punish Honey, / It only sweeter grows." At the same time, in speaking such a law, this creature of milk and honey initiates the reeducation and redemption of Godfrey Cass: the cultural code of Deuteronomy speaks through her, suggesting that, even if she is a Christmas child, she is as much a daughter of the Old Testament as of the New, of the first telling of the law as of its second telling.[18]

Happy and dutiful as she is, however, Eppie is not perfectly contented, for she has a small fund of anxiety that is pledged to her other parent—her lost mother. This intermittent sadness, which manifests itself as a preoccupation with her mother's wedding ring, directs our attention to a strange disruption at the center of *Silas Marner*: the history of Eppie's dead mother. On the surface, of course, the ring Silas has saved for his adopted daughter is an aptly ironic symbol of that repressed plot, since there never was any bond beyond an artificial one between Molly Farren and Godfrey Cass, the lawless father "of whom [the ring] was the symbol." But Eppie's frequent ruminations on the questions of "how her mother looked, whom she was like, and how [Silas] had found her against the furze bush" suggest that there is something more problematic than a traditional bad marriage at issue here. As so often in this "legendary tale," what seems like a moral point also offers an eerily accurate account of what Freud sees as the inexorable psychosexual growth and entry of the daughter into a culture shaped by the codes of the father. "Our insight into [the pre-Oedipus] phase in the little girl's development comes to us as a surprise, comparable . . . with . . . the discovery of the Minoan-Mycenaean civilization behind that of Greece," remarks Freud, explaining that "everything connected with this first mother-attachment has . . . seemed to me . . . lost in a past so dim and shadowy . . . that it seemed as if it had undergone some specially inexorable repression."[19]

Indeed, Molly Farren *has* undergone a "specially inexorable repression" in this novel. Three or four pages of a single chapter are devoted to her, though her damned and doomed wanderings in the snow strikingly recapitulate the lengthier wanderings of fallen women like Hetty Sorel and Maggie Tulliver. I suggest that Eliot attempts this drastic condensation precisely because *Silas Marner*, in allowing her to speak symbolically about the meaning of daughterhood, also allowed her to speak in even more resonant symbols about the significance of motherhood. What she said was what she saw: that it is better to be a daughter than a mother and better still to be a father than a daughter. For when the Deuteronomy of culture formulates the incest laws that lie at the center of human society, that severe code tells the son: "You may not have your mother; you may not kill your father." But when it is translated into a "Daughteronomy" preached for the growing girl, it says: "You must bury your mother; you must give yourself to your father." Since the daughter has inherited an empty pack and cannot *be* a father, she has no choice but to be *for* the father—to be his treasure, his land, his voice.[20]

Yet, as Eliot shows, the growing girl is haunted by her own difficult passage from mother to father, haunted by the primal scene in the snow when she was forced to turn away from the body of the mother, the emblem of nature which can give only so much and no more, and seek the hearth of the father, the emblem of culture that must compensate for nature's inadequacies.[21] This moment is frozen into the center of *Silas Marner* like the dead figure of Molly Farren Cass, whose final posture of self-abandonment brings about Eppie's "effort to regain the pillowing arm and bosom; but mammy's ear was deaf, and the pillow seemed to be slipping away backward." Indeed, for women the myth that governs personality may be based on such a moment, a confrontation of the dead mother that is as enduring and horrifying to daughters as Freud (in *Totem and Taboo*) claimed the nightmare of the dead father was to sons. Finally, the garden that Eppie and Silas plant at the end of the novel memorializes this moment. " 'Father,' " says the girl "in a tone of gentle gravity . . . , 'we shall take the furze bush into the garden' "—for it was against the bush that Molly died. Now, fenced in by the garden of the law, the once "straggling" bush will become a symbol of nature made meaningful, controlled and confined by culture.

In the end, then, it is *Silas Marner*, the meek weaver of Raveloe, who inherits the milk and honey of the earth, for he has affirmed the Law of the Father that weaves kin and kindness together. Not coincidentally, when Silas' adopted daughter's engagement to Aaron knits him definitively into the world, Dunstan Cass' skeleton is uncovered and the gold is restored: since Silas has been willing to give his treasure to another, his treasure is given back to him. The intricate web of nemesis and apotheosis that Eliot has woven around Silas reminds us, moreover, that the very name "Raveloe" preserves two conflicting meanings along with an allegorical pun on the word "law." According to *Webster's*, to "ravel" means both to "entangle" or "make intricate" and to "*un*ravel" or "disentangle." And indeed, in this "legendary" domain the nots and knots of the law are unraveled—untangled and clarified—in an exemplary manner, even while the *Ravel* or entanglement of the *Law* weaves people together with Rainbow threads of custom and ceremony.

Finally, too, all is for the best in this domain because this tale of ravelings and unravelings has been told both by and about a daughter of wisdom. Indeed, though Silas as Job is, of course, no Jove and the daughter of his single parenthood is no Minerva, the structure of the relationship between innocently wise Eppie and her lawful father repeats the structure of the relationship between the goddess of wisdom and her law-giving father, just as the frozen burial of Molly Farren Cass affirms the fateful judgment of the *Oresteia* that the mother "is not the true parent of the child / Which is called hers."[22] In Hélène Cixous' wry words, there is "no need for a mother—provided that there is something of the maternal: and it is the father then who acts as the mother."[23] With no Eumenides in sight, the redeemed land of Raveloe belongs to fathers and daughters. It is no wonder that Wharton begins her re-visionary *Summer* with Charity Royall, an angry transformation of Eppie, trapped in a library ruled by a plaster bust of Minerva.

Writing to Wharton in 1912 about *The Reef,* perhaps the most Jamesian of her novels, Henry James thought of Eliot and suggested that his friend's re-visionary clarification of Eliot's message was so radical that the American writer had made herself, metaphorically speaking, into her English culture-mother's primordial precursor. "There used to be little notes in you that were like fine benevolent finger-marks of the good George Eliot—the echo of much reading of that excellent woman," he told Wharton. "But now you are like a lost and recovered 'ancient' whom she might have got a reading of (especially were he a Greek) and of whom in her texture some weaker reflection were to show."[24] In fact, James' remarks were more prophetic than analytic, for if the not altogether successful *Reef* was quasi-Jamesian rather than proto-Eliotian, the brilliantly coherent *Summer* does surface the *Ur*-myth, and specifically the dark "Daughteronomy," on which *Silas Marner* is based.

It may seem odd to argue that *Summer*, a sexy story of an illicit love affair, has anything in common with Eliot's pedagogically respectable *Silas Marner*. Yet, like *Silas Marner*, *Summer* is a family romance which also incorporates a female *Bildungsroman*, the account of a daughter's growth to maturity. As in *Silas Marner*, too, both the covert symbolic romance and the overt educational *roman* are resolved through the relationship between an adopted daughter and a man who seems to act as both her father and her mother. Again, like *Silas Marner*, *Summer* broods on the winter of civilization's discontent and the summer of reproduction; in doing so, moreover, Wharton's romance, like Eliot's fable, explores events that are situated on the margins of society, where culture must enter into a dialectical struggle with nature in order to transform "raw" female reality into "cooked" feminine sex roles.[25] In addition, as a corollary of this exploration, *Summer*, like *Silas Marner*, traces the redemption the father achieves through his possession of the daughter. Finally, therefore, the two novels illuminate each other with striking reciprocity: in the conciliatory coziness with which it evades desire, *Silas Marner* is the story Wharton might have liked to tell, while in the relentless rigor with which it renounces desire, *Summer* is the tale Eliot may have feared to confront.

As James' remark about her "ancient" quality implied, Wharton had begun to become a fierce mythologist by the time she wrote this short novel; in particular, she had started to read Joseph Conrad, whose grasp of archaic symbolism she much admired and imported into *Summer*, strengthening her implicit reading of *Silas Marner* with a quest plot that mimics the psychic journey at the heart of his *Heart of Darkness*. Thus, as in Sylvia Plath's poem "The Colossus," from which I have drawn an epigraph, "a blue sky out of the Oresteia" does arch over *Summer*, infusing and illuminating every detail of a mythic narrative that revolves around three figures: a father who "all by [himself is] pithy and historical as the Roman Forum," a daughter who marries the "winter of [his] year" as helplessly as Aeschylus' Electra and Plath's "Electra on Azalea Path" marry the shadow of Agamemnon, and a dead mother who must be as definitively consigned to barren ground as Clytemnestra or the Eumenides.[26] Appropriately enough, therefore, *Summer* begins as its heroine, teenage Charity Royall, walks down the main street of the New England village of North Dormer to her part-time job in a library presided over by a plaster cast of "sheep-nosed" Minerva, the divine daddy's girl who resolved the *Oresteia* by ruling in favor of "the father's claim / And male supremacy in all things." A representative of nature bewildered by culture, Charity is a sort of foundling who, we learn, was "brought down" from a nearby mountain (always mysteriously called "the Mountain," with an ominous capital *M*) when she was very little, an origin which places her among the "humblest of the humble even in North Dormer, where to come from the Mountain was the worst disgrace." At the same time, however, both her job as librarian and the odd fact that she keeps the lace she is making "wound about the buckram back of a disintegrated copy of 'The Lamplighter'" significantly qualify her humbleness. For, like Eliot's Eppie and like Gerty, the heroine of Maria Cummins' 1854 bestseller, Wharton's Charity is the ward of a solitary older man who dotes on and delights in her youth, her dependence.[27]

Where both Eliot's *Silas Marner* and Cummins' Trueman Flint are sympathetic men almost from the first, however, Charity's guardian is an equivocal figure, and his difference begins to reveal the secret dynamics such apparently divergent works as Cummins' and Eliot's novels share with Wharton's. For Lawyer Royall, says the narrator of *Summer,* "ruled in North Dormer; and Charity ruled in lawyer Royall's house . . . But she knew her power, knew what it was made of, and hated it." *Lawyer* Royall: so far as we know, this "magnificent monument of a man" has no other name. Indeed, as Charity's father/guardian/suitor and (eventually) husband, he is, ultimately, no more than the role his professional title and allegorical surname together denote: a regal lawgiver, a mythologized superego whose occupation links him with the library and with culture, that is, with the complex realm of patriarchal history that both puzzles and imprisons the wild child he is trying to make into a desirable daughter/bride.

Even while he is a "towering" public man, however, Lawyer Royall is a notably pathetic private man. From the first, Wharton deconstructs the colossus of the father to make explicit the ways in which this paradigmatic patriarch is as dependent on his Charity as *Silas Marner* was on his Eppie or, indeed, as Agamemnon was on Iphigenia or Electra, Oedipus on Antigone and Ismene, or the biblical Jephthah on his (nameless) daughter. To begin with, we learn that Charity had long ago perceived Lawyer Royall as "too lonesome" for her to go away to school; later, more dramatically, we discover that his "lonesomeness" manifested itself in an abortive attempt to rape her. Finally, we are told that it was this episode which drove the girl to try to establish her independence by taking her deathly job in the library. But, of course, this attempt at escape, as in some Sophoclean case history, simply impels her even more inexorably toward her fate.

For it is in "Minerva's" library that Charity meets her lover-to-be, a handsome architect named Lucius Harney—a far more glamorously equivocal representative of culture than the aging Lawyer Royall. Town-bred, easy with books, this dashing young man is culture's heir; at the same time, he is a golden boy whose "lusciousness," as Andrea Hammer has observed, links him to nature, even seems to make him nature's emissary—and that is why *he* is an equivocal figure. Young, sensual, magnetic, he is frequently associated with the grass, the sky, the "flaming breath" of summer; indeed, he and Charity conduct their affair while he is "camping" halfway up the Mountain in a little abandoned house surrounded by a fallen fence, "crowding grasses," and rosebushes that have "run wild."[28] That he is often connected in Charity's mind with her mysterious Mountain relative Liff Hyatt, whose initials echo his, seems at first to suggest, moreover, that, like Liff, Lucius is a brother figure—and his earliest advances *are* described as "more fraternal than lover-like."[29] Yet, just as Eppie Marner's marriage to the brother figure Aaron also marries her definitively to her father Silas, so Charity's apparently illegitimate romance with Lucius Harney moves her inexorably into the arms of Lawyer Royall, and this not just because it is Lawyer Royall who marries her to "rescue" her from unwed motherhood but because it eventually becomes plain that even Lucius Harney's desire for her is entangled in feelings of rivalrous identification with the patriarchally "majestic" lawyer.

For Charity, in every sense of that word, must be given to the father. And, as *Summer*'s denouement finally makes clear, even while Lucius Harney has seemed to act against the patriarchal Royall, he has also acted *for* the lawyer, appearing as if by magic in the library to deflower Charity and impregnate her so that she is at last ready for the marriage to her guardian that she had earlier persistently refused. Indeed, it is arguable that throughout the affair in which he seems to have functioned as nature's emissary by drawing the girl into the wilderness of her own sexuality, Harney has really performed as culture's messenger and, specifically, as a vivid and vital "Phallus" whose glamour seduces the daughter into the social architecture from which she would otherwise have tried to flee. For in patriarchal marriage, says Wharton's plot, the brother/equal inevitably turns into the father/ruler. Not surprisingly, therefore, when Charity and Lawyer Royall start on their journey toward the allegorically named town of *Nettle*ton, where the girl's sexual initiation began and where she is finally going to be married to her legal guardian, Charity briefly imagines that she is "sitting beside her lover with the leafy arch of summer bending over them." But "this illusion [is] faint and transitory" because it implies a deceptive liberty of desire. As Wharton reluctantly observed, the daughter's summer of erotic content blooms only to prepare her for what Dickinson called "a Doom of Fruit without the Bloom"—an autumn and winter of civilized discontent in which, like her precursor, the first Mrs. Royall, she will be "sad and timid and weak." As in Wharton's pornographic "Beatrice Palmato" fragment—a more melodramatic tale of father-daughter incest which makes overt some of the psychodynamics that even in *Summer* are only covert—the symbolic father will "reap [the] fruit" borne from the son/lover's deflowering of the daughter.[30]

Charity does, however, make one last frantic effort to flee the wintry prison house of culture that is closing around her, and that is in her wild pilgrimage up the Mountain in search of her mother. As the girl's affair with Lucius Harney has progressed, she has become increasingly concerned about her origins and begun to try, the way Eppie did in *Silas Marner,* to explain to herself what it means both to have and to be a mother. Finally, when she realizes she is pregnant, she also understands that there is "something in her blood that [makes] the Mountain the only answer to her questioning," and in an astonishing episode, which includes some of the most fiercely imagined scenes in American fiction, she journeys toward the originary heart of darkness where she will find and lose her mother.

Appropriately enough, Charity's mother's name is *Mary* Hyatt. Equally appropriately, Charity arrives in the outlaw community on the Mountain only to discover that the woman has just died. It is as if the very idea of the daughter's quest must necessarily kill her female progenitor, not only to emphasize the unavailability of female power but also to underscore the Oresteian dictum that "The mother is not the true parent of the child / Which is called hers. She is [merely] a nurse who tends the growth / Of young seed planted by its true parent, the male."[31] Worse still, this anti-Virgin Mary is not only dead, she is horrifyingly dead, dead "like a dead dog in a ditch," "lips parted in a frozen gasp above . . . broken teeth," one leg drawn up under a torn skirt and the other "swollen glistening leg" flung out, "bare to the knee," in a death paroxysm that parodies the paroxysm of birth and suggests the nausea of nakedness in which the flesh of the mother expels and repels the flesh of the child. As Mr. Miles, the clergyman who ascends the Mountain only for funerals, prepares to bury the woman's uncoffined body in frozen ground, nameless and indistinguishable squatters, Charity's undefinable relatives, squabble over the pitiful furnishings in the shanty where Mary Hyatt died on a mattress on the floor. Nothing, they say, was hers: "She never had no bed"; "And the stove warn't hers." Nor does the reading of the Bible, the Book of patriarchal Law, offer any hope of redemption for the dead woman. When Mr. Miles intones, "Yet in my flesh shall I see God," Charity thinks of "the gaping mouth and stony eyes [and] glistening leg," and when he proposes that Jesus Christ shall change this "vile body that it may be like unto His glorious body," a last spadeful of earth falls heavily "on the vile body of Mary Hyatt."

Where women poets from Elizabeth Barrett Browning to Emily Dickinson transformed mothers into "multitudinous mountains sitting in / [A] magic circle, with [a] mutual touch / Electric," and "Sweet

Mountains" into "Strong Madonnas," Wharton, like her culture-mother George Eliot, saw the mother as blind, deaf, and stony and the maternal Mountain as a place of mourning.[32] As if Eliot anticipated the French feminist psychoanalyst Christiane Olivier's contention that the mirror which man holds toward woman "contains only the image of a dead woman" and, more specifically, a dead Jocasta, the morbid moment of Molly Farren Cass' death in the snow and her daughter Eppie's discovery that "mammy's ear was deaf" is—as we saw—frozen into the center of *Silas Marner*.[33] Similarly, frozen into the center of *Summer* is the moment of Mary Hyatt's burial in the snow and her daughter Charity's mortifying discovery that there is no salvation from or for her mother's "vile body."

Neither is there salvation or even significant charity for Charity from other women in the novel. To be sure, one of the girl's unnamed relatives—Liff Hyatt's mother—lets her spend the night on a mattress on the floor "as her dead mother's body had lain," but as that simile suggests, such an act of kindness only promises to induct Charity into the "passive promiscuity" lived by the matriarchal horde on the Mountain, a life entirely outside the comforts and controls of culture, a life in which the mother—possessionless and unpossessed—is "glad to have the child go." As for the other women, the semi-senile figure of Verena Marsh, the Royalls' housekeeper, "with her old deaf-looking eyes" foreshadows the blind deaf stony figure of Charity's mother; the "fallen" Julia Hawes and her impoverished sister Ally, together with the "indestructible" Annabel Balch, reemphasize women's dependence on male legal and financial protection; and the pseudo-motherly abortionist, Dr. Merkel, suggests that a daughter who wants to live apart from the father must kill her baby or else, like Mary Hyatt, be "cut down" and killed by the "savage misery" of a life apart from culture.

Taken together, therefore, the decisions and destinies of all of these women italicize Charity's own perception that "in the established order of things as she [knows] them, [there is] no place for her individual adventure." In fact, the pregnancy that signals her transformation from girl to woman, from daughter to mother, has so severely depersonalized her that she feels herself "a mere speck in the lonely circle of the

sky." Like dead Mary Hyatt, she has nothing and is nothing but a vessel for her child; thus the impersonal biological imperative of the coming life is, as Wharton brilliantly puts it, "like a load that [holds] her
down, and yet like a hand that pull[s] her to her feet." The annunciation
of summer, Charity discovers, inexorably entails the renunciation that is
winter, a divestment of desire that definitively prepares her for her final
turn toward the rescuing father. Fated to move from father to library to
lover to father, she goes to Nettleton and marries her guardian. And by
now even the Romantic nature she had experienced with her lover has
been transmuted into culture—that is, into a set of cultural artifacts: an
engraving of a couple in a boat that decorates her bridal chamber, and a
pin set with a lake-blue gem which implies that in the bloomless winter
of her maturity the lake itself must turn to stone.

But if a stone is all Charity has, Charity is what Lawyer Royall has,
an emblem of redemption he needs as much as *Silas Marner* needs "his"
Eppie. For if, as Freud argues, the girl arrives at "the ultimate normal
feminine attitude in which she takes her father as love-object" only after
"a lengthy process of [symbolically castrating] development" which, in
Helene Deutsch's words, "drive[s]" her "into her constitutionally pre-
determined passive role," then the daughter's desire for the father must
be understood to be, like Charity's need for Lawyer Royall, constructed
by a patriarchal order that forces her to renounce what might be more
"natural" desires—for lover/brother, for mother, for self.[34] But as the
ambiguous allegory of Charity's name suggests, the father's desire for
the daughter is inevitable, a desire not only to give but to receive charity. Standing outside the girl's room after proposing to her (and being
rejected) for the second time, Lawyer Royall seems to understand this:
"His hand on the door knob[,] 'Charity!' he plead[s]." For not only is the
"daughter" a milk-giving creature, a suitably diminished and dependent
mother, she is also, as a living manifestation of the father's wealth, the
charity to which he is culturally entitled.

Finally, therefore, from Charity's point of view, *Summer* is very much
a novel about both renunciation and resignation. When her last hope
for escape is buried with her mother, she must resign herself, or, rather,
reassign herself, to her symbolic father.[35] After her marriage she will be

Charity Royall Royall, a name whose redundancy emphasizes the pro-
prietorial power by which her guardian/husband commands her loyalty.
But from Lawyer Royall's point of view or, for that matter, from Lucius
Harney's, *Summer* is a novel about assignment—that is, about the roles of
cultural authority to which men are assigned and about the women who
are assigned—marked out, given over—to them to signify that authority. No wonder, then, that Lawyer Royall's first gesture after his marriage
to Charity is to give his new bride the munificent sum of forty dollars to
buy clothes so that, like an illustration from Thorstein Veblen's *Theory of
the Leisure Class,* she will prove his wealth by "beating" all the other girls
"hollow." "Of course, *he's* the book," said Wharton enigmatically about
Lawyer Royall.[36] Consciously, she no doubt meant that he is the novel's
most complex personality—indeed, its only Jamesian adult—and therefore the only character whose redemption is worth tracing in detail. But,
less consciously, she might have meant that, as law-giving patriarch, he
is the "book" in which Charity's fate must be inscribed; for it is, after all,
the text of his desire that determines the destiny of hers.

Apart from fictions like *Silas Marner* and *Summer,* what evidence have
we that father-daughter incest is a culturally constructed paradigm of
female desire? Equally to the point, what proof is there that the father
may need, even desire, the daughter at least as much as she needs him?
Though psychoanalytic and sociological replies to both of these questions have been disputed, many answers have been offered, particularly in recent years. From Phyllis Chesler to Judith Lewis Herman,
for instance, feminist theorists have argued that in a patriarchal culture women are encouraged by society, in Chesler's words, "to commit
incest as a way of life." "As opposed to marrying our fathers, we marry
men like our fathers," Chesler declares, "men who are older than us,
[and] have more money [and] more power [and are taller]." Similarly,
in her study of literal father-daughter incest, Herman claims that "overt
incest represents only the furthest point on a continuum—an exagger-
ation of patriarchal family norms, but not a departure from them."[37]
Less extravagantly but along the same lines, Nancy Chodorow has

observed, following Talcott Parsons, that "father-daughter incest does not threaten a daughter [with a return to infantile dependency] in the same way" in which "mother-son incest . . . threatens a son," so that "mother-son and mother-*daughter* [not father-daughter] incest are the major threats to the formation of new families (as well as to the male-dominant family)."[38]

Nor are any of these views incompatible with Freud's own belief that what he called the "female Oedipus complex"—the process through which the little girl relinquishes her earliest mother-attachment and transfers her affection to her father—is both the end result of an extraordinarily difficult procedure and, as he puts it, a "positive" development. Only by a "very circuitous path," he admits in his late essay "Female Sexuality" (1931), does the girl "arrive at the ultimate normal feminine attitude in which she takes her father as love-object." And because *her* Oedipus complex (unlike the boy's) represents the "final result of a lengthy process . . . it escapes the strong hostile influences which, in men, tend to its destruction"—that is, because the female Oedipus complex is not destroyed but created by the "castration complex" (which signifies the recognition of sexual difference), many women, in Freud's view, never surmount the female Oedipus complex at all and perhaps never should.[39]

As the researches of Judith Herman and Lisa Hirschman have shown, however, and as Deutsch argued, the desire of the father for the daughter is frequently complicitous, even essential in constructing the desire for him that she manifests in the "positive" female Oedipus complex. Proposing a theory of what has come to be called "reciprocal role learning," Deutsch suggested in *The Psychology of Women* that the father functions "as a seducer, with whose help the girl's aggressive instinctual components are transformed into masochistic ones." Recent investigators have suggested that girls do "learn to behave in a feminine fashion through complementing the masculine behavior of their fathers." Tellingly, though, "there is no evidence that reciprocal role learning is of any significance in the development of masculinity."[40] In other words, boys are not encouraged to learn to be boys by responding with precocious virility to seductive behavior by their mothers. This last point, however, leads to my second question—What proof is there that the father needs the daughter at least as much as she needs him?—and to a related query—Why *should* the father desire the daughter? If men have not developed masculinity through reciprocal role learning with mothers, why should they interact "reciprocally" with their daughters? I have extrapolated from my readings of *Silas Marner* and *Summer* the idea that the father needs the daughter because she is a suitably diminished "milk giver," a miniaturized version of the mother whom patriarchal culture absolutely forbids him to desire. Beyond the often ambiguous configurations that shape literary texts like Eliot's and Wharton's, there is considerable evidence that this is so.

The empirical investigations of Herman and Hirschman, for instance, have yielded crucial information: in studying surveys of "white, predominantly middle-class, urban, educated women" these clinical psychologists discovered that "between four and twelve percent of all women reported a sexual experience with a relative, and one woman in one hundred reported a sexual experience with her father or stepfather." Examining individual incest cases, moreover, they learned that, often because of a wife's illness, absence, or alleged frigidity, a father had transferred his affections to his daughter in an attempt "to continue to receive female nurturance." More generally, they observed that "in the father's fantasy life, the daughter becomes the source of all the father's infantile longings for nurturance and care. He thinks of her first as the idealized childhood bride or sweetheart, and finally as the all-good, all-giving mother." Reasoning both from anthropological studies and from the Bible, they conclude that "in patriarchal societies [where] the rights of ownership and exchange of women within the family are vested primarily in the father[, t]hese rights find their most complete expression in the father's relationship with his daughter" because—of all female relatives—"the daughter belongs to the father alone." They then cite a key passage from Leviticus in which, while forbidding sexual union with every other female blood relative or in-law, "the patriarchal God sees fit to pass over father-daughter incest in silence."[41]

Freud's theories of psychoanalysis began, of course, with the hypothesis that just such incest was the root cause of the hysteria manifested by the female patients he and Josef Breuer treated in the 1890s. But traditional interpretations of the history of psychoanalysis propose that, as Diane Sadoff puts it, "Freud realized that his female patients' stories of remembered paternal seduction did not necessarily report reality and may have reported fantasy [so that] the scene of paternal seduction retroactively seeks to represent and solve a major enigma confronting the daughter: the origin or upsurge of her sexuality." In fact, explains Octave Mannoni, "the theory of trauma, of the seduction by the father . . . served as [Freud's] defense against knowledge of the Oedipus complex." Even the feminist theorist Juliet Mitchell acquiesces in this view, observing that "the fact that, as Freud himself was well aware, actual paternal seduction or rape occurs not infrequently, has nothing to do with the essential concepts of psychoanalysis" (which are, after all, founded on the hypothesis of filial rather than paternal desire). Yet, interestingly enough, we have from the Father of Psychoanalysis himself strikingly direct evidence of the reality of paternal desire.[42]

In May 1897, shortly before abandoning his theory that hysteria was caused by paternal seduction or rape, Freud had a dream about "feeling over-affectionately towards" his oldest daughter, Mathilde. "The dream," he wrote to his friend Wilhelm Fliess, "of course fulfills my wish to pin down a father as the originator of neurosis and put an end to my persistent doubts." Yet, on the one hand, the experience clearly troubled him, while, on the other hand, it does seem to have functioned as a screen for what troubled him even more: the sequence of dreams and memories Freud recorded in the letters of spring–summer 1897 shows that many of the psychic events he examined as part of the self-analysis he was conducting at this time had to do with desires for or anxieties about mature women—his mother or figures for her. The sequence culminated in his crucial speculation that "(between the ages of two and two-and-a-half) libido towards *matrem* was aroused" at a time when he "had the opportunity of seeing her *nudam.*" Embedded in this dramatic series of reveries is his equally dramatic decision that though "in every case [of female hysteria] blame was laid on perverse acts by the father . . . it was hardly credible that perverted acts against children were so general," a decision that, despite its negative implications for a career he had been building on theories about paternal seduction, left him feeling inexplicably exhilarated.[43]

Careful analysis of these materials suggests that Freud's brilliant self-interrogations both reveal and conceal a slippage in his thinking. His no doubt accurate discovery of feelings for his mother is quite unaccountably associated with the notion, which he later repudiated, that his female patients would naturally have had equivalent desires for their *fathers*. That even as he surfaced his own Oedipal wishes, he may have disguised them (for instance, reporting awful dreams about an ugly elderly nurse who washed him in "reddish water") implies his own *resistance* to these wishes, however, a resistance also expressed in his dream of Mathilde. As Mitchell observes, even "Freud . . . found it more acceptable to be the father than the incest-desiring or rival-castrating son—as do most men." Thus the theory of paternal seduction appropriately led to Freud's understanding of the son's desire for the mother, of which the father's desire for the daughter is a belated but more socially acceptable transformation. Nevertheless, the father's desire for the daughter was not so acceptable to Freud that he could persist in his "wish to pin down a father as the originator of neurosis." Rather, having admitted his own filial desire, he seems to have wished to "pin down" daughters as equivalent sources of desire. Yet as his later formulations of female psychosexual development were to suggest, erotic feelings of daughters for fathers symmetrical with those of sons for mothers were not necessarily implicit in the accounts of paternal seduction that he called his patients' "fantasies." In fact, as recent reports about the unpublished portions of his letters to Fliess, along with analyses of the alterations and evasions in *Studies on Hysteria* have suggested, Freud himself was, in Mitchell's phrase, "well aware" that many of these patients were not fantasizing, that they actually had been seduced or in some sense seductively manipulated by their fathers or by father figures. Their "hysteria" may therefore have constituted not a rejection of their own desire but a refusal of the paternal demands that not only their own families but also their culture defined as psychologically "right." Even so early in his career, in other words, Freud's fruitful transformation of speculations about father-daughter seduction into a theory about son-mother incest, with its corollary evasion of a theory of father-daughter desire, expresses his proleptic awareness that he would eventually have to construct a far more complicated model of female psychosexual development in order to trace the girl's "circuitous path" to what he was to define as mature (heterosexual) femininity.[44]

That path, with its obstacles, its terrors, and its refusals, is the road studied in *Silas Marner* and *Summer*—in *Silas Marner*'s exploration of the powers the daughter gives the father and in *Summer*'s examination of the powers the father takes away from the daughter. But of course countless other literary texts—written by both men and women—focus on the submerged paradigm of father-daughter incest that shapes the plots and possibilities inscribed in these novels. From the *Oresteia*'s repudiation and repression of the matriarchal Furies and its concomitant aggrandizement of Athene, the dutiful father's daughter, to *Oedipus at Colonus*' praise of Antigone and Ismene, the two loyal daughters who have been their father's sole guardians in the blinded exile to which his incestuous marriage with his mother condemned him, Greek literature consistently valorizes such a paradigm. That Oedipus' daughters, in particular, functioned as their father's "eyes" reminds us, moreover, that "the word for daughter in Greek is *Kore*, the literal meaning of which is pupil of the eye."[45] Similarly, the violent obliteration of the mother in these works and many others recalls one version of the story of Athene's origin: after raping Metis the Titaness, the father-god *swallowed her*, having heard that, though she was now pregnant with a daughter, she would bear a son who would depose him if she had another child; then, "in due time . . . seized by a raging headache," he himself gave birth to Athene, who "sprang fully armed" from his skull.[46] In just the way that Antigone and Ismene properly replace Jocasta as Oedipus' helpmeets—indeed, as the "eyes" who, according to Freud, would signify his continuing sexual potency—so Athene supplants Metis as Zeus' true child/bride.

To be sure, these archaic texts enact the prescriptions and proscriptions of patriarchal culture with exceptional clarity; yet such imperatives also underlie a surprising number of other, later works, ranging from Shakespeare's *King Lear* to Percy Bysshe Shelley's *Cenci*, from Mary Shelley's *Mathilda* to Christina Stead's *Man Who Loved Children*, from some of Sylvia Plath's and Anne Sexton's most striking poems to Toni Morrison's *Bluest Eye*. Whereas the stories of such heroines as Antigone and her later, more angelically Victorian avatar Eppie Marner—the creation of a novelist long haunted by Antigone—had recounted the daughter's acquiescence in her filial destiny, however, these works, like Wharton's *Summer*, record her ambivalence toward a fate in which, as Beatrice Cenci cries, "all things" terrifyingly transform themselves into "my father's spirit, / His eye, his voice, his touch surrounding me."[47] Specifically, in each of these works a father more or less explicitly desires a daughter. His incestuous demands may be literal or they may be figurative, but in either case the heroine experiences them as both inexorable and stifling. Thus, in each work the girl struggles with more or less passion to escape, arguing that "I love your Majesty according to my bond, no more, no less." And in almost all of these works, she discovers, finally, just what the nature of that bond is: no more, no less, than—on the one hand—death or—on the other hand—a surrender to the boundless authority of paternal desire that governs the lives of mothers and daughters in what Adrienne Rich has called "the kingdom of the sons" and the fathers.[48] Indeed, in the few works (for instance, Plath's "Daddy" and Stead's *Man Who Loved Children*) where the daughter neither dies nor acquiesces, she becomes a murderess and an outlaw.

Reducing the plot, as fairy tales so often do, to its most essential psychic outline, a narrative recorded by the Brothers Grimm provides a resonant summary of the father-daughter "story" I have been exploring here. The fairy tale "Allerleirauh" (which means "many different kinds of fur") introduces us to a king whose dying wife has made him promise not to remarry unless he can find a new bride who is as beautiful as she is and who has "just such golden hair as I have."[49] Grief-stricken, the king keeps his word until one day he looks at his growing daughter, sees that she is "just as beautiful as her dead mother, and ha[s] the same golden hair," "suddenly [feels] a violent love for her," and resolves to marry her. Shocked, the daughter tries to escape by setting him impossible tasks—she asks for three magical dresses and "a mantle of a thousand different kinds of fur"—but when he fulfills her requests, she has no choice but to run away. Taking her three dresses and three tiny domestic treasures, she wraps herself in her fur mantle and escapes to a great forest. There she is asleep in a hollow tree when "the King to whom this forest belong[s]" passes through with some huntsmen who capture her, thinking she is "a wondrous beast." When she tells them she is simply a poor orphan child, they bring her to this king's palace, where they set her to work, like Cinderella, in the kitchen.[50]

Of course, however, the king at this palace soon manages to discover her identity. He gives a series of three feasts, at each of which she appears in one of her magic dresses; he admires the soup she cooks while she is disguised in her furry Cinderella garb; and he finally manages to tear off her protective mantle, revealing her magic dress and her golden hair so that, in the words of the story, "she [can] no longer hide herself," and the pair are wed soon after this epiphany. Like such texts as *Summer, Mathilda,* and *The Cenci,* then, this tale records the case history of a daughter who tries to escape paternal desire, and like the heroines of many such works (for instance, Charity Royall journeying to the Mountain), the "fair princess" who becomes "Allerleirauh" flees from culture (her father's palace) to nature (the great wood), trying to transform herself into a creature of nature (a "hairy animal") rather than acquiesce in the extreme demands culture is making upon her.[51] Like a number of the other protagonists of these stories and case histories, however, Allerleirauh cannot altogether abandon the imperatives her culture has impressed upon her: she brings with her the three magical dresses and the three domestic tokens which will eventually reveal her identity and knit her back into society. Like countless other heroines in such tales, moreover, she is motherless, a fact which, the story emphasizes, has brought about the seductive paternal persecution she is trying to evade. Finally, like that of so many of these heroines—perhaps most notably *Silas Marner*'s Eppie—her function as a "treasure" to both kings is manifested by the golden hair she is at last unable to conceal.

That there are in fact two kings in "Allerleirauh" may at first seem to controvert my argument that this tale offers us a paradigm of the prescription for father-daughter incest that lies at the heart of female psychosexual development in patriarchal society. Not just the princess but also the first king's courtiers, after all, express dismay at his desire to marry his daughter. In addition, the second king is distinguished from the first by a restrictive clause: he is not "the king, who owns this forest"—that is, the king from whose palace Allerleirauh has just fled—but, rather, "the king who owns this forest." Yet structurally and psychologically, if not grammatically, the two kings are one: paternal figures from both of whom the "fair princess" tries to escape, though not, perhaps, with equal vigor. In fact, for all practical purposes, the distinction between the two is best expressed by a single comma, the linguistic mark that marks the difference between illegitimate and legitimate incest, a difference Allerleirauh herself involuntarily acknowledges by the ambivalence with which at one moment she decks herself in glorious apparel and then, soon after, retreats into her old life as a wild child.

To be sure, given such ambivalence, some readers might see this tale simply as an account of the advances and retreats through which an adolescent girl comes to terms with her own mature desires. At the same time, however, what gives the tale a good deal of its force is the fatality it shares with subtler works like *Silas Marner* and *Summer*—specifically, a fatality provided by the *mother's* complicity in her daughter's destiny. For it is, after all, Allerleirauh's mother who has set the girl's story going with her admonition to the father that he must marry only a bride as beautiful as she. Lost to the daughter, like Molly Farren Cass and Mary Hyatt, she nevertheless rules her daughter's life with the injunctions of the culture-mother: "You must bury your mother, you must give yourself to your father." In such novels as *Silas Marner* and *Summer*, the authors themselves replace her, splitting the maternal function between the ignominy of the dead mother and the qualified triumph of the male-identified maternal authority. But in all of these stories, as even in more apparently rebellious works, the text itself discovers no viable alternative to filial resignation. Certainly, paradigmatic culture-mothers like Eliot and Wharton do not suggest (at least not in such resonant works as *Silas Marner* and *Summer*) that the daughter has any choice but that of acquiescence.[52] Though the "empty Pack" of daughteronomy may be heavy, as Dickinson saw perhaps more clearly than they, it is vain to "punish" the cultural "Honey" it manufactures; for the daughter who understands her duty and her destiny, such honey "only sweeter" grows. Under "a blue sky out of the Oresteia," Eppie Marner, Charity Royall, and the fair princess Allerleirauh, along with many others, and each in her own way, obey the implicit command of patriarchal society and marry the winter of the Father's year.

—1985[53]

POTENT GRISELDA

Male Modernists and the Great Mother

Yea, like bees in and out of a hive, we come backwards
and forwards to our woman . . . we are bees that go
between, from the flower home to the hive and the Queen;
for she lies at the centre of the hive [and] in her all things
are born, both words and bees.

—D. H. LAWRENCE, FOREWORD TO SONS AND LOVERS

Man has fallen. It would be difficult to point to a man
in the world today who is not subservient to the great
woman-spirit that sways modern mankind.

—D. H. LAWRENCE, "THE REAL THING"

"The modern young man is not afraid of being petticoat-ruled," declared D. H. Lawrence in his late essay "Matriarchy." "He is afraid of being swamped, turned into a mere accessory of bare-limbed swooping woman . . . He talks rather bitterly . . . about matriarchy, and rather feebly about man being master again. He knows perfectly well that he will never be master again."[1] Such an admission from our century's major acolyte of the phallic mysteries and of the lordly "men in whom the gods are manifest" may seem somewhat surprising. Yet in his presup-

274

positions about the power of female (pro)creativity the masculinist and often misogynistic Lawrence was oddly close to his quasi-feminist friend the poet H. D. Indeed, as perhaps the paradigmatic modernist theoretician of sexuality, he frequently articulated ideas about the primacy of maternity that also represented the views of such equally unlikely contemporaries as Isadora Duncan and James Joyce, both of whom within the same decade expressed almost the same sentiment on what was for these avant-garde revolutionaries a peculiar subject. "*Amor matris,* subjective and objective genitive, may be the only true thing in life," said Stephen Dedalus in *Ulysses* (1922), as if anticipating Lawrence's plaintive "Matriarchy," and through him his creator, James Joyce, also spoke. Five years later, Isadora Duncan, writing in *My Life* (1927), asked a rhetorical question that implied the same speculation. "Is it that in all the universe there is but one Great Cry containing Sorrow, Joy, Ecstasy, Agony, the Mother Cry of Creation?"[2]

Radical and rebellious as they were, neither Duncan nor Dedalus (nor Joyce himself nor H. D. nor Lawrence) can be seen as merely restating typical nineteenth-century verities about Home, Hearth, and Mother. Certainly, naked beneath her Grecian veils, Isadora would seem to have dramatically escaped the decorous cult of True Womanhood, while H. D., living out a liberated expatriatism, could hardly be defined as a hierophant of Mrs. Beeton's Good Housekeeping. Similarly, the mature Joyce and his youthful alter ego, Stephen—both busily inventing fictions of fatherhood—were nothing if not cynical about the claims of the maternal Angel in the House. Stephen, indeed, fantasized his rejection of Catholicism as an act of matricide, and Lawrence's gloomy assertion in "The Real Thing" that "man has fallen," together with the rhetoric of fear and resignation that he deploys in "Matriarchy," brings to the surface an anxiety that underlies Joyce's claims, if not H. D.'s or Duncan's. Nevertheless, whether anxious or ecstatic, all four of these figures were shaped by a cultural context that defined motherhood as the ontological fact from which all other facts, fictions, and myths arise.

Why and how did these disparate artists come to create so mystical and metaphysical a definition of female sexuality and more specifically of motherhood? Furthermore, what were the aesthetic implications of such a definition? I will argue here that all were reflecting a general transformation in what Michel Foucault has called the "history of sexuality," a transformation that can be more clearly, if less surprisingly, traced in the treatises of speculative anthropologists from Bachofen to Frazer and Harrison to Briffault, Graves, and Neumann. For women artists— particularly for feminist modernists—this sociocultural change had a number of empowering consequences, as I will argue in the next chapter. For their male (and often masculinist) modernist contemporaries, however, such a change posed crucial problems, implying as it did an important set of unmanning transformations not only in Western culture's biological and anthropological valuation of motherhood but also in those sexual metaphors for creativity through which so many writers have traditionally expressed their deepest feelings about their own nature and the nature of their own art. Because Lawrence's self-analyses were always so frank in their confrontation of the psychodynamics that other poets and novelists only more hesitantly explored, some of his works, and in particular his middle-period novella "The Ladybird," may allow us clearly to chart both the anxieties induced in men by the newly conceived potency of H. D.'s "Early Goddess . . . , the first love, Maia, mama, Mutter," and the aesthetic maneuvers through which they defended themselves against such anxieties.

Throughout much of the nineteenth century, of course, as throughout much of Western literary history, the power of the literary artist to create texts was metaphorically equated with the power of men to engender children and/or the power of God the Father to generate both the world and the Word, both the Book of Nature and the Book of Judgment. The human author of poems and plays, that is, usually seemed to male writers who worked in the masculinist traditions of what Gertrude Stein called "patriarchal poetry" to be a kind of copy or shadow of that cosmic Author who fathered all things and from whom, ultimately, all authority sprang. Thus there has long been a secret or subliminal sense in which a writer's pen somehow "stood" for his penis (and here a pun may or may not be intended). As recently as 1886, even the withdrawn and submissive clergyman Gerard Manley Hopkins declared that the artist's "most essential quality [is] masterly execution, which is a kind of male gift, and especially marks off men from women, the begetting of one's thought on paper, in verse, or whatever the matter is."[3]

More recently, this idea that, as Hopkins also put it, "the male quality is the creative gift," has been explored by such critics as Jacques Derrida and John Irwin. In particular, both of these men, along with many other contemporary thinkers, speculate upon the notion that "the hymen is the always folded . . . space in which the pen writes its dissemination" and that the creative act involves, a relationship between "the phallic pen" and "the 'pure space' of the virgin page."[4] In elaborating this argument, moreover, both implicitly allude to the old biological model in which the female is merely a passive vessel upon which and in which the male acts. Acquiescing in male desire, suffering the consequences of man's will, woman, according to this ancient paradigm, is and should be no more than a patient Griselda, like the bizarrely submissive wife of Walter, Marquis of Saluzzo, in Boccaccio's and Chaucer's stories, who bears her lord's children only to lose them to his specially defined *droit du seigneur*. Whether she is, as in the current formulation, a blank page, or, as in older terms, an empty vessel, Griselda's story tells us that woman should be humble because she is inert. Man generates life, she receives it; he defines it, she contains it; he imagines it, she embodies it. Familiar notions, for from the fourth century B.C. until at least the eighteenth century, most European medical metaphysicians accepted the "highly influential concept of the relative roles of male and female in development," which Aristotle postulated in his *Generation of Animals*: males were believed to provide "the form, at once formal, efficient, and final cause" and females no more than "the substance, the material cause, for the new organism."[5]

During the seventeenth and eighteenth centuries, moreover, as proponents of the infant science of embryology took up the concept of "preformation"—that is, the notion that, as Seneca had written in the first century, "in the seed are enclosed all the parts of the body of the man that shall be formed"—thinkers such as Dalenpatius, Leeuwenhoek, and Leibniz actually argued that tiny homunculi sprang fully formed from male penises to be lodged temporarily in female bodies, which acted as little more than "homely foster nurses" (to quote Wordsworth) or large incubators. Yet though such an extreme devaluation of even the biological role of the female may now seem absurd, it is, after all, only another version of the famous judgment Apollo issues at the end of the *Oresteia*, an assertion that has often been seen as one of the founding statements of Western patriarchy: "The true parent is he who mounts, the mother is not the parent at all." For as Neumann observes, a patriarchate traditionally postulates "that the male seed is the creative element while the woman . . . is only its temporary abode and feeding place." In fact, to translate biological terms back into literary metaphors again, the woman is simply a blank—or in Irwin's phrase "virgin"—page on which the male body inscribes the word made flesh of a new generation.[6]

There is a significant difference, however, between such a metaphor as it is ironically examined by, say, Derrida and Irwin, and the metaphor as it was more confidently expressed by earlier thinkers from Aristotle to Chaucer's clerk to Hopkins. For what intervened between these two sets of theorists was an epoch that became increasingly aware of female power, increasingly conscious that it might be possible to define the female vessel, rather than the male seed, as the actively creative agent both in life and in art, possible to reimagine Griselda as positively potent rather than merely patient. Indeed, it might be possible, as Neumann notes, to describe the male seed as itself no more than a function of the great transformative female vessel. "In the matriarchal world," he declares,

> the woman as vessel is not made by man or out of man or used for his procreative purposes; rather, the reverse is true; it is this vessel with its mysterious creative character that brings forth the male in itself and from out of itself. Bachofen rightly pointed out that in the matriarchate man is looked upon as a sower, but he did not perceive the radical meaning of this image, in which the man is only an instrument of the earth and the seed he sows is not "his" seed but earth seed.[7]

Whether or not it is objectively "true," Neumann's notion that woman as mother goddess might once have been a historically and theologically significant force—that, in Lawrence's phrase, modern generations might be "the embodied ideas of our grandmothers" rather than of our grand*fathers*—was a new idea that developed along with (and no doubt in part because of) the new sciences of embryology and anthropology, as well as the new movements of feminism and Romanticism, in the late eighteenth century and the first half of the nineteenth century, and it is an idea that has had far-reaching implications for literary artists of both sexes. For until that crucial turn of the century, just as physicians imagined the generation of animals very differently from the way in which nineteenth- and twentieth-century embryologists conceptualize the process, so philosophers and scholars imagined prehistory very differently from the way theorists of matriarchy from Bachofen to Harrison, Briffault, and Neumann do. Whether they were "classical" Greeks or Renaissance classicists, their originary age, Golden or Iron, was on the whole as patriarchal as the society in which they lived.[8]

The impulse to question the notion that prehistory was necessarily patriarchal—with patriarchy, indeed, a sort of Platonic form of all society—can no doubt be traced back, first, to the work of speculative anthropologists like Bachofen, Frazer, and Harrison, along with the research of field ethnologists such as Lewis Morgan and Bronislaw Malinowski, who began exploring the differences between both historically and geographically distinct cultures and in doing so revealed that human social structures may be—and may always have been—fluid rather than fixed, unlike rather than like; second, to the work of embryologists such as Wolff and Baer, whose studies of the epigenesis of the fertilized egg emphasized both the power of the female "seed" and the importance of the transformative process that takes place in, and is facilitated by, the female body; and, finally, of course, to the work of Darwin himself, whose large-scale application of the idea of process to all of biological "history" set off, as Gordon Rattray Taylor remarks, "a series of attempts to draw up schemes designed to account for the whole development of human society, [schemes that] represented the application of the idea of evolution . . . to society as a whole."[9]

Taken together, the researches and hypotheses of these thinkers suggested that traditionally patriarchal visions of a fixed prehistory reflecting the modes and fixtures of "modern" society, like the patriarchal biology with which they were (consciously or not) associated, had been in some sense illusory. "The absolute antithesis between our present-day thinking and that of antiquity," wrote Bachofen in the introduction to his massive and groundbreaking *Mother Right* (1861), "is nowhere so startlingly disclosed as in the field upon which we are entering"—the field, that is, of the relations between, and especially the relative positions of, the sexes. Some forty years later, in her superbly argued *Prolegomena to the Study of Greek Religion* (1903)—about which Joseph Campbell remarks that "if Bachofen's name were mentioned anywhere in its pages [it] might be read from beginning to end as an intentional celebration and verification of his views"—Jane Ellen Harrison observed that though "our modern patriarchal society focuses its religious anthropomorphism on the relationship of the father and the son," the civilization of pre-Homeric Greece "is quite other than patriarchal." Subversively tracing the evolution of patriarchal Olympus from matriarchal Eleusis, she drew upon the findings of Sir Arthur Evans, who had begun to excavate the ruins of Cretan Knossos, to support her theories, exuberantly exclaiming that "in Crete most happily the ancient figure of the mother has returned after long burial to the upper air." For her, as for Bachofen before her and Briffault after her, the Great Mother, the Lady of the Wild Things—whether in her incarnation as Demeter/Kore, as Isis, as Aphrodite, or as Semele—was in earliest theology the only true and primordially potent parent of everyone.[10]

The work of speculative thinkers such as Harrison and Bachofen was not, of course, in a scientific sense "empirical"; rather, it was based on the painstaking interpretation of what Bachofen himself called "a vast heap of ruins," and it is questionable whether either the Swiss jurist or the English scholar knew much about the advances in embryological theory that accompanied and in a way offered a counterpoint to their research. Yet it seems more than coincidentally significant that even among preformationist biologists who believed the human infant to be contained as a tiny homunculus in egg or sperm, the "ovists" had defeated the "animalculists" by the middle of the eighteenth century, that by the end of the century Caspar Friedrich Wolff's theory of ovular epigenesis (substituting active process for static "preformation") had been widely accepted, and that by the end of the nineteenth century, in just the years when Harrison was writing her *Prolegomena,* experimental embryologists like Roux (1888), Driesch (1891), Endres (1895), and Spemann (1901, 1903) had established the nature of the cleavage by which the egg/embryo manifests its developmental potency. Clearly, from a medical point of view, such laboratory research definitively superseded the ancient a priori assertions of Aristotle and of Aeschylus' Apollo.[11]

That such research constituted a kind of resonant accompaniment to the mythography of Bachofen and Harrison is made clear from a central symbol studied in Bachofen's first book. An *Essay on Ancient Mortuary Symbolism* (1859), which acted as an overture to *Mother Right,* featured an analysis of "The Three Mystery Eggs" found in an Etruscan tomb. Here, as if intuiting modern embryology's refutation of the Aristotelian reproductive model, the future theorist of matriarchy noted that "in religion the egg is a symbol of the material source of all things . . . which brings forth all life from out of itself," adding that "the phallic god, striving toward the fertilization of matter, is not the original datum: rather, he himself springs from the darkness of the maternal womb" and merely "stands as a son to feminine matter." Similarly, and as if to reinforce the revisionary biomythology implicit in this first of Bachofen's interpretive hypotheses, Harrison concluded her *Prolegomena* with a study of the crucial importance of "one characteristic Orphic element, the cosmic egg." Thus, in the very years when Gerard Manley Hopkins, celebrating the "male" creative "gift," defined failed poems as analogous to "hens' eggs that are good to eat and look just like live ones but never hatch," both mother and egg, womb and womb fruit, were being radically redefined and reempowered. Inevitably, such a drastic reversal of traditional assumptions about the origin and history of physical creativity would seem to have necessitated drastic reversals in just the sorts of metaphors for aesthetic creativity that Hopkins was elaborating.[12]

To be sure, as Terry Castle has shown in "Birth *Topoi* and English Poetics, 1660–1820," a trope of literary maternity had long complemented and supplemented the patriarchal trope of literary paternity.[13] Paradoxically, however, Castle's study illuminates one constant, one term of the childbirth metaphor that did not and could not change until the mid-nineteenth century: its underlying assumption that, whether for better or worse, the literal or literary "mother" of a child is merely an inert vessel. But what happened to this view when biology and anthropology conspired to suggest that the energetic darkness of the mother, rather than the apparently commanding lucidity of the father, might be both primordial and primordially authoritative? What happened when it became clear that neither womb nor egg are passive but that instead they, and their bearer, might manifest an ontologically "wise" activity? I would argue that by the end of the century most male artists had begun to approach the childbirth metaphor with a new wariness; furthermore, that in many of these artists and thinkers—and perhaps most clearly in Lawrence—we see a defensive movement toward devaluation of the female expressed not for the most part (like the eighteenth-century satirists' revulsion against witless pregnancy) through an articulation of the physical horror of maternity but rather through a more generalized expression of dread; and that, paradoxically, we see at the same time an acknowledgment of the male subject's dependence on female, and specifically maternal, power.

Not insignificantly, it is among male anthropological and psychoanalytic theorists of maternity that we can first trace such equivocal manifestations of dependency and dread. Bachofen himself, after all, even while excavating and acclaiming the civilizing virtues and primordial authority of "Mother Right," anxiously insisted that this "lunar" stage in human social evolution had necessarily to be replaced by the more spiritual "solar" stage of "Father Right." Similarly, Neumann, following Jung and Briffault, located the "origin and history of consciousness" in the solar hero's separation from, and attack upon, the engulfing darkness of the Great Mother. At the same time, from a different intellectual perspective, but with apparently equal anxiety, Freud, committed archaeologist though he was, managed to construct ontogenetic theories of sexuality that until quite late avoided any recognition of a "Minoan/Mycenaean" matriarchal stage in either culture or the individual while defining the vagina in neo-Aristotelian terms as "nonexistent"—an absence or blank—for much of the young girl's life and as, later, no more than a passive home, refuge, or "asylum" for the aggressively generative activity of the penis.[14]

Small wonder, given such theoretical contexts, that the texts of male artists dramatically reproduced the reactions of men like Bachofen, Neumann, and Freud to contemporary discoveries about female reproductive authority. From Henry Adams' nervous assertion that "the proper study of mankind is woman"—the "virgin" who represents "creative energy, the life force"—to Robert Graves' book-length meditation on the often frightening priorities of *The White Goddess* and Philip Wylie's fascinated catalog of the improprieties of "mom-ism," English and American men of letters simultaneously revised, resisted, and rejected theories about female (pro)creativity that put them, as engendered males, in surprising positions. Conceding, with Lawrence, that "we are in for the monstrous rule of women, and a matriarchy," such thinkers often tried to persuade themselves, again with Lawrence, that "Courage! Perhaps a matriarchy isn't so bad after all." But they knew that their situation was radically new, if not "bad." Certainly, for male modernists Bachofen's concept of the Great Mother and her "cosmic egg" implies that the very pages on which supposedly patriarchal authorities inscribe the texts of royal desire, like the vessels presumably possessed by lords like Griselda's Walter, are not only autonomously powerful; they may be text(iles) created by a spinning sisterhood of women, for, as Bachofen observes, in the earliest religions "the spinning and weaving of the great nature mothers . . . represents the creative, formative power of nature." But just as women spin the textiles that clothe and enclose men while creating the bodies men wear, so too they may conceive and give birth to the texts men read. In that case, however, no woman is ever metaphorically a blank or virgin page. On the contrary, every woman is always potentially both the author of the page and of the page's male reader/critic. She is primary; he is secondary; she makes the plot; he enacts it; she delivers both texture and text, he interprets it. In fact, many a modernist male uneasily decided that, as Lawrence put it, "All this talk of young girls and virginity, like a blank white page on which nothing is written, is pure nonsense."[15]

As I have already observed, Lawrence is the archetype of the male

modernist I have been describing here, a literary theorist and metaph-
orist who implicitly believes in the Great Mother's power even while he
explicitly dreads and rejects it. Famously misogynistic and, in rhetoric,
fiercely, almost fascistically patriarchal, he is nevertheless the author of
books whose very titles—*Sons and Lovers, Women in Love, Lady Chatterley's Lover*—are haunted by female primacy, by the autonomous sexual energy of the goddess. "All women are giantesses in their natures," he
once remarked, and though he attacked the role reversals of "cocksure
women and hensure men," serious readers of his fiction and poetry must
also inevitably conclude that, as one male Lawrence scholar recently
quipped, "For Lawrence man is always the second sex." Indeed, it is possible to speculate, as Anne Smith has, that "Lawrence's God was Woman,
Woman, moreover, as Magna Mater."[16]

No doubt a number of personal and historical factors contributed
to such a position, factors quite distinct from the transformations in
biomythology brought about by the researches of nineteenth-century
anthropologists and embryologists. Lawrence's own psychosexual
development was, after all—as everyone knows but no one more clearly
than he—marked and perhaps marred by the long enthrallment to his
mother that made him for many years an "Oedipus in Nottingham."
In addition, he was exceptionally conscious that he was living in an
age of unprecedented feminist emancipation. As he put it, "Perhaps the
greatest revolution of modern times is the emancipation of women; and
perhaps the deepest fight for two thousand years and more has been
the fight for woman's independence or freedom, call it what you will.
The fight was deeply bitter, and, it seems to me, it is won." Yet Lawrence's keen awareness of these two points might have been very differently articulated had it not been shaped and shadowed by an equally
keen grasp of the implications of woman's newly defined (pro)creative
potency.[17]

As Martin Green has brilliantly demonstrated, the young poet-
novelist was quite early and quite specifically influenced by the thinking of the circle of German intellectuals who called themselves "Die
Kosmiche Runde" when he eloped with Frieda Weekley-Richthofen,
whose sometime lover Otto Gross was a member of the group. "The

Cosmic Circle," notes Green, "stood for life-values, for eroticism, for the value of myth and primitive cultures [and] for the primacy of the female mode of being. The major outside impulse to the development of their ideas came from the Swiss scholar, J. J. Bachofen." In fact, Green argues, "It is surely undeniable that Lawrence was working in the same direction and the same mode of thought as Bachofen," for though the English writer may never have read *Mother Right*, "Frieda's incarnation and enactment of the matriarchal idea" would have been powerfully significant to him. In any case, however, as I have tried to show, the vision of woman as potentially a "giantess" was both new and crucial, so much so that even without the filtering through of specific concepts from the *kosmiche Runde* Lawrence would have been as struck as many other modernists were by a transformed sense of the implications of female sexuality. Thus, in combination with his sense of female domination in both private and public history, it was this vision of woman's primacy that finally determined the nature of the biomyths he himself can be said to have made in response to (and in defense against) all these factors. For as Bruce Clarke observes in a fine meditation on the way in which "Lawrence's sexual affiliations are exquisitely conflicted," this phallic philosopher's "word-demon is a male grasped by a female principle, a logos spermatikos both possessed and empowered by the womb."[18]

Exploring the "female principle" not long after experiencing the unmanning trauma of World War I, Lawrence wrote a novella that perfectly illustrates the sexual paradoxes he also recorded in many other stories, poems, and essays. "The Ladybird" was first published in 1923 in a volume that included as well "The Fox" and "The Captain's Doll," two more novellas about the relationship between female power and male anxiety or anger. Set in war-torn London around 1918, it is the tale of a mystical and mysterious encounter between a small, dark, "elfish" German prisoner of war named Count Johann Dionys Psanek and a tall blond English beauty named Lady Daphne Apsley. Because she is Daphne and he is Dionys, because she is flower-like and pale, while he is dark and lordly with a "devil" of rebellion in his blood, the tale has frequently been read as yet another of Lawrence's "leadership" fictions, and in this light (or darkness) as yet another Lawrencian re-vision of the ancient myth of the marriage of Pluto and Persephone, a romance with which the author of *The Plumed Serpent* had long been obsessed. And certainly the Pluto-Persephone marriage of darkness, with its mystification of phallic power, is an important motif in "The Ladybird." What is just as important, however, is an exposition of female power, power that is shown as essential for and prior to the Plutonic myth of male energy. In fact, in "The Ladybird" Lawrence clearly, if not consciously, suggests that female power creates male energy.

The story itself can be easily summarized. Daphne's mother, Lady Beveridge, has lost her two sons and her brother in the war, but like a philanthropic "Mater Dolorosa," she persists in visiting a prison-hospital where the "enemy sick and wounded" are incarcerated. There she encounters Count Johann Dionys Psanek, whom she had known before the war, and there she soon brings her daughter, of whom Dionys had once been fond: for Daphne's seventeenth birthday, in fact, Dionys had given the girl a thimble decorated with the Psanek crest, "a gold snake at the bottom, and a Mary-beetle of green stone at the top."[19] Now, however, the imprisoned aristocrat appears to have been fatally wounded, and Daphne herself is ill, her husband Basil "missing in the East," her baby "born dead," and her "two darling brothers dead." Nevertheless, she begins regularly to visit Dionys and, as she does, both slowly recover their strength. Daphne, in particular, who has from the first seemed "looming" by comparison with the delicately formed count, takes on healing power, so that Dionys begs her to "let me wrap your hair round my hands like a bandage," explaining that "I feel I have lost my manhood for the time being." Finally, reminding her of the gift he had given her when she was a girl, he asks her to sew him some shirts, using the Psanek thimble. After some difficulty, she does this and then sews some shirts for her wounded husband Basil, who has now been found and released through a prisoner exchange.

A handsome Englishman, Basil is "the true Dionysos," thinks Daphne, "full of sap, milk and honey, and northern golden wine." When he returns from the war, scarred and strange, she devotes herself to him, though she is somewhat frightened by his worshipful passion. Eventually, however, she takes him to see Count Dionys, and, oddly enough, the two become friends, although, even more oddly, their relationship only prospers when Daphne is in their presence "to complete the circuit." After the armistice of 1918, Dionys is freed, and Basil invites him to visit Thoresway, the ancestral home of Daphne's family. There Daphne hears him crooning ancient songs in his room at night and, drawn irresistibly to "the thin thread of his singing," she goes to him in the dark and they consummate their mystic marriage. At the tale's end, he leaves to return to his homeland but promises her that he will await her in the kingdom of death, for though she is still by day the wife of Basil Apsley, she has become "the night-wife of the ladybird."

Obviously, with what F. R. Leavis calls its tone of "solemn poetic—even prophetic—elevation,"[20] this consciously legendary and carefully symbolic story intends to convey a number of messages. Thus, the shadowy coupling of Daphne and Dionys suggests the mystic marriage of Pluto and Persephone, while the tense friendship of Basil and Dionys functions as a neo-Nietzschean comment on the Apollonian and Dionysian modes of being that the two men incarnate. Glowing and golden, polyandrous Daphne's day-husband is a lucid young man whose way of thinking is purely Apollonian—rational, spiritual, transcendent—so that her temporary identification of him with Dionysos seems ironically mistaken. His name, Basil, means royal or kingly—again, Apollonian—but also associates him with both the medicinal herbs of Apollo and the pot of basil in which Keats' Isabella kept the severed (that is, the disembodied) head of her lover. Conversely, and not surprisingly, if Basil is Apollonian, Dionys is Dionysian. His full name, Johann Dionys Psanek, is one to which he is so intensely attached that the humiliation of defeat causes him to want to change it, and indeed, each part of the name reinforces its almost liturgical significance. "Johann," or "John," for example, recalls both the John who prophesied in the wilderness and the John who envisioned the Bible's Apocalypse. But the Count's other two names tell us that this John is not a prophet of the Law of the Father but of the transformative Rule of the Mother. For "Dionys" does not just recall but literally signifies the darkly demonic fertility god of *The Bacchae,* and "Psanek" means "outlaw" (as Lawrence pointedly tells us), intensifying the air of Dionysian lawlessness and irrational sensual/Satanic energy that clings to this small, "aboriginal"-seeming and somewhat animal-like Middle European aristocrat.

Our sense of Dionys's hellish, anti-Apollonian power is also enhanced by a number of passages that link him with Dracula, the demonic vampire who had long been a Dionysian/Gothic fixture not just in Bram Stoker's novel but also in countless theaters by the time Lawrence wrote "The Ladybird." For instance, besides coming, like Dracula, from "one of those curious . . . aboriginal races of Central Europe," Dionys has "something ages old in his face" and confesses that "I would not mind if they buried me alive, if it were very deep, and dark, and the earth heavy above." Several times, moreover, we are told, as we are about Dracula, that Dionys has "strong white teeth that [seem] a little too large, rather dreadful." And like Count Dracula (whose name is significantly similar to his), Count Dionys belongs by inheritance to a secret society, a night cult that believes "we've got the world inside out. The true living world of fire is dark, throbbing, darker than blood. Our luminous world that we go by is only the reverse of this." Finally, indeed, like both the classical Dionysos and the Victorian Dracula, Count Dionys is a votary of the mysteries of the blood, a prince or priest of what Lawrence was eventually to call "blood-knowledge, the great dark knowledge you can't have in your head."[21]

But as Dionysos' female followers knew, as Frazer, Harrison, and others noted, as the story of Dracula's arrival in England on a ship called the *Demeter* suggests, and as—in spite of his overt phallocentrism—Lawrence shows in "The Ladybird," the mysteries of the blood are female mysteries: they are the rites of female creativity. (In fact, as intellectual categories even the Nietzschean concepts of "Apollonian" and "Dionysian" modes of being are notions borrowed from Bachofen's analysis of "Mother Right.")[22] Thus, behind the screen of masculinist rhetoric with which Lawrence surrounds handsome, Apollonian Basil and pharaoh-dark Dionysian Dionys, "The Ladybird" is a tale of female power, a story of how tall, moon-pale, flowering Daphne sews both her war-torn husbands together using a thimble whose crest of snake and ladybird symbolizes the archaic transformative energy of the Great Mother.

From the first, Daphne is associated with a strong maternal line. She has lost her two brothers and her uncle, and she frequently appears alone in the company of her "Mater Dolorosa," whose husband, a gloomy and feckless earl, is always "standing aside, in the shadow." Quite early in the story, too, Lawrence describes "the curious distraught slant of her eyes [that] told of a wild energy dammed up inside her"—the furious energy, we soon infer, of a Maenad, a participant in female mysteries whose powers have been denied outlet in a war-torn, Apollonian/patriarchal society. Later, moreover, Basil calls her—besides Venus, Aphrodite, and Proserpine—Astarte, Cybele, and Isis, a "long, limber Isis with sacred hands." Though there is some indication that Lawrence is trying to undermine Basil by sardonically suggesting that he is a mere woman worshiper, we must ultimately—as Lawrence himself once remarked—trust the tale, not the teller. And this tale tells us that Daphne *is* a kind of Isis, a mother-goddess who, having lost her own child, re-creates him in the shape of small, perfectly formed Count Dionys, the demonic scion of the womb of night.

"I have lost my soul, and I can't stop talking to you," cries Dionys to Daphne on one of the occasions when she comes to the hospital to "put" him in the sun. Imprisoned first in her country and later in her ancestral home, he is continually at her mercy throughout the tale. In fact, though he tells Daphne that she almost looks as though "the Evil One" had cast a spell on her, he himself, in his imprisoned passivity, seems like the one on whom a spell has been cast, the one who is inescapably at Daphne's womanly mercy. But most of all he is at her mercy in his need for her to perform the central ritual of sewing by which, and only by which, he is ultimately to be re-created.

"Sew me a shirt that I can wear," he begs Daphne, explaining that "I am a prisoner in other people's clothes, and I have nothing of my own." His urgent, almost prayerful request implies that in "losing his shirt" he has somehow lost both his essential body and his essential identity, his shape and his name. Like Osiris, another ruler of the dark underworld kingdom of whom he is also an avatar, he has been unmanned and fragmented by his enemy; like John the Baptist, as well as Keats' "basil," he has been figuratively speaking decapitated or castrated, and he can only be restored through the creative activity of this moon-luminous woman who is not just Basil's but his own "long limber Isis." She it is who must sew together the scattered pieces, she who must re-create the lost bruised phallus that exists—so the myth implies even if Lawrence refuses to admit it—for her, rather than she for it. For if, like Osiris' Greek parallels Orpheus and Dionysos, or like the prophet who was Salome's victim, Dionys might once have been rended by women (by, for instance, the indifferent wife who left him during the war), he can also only be mended by women. Indeed, Dionys' descriptions of his family make his heritage sound quite as matrilineal and matriarchal as Daphne's, since the chief Psanek (or "outlaw") tradition he mentions is the one in which "my mother sewed for me. And after her, my mother's sister, *who was the head of my house*" (emphasis added). No father is mentioned, no brothers, no uncles. Only the mother and the matrilineal aunt, a spinning sisterhood who worked with the *lady*bird, or "Marien-beetle," at their fingers and embroidered that symbol onto the Diony-sian young man's shirts.

Interestingly, Dionys describes himself as going like a bride to his marriage with a sort of dowry of sixty shirts, provided by his mother and his aunt. Thus when tall Daphne finally mates with this dark doll of a prisoner, it seems natural to think of him as *her* consort, a son/lover whom she has first birthed and then wed in the tradition of the Great Mother that speculative anthropologists from Bachofen to Neumann describe so well. In this connection, it is significant that Frazer (whose *Golden Bough* might have been one of Lawrence's sources for information about Dionysos) recounts a version of the Dionysos story in which Persephone is the god's *mother*, and another version of the story in which "Demeter, his mother, pieced together his mangled limbs and made him young again." Similarly, Harrison (whose *Prolegomena* might have been another of Lawrence's sources) observes that "an important feature of Dionysiac religion was the rending and death of the god" and notes also that "there was some sort of resurrection of the god, a new birth as a little child," for despite the patriarchal revisionism that was later to describe the infant vine god as reborn from Zeus' thigh, "it is at once a cardinal point and a primary note in the mythology of Dionysos that he is the son of his mother." Taken together, all of these allusions and images suggest that Daphne is not Persephone as daughter but Persephone/Demeter/Isis as mother: she is the mother goddess, Dionys is the priest of maternal darkness; she is the Great Mother, Dionys the diabolical/Dionysian child whom the divine woman in her "indomitable" calm sometimes chooses as consort.[23]

Finally, in fact, this English Isis is not only a revisionary Daphne but also, just as importantly, a version of Ariadne, the bride of Dionysos who spins and guards the sacred thread, the clue to the passage of blood that is the labyrinth of birth and death. Only, as Lawrence characterizes her, despite (or perhaps because of) his anxiety about the mother goddess, this Ariadne does not merely rescue the Apollonian Theseus (to whom Basil bears some likeness); she also rescues Dionysos, rather than being rescued by him. Thus, in their helpless dependence on her maternal stitchery, both the dark husband and the light husband, the ruler of the day and the night king, are brothers under the skin. Without her, neither has power. With her to "close the circuit" of their brotherhood, they are energetic companions. For like Demeter—about whom Harrison reminds us that "the Mother herself keeps ward in the metropolis of the dead" and therefore "the Athenians of old called the dead 'Demeter's people' "—Daphne rules both realms and enables her consorts to see that, in the creative embrace of the mother, death and eternity might well become, as Basil says, "the same thing."[24]

What reinforces this argument about Daphne's creative authority is the fact that, besides the Greek myths that obviously play so important a part in any consciously literary tale about people named Daphne and Dionys, another story lies behind or within the plot of "The Ladybird." Appropriately enough for a novella about a German prisoner of war, it is a Grimm German fairy tale entitled "The Six Swans." And unlike many of the better-known Grimm stories, which are so often about helpless maidens such as "Snow White" and "Sleeping Beauty," this one is a story about female power. Specifically, and centrally, it is about the power of a princess whose six brothers have been transformed into swans by a wicked stepmother and who alone has the ability to redeem their humanity by sewing them "six little shirts of starwort,"[25] which will change them back into princes, a task that, after many trials, she accomplishes. But "The Six Swans" is also about other manifestations of female power. Fearing the animosity of his new queen, for instance, the children's royal father has hidden them away so deep in the forest that he himself can only find them with the aid of a magic ball of yarn given him by a wise woman— an emblem of female knowledge that recalls Ariadne's power over the labyrinth. In addition, the malevolent queen who is the story's villainess manages the first metamorphosis of the young princess by herself sewing magic shirts that turn them *into* swans—a point suggesting that the bodies of the boys have become passive artifacts in a duel between two spinning seamstresses, a good fate and an evil fate.

Finally, then, this resonant German folktale is in some sense an extended meditation on what Bachofen called "the spinning and weaving of the great nature mothers," on the "thread" of life over which the female has ultimate control, and on the primordial authority of the maternal seamstress, from whom, in the view of early religion, all creatures "have the subtle web of their body, which she fashioned with unparalleled mastery in the dark womb of matter."[26] In particular, the central symbolic act of sewing, performed by the swans' sister, is here, as Daphne's sewing is in "The Ladybird," the ultimate sign of female creativity. Like Isis putting her brother/lover Osiris back together again, like Demeter reconstructing her son Dionysos, the swans' sister does for her brothers what all the *king's* horses and all the king's *men* could not do for that sad egg Humpty Dumpty: she brings about a resurrection.

Significantly, moreover, the swans' sister's mode of re-creation is neither passive nor receptive, as woman's sexual/maternal power was traditionally thought to be. On the contrary, while her brothers are helpless in the grip of circumstances, the young seamstress seeks and seizes their salvation, using active transformative energies to make something new and magically alive—new shirts, new bodies—from apparently inert materials. Finally, too, it is significant that even those materials may not be quite as inert as they seem, that they are both biologically alive and uniquely hers. In fact, it seems like still another emblem of maternity that this modest yet potent Griselda creates the boys' fleshly costumes of humanity not from ordinary cloth but from flowers that grow in a forest where women and women alone—she, the wise woman, her stepmother—hold sway.

To be sure, "The Six Swans" does define the swans' sister as a kind of "Griselda"—she must be silent while she sews, she is assaulted by a kind of wicked stepmother, and so on—and thus hedges her round with doubts and fears, anxieties and contradictions, but her power is nevertheless there, crucial, incontrovertible. And to Lawrence such power seemed equally crucial and incontrovertible, though he frequently tried to seal it off from consciousness or at least to fence it in with deceptively phallocentric rhetoric. Yet that Dionys must beg Daphne to sew his shirts using a thimble crested with a ladybird and a snake, an emblem of the goddess together with the priapic creature that was traditionally her attendant, tells us that, at least in the part of his mind that thought in symbols, Lawrence knew whose power he was confronting in this story. Moreover, there is even some indication that, consciously or not, he may have been thinking not just of the myth of Dionysos but also of the fairy tale of "The Six Swans" when he imagined his confrontation of maternal creativity. For toward the end of "The Ladybird," Dionys calls Daphne to him—invokes her, as a priest would his deity—by singing a song about the king of the *swans,* whose bride had left him for a human but who "called her to come back, *or else he would die,*" and she is drawn by the "thin thread of *his* singing," a defensive displacement of the female fate symbol that nevertheless suggests he is about to give her another opportunity for re-creative sewing even while it also recalls both Ariadne's thread and the wise woman's ball of yarn in "The Six Swans." Finally, therefore, though the mythic transformations in Dionys' song are different from those in Grimm's story, the theme of the swan's redemption and restoration through the primacy of the ladybird of female potency is exactly the same in both the old fairy tale and the modern novella.

Haunted by female primacy, how did Lawrence establish his own personal and literary authority over the power of the woman upon whom he saw himself as, like all men, dependent for life and limb? To begin with, more than most modernists—perhaps because he had had so famously and for so long to struggle for emotional freedom from both the specter and the reality of his own mother—he frankly revealed his dependency on the creative energy of symbolic mothers such as Daphne Apsley. At the same time, however, he enacted his dread of female power and fought to liberate himself from its threat to his autonomy with special inventiveness and fervor. Thus, no doubt influenced by the real rise in female assertiveness that accompanied the birth of the feminist movement and the entrance of women into the professions, as well as by the work of mythographers like Bachofen, Frazer, and Harrison, he conceded in his late essay on "Matriarchy" that "we are drifting into" a state of "Mother-rule": "No good trying to stem the tide. Woman is in flood."

Yet even while he affirmed that "it is nothing but just" if women "form themselves into a great clan, for the preservation of themselves and their children," Lawrence also proposed a kind of masculinist separatism brought about through the revitalization of the primitive institution of the men's house, arguing that men need "a new foregathering ground, where they can meet and satisfy . . . deep social needs . . . which can only be satisfied *apart from women*" (emphasis added). The polarities articulated here—on the one hand, a reluctant acquiescence in female authority, on the other hand, a resistant attempt at independence of female authority—were paradigmatic throughout his literary career. For, with Goethe's Faust, Lawrence early knew that the time had come for him, as for most of his contemporaries, to encounter "The Mothers" and their meaning: "The unacceded, / The inaccessible . . . , the never-pleaded" fact of female creative energy. But, also with Faust, he might have almost involuntarily exclaimed, "The Mothers! Still it strikes a note of fear. / What is this word that I am loathe to hear?"[27]

From *Sons and Lovers* through *Women in Love* and *Lady Chatterley's Lover*, therefore, Lawrence enacted a profound ambivalence toward both real mothers and Great Mothers. The Paul Morel who devoutly promises his mother that "I'll never marry while I've got you" is paradoxically identical, after all, with the Paul Morel who achieves his (and her) "release" from the matriarchal bonds of their love by feeding her a "bitter" draught of poisoned milk. Similarly, the Lawrence who, in a curious inversion of Hopkins' vision of infertile "hens' eggs," wrote to Gordon Campbell in 1914 that "there is no getting of a vision before we get ourselves *fertilized by the female*" (emphasis added) is the same novelist who was, a year later, to create the dramatic scene in which Rupert Birkin, his surrogate self in *Women in Love,* passionately stones the reflection of the moon in Willey Water, muttering "Cybele—curse her! The accursed Syria Dea!"[28]

But it is in later, more overtly allegorical or mythic works that Lawrence's anxieties achieve both their fullest expression and their most imaginative resolution. In "The Captain's Doll," for instance, a novella that appeared in the same volume with "The Ladybird," he told in different terms and with a different emphasis another story about the "shock and fear" that the very name of "the Mothers" inspired in so many modernists. In this tale, however, female creative power is more bitterly described, and it is definitively defeated. The doll of the story, for instance, is not a soldier's girlfriend, as the title may suggest. Rather, it is a playful miniature effigy that Hannele—Countess Johanna zu Rassentlow, an aristocratic German dollmaker—has made of Alexander Hepburn, a Scottish officer with whom she is in love. Hepburn is married to a domineering but genteel little woman very much like Mrs. Morel in *Sons and Lovers* or Lawrence's own mother. When this woman discovers the doll in the countess's shop, she tries to buy it. Thus the love triangle in which the two women are engaged in a struggle for possession of the captain soon becomes also a triangle in which these sinister "mothers" battle for the doll to which they have reduced him.

By the end of the story, however, Hepburn's wife is dead ("fallen" from a third-story window under suspicious circumstances) and Hannele has lost the doll. In a ritual climb up a very female-sounding glacier not unlike the Swiss "Mer [*Mère*] de Glace," Hepburn triumphs over the "gills" and clefts, the "immense depths" and crevices in the "huge body of the soft-fleshed ice," the body, so it seems, of the "Terrible Mother." And informing the repentant Hannele that he now wants "a sort of *patient Griselda* [emphasis added], I want to be honoured and obeyed. I don't want love," he exacts her promise that she will go with him to Africa. There he is, significantly enough, planning to "do a book on the moon" that will no doubt be a scientific attempt to murder the mother goddess by dissecting her.[29]

Rather differently, but with a similar intent, two poems from Lawrence's great middle-period collection, *Birds, Beasts and Flowers,* deal specifically but defensively with the Eleusinian mysteries and with "the female mystery" of the "ripe womb." In the first, "Purple Anemones," the flowers of "Sicily, on the meadows of Enna," are characterized variously as "hell-hounds" or "little hells of colour" that have "risen in pursuit" of the "husband-snared hell-queen," Persephone, who is trying in vain to return to her mother. Revising Eleusis to update it, the poet describes "Madame Ceres" and her daughter as "two enfranchised women" and warns them that "the enemy is upon you." Clearly, despite the concessions he was later to make in his essay on "Matriarchy," he has not the slightest sympathy here for "poor Persephone and her rights for women." At the same time, however, he is almost feverishly aware how vigorous a defense he himself, and the male "husband-blossoms" he makes into his agents, must conduct against the "Mother Right" these two goddesses represent. *"At 'em, boys, at 'em! . . . Smell 'em, smell 'em out!"* he snarls, his words italicized as if to emphasize the strenuousness that must mark the male hunt for patriarchal authority in a possibly matriarchal new age.[30]

Again, with the same fervor but with an even deeper acquiescence in the transformative "secret" implicit in the "inward" flowering of the "ripe womb," he writes in "Figs" of that fruit's "symbolic" power, its "covert nakedness, / where," as if in an illustration of the discoveries of nineteenth-century embryologists, "everything happens invisible, flowering and fertilisation and fruiting." Yet here, too, he has to defend himself against the secret, sacred power of the "female mystery," and he does so by predicting the inexorable corruption implicit in that mystery. When the fig is "over-ripe," "she" bursts "to give up [her] ghost," and becomes a kind of "prostitute . . . , making a show of her secret." Worse still, like that emblematically female fruit, modern women, with their demands for matriarchal power, have "fallen over-ripe" and "bursten into self-assertion." But, insists Lawrence, "ripe figs won't keep," so by analogy, assertive women, like their matriarchal foremothers, are doomed to a rottenness in which their rule will inevitably be superseded by the less fleshly, more transcendent state that Bachofen called "Father Right" and that Jacques Lacan has more recently called "the Law of the Father."[31]

Finally, however, Lawrence could not remain content with purely polemical defenses like those he mounted in "Figs" and "Purple Anemones" and, to a lesser extent, in "The Captain's Doll," for given the aesthetic honesty that characterized so much of his writing, his sense of the primacy of female power was too haunted and haunting to allow him to escape for long into rhetorical rationalization. Thus, in the complex of late works constituted by *The Escaped Cock, Lady Chatterley's Lover,* and *Etruscan Places,* he affirms matriarchal authority more humbly than ever before while definitively creating the only theology he can imagine to oppose it: the religion of the phallus. "The goddess is great," concedes the risen "Jesus" of *The Escaped Cock* on his first encounter with the priestess of Isis who will resurrect his fallen manhood, and later "Great is Isis!" he exclaims. "In her search she is greater than death . . . All men praise thee, Isis, thou greater than the mother unto man." Yet this story, which celebrates "the mysterious fire of a potent woman" and the "fulness of the woman . . . , the soft white rock of life" was also, according to Earl Brewster, called *The* Escaped *Cock* (emphasis added) because it was inspired by "a little shop, in the window of which was a toy white rooster *escaping* from an egg" (emphasis added). For Lawrence, obviously, that "toy" cock became a triumphant phallus that, anxiously asserting (with "the man who died") that "I am risen," he set against what he really believed to be the primal power of the womb.[32]

Indeed, it might even be said that, for Lawrence, the phallus almost always functions as a kind of substitute baby, in an ironic reversal of Freud's dictum that for women the baby functions as a kind of substitute phallus. Miniature but autonomous, it is "his" mysterious product even while it has its own separate life, its own separate and nameable identity ("John Thomas"). As "Jesus" punningly cries "I am risen" in *The Escaped Cock,* he feels, just as punningly, "his own sun [son] daw[n], and sen[d] its fire running along his limbs." Similarly, in *Lady Chatterley's Lover,* where the paralyzed Clifford Chatterley has been definitively immobilized by the seductions of the Magna Mater in the person of Ivy Bolton, the sexually victorious Mellors croons to his John Thomas as a woman might to her child. "Ay, ma lad," he murmurs, "tha'rt theer, right enough. Yi, tha mun rear thy head! Theer on thy own, eh? an 'ta'es count o' nob'dy?" reminding his baby/phallus of "his" origins ("tha's dipped me in again") even as he nurses "his" individuality ("Art boss of me?").[33] At the end of that novel, moreover, when Connie is left, like the priestess of Isis in *The Escaped Cock,* satisfyingly pregnant, the book's hero can do no more than ask her to meet him at an allegorical tavern hopefully called "The Golden Cock in Adam Street."

Finally, in *Etruscan Places,* viewing and reviewing the very tombs that had inspired Bachofen's ideas about "The Three Mystery Eggs" less than a century earlier, Lawrence perfunctorily acknowledged the powers of the womb ("the ark of the covenant, in which lies the mystery of eternal life"), the egg ("the egg of resurrection, within which the germ sleeps as the soul sleeps in the tomb") and the egg-like *"patera* or *mundum"* ("the plasm . . . of the living cell, with its nucleus, which is the indivisible God of the beginning and . . . which yet divides and subdivides") but devoted his closest attention to the phallus, which he saw as both born from and standing against these female symbols. Unlike Bachofen—almost, in fact, as if responding to Bachofen—he declared that "the thing that impresses one in the very first five minutes . . . in an Etruscan necropolis [is] the phallic symbol," and as he journeyed deeper into the tombs, he saw that symbol manifested in divine creatures like the dolphin ("carrying the fiery spark of procreation down into the wet darkness of the womb") and the "hot, soft, alert duck" ("symbol of a man's own phallus and phallic life") as well as, more grandiosely, in the Etruscan kings "who are gods by vividness, because they have gathered into themselves core after core of vital potency from the universe" and the Etruscan institution of the "*Lucumo* . . . , sitting very noble in his chariot driven by an *erect* chario-teer" (emphasis added), the Lucumo who was "divine . . . within another world of power." That last phrase, indeed, is a crucial one, for Lawrence ultimately and rather desperately opposed to the authoritative "Lady-bird" of female creativity "another world of power" whose source was fictive and whose trappings were elaborately fictionalized. In that ges-ture, conceding the primacy of the "second sex" and the secondariness of the "first sex," the authority of the female and the otherness of the male, he formulated a defense against the Great Mother that male modernists from Yeats and Joyce to Eliot and Stevens also attempted to raise.[34]

Certainly Yeats, despite (or perhaps because of) his years of ambivalent devotion to the powerful Maud Gonne, raised such defenses even while making similar concessions. Throughout his middle and late career, of course, he consistently drew upon the metaphysical "system" of *A Vision*, which, as if anticipating the Celtic matriarchalism of Graves' *The White Goddess*, he had based upon the "phases of the moon." But particularly in a late poem called "The Crazed Moon," he analyzed the specifically maternal primacy of *his* white goddess, describing the contrast between a rotting matriarchal age (like the world of Lawrence's "Figs") in which "Crazed through much child-bearing / The moon is staggering in the sky" so that her male as well as female subjects are "moon-struck by the despairing glances of her wandering eye," and by the days of the moon/woman's primordial authority, when "in all her virginal pride" she "trod on the mountain's head" and "every foot obeyed her glance!" Again, in "To Dorothy Wellesley," a poem from almost the same period, Yeats assured a woman writer whose work he much admired that she should await a visit from (in a phrase echoing the re-visionary evaluations of the *Oresteia* formulated by Jane Harrison) "that great family / Some ancient famous authors misrepresent, / The Proud Furies, each with her torch on high."[35]

At the same time, however, Yeats was as ambivalent as Lawrence about the resurrection of the Furies. If his Cuchulain was at one point redeemed by the matriarchal energies of his motherly wife Emer, that hero was also destroyed by the insidious intentions of Terrible Mothers like the warrior Queen Aoife and the crow-headed death goddess, the Morrigu. Furthermore, for his own daughter Yeats famously wished nothing more than that she should become a "flourishing *hidden* tree" (emphasis added), a beautiful but modest Daphne without the primally regenerative creativity of "The Ladybird's" Daphne Apsley. Imagining moments of annunciation and impregnation, moreover, he wishfully transformed virgin mothers into the inert vessels for male authority ("Did she put on his knowledge with his power / Before the indifferent beak could let her drop?") that Apollo had claimed they were in the *Oresteia*, so that not egg but phallus engenders the sexually burning towers and broken walls of history. Finally, and perhaps at his most defensive, he assumed the creative authority of maternity into an ostensibly androgynous but essentially male divinity, celebrating in "Supernatural Songs" the "He"/God who "holds him from desire, all but stops his breathing lest / Primordial Motherhood forsake his limbs."[36]

That last maneuver—the imagining of a sacred male motherhood—is one Lawrence apparently never thought of, but it was an obvious resort for Yeats, who, despite his sense of Leda's dumb passivity, always brooded on the question of the virgin mother's power, wondering in "Supernatural Songs" "What sacred drama through her body heaved / When world-transforming Charlemagne was conceived?" For his countryman James Joyce, moreover, such a maneuver was almost a first resort. The very Stephen Dedalus who asserts in *Ulysses* that "*Amor Matris . . .* may be the only true thing in life" is, after all, merely an older version of the Stephen Dedalus who, at the end of *A Portrait of the Artist as a Young Man,* gives birth to a villanelle conceived in "the virgin womb of the imagination" as if to propose a specifically modernist re-vision of the old trope of literary maternity. As Joyce's surrogate self, moreover, he is also simply another version of the Richard Rowan who, in a canceled passage from *Exiles,* gives birth to his wife and "character" Bertha, and he is an alter ego, too, of the "new womanly man" Leopold Bloom, who, comically exclaiming "O I so want to be a mother," manages in "Nighttown" to bear "eight male yellow and white children . . . with valuable metallic faces" and then is burned as a witch. Finally, in the sense that such fantasies suggest a desire not only to have a womb but to be in a womb, they are associated with characters who share the desire for regeneration not just *as* but *in* the female body that the young James Joyce expressed in a 1909 letter to Nora Barnacle: "O that I could nestle in your womb like a child born of your flesh and blood, be fed by your blood, sleep in the warm secret gloom of your body!"[37]

As Richard Ellmann observes, such an ecstatic vision of a return to the warm stasis of the womb, where the growth of the "manchild" could be facilitated (but not threatened) by the mother's nurturing autonomy, foreshadows Joyce's later subtextual metaphor of Stephen Dedalus as "an embryo," with *A Portrait* being the account of "the gestation of a soul," and it also prefigures the author's description of Leopold Bloom, returned to Molly's bed, as "the childman weary, the manchild in the womb." At the same time, moreover, it predicts the obsession with embryology that seized the author of *Ulysses* as he labored on the "Oxen of the Sun" section of that novel. As Ellmann notes, and as the physician J. B. Lyons has extensively documented, Joyce intended this episode, set in the Dublin Lying-In Hospital, to suggest that human ontogeny recapitulates linguistic phylogeny by displaying a parallel between the evolution of English style and the development and birth of the "manchild" who is delivered from the prostrate body of one Mina Purefoy at the end of the chapter. Thus he took elaborate notes from a textbook of embryology in order to produce a "gestation chart," which he "kept before him" during the writing of the section; declared that "the art" of the episode was medicine, while its "organ" was the womb; and explained to Frank Budgen that "Bloom is the spermatozoon, the hospital the womb, the nurse the ovum, Stephen the embryo," adding, "How's that for high?" And certainly, in the intensity with which he pursued the conceit of linguistic evolution as embryological growth, Joyce would seem to have carried the trope of literary maternity to new "heights." Implicit in his heightening of that metaphor, moreover, would seem to have been the kind of profound "womb envy" that Robert Graves, in *Goodbye to All That*, attributes to the nameless Frenchman of whom Graves' mother reported that he "died of grief because he could never become a mother."[38]

Yet even while, like Lawrence, he expressed his dependence on the literary as well as the literal implications of woman's newly empowered biology, Joyce, again like Lawrence, defended himself vigorously against that biology. Unlike Lawrence, he did not set a phallus/baby against the woman's baby/phallus, but as if himself recapitulating the evolution Bachofen postulated for all human society, he did implicitly oppose a "higher" fiction of paternity to the "lower" factuality of maternity. "The progress from the maternal to the paternal conception of man forms the most important turning point in the history of the relations between the sexes," declared Bachofen in his introduction to *Mother Right*, adding:

> *Standing in no visible relation to the child [the father] can never, even in the marital relation, cast off a certain fictive character. Belonging*

to the offspring only through the mediation of the mother, he always appears as the remoter potency [and] discloses an immateriality over against which the . . . nourishing mother appears as matter [so that] the triumph of paternity brings with it the liberation of the spirit from the manifestations of nature.[39]

These words seem almost to gloss, and may well stand behind, the famous meditation on paternity as "a mystical estate, an apostolic succession . . . , a legal fiction" with which Stephen Dedalus introduces his theories about Shakespeare in the "Scylla and Charybdis" section of *Ulysses.* But the assumptions they embody also underlie almost all of Joyce's manifestations of "womb envy," for in every case this neo-Homeric Irishman subverts (as Homer himself might have) what would seem to have been his own inclination to celebrate the principles and powers of Mother Right.

The poem that is "made flesh" in the "virgin womb" of Stephen Dedalus' imagination is, after all, a banal and sentimental villanelle, a parody of some of Yeats' more mannered early works, written in praise of a neo-Swinburnian femme fatale. Soon after writing this pastiche, moreover, the artist-hero realizes he must leave both mother and motherland, and, escaping like Lawrence's cock from the egg of his former life, calls upon the proper deity—"old father, old artificer"—to "stand" him "in good stead." Similarly, the Bertha whom Richard Rowan conceives and bears in the womb of *his* imagination is a character whose contrived faithlessness attests to his own perversity, in particular his own perverse desire for emasculation. Again, Leopold Bloom's childbearing is almost immediately followed by his scornful juxtaposition of the phrases "Laughing witch!" and "The hand that rocks the cradle," and it is set in the context of a whorehouse ruled by a Circe who is a decidedly Homeric and horrifying temptress, though she might once have been a fertility goddess and her subject pigs might once, as Harrison shows, have been *pharmakoi,* sacred sacrificial animals. Finally, and perhaps most tellingly, Joyce's excursion into embryology in the "Oxen of the Sun" issued in what was perhaps his most powerful defense against female power, for in his schema of literary childbirth—"Bloom . . . the spermatozoon, the hospital the womb, the nurse the ovum, Stephen the embryo"—there was, paradoxically enough, no room whatsoever for Mina Purefoy, the laboring mother, whose son, English literary history, emerges to cheers of "Hoopsa Boyaboy Hoopsa" into the "All-father's air" (and as the Allfather's heir) with the Carlylean comment that his only begetter, Theodore Purefoy, is "the remarkablest progenitor barring none in this chaffering allincluding most farraginous chronicle."

These virtually simultaneous assertions of dependency and dread exhibited by male modernists like Lawrence, Yeats, and Joyce could easily be traced in the works of many of their contemporaries. Certainly T. S. Eliot revealed a characteristic ambivalence toward the metaphor of literary maternity, and toward the Great Mother whose newly defined potency informed that metaphor, when he replied to Conrad Aiken's praise of his 1920 *Poems* with a page torn from *The Midwives' Gazette* on which were underlined the words "blood, mucus, discharge, purulent offensive discharge,"[40] and certainly he expressed the same ambivalence when he rewrote the *Oresteia* in *The Family Reunion* to force his Harry, Lord Monchensey, to be haunted by the horror of the matriarchal Furies even while, in the same years, he struggled in "Ash Wednesday" to free himself from the sensual seductions of the mother goddess's "brown hair across the mouth blown" and to find a transcendent Mother's "Garden / Where all Love *ends*" (emphasis added). Similarly, Eliot's American antagonist William Carlos Williams seems to have had to cope with an equally fierce ambivalence toward female sexual potency. As a practicing physician, after all, he knew as much as any man could about the deliveries and deliverances of birthing women, yet his "Paterson," like Blake's "Albion," is a male spirit of place created in the image of a Father God-like giant.

But perhaps the motions of the mind that marked the work of one apparently unlikely modernist poet can serve to summarize the equivocations of all these men. With his celebrated proclivity for "musing the obscure" and tracing the ambiguities of the relationship between the "blue guitar" of the imagination and the ontological "rock" of reality, Wallace Stevens would seem to have been a philosopher-poet purely detached from the exigencies of sexuality. Yet even while he shaped a paean to the power of the muse, "the one of fictive music" whom he defined as "sister and mother and diviner love," and even while he prayerfully praised the creative authority of a deific woman singing on the shore at Key West ("She was the single artificer of the world / In which she sang"), Stevens gradually began to express ever intenser anxiety about the Great Mother's primal energy, so that, moving through a famously fearful assertion in "Sunday Morning" that "Death is the mother of beauty / Within whose burning bosom we devise / Our earthly mothers, waiting, sleeplessly," he finally arrived, in an extraordinary late poem called "Madame La Fleurie," at a vision of the earth/mother's *vagina dentata* not unlike that expressed in Robert Bly's much later description of "The Teeth Mother Naked at Last." Dying and returning to the womb/tomb of the figure whom Neumann, before Bly, called "the Terrible Mother," Stevens' poet recognizes that "His grief is that his mother should feed on him, himself and what he saw, / In that distant chamber, a bearded queen, wicked in her dead light." Against such a neo-Bachofian vision of primordial female authority (and female eschatology), he set, like Joyce and like Bachofen himself, a transcendent masculine construct, a "Supreme Fiction" of the (male) poet whose simultaneous alienation from and reimagining of that "fat girl" the sensible world made him explicitly into "major man" and implicitly into a masterful Apollo who represented, like Bachofen's primal father, "the liberation of the [male] spirit from the [female] manifestations of nature."[41]

Because Lawrence was never convinced, as Stevens was, of "The Pure Good of Theory," he never defended himself with such openly metaphysical abstractions against the "Madame La Fleurie" whose hegemony he also acknowledged. Yet his self-preserving maneuvers can be seen as analogous to the American poet's more disguised celebrations of aesthetic "virility." Concretely described, vitally embodied, the Etruscan king toward whom he nostalgically yearns paints himself "vermilion like the throat of dawn" until he is so "red and utterly vivid" that he has become not just, as Lawrence declares, "god's body" but more specifically god's phallus, a phallus whose power to reengender the ancient texts and textures of the world would seem to offer some hope of reducing Griselda's new potency to passive patience and reachieving the old "mastery that man must hold." At the same time, though, possessed by (rather than possessing) the womb, Lawrence ultimately and explicitly concedes—as Stevens, Yeats, and even Joyce more covertly do—that he must acquiesce in its power. More, if he finally implies that, as he says in "Matriarchy," "man will never be master again," he hints, after much internal struggle, that such a change may be for the best. In one of his last and most poignant poems, in fact, he reimagines himself as a Dionys even weaker and needier than the dark hero of "The Ladybird." Invoking the primal creative energies of the Great Mother, he addresses her lunar avatar—"Moon, O Moon, great lady of the heavenly few"—and begs her to

> *give me back my lost limbs*
> *and my lost white fearless breast*
> *and set me again on moon-remembering feet*
> *a healed, whole man, O Moon!*[42]

To him, as to H. D., Isadora Duncan, James Joyce, and so many other major modernists, it must often have seemed that in the end only "the first deity . . . , the first love, Maia, mama, Mutter" could both cure the body and re-create the soul.

—1985

MOTHER RITES

Maternity, Matriarchy, Creativity

*Beneath every temple to Zeus . . . there was found on
excavation without exception, some old cell or cellar or the
rough ground-work of some primitive temple to the Early
Goddess . . . , the first deity, the primitive impulse, the
primitive desire, the first love, Maia, mama, Mutter, mut,
mamalie, mimmie, Madre, Mary, mother.*

—CANCELED PASSAGE FROM H. D., *THE GIFT*

If, from Bachofen to Joyce to Stevens, male thinkers opposed the "supreme fiction" of fatherhood to the realities of maternity, how did women theorists respond to nineteenth- and twentieth-century revisions of the Great Mother? Given the shift from a biomythology based on woman's powerlessness to one founded in a sense of her power, women of letters might well have derived female metaphors for literary creativity from the speculations of anthropologists and the researches of embryologists. But the case isn't so simple, for, even more than the male artist, who is only daunted by the Great Mother after a particular complex of conditions have strengthened her image, the woman artist can only be empowered by a trope of literary maternity when special circumstances have combined to give that trope visionary meaning for her.

To be sure, a number of Romantic and Victorian women writers strove to imagine maternity as a figure for creativity. In her preface to *The*

Last Man (1826), for instance, Mary Shelley characterized the womb-like cave of the Cumaean Sibyl as a place of female power and presented the act of sewing together the prophetess's scattered leaves as a paradigm of creativity. Similarly, in *The Professor* (1857) Charlotte Brontë's heroine celebrates the return of love after a long interlude of sorrow by reciting "Milton's invocation to that heavenly muse, who . . . had taught the Hebrew shepherd how in the womb of chaos, the conception of a world had originated and ripened." Ten years later Elizabeth Barrett Browning created in *Aurora Leigh* an artist-heroine who referred to her unsuccessful poems as "embryos whose heart had not yet beat" and not long after this "verse-novel" took the English-speaking world by storm, Barrett Browning's American disciple, Emily Dickinson, wrote reverently of "the Word made flesh," described spring as the time "when the Eggs fly off in Music," and declared her devotion to goddess-mountains whom she named "My strong Madonnas."[1]

Nevertheless, as Nina Auerbach has observed, the metaphor of literary maternity has always been a problematic one for women, who have every reason to agree with this critic's warning that it is "misleading to yoke artistic and biological creativity" since, as the psychoanalyst Robert Seidenberg points out, "without in the least knocking the values and delights of having babies, writing books would seem to be another thing again." Both Auerbach's and Seidenberg's comments imply the difficulty women artists have with this trope. When employed by men, the concept of aesthetic maternity inevitably remains metaphoric. When employed by women, however, the metaphor of maternity can be ambiguous, for it is always in danger of crossing the shadow line from the literary to the literal. While even literal begetting is always in some sense mysteriously fictive, literal birthing is always relentlessly material (a truth of which the very word "*material*" reminds us). As a material process, moreover, birthing is associated with just those bodily issues—what T. S. Eliot, quoting *The Midwives' Gazette,* called "blood, mucus, discharge"—that the artist seeks to transcend: the uncontrollable cyclical repetitiveness of nature, the insistently "bestial floor" of blood and flesh, the inextricable fusion of sex and death which simultaneously creates and annihilates "those dying generations." Sociohistorically, too, the materiality of maternity has meant not only what Beauvoir calls woman's "enslavement to the species," it has also meant an identification of woman with nature which, as Sherry Ortner has argued, seemed logically to entail her universal subordination in culture.[2]

If we return briefly to the Grimm fairy tale of "The Six Swans," for instance, we can see that, despite its affirmation of female creative power, the story doesn't present such power as unqualifiedly positive. Significantly, a stipulation of the swans' sister's magic is that she must remain "mute as a fish" while she sews her brothers the shirts that will revive their humanity. In addition, a subplot of the tale turns on her marriage to a king whose jealous mother steals the queen's three newborn children, smears the young woman's mouth with blood while she sleeps, and accuses her of "being a man-eater," a charge against which she cannot defend herself because of her vow of silence. Thus from the first the task of the swans' sister entails great suffering. Not only has she lost her brothers, but she is also forced to redeem them in "dumbness" and secrecy; until the very end of the story, in fact, no one comprehends her creative energy, so that even though she is really active she seems passive—a patient Griselda rather than a potent one—just as the body of the pregnant woman appeared merely passive to medical scientists until recent centuries.

Again, powerful though it proves, the art of sewing by which the swans' sister delivers her brothers from their animal bondage is a female domestic labor, and hence a secondary, devalued activity. Sewing and suffering in silence and submission, this magical queen reenacts the fate of the woman, who must, says the Bible, bring forth children "in sorrow." Worse still, the silence imposed on her separates her from her newborn children, whose disappearance suggests that to give birth is to give birth into death, while the threat of execution that constantly hangs over her implies that to give birth is to risk—and to be thought deserving of—death. Further, the animosity of the two stepmothers— the rage of the one who makes the deadly shirts, and the malevolence of the one who smears the queen's mouth with blood—reminds us that, as Neumann notes, the power of the Mother has always appeared ambiguous: a power to kill as well as a power to create, a murderous energy for devouring and deconstruction as well as a benevolent energy of creation and reconstruction. Like the poisoned shirt that Deianeira weaves for Hercules, the shirt of flesh that woman sews for man is the garment of mortality, and, like menstrual blood, the blood around the swans' sister's mouth (suggesting a *vagina dentata*) hints at what Adrienne Rich reports her own mother as calling "wasted baby." Finally, from a feminist perspective, the idea that the swans' sister must endure her sufferings to serve men—her brothers and her husband—implies that she has been forced to use her transformative power only as an agent of patriarchal culture, for the sake of male survival rather than female assertion. It suggests, in other words, that she is, exactly in Beauvoir's sense, a "slave to the species."

The dissonances of this tale help illuminate paradoxes experienced by many feminists. For instance, even while exulting in Arthur Evans' recovery of the Great Mother as "too good to be true," Jane Ellen Harrison, the theorist of matriarchy, also praised the "miracle" by which she herself had "escaped marriage," explaining that the "family life" associated with the uneasy "role of wife and mother" might be "a private hell."[3] True, the turn-of-the-century birth control movement gave the most advanced women a chance to moderate the conditions of that "hell." Meditating on Victorian childbearing and the modern possibility of escape from such an involuntary servitude to biology, Virginia Woolf implied in 1928 that a womb of one's own might well lead to a room of one's own. Yet the birth control movement was frequently greeted with the kind of male hostility that evokes female anxiety. Even the lapsed Catholic James Joyce, after all, prefaced his plans for the "Oxen of the Sun" with a declaration that "the idea" behind this exercise in embryology was "the crime committed against fecundity by sterilizing the act of coition," and as if to concede that she, at least, understood the implications of this position for women like herself, his patroness Harriet Weaver offered an assessment of his "Lying-in Hospital" quite as bitter as Jane Harrison's appraisal of marriage-and-motherhood: "I think this episode might also have been called Hades for the reading of it is like being taken the rounds of hell."[4] Considering the strength of patriarchal institutions—the male gynecological establishment whose wisecracking medical students celebrate their sexuality over the prostrate body of Mina Purefoy, the bourgeois family that relegates woman to the nursery and the parlor—most women could not realistically affirm the powers of the Great Mother, even when birth control had ostensibly given them a power of choice over their own reproductive capacities. Still less could they realistically draw the parallel between literal and literary childbirth that came so naturally to such diverse male artists as Shelley and Joyce.

If we look, therefore, at "realistic" novels by women we find few instances of heroines who are empowered by either the image or the actuality of maternity. Ensnared in the logic of circumstance, women novelists cannot break free of the qualifications implicit in the mimetic imperative. From Kate Chopin's Edna Pontellier to Nella Larsen's Helga Crane and Sylvia Plath's Esther Greenwood, their protagonists frequently see childbirth as part of a patriarchal "plot" designed to keep woman subordinate. The female-authored *Künstlerroman*, moreover, almost always emphasizes the dissonance, rather than the consonance, between aesthetic and biological creativity. A male hero may be empowered by female reproduction in female-authored works, as Vance Weston is by Halo Spear's maternity in Edith Wharton's *The Gods Arrive* (whose gods, Elizabeth Ammons suggests, are "the Mothers" of Goethe's *Faust*). But even such a figure is equally likely to be trapped by some woman's maternity, as Newland Archer is by his wife May's pregnancy in Wharton's *Bildungsroman The Age of Innocence* or as, in a sense, Professor St. Peter is by the demands of his family in Willa Cather's elegiac novel *démeublé The Professor's House.*[5]

As for female heroes in such works, they consistently make themselves into artists by insisting upon Auerbach's refusal to "yoke artistic and biological creativity." Thus Willa Cather's Thea Kronborg becomes, as her name indicates, a goddess/artist when she plays the role of Fricka—that paradigmatic Wagnerian wife—onstage but not in real life. Similarly, artist-heroines like Dorothy Richardson's Miriam Henderson and May Sinclair's Mary Olivier deliver themselves from what they see as their own mothers' social as well as biological confinement by remaining obdurately unmarried, while most famously, Virginia Woolf's Lily Briscoe achieves the aesthetic vision that she transcribes in her painting at the end of *To The Lighthouse* when she distances herself from Mrs. Ramsay's archaic command of "Marry, marry!" to realize that "life has changed completely" so that "she stood here painting, had never married." As if echoing Jane Harrison's pleasure in the "miracle" that had kept her from marriage, Lily rejoices in having "triumphed over Mrs. Ramsay," whose muse-like maternity empowers her art as Halo's empowers Vance's, but whose reproductive life provides no model for either this modern artist's personal progress or her aesthetic practice. And Louie Pollit, the fledgling writer-heroine of Christina Stead's *The Man Who Loved Children,* even has to murder her horrifyingly fertile stepmother— a woman with the allegorical nickname of "Henny"—in order not just to triumph over but to annihilate the threatening materiality of Henny's mindless maternity.

Finally, that many female artists were unnerved by what Harriet Weaver saw as the "hell" of the Lying-In Hospital is emphasized by the wounds with which they associate the sexuality that issues in the confinement of that hospital. Lily imagines Paul Rayley's erotic energy as the "roar and crackle" of a savage fire that "repel[s] her with fear and disgust," and Woolf juxtaposes the artist's memories of Mrs. Ramsay with a brief, chilling description of "the mutilated body" of a fish "Macalister's boy" is using "to bait his hook with." Indeed, as early as *The Voyage Out,* Rachel Vinrace, the young pianist who might have been the subject of a *Künstlerroman* had Woolf kept her alive, connects sexuality with terrifying subterranean tunnels and "vaults"; arguably, indeed, she's killed by sexuality, for she dies of a tropical fever contracted during the trip up the Amazon on which she became engaged to Terence Hewet. And in Sylvia Plath's *The Bell Jar,* the young writer Esther Greenwood (whose name Plath derived from playful musings on the image of the mythic but dead woman poet Woolf called "Shakespeare's sister") experiences her first "deflowering" encounter with sexuality as a literal wound, a hemorrhage which, she says sardonically, made her "part of a great tradition." To transcend the ills of this tradition and create a greater one of her own, Esther must be reborn into a new virginity. Checking her clothes as she prepares for her final interview at the sanitarium where she has been sequestered, she involuntarily thinks, "Something old, something new," then, as if echoing Jane Harrison and Lily Briscoe, she urgently reminds herself, "But I wasn't getting married."

To consider Plath, however, is to recall that some women have been empowered (as Auerbach seems to believe women never can be) by the trope of maternity, for even while *The Bell Jar* records a revulsion from sexuality and childbirth, countless Plath poems—as we have seen—celebrate the empowering possibilities of female biology, and praise the divinely fertile queen bee whom this woman poet defines as her true "Self." Given the negation of such ideas enacted in so many female *Künstlerromane*, what circumstances could have made them positive? I want to suggest that the conditions under which the trope of maternity becomes plausible to women are—in the largest sense—generic. If male artists required a nexus of anthropology and biology in order both to acknowledge and to defuse the idea of female reproductive power, female writers needed not only such a nexus but also a genre in which that interconnection could be translated into hopeful imaginings. Thus, literary women had to move beyond the "realistic" novel, with its duplication of the sociocultural knots and nots of gender, into less mimetic genres—specifically into fantasy and lyric (or in a few cases epic) poetry—before they could allow themselves dreams about the authority of the Great Mother, for in order to envision childbearing as empowering they required the freedom to envision a context in which such a biological process could signify empowerment. For men, the mere threat of maternal primacy often fostered anxious visions, but women were more skeptical, separating imaginings of what might be from records of what is. Thus in different works by the same woman writer—Harrison's memoir and her *Prolegomena,* Plath's novel and her poems—we find quite dissonant confrontations of the Great Mother.

Sometimes women artists even seem consciously to address such dissonances in a single work, proposing and then revising a conclusion to which they have come when writing in a different genre. Plath's "Two Sisters of Persephone," for instance, juxtaposes the unmarried intellectual woman (Lily Briscoe or Jane Harrison) with the pregnant mother goddess (Mrs. Ramsay or Harrison's Demeter). Here, however, the child bearing "sister of Persephone" becomes jubilantly fertile— "Grass couched in her labor's pride / She bears a king"—while the self-preserving spinster becomes "rat-shrewd," this because the liberation of the lyric from the limits of "realistic" fiction guards the poet against a disturbing literalization of the metaphor of maternity. In addition, what guards Plath's positive sister of Persephone against the degradations of the "bestial floor" which threaten, say, Mrs. Tomolillo (or Esther Green-wood) in *The Bell Jar* is the alternative metaphoric "floor" provided by the myth of Persephone and Demeter that shapes this poem.

Much modernist prose fiction is, of course, founded in myth. But as that notable novelist-mythographer D. H. Lawrence once observed, the ostensibly "realistic" novel is always qualified and ironic in its use of myth or indeed of any overarching theme or metaphor: "If you try to nail anything down in the novel, either it kills the novel or the novel gets up and walks away with the nail." Thus Leopold Bloom is both a serious reincarnation of Ulysses and a comic comment on the impossi-bility of that hero's metempsychosis; Kate Leslie in *The Plumed Serpent* becomes the fertility goddess Malintzi even while complaining "I've had it put over me"; Mrs. Ramsay is both a redaction of the Great Mother and a reflective critique of such a figure. In every case, the novel (or nov-elist) has simultaneously flourished and "walked away with" the nail of myth. However, as we can see from the tentative moments of empower-ment explored by nineteenth-century writers, women artists can turn to fantasy—to dream visions (Mary Shelley), to revisionary interpretation (Charlotte Brontë), to extended metaphor (Elizabeth Barrett Browning), and to visionary lyric (Emily Dickinson) in order to construct a world in which maternity could inspire the female imagination. Given a revised biomythology, women of letters could elaborate such fantasies in celebra-tions of the power of the Mother and the potency of her womb. Signifi-cantly, then, modern women artists who valorize maternity and in some cases "yoke artistic and biological creativity" are poets (H. D., Plath, Rich, Lorde, Levertov), fantasists (Gilman in *Herland,* Woolf in *Orlando,* LeGuin in *The Left Hand of Darkness*), surrealists (Fini, Carrington), and what for want of a better phrase I will call utopian interpreters (Duncan, Harrison). These writers employ a rich range of strategies as they explore the mystery of maternity; often, indeed, a single woman will draw upon metaphors that exploit the Great Mother's power in notably different ways. But the spectrum of their matriarchal imaginings has a subtle coherence.

Starting with revisionary interpretations of the myth of Maenadic autonomy that underlies Euripides' *The Bacchae* and against which Lawrence struggled in "The Ladybird," women writers have elaborated ever more fantastic conceptions of female (pro)creativity. For turn-of-the-century artists, feminist modernists, and a number of Second Wave feminists the idea of such creative energy multiplied magically. One could write as a "Maenad" or about the "long, long dances" of the matriarchal Maenads. One could write as the Great Mother herself or one could write about the daughter's privileged relationship with that mysterious goddess/muse. One could write about the connections between lover/ muse and goddess/muse that such a relationship made possible. One could write about the victorious (and sometimes vengeful) female community devoted to worship of the mother goddess. One could write about the paradoxical gynandry—the incorporation of male power into female potency—implicit in the autonomy of the Great Vessel that is the goddess's womb. And one could write about the womb itself as a mystically (pro)creative organ, a womb detached both from "blood, mucus, discharge" and from "enslavement to the species" and therefore an agent of imaginative energy. Reviewing each of these quite distinct strategies individually, we'll see that in all cases, art was generated by a revision of literal anatomy that promised a new literary destiny.

To begin with, for turn-of-the-century women writers and a number of their descendants the myth behind both *The Bacchae* and the Eleusinian mysteries with which the Dionysian mysteries were associated became as crucial as, say, the Oedipus story was for Freud. From nineteenth-century studies of the rites at Eleusis and from the "Homeric Hymn to Demeter" that celebrated the narrative on which they were based, women writers derived a new sense of the primacy of the mother-daughter bond dramatized in the tribulations and triumphs of the great goddesses Demeter and Persephone. And at the same time, from the archaic configurations of *The Bacchae*, revisionary feminists excavated not the glamour of Dionysos but the glory of the female hierophants whose prideful nursing bestowed such an aura upon him, not the cautious wisdom of Tiresias but the ferocious passion of Agave. Indeed, as their celebrations imply, *The Bacchae* is in some sense the play Freud avoided when he chose Sophocles' *Oedipus Tyrannos* as the tragedy that articulated his paradigm for the dilemma of human psychosexual development. Certainly the plot of the work would seem, in a resonant rearrangement of the Oedipus story, to have explored some of the sexual anxieties Freud read into that narrative: first, the loss or absence of the empowering, socially legitimate father; second, the alarming liberation of female (and specifically maternal) desire; and third, most drastically, the engulfment and destruction of the patriarchally legitimate son, the "daddy's boy," by a mother who is enthralled to the ecstasies offered by the illegitimate, matriarchal son, the "mama's boy." For Dionysos, after all, has come to Thebes in his significantly effeminate guise as a "Lydian stranger" in order to vindicate the name of his dead mother, the quasi-earth goddess Semele, whose sisters, Cadmus' other daughters, have denied her legitimacy and desecrated her tomb in their acquiescence to a patriarchal order that has superseded the matriarchal culture she originally represented.

The tragedy that ensues—Dionysos' vindictive transformation of Pentheus into a helpless transvestite, Agave's rending and decapitation/ "castration" of her legitimate son during a nightmarish vision of him as a threatening "Lion"—thus enacts male anxieties about matriarchal fury that Euripides and his contemporaries shared, and that Freud may have inherited. Not only is the god Dionysos a tool of the mythic dead mother Semele (who may even be said to parallel the mythic dead father of *Totem and Taboo*), but Pentheus, the "good" son who could be said to incarnate the "law of the Father," is the drama's *pharmakos*, rather than Jocasta, the *pharmakos* who must be sacrificed in the *Oedipus* in order to purge the son of his illicit desire. Moreover, despite the penance Euripides imposes on the filicidal Agave in the last scene of *The Bacchae*, the matriarchal Dionysos and his raging women attendants are left in power at the end of the play. Indeed, in a reversal of the satisfactorily patriarchal denouement of the *Oedipus* (where Thebes is purified both of Oedipus's sinister mother and of his incestuous mother-longing) and of the equally patriarchal conclusion of the *Oresteia* (where the matriarchal Furies are imprisoned deep in the earth), this idiosyncratic and ambiguous drama offers an ending in which the patriarchal Cadmus and his once (and now again) loyally submissive daughters are driven into exile, while Dionysos and his women resume what appears to be an archaic ascendancy.

Late in her life Freud's female disciple Helene Deutsch wrote a study of the Dionysian and the Apollonian—categories which had obsessed nineteenth- and twentieth-century thinkers from Nietzsche on but which they had usually seen as gender-neutral—in which she examined just these issues. She divided her work into two sections, the first an analysis of Dionysos as "The Son Who Saves" the mother, and the second a meditation on Apollo as "The Son Who Kills" the mother, and noted that in rebuking Agave by releasing her matriarchal Furies, the Dionysos of the Bacchae redeems the ancient goddess Semele. Thus, observes Deutsch, "he appears as a great social revolutionary—the first feminist in the history of mankind—in order to free the enslaved women." Even though such a reading was available to the hermeneutic strategies of a fellow analyst, however, Freud ignored *The Bacchae*'s paradigmatic potential. As an amateur archaeologist and brilliant mythographer who withdrew with anxious disingenuousness both from "the great mother-goddesses" for whom he could find no "place" in his myth of social origins, and from what he saw as the castrating demands of contemporary feminists who appeared to be the descendants of such matriarchal figures, he had to renounce the raging relics of the Great Mother that this play preserved in favor of stories that emphasized a "normative" transference to the father.[6]

But it was just these relics, and especially the female community they symbolized, that inspired fin de siècle and modernist women to fantasize about the drama. Believing that, as Deutsch was to put it, Dionysos "did a lot for progress and . . . his statue ought to be . . . at the entrance to girls' dormitories," these women not only celebrated the power of the Bacchantes, they also meditated on the play's eloquent, oddly nostalgic depictions of the Bacchantes' life in their liminal, liberating "dormitory" on the mountains; they brooded on the wonders worked by this sisterly band Gilbert Murray's translation of the play defined as "the wild white women"; they dreamed of the escape from the distaff promised by the Bacchantes' timbrels and their mysteries; and they even fantasized about the transgressive, implicitly lesbian love experienced by Dionysos' attendants when "wrapped" in the "flame . . . of Bacchos." Isadora Duncan confesses in *My Life,* for instance, that when she and her brother Raymond landed in Greece for the first time, "half-mad with joy" at finally reaching the land of their dreams, they hoped their singing might "awaken Dionysus and his sleeping Bacchantes." The chorus she remembers wanting to chant was the famous invocation from *The Bacchae:* "Up, O Bacchae, wife and maiden, / Come, O ye Bacchae, come . . ."[7] Throughout her career, moreover, this self-dramatizing artist was to imagine herself as a "vine-wreathed Bacchante drenched with wine" or an "aggressive Bacchante" even while she also identified the passion, pain, and power of her maternity with "the Mother Cry of All Creation." Her absorption in Euripides' play isn't surprising, however, when we consider that her London "instructor" in the classics was none other than Jane Harrison, who imparted her evolving theories of the Great Mother to the young American, guided her "through the Greek collection at the British Museum," and chanted Greek lyrics in the background while the barefoot dancer performed in filmy neo-Thracian veils.

For Harrison's *Prolegomena* is a book haunted by both *The Bacchae* and the Bacchae, a book whose longing for the lost primacy of the Great Mother—for, say, Semele, the "ancient Thracian earth goddess" who gave birth to Dionysos only to be "effaced by the splendor of the Hellenic Zeus" as "matriarchy pale[d] before the new order of patriarchy"—is always associated with the yearning of the Bacchae for the wild freedom of their revels on the mountain. Meditating on the Maenads' desertion of home and husbands for their Dionysian worship, Harrison quotes "the lovely song" that Euripides writes for them:

> *Will they ever come to me, ever again,*
> *The long, long dances,*

On through the dark till the dim stars wane?
Shall I feel the dew on my throat and the stream
Of wind in my hair? Shall our white feet gleam
    In the dim expanses?

and clearly the song represents her own paean to the "miracle" of liberation from marriage. Clearly, too, her interpretation of "the long, long dances" that expressed such freedom provided a compelling model for Isadora Duncan's own "long, long dances."[8]

Elsewhere in the *Prolegemona*, Harrison makes plain her belief in the gravity as well as the glamour of the "hieratic state of holy madness" that marked the Bacchantes' Dionysiac possession. Noting that "it is refreshing to turn from the dissolute crew of Satyrs" to the Maenads, she insists that these "women-attendants of Dionysos" were no "mere female correlatives of the Satyrs." Rather, they were nurses and worshipers, priestesses and prophetesses, said to have "miraculous magnetic powers." Where other writers on Dionysos (for instance, Walter Otto) stress his bond with the father—his "second birth" from Zeus' thigh—and the phallic power manifested in his epiphany as a raging bull or a roaring lion, she deemphasizes such masculinity, dismissing his relation to Zeus as "slight and artificial": Dionysos, she notes, is "essentially the son of his mother" for "Zeus the Father will have no great Earth-goddess, Mother and Maid in one, in his man-fashioned Olympus"; indeed, to Zeus, "the archpatriarchal *bourgeois,* the birth of the first woman [Pandora] is but a huge Olympian jest." Thus this proto-feminist classicist centers an important part of her discussion on "Dionysus Liknites," the cradle-bound baby whom the Maenads "tend" even while they "suffer his inspiration."[9]

At the same time, Harrison celebrates the female bonding that the travels of the Bacchantes often elicited, retelling "the pleasant story of the Thyiades and the women of Phocis," an episode in which the women of Amphissa silently guarded a group of Maenads (here called Thyiades) as they slept exhausted in the agora of a strange and possibly hostile city. Finally, speculating on modern reactions to the escapes from domesticity that Maenadic women enacted, she defends their autonomy against both puritanical disapproval and patriarchal skepticism, observing, "We are so possessed by a set of conceptions based on Periclean Athens . . . that we are apt to dismiss as 'mythological' whatever does not fit into our stereotyped picture," but adding, with a note of exultation, that "however much the Macedonian men disliked [their wives' and daughters'] orgies, they were clearly too frightened to put a stop to them," for "the women were possessed, magical, and dangerous to handle." In conclusion, indeed, she speculates sorrowfully that Solon's reaction against such female "excesses" constituted a set of "dreary regulations [among which] comes the characteristically modern touch that they are not to go out at night 'except in a carriage and with a light before them.' "[10]

For Harrison, then, as perhaps later for Deutsch, the Maenads are madwomen (the term "Maenad" literally means "madwoman") but they are very different from the madwomen we have been accustomed to encounter, say, in Victorian England. Where Charlotte Brontë's Bertha Mason Rochester, for instance, is reduced by rage and desire to mad mutterings and secret subversive wanderings in her husband's house, these "madwomen" openly express their feelings, chant their longings in great choruses, and dance together the "long, long dances" of pleasure. Where Bertha Mason Rochester exists primarily as an id implicit in the household who must be tended as a beast is tended, these "madwomen" must be attended to, for they tender new life to the god. Indeed, where Bertha Mason Rochester has no issue and thus no creative power, these "madwomen" incarnate the power of incarnation. Finally, where Bertha Mason Rochester is isolated in the attic, these "madwomen" deliver themselves into an all-female community which maintains itself far from the "dreary regulations" of patriarchal culture, in passionate collaboration with nature, on a mountain sacred to the Great Mother. Thus Harrison's regeneration of these archaic figures marks a major shift in the female tradition from the subtle duplicity of nineteenth-century women novelists who overtly acquiesced in oppressive constraints while creating lonely and apparently mad characters who covertly challenged such constraints, to the sisterly complicity of fin de siècle and modernist artists who openly rejoiced in the possibility of a female "world elsewhere" in which there would be no constraints.

Quoting one of the messenger's key speeches from *The Bacchae*, Harrison alludes to this place—"I have seen the wild white women there, O king . . . and come to tell thee how / They work strange deeds"—and hints at her own yearning for it. And explaining in a footnote the "two-fold connotation . . . purity and inspired madness" of the "wild white women," she justifies their ecstatic mysteries and mysterious ecstasies.[11]

Where the great J— H— herself" of Virginia Woolf's *A Room of One's Own* theorized the matriarchal significance of *The Bacchae*, other women artists besides Isadora Duncan were equally obsessed by the play and its imagery. As far back as the 1850s, Emily Dickinson had written yearningly of a "mystic green" where "maids . . . keep their Seraphic May" and are "by men unseen" as they perform "dance and game, / And gambol I may never name." Praying "Like thee to dance—like thee to sing," the American poet may well have been thinking of "the long, long dances" of *The Bacchae*, and her longing surely foreshadowed Harrison's equally vivid nostalgia. As if to make explicit the allusion implicit in Dickinson's poem, and perhaps even referring to the same translation of the play that Harrison cites, the English writer Mary Elizabeth Coleridge celebrated Euripides' implicitly feminist utopia-on-the-mountain in a poem she published in 1908:

> *Where dwell the lovely, wild white women folk,*
> *Mortal to man?*
> *They never bowed their necks beneath the yoke.*
> *They dwelt alone when the first morning broke*
> *And Time began.*[12]

As dangerous ("mortal") to men as Agave and her sisters are to Pentheus, these women are threateningly Medusan, for, as the last stanza of Coleridge's poem relates, when "One of our race, lost in an awful glade, / Saw with his human eyes a wild white maid, / . . . gazing he died." At the same time, they are Amazonian: "Taller are they than man," says Coleridge, and "The deadly shafts their nervous hands let fly / Are stronger than our strongest." More marvelous still, they speak a "language strange" as that uttered by Keats' fatal "belle dame sans merci"—a literal "mother tongue." "Their words are not as ours," explains Coleridge. In fact, their "war cry of the storm" is closer to the winds and waves of nature: the "waves of Ocean" and "the language of the snow / Falling on torrents" represent the "tongue they speak." Finally, while these "wild white women" are as pure as Harrison's Bacchantes, their autonomous desire symbolizes the sexuality associated with the Great Mother. "They never sinned," Coleridge insists, but at sunset, "their tresses they unbind / And fling their girdles to the Western wind, / Swept by desire." And "Lo, maidens to the maidens then are born"! In an apotheosis of the Maenadic dream, these are children only of woman and nature—a fantastic phenomenon in which their utopian strength, along with that of their mothers, resides. Dancing and delighting in a world inimical to man, these Bacchic women offer perhaps the most positive interpretation possible of the female community that Euripides' play seemed to some to imply, for their utopia is not only self-empowering, it is also self-perpetuating, parthenogenetic.

Few other feminist writers surfaced such fantastic implications from *The Bacchae,* but a number of others were haunted by the play's possibilities. In 1919, for instance, May Sinclair created in *Mary Olivier* an artist-heroine whose escape both from marriage and from her own enthrallment to the chafing demands of a frustrated mother was facilitated by her successful translation of *The Bacchae.* Even while, like many other protagonists of womens' *Künstlerromane,* Mary has to reject the "soft, annihilating feet" of the "realistic" mother, she gives birth to herself by reimagining the poetic "feet"—the newly vital meters—of the Great Mother, and particularly the choruses that mark *The Bacchae:* "verse that could be chanted; that could be whispered, shouted, screamed as they moved. Agave and her Maenads. Verse that would go with a throbbing beat, excited, exciting; beyond rhyme. That would be nearest to the Greek verse." And in her 1931 *Red Roses for Bronze,* the American poet H. D. translated a series of choruses from *The Bacchae,* including the "lovely song" of "the long, long dances," which she rendered in the kind of "excited, exciting" meters—liberated from the constraints of rhyme, pulsing with pleasurable repetition—that Mary Olivier had decided to use:

Again,
again in the night,
shall I beat white feet in delight of the dance
to Dionysos? . . .
shall I lie in the meadows sweet, escaped,
escaped from the lot
of men . . . ?

Most of the other choruses H. D. chose to translate propose equal empowerment for women, for they include a paean to the "blessed, blessed spirit / who seeks the mountain goddess, / Cybele mother-spirit," an invocation to "Thebes, / Semele's nurse" to "crown yourself / with pine branch, with ivy . . . on the hills" where the Bacchantes "dance in sacred faun-pelt" and "the fields drip . . . honey / and wine / and white milk," and an injunction to "Stalk, / stalk the prey . . . track Pentheus down, / the clown, / mimic in woman's dress." Indeed, freely diverging from the Greek text along with the Murray translation, H. D.'s versions of *The Bacchae* are, like Mary Olivier's fictive verses, as much interpretations as translations, for their shrieking, pounding repetitions ("blessed, blessed," "crown, / crown," "Stalk, / stalk") emphasize the unleashed rage as well as the unleashed delight of women who "whisper, shout, scream as they move" into a fantasy of desire "beyond" the confining symmetries of rhyme and reason—and realism.

Finally, as if to comment on the Maenadic interpretations of feminist/modernist precursors, Plath in 1960 incorporated a dramatic monologue called "Maenad" into her sequence "Poem for a Birthday." But where the writings of earlier women had emphasized the energy of Dionysos' worshipers, her ambivalent account of a Maenad's madness stresses the speaker's pain, passivity, bewilderment. Speaking as, in a sense, an "Elektra on Azalea Path" still enthralled by "Daddy's" rules, Plath dramatizes the agony of transformation into something other than a dutiful daughter, a metamorphosis whose difficulties she was about to describe in novelistic terms in *The Bell Jar*. Her Maenad's monologue begins wistfully: "Once I was ordinary: / Sat by my father's bean tree / Eating the fingers of wisdom." As the poem progresses,

however, she describes the process of "becoming another" as a horrifying one:

> *Dog-head, devourer:*
> *Feed me the berries of dark.*
> *The lids won't shut. Time*
> *Unwinds from the great umbilicus of the sun*
> *Its endless glitter.*
>
> *I must swallow it all.*

Even the ordinarily Apollonian sun is disturbingly matriarchal here; its
"umbilicus" feeds the speaker with an "endless glitter" while the related
realm of darkness is inhabited by monsters ("Dog-head, devourer") and
promises an insomniac confrontation of frightening, even cannibalistic
desires—the omophagia, for instance, that lurks behind Agave's rending of Pentheus. In the piece's last stanza, even the sisterhood of the Bacchantes has become disturbing, as the speaker wonders "who are these
others in the moon's vat?" and begs "Tell me my name."

Precisely because it implies a patriarchal reading of *The Bacchae* that
"blackens" the Bacchantes by emphasizing the torment rather than the
liberation of Agave's madness, Plath's poem reminds us that all of these
women's transformations of the Dionysos myth *are* readings, that is to
say, interpretive fantasies. It reminds us too, therefore, that given the
urgency of literary women's needs for fantasies about maternal potency
which would redefine female biology in a utopian social context, no
single myth could offer universal energy. If literary men had to defend
themselves against what they saw as the creative potential of the Great
Mother through a variety of strategies, women had, even more vigorously because more desirously, to resurrect that potential through a fluid
multiplicity of imaginings.

Thus the powers that Mary Elizabeth Coleridge ascribed to her
"wild white women," at an apex of feminist interpretations of Euripides,
are diffused in other feminist/modernist works into a number of related
fantasies. As Judith Kroll's *Chapters in a Mythology* demonstrates, for

instance, Sylvia Plath's mature poetry often depends for allusive substructure on the matriarchal theories of Robert Graves, which may themselves have been influenced by the revisionary feminism of Graves' sometime collaborator, the poet Laura Riding. Plath and Ted Hughes studied *The White Goddess* together at a crucial point in the poet's artistic development. In fact, Plath's conception of "Maenad" may well have been influenced by Graves' magisterial insistence that "no poet can hope to understand the nature of poetry unless he [*sic*] has had a vision of the Naked King crucified to the lopped oak, and watched the dancers [chanting] 'Kill! kill! kill!'" At the same time, however, Plath's anxiety about the metamorphosis her speaker experiences as, in Hughes' phrase, "she goes under the fury" may well have been exacerbated by another of Graves' assertions: his claim that "the archives of morbid pathology are full of Bassarid case histories. An English or American woman in a nervous breakdown of sexual origin will often instinctively reproduce in faithful and disgusting detail much of the ancient Dionysiac religion."[13]

Given such a guilt-inducing interpretation of *The Bacchae*, it makes sense that Plath chose to extrapolate a different fantasy from Graves' writings in order to rehabilitate a poetic "self" who was also a mythical "queen." Meditating on his famous dictum that "it is the imitation of male poetry that causes the false ring in the work of almost all women poets," she evidently also brooded on his injunction that "a woman who concerns herself with poetry" and does not want to be "a silent Muse" should "be the Muse in a complete sense . . . and should write . . . with antique authority," and seems to have sought to achieve such authority first, through her studies of the mythic matriarchs Graves mentions, second, through meditations on her own experiences of childbirth, and third, through an identification with images of the Great Mother. Whether consciously or not, she undertook this task of poetic self-transformation at just the time when her renewed analysis with Dr. Ruth Beuscher was surfacing her revulsion toward a childhood she saw as having been spent, after her father's death, "in a smarmy matriarchy . . . a family full of women. So many women, the house stank of them." Thus the dialectic between her negative definition of the "matriarchy" in her own life and her positive evaluation of the mythic matriarchy proposed by Graves emphasizes once again the polarities of "realism" and "fantasy" between which women writers have oscillated as they struggled to reimagine female (pro)creation.[14]

As Kroll long ago noted, works as diverse as "The Beekeeper's Daughter," "Poem for a Birthday," "The Rival," "The Other," "The Moon and the Yew Tree," and "Lady Lazarus" are all in one way or another informed by paradigms Plath drew from Graves' book or from analogous studies by Frazer (and possibly, though Kroll does not mention her, Harrison). In a few key poems, however, we can trace the poet's development of the mother/muse into a fantasy of female power that unleashed the energies of her later years. As early as 1956, her "Two Sisters of Persephone" had articulated a dream of female "labor's pride," and by 1960, not long after she had completed her ambivalent "Poem for a Birthday," Plath was using a metaphor of maternity as creativity in "Stillborn," a sardonic lament for poems that "do not live" though "their mother," who is "near dead with distraction," lavished love on them. If maternity is equivocal in this work—the mother has not yet achieved the power to infuse life into her aesthetic offspring—it rapidly becomes demonic from here on, and it seems to do so as Plath's own experience of childbearing provided her with a sense of the creative process she could mythologize in poems even while she recorded literal struggles with nursing and child care in "realistic" letters, journals, and stories.

"Magi" (late 1960), for instance, comically repudiates "abstracts" which "hover like dull angels" over her daughter's crib, while "Morning Song" and "Barren Woman," written within two days of each other early in 1961, tentatively celebrate the mysteries of maternity. Then, in "Elm" and the verse play *Three Women*, Plath began to use dramatic masks to speak for and as the Great Mother, expressing the anxiety as well as the exuberance evoked by the goddess's power. Finally, in the late poems of the bee sequence she discovered an affirmatively Maenadic self who was "a queen . . . with her lion-red body, her wings of glass": a self released, like Agave and her sisters, from "the engine that killed her— / The mausoleum, the wax house." That this self is also described as "terrible" should be understood to mean that she is "terrible"—awesome—in her creative power even while it may also suggest that it is "terrible"—awful—to be and be near her. For as Harrison reminds us in passages from the *Prolegomena* that not only gloss Plath's poem but might have actually served as sources for this poet's resonant bee-imagery, ancient priestesses were often figured as bees. The "three maiden prophetesses" known as the Thriae (whose "inspired, impassioned" song was the primordial verse form called "the thriambos")

> *are nurses like the Maenads, they rave in holy madness . . . but their inspiration is not from Bacchos, the wine-god . . . it is from . . . an intoxicant yet more primitive, from honey. They are . . . "Melissae," honey-priestesses, inspired by a honey-intoxicant; they are bees, their heads white with pollen; [and] not only the priestesses of Artemis at Ephesus were "Bees" but also those of Demeter, and, still more significant, the Delphic priestess herself was a Bee . . . With all these divine associations about the bee . . . it is not surprising that she was figured by art as a goddess and half human.*[15]

Perhaps, newly separated from her marriage, Plath excavated this material and used it to mark a metamorphic moment when, as Graves had admonished the woman poet to do, she herself became the goddess, uttering a *thriambos* of female triumph. Thus, in "Wintering"—the poem with which the original *Ariel* was supposed to conclude—she exulted that "the bees are all women, / Maids and the long royal lady. / They have got rid of the men," for the sacred hive, as Harrison envisions it, is as much a woman's place as the Bacchanalian mountain of the Great Mother. In fact, Harrison offers a connection between these two female utopias that once again glosses the self-transformation Plath accomplished through matriarchal fantasies. Analyzing the "splendid poetry" Euripides wrote in the *Hippolytus* about Dionysos' mother, Semele, Harrison quotes a passage that characterizes the persona Plath adopted: like the queen-self of "Stings," Dionysos' earth goddess-mother in her role as "Bride of the bladed thunder" is in every sense fertile—"her breath is on all that hath life"—and like Plath's unleashed female comet, "she floats in the air, / Bee-like, death-like, a wonder."[16]

Plath's strategies are not unique. Throughout the last century a number of women poets employed allusion and fantasy to move beyond the particular paradigm of *The Bacchae* which had been so useful to their precursors, in order to continue countering the "realistic" implications of maternity while energizing their verse with its metaphors. Revisionary mythology has long been a distinctively feminist genre, but interestingly, in relation to the equivocal problem of the Great Mother, many women writing in this genre chose, as if following Graves' advice, to speak *as* the *Great Mother* or one of her acolytes. In the 1920s, for instance, H. D. included a sequence of soliloquies titled "Demeter" in *Heliodora and Other Poems* (1924). Here, assuming the "antique authority" of the primordial matriarch, she proclaimed that "Men, fires, feasts" are "Useless to me who plant / wide feet on a mighty plinth," and affirming the autonomy of maternal creativity ("am I a spouse . . . am I a woman, or goddess or queen, / to be met by a god with a smile—and left?"), she reminded her votaries (and readers) to "keep me foremost, / keep me before you, after you, with you." Clarifying the link between this incarnation of female (pro)creation and the Dionysian mysteries she was to explore in her translation of *The Bacchae* choruses, she had her Demeter declare that "the child of my heart and spirit / is . . . the unclaimed Dionysos."

H. D. composed this work not long after she had had several terrifying experiences with literal maternity: her first child was stillborn during World War I, and the birth of her second—resonantly named Perdita—coincided with a severe attack of influenza and the definitive breakdown of her marriage to Richard Aldington. Years later in *The Gift* she was to record a childhood anxiety about motherhood that would seem almost to have predicted such traumas: "It is terrible to be a virgin because a virgin has a baby with God." Once again we see that when the implications of the myth of the Great Mother are literalized in reality, they are disturbing; but when the myth transforms reality into fantasy, its lineaments strengthen poems. For H. D. this myth became a source of almost limitless poetic energy, a major theme of her life/work.[17] Seven years after the appearance of "Demeter," for instance, she offered several key reworkings of the matriarchal voice-of-authority in *Red Roses for Bronze*, the same volume in which she published her translations from *The Bacchae*. Her "Wine Bowl," for example, is a magnificent incantation uttered by a sorceress who declares that "in my skull / where vision had *birth* (emphasis added) / will come wine"—and song. Similarly, her "The Mysteries," a sequence that concludes this 1931 collection, once more assumes the mystic voice of the Eleusinian earth mother herself:

> *Demeter in the grass*
> *I multiply,*
> *renew and bless*
> *Iaccus in the vine;*
> *I hold the law,*
> *I keep the mysteries true . . .*

From Adrienne Rich to Audre Lorde, contemporaries of Plath's worked in this mode that H. D. may be said to have pioneered. Rich, for instance, spoke as a Maenadic initiate in "I Dream I'm the Death of Orpheus," and in "From an Old House in America" she transported the Great Mother to the New World, declaring in Whitmanesque cadences that "my body [is] a hollow ship bearing songs to the wilderness."[18] With more openly mythic emphasis, Michele Murray wrote as "The Woman Who Lives Inside the World" in her collection *The Great Mother and Other Poems.* "I am the one who is inside you / kerchiefed / uttering a blessing," she asserts, imagining her queenly speaker-self as muse for herself as well as others. Diane Wakoski fantasized on the sacred significance of the name Diane, describing herself as sister to "an ancient priestess / whose tears make the spider lilies grow" while arguing that "I am / also a rule of the sun." Similarly, Audre Lorde speaks as a fierce goddess in "The Women of Dan Dance with Swords in their Hands to Mark the Time When They Were Warriors," claiming the Great Mother's dual powers of creator and destroyer. And in *Surfacing,* an ostensibly "realistic" novel about a heroine's Freudian search for her dead father, Margaret Atwood—who would later explore the dystopian pains of maternity in *The Handmaid's Tale*—offered her narrator/protagonist the Maenadic grace of a matriarchal fantasy. Going "under the fury" of a willed rever-sion to wildness, this illustrator of children's books and sometime artist of Easter eggs employs a lover as an instrument of impregnation during an act of ritual intercourse, imagining how "the baby will slip out easily as an egg, a kitten . . . it will be covered with shining fur, a god."

Though Atwood's novel concludes—as I am suggesting "realis-tic" novels must—in an open-ended compromise with reality ("we will probably fail, sooner or later"), her moment of apparently "mad" fantasy yields her not only a vision of a baby god but also an epiphany of her lost mother as a Lady of the Wild Things, silently feeding the birds. Such a revelation suggests yet another series of strategies by which women poets and fantasists have empowered their art through the metaphor of the Great Mother: distancing themselves from the goddess in order to envision and thereby revitalize her image not from the inside but from the outside, not as her avatar but as her daughter/lover. For if speak-ing as the Mother or one of her Maenadic incarnations bestows author-ity on the female imagination, counting the ways of her love confirms the woman artist's privileged participation in a communion of goddess/muse/mother and writer/daughter that suggests not only the possibility of a literary matrilineage but also an aesthetic/erotic marriage of daugh-ter and mother, woman (poet) and woman (muse).

Graves' admonition to women writers entails, after all, certain risks, for it is prefaced by disturbing alternative: "A woman who concerns her-self with poetry should . . . either be a *silent Muse* . . . or write . . . with antique authority" (emphasis mine). But might there be a kind of silence implicit even in the voice of antique matriarchal authority? What if by metamorphosing into the mother goddess the woman writer makes her-self into a musing voice not for women but for men, merely the voice, that is, of an attendant nurse of "Dionysos Liknites," the cradled god growing toward his own male power? One way to avoid such a dilemma is to step outside the mother goddess so as not to *be* her but, more cru-cial, to *have* her. For only if she is other can the goddess love you; union with her energy is only possible, paradoxically, through separation from her body, which becomes a country for you only when you are not *it* but *of* it. In a sense, you can only, in fact, be in the goddess's body if first you are out of it, just as she can only enter and inspire you if she has been apart from you.

Such an almost mystical notion of maternal/filial separation-leading-to-union was expressed in psychoanalytic terms by Nancy Chodorow in *The Reproduction of Mothering,* a classic study whose theoretical substratum elaborated a metaphor of the "fluid boundaries" that simultaneously unite and divide daughters and mothers. Putting aside questions of the empirical validity of Chodorow's claims about the special pre-Oedipal relation between women and their female babies just as I have put aside appraisals of the anthropological accuracy of Bachofen's theories, I suggest that Chodorow's system is part of the same complex of desirous fantasies that impelled numerous poems of mother-daughter goddess-poet intercourse such as, say, Levertov's "Song for Ishtar" and her "The Goddess," H. D.'s *Trilogy,* Rich's "Sibling Mysteries," Lorde's "From the House of Yamanja," and Renée Vivien's "Returning to Mytilene," as well as epiphanies of the mother goddess in significant prose writings. Of these works, Denise Levertov's "Song for Ishtar" provides a paradigm:

> *The moon is a sow*
> *and grunts in my throat.*
> *Her great shining shines through me*
> *so the mud of my hollow gleams*
> *and breaks in silver bubbles.*
>
> *She is a sow*
> *and I a pig and a poet.*
>
> *When she opens her white*
> *lips to devour me I bite back*
> *and laughter rocks the moon.*
>
> *In the black of desire*
> *we rock and grunt, grunt and*
> *shine.*

Imagining herself as a totem of the goddess, perhaps as one of the sacred pigs central to the rites at Eleusis that Harrison studied, Levertov also defines herself as a lover/hierophant of this divine moon-mother's magic, and in a revisionary reversal of the traditional image of the sow who eats her farrow, she strips away what is implicitly, at least, a male anxiety about the mouth of the mother to reveal female exuberance. For as she engages in an act of ritual intercourse not (like Atwood's) *as* the goddess but *with* her, Levertov stresses both the separation and the similarity of this erotic mother-daughter pair. If one has a *vagina dentata*, so does the other ("When she opens her white / lips to devour me, I bite back"), but neither is sinister; rather, both are instruments of delighted love play ("Laughter rocks the moon") which enhances the mutual but differentiated desire of goddess and worshiper, (female) lover and (female) beloved ("In the black of desire / we rock and grunt, grunt and / shine").

Finally, then, as she is paradoxically impregnated by femaleness, this poet who early in her career produced a lyric meditation on the "Girlhood of Jane Harrison" as a fluent "outleaning from indoor darkness / to garden darkness" reestablishes the fluid boundaries between mother/muse and poet that markedly dissolve and reform throughout "The Goddess," perhaps her most well-known poem-about-poetry. In this piece, the speaker imagines another sort of divine rape by the power of the Great Mother ("She in whose lipservice / I passed my time"). "Coming" upon the poet "where I lay in Lie Castle," this potent figure flings the speaker through wall after wall into a fertile forest where, like a latter-day Persephone, "I bit on a seed and it spoke on my tongue." Yet unlike the six fatal seeds that in effect "spoke" to the mythic Persephone of Hades' power to assault and imprison, Levertov's seed "spoke" of Demeter,

> *without whom nothing*
> *flowers, fruits, sleeps in season,*
> *without whom nothing*
> *speaks in its own tongue but returns*
> *lie for lie . . .*

Spoke, that is, of the goddess who is the other and who is therefore the emblem of just the linguistic separation that provides linguistic inspiration.

Though few other writers have produced texts that enact the eroticism of the woman artist's aesthetic bond to the mother/muse quite as romantically as these two works by Levertov, many others have similarly distanced the goddess in order to evoke her inspiration. H. D.'s vision in *Tribute to the Angels* of the lady who "carries over the cult / of the *Bona Dea*" while simultaneously bearing "the unwritten volume of the new" recounts a moment of ecstatic contemplation that is also an epiphany of aesthetic consolation, as does her incantatory excavation in *The Gift* of culture's matriarchal substratum: "the first love, Maia, mama, Mutter, mut, mamalie, mimmie, Madre, Mary, mother." In another mode, throughout her autobiographical *Künstlerroman HERmione,* this life-long devotee of Mary/*mère*/*Mutter* meditated on the fluid boundaries between female self and female lover/other—"I know her. Her. I am Her. She is Her. Knowing her, I know Her"—as if to gloss such passages from *Trilogy* and *The Gift* while enacting again the paradoxical need for a separation that empowers erotic/aesthetic union.

Working both in words and paint, contemporaries of H. D.'s, notably the feminist surrealists Léonor Fini and Leonora Carrington, offered perhaps more nakedly fantastic contemplations of the goddess and her (pro) creative power. As Gloria Orenstein has observed, Fini's "world is a matriarchy"; she "presents the Alchemist as woman and identifies the womb as the alchemistic retort in *La Dame Ovale*" while such works as "*The Spinner* and *The Seamstress* also depict the archetypal feminine principles of the Great Mother" who "weaves the web of new life as she creates the fabric of the child within her body." Deploying the same dream strategies, Fini's sister surrealist Leonora Carrington dwells on images of the Black Swan ("the secret sign of the Goddess of the Old Religion, to which all women belong"), designs a Women's Liberation poster which "depicts the rising of the new woman as the goddess resurrected," and repeatedly returns in writings and paintings to "the female symbol of the egg" as if to emphasize just the coincidence of anthropology and embryology that underlies so many male and female meditations on matriarchy.[19]

As Orenstein notes, many of Fini's latest paintings "explore . . . the theme of lesbianism," surfacing the eroticism implicit in all of these fantasies about the goddess. But of course some of the best-known twentieth-century writing about maternal (pro)creativity was produced by Rich and Lorde, who moved from incantatory evocations of the mother like the affirmative conclusion of Rich's "Sibling Mysteries" ("the daughters were to begin with / brides of the mother") or the pulsing climax of Lorde's "From the House of Yamanja" ("Mother I need / mother I need / mother I need your blackness now / as the august earth needs rain") to aesthetic consummations made possible by the body of the lover/other. "My body / writes into your flesh / the poem / you make of me," Lorde declares in the punningly titled "Recreation," adding, just as punningly, "I made you / and take you made into me." Made by, for, and in a maid, the poet is herself re-made as the maiden acolyte of the mother. Similarly, Rich dreams in "Twenty-One Love Poems" of her lover piecing together "the fine, needle-like sherds of a great krater-cup / bearing on its sides / figures of ecstatic women striding / to the sibyl's den or the Eleusinian cave" even while she desires those "slender fingers" in her own "rose wet cave," adding that "when away from you I try to create you in words." An emblem of linguistic as well as sensual desire, the mother goddess is distinct from a lover for Rich and Lorde, as she is not for Levertov; nevertheless, she continually resolves into a beloved whose musing makes such musings possible, since, as Rich asserts, "it is the lesbian in us" who fantasizes a return to matriarchal creativity because she knows she is "of woman born."

Although Rich and Lorde, along with such contemporaries as Olga Broumas and Judy Grahn, represent the so-called Second Wave of feminism in their commitment to a lesbian aesthetic based on reenvisioning the mother goddess, they were also quite consciously working in a tradition that goes back at least as far as Sappho, whose Orphic/Dionysian community of women on Lesbos was elegantly analyzed in the nineteenth century by Bachofen himself. In the chapter of *Mother Right* titled "Lesbos," he discussed the simultaneously erotic and aesthetic "nature of Sapphic exaltation," noting that "to overlook the religious idea"—an idea analogous (and prior) to the Orphic mysticism that pervades, say, Plato's

Symposium—"is to miss its chief beauty," and stressed that "Singing both nature and womanhood, Sappho encompasses all sides of the goddess she serves." The "sublimity of [Sapphic] woman," he wrote, "is a consequence of her relation to the hidden doctrine" of matriarchal mystery: "the mystery is entrusted to the woman; it is she who safeguards it and administers it, and she who communicates it to men."[20]

Bachofen's theories prefigure the images and metaphors of one of Rich's and Lorde's more recent precursors: Renée Vivien, a poet who, as Susan Gubar has pointed out, made Sappho into the kind of muse/mother that, say, Ishtar is for Levertov. For Vivien, however, the powers of the goddess are so manifold that she can divide and arrange them into what amounts to a feminist chain of Being, a kind of womanly neo-Platonic hierarchy in which her human lover (in real life Natalie Barney) becomes a magical being not unlike Dante's Beatrice, a "Lorelei" who leads her toward "Lesbos of the golden flanks" and from there to Sappho, the spiritual/erotic mother who herself mediates the ultimate power of the goddess Aphrodite. Explaining that "Certain among us have conserved the rites" of Lesbos and "our loves have the white feet of the Kharaties," Vivien clarifies the hermetic correspondence between her living love and the mythic love of Sappho's lesbians: "Our bodies are for their bodies a reflecting mirror."

At the same time, Vivien also yearns in "Come, Goddess of Kurnos . . ." for the Maenadic freedom that Jane Ellen Harrison and Mary Elizabeth Coleridge celebrated:

> *Pour the wine of Cyprus and the wine of Lesbos,*
> *Whose hot language smiles and insinuates itself,*
> *And, the hour being sacred to the red Dionysus,*
> *Take the fragrant lilac and dance, fiery and nude.*

Thus Vivien's redemptive "Lesbos of the golden flanks" is not only a maternal body which promises erotic communion—an "Isle melodious and favorable to caresses"—it is also a maternal land that promises to "give us back our ancient soul" in a blessed female community not unlike the place inhabited by Coleridge's "wild white women."

For some literary women, the image of the Great Mother inspired such a dream of community even more than it did for Vivien, Coleridge, and Harrison. Displacing the power of the goddess onto the structures of desire that bond her acolytes into Amazonian bands, writers from Charlotte Perkins Gilman to Isak Dinesen to Monique Wittig describe utopias that center on the divine autonomy of the female body, the fierce creativity of womb or vulva. Nor do these artists necessarily locate their dream lands in the nostalgic Greece celebrated by Harrison and Vivien, although it is likely that many were at least inspired by Harrison's revisionary researches. In *Out of Africa* Dinesen, for example, has a fleeting epiphany of the possibility of such a community in an African harem:

> *Within this enclosed women's world . . . behind the walls and fortifications of it I felt the presence of a great ideal, without which the garrison [of women] would not have carried on so gallantly; the idea of a Millennium when women were to reign supreme in the world. The old mother at such times would take on a new shape, and sit enthroned as a massive dark symbol of that mighty female deity who had existed in old ages, before the time of the Prophet's God.*

Encompassing past and future, resurrection and redemption, Dinesen's vision of an African queendom prefigures the dream Dahomey of Lorde's liberated women warriors as well as the euphoric nowhere inhabited by Wittig's more hellenized *Guérillères*. More strikingly, Dinesen's epiphany foreshadows the revelation of female power that Anne Sexton records in "Somewhere in Africa," her elegy for her teacher John Holmes:

> *Let God be some tribal female who is known but forbidden.*

> *Let there be this God who is a woman who will place you*
> *upon her shallow boat, who is a woman naked to the waist,*
> *moist with palm oil and sweat, a woman of some virtue*

and wild breasts, her limbs excellent, unbruised and chaste.
Let her take you. She will put twelve strong men at the oars
for you are stronger than mahogany and your bones fill
the boat high as with fruit and bark from the interior.
She will have you now, you whom the funeral cannot kill.

John Holmes, cut from a single tree, lie heavy in her hold
and go down that river with the ivory, the copra and the gold.

The indefinite location of Sexton's vision ("somewhere in Africa") echoes the indefinite chronology of Dinesen's vision (a future "Millennium," the "old ages" of a distant past), just as her powerful "God who is a woman" corresponds to Dinesen's "Mighty female deity." At the same time, her poem provides a simultaneously male and female perspective on the Great Mother. For even while her stately stanzas (formally unusual for her) express her own yearning for the intercession of a divine woman, they also articulate her desire for this goddess to empower *her* but also, curiously, to simultaneously cradle and disempower the man she mourns. On the one hand, that is, Sexton seems to want (as Levertov and others do) to be "taken" by the goddess; on the other hand, she wants the goddess to "take" (and take away?) the male body of John Holmes, who is here reduced to an ivory cargo as inert as, say, Conrad's Kurtz becomes.

But in elaborating such a notion of the Great Mother's differing stances toward women and men, Sexton was not just echoing Dinesen; quite unconsciously, perhaps, she was recapitulating a theme that had concerned the turn-of-the-century feminist Charlotte Perkins Gilman. For in *Herland,* her 1915 utopia-of-women, Gilman employs a male narrator to describe a country devoted to the worship of a mother goddess, inhabited by "the marching stateliness of . . . great mothers," and perpetuated by maternal parthenogenesis. Paradoxically, moreover, her use of such a narrative perspective allows her to enact a double fantasy far more explicit than Sexton's. For even while Gilman describes with a certain vengeful pleasure the moments in which her masculine adventurer and his two companions are "taken" by these quasi goddesses—each of them at one point "seized by five women . . . and borne onward . . . struggling manfully, but held secure most womanfully, in spite of our best endeavors"—she also uses the narrator's gradual reconciliation to his incarceration in Herland to express her own desire to be "taken" by the mother. Love in Herland, she has him explain, "gave me a queer feeling, way down deep, *as of the stirring of some ancient dim prehistoric consciousness* [italics mine] . . . It was like—coming home to mother." On the one hand, therefore, this narrator's confinement in a "structure . . . built like the pre-Incan architecture in Peru, of enormous monoliths" turns *him* into a kind of cargo as passive as Sexton's John Holmes, but on the other hand his account of the "Goddess of Motherhood" whose matronage empowered the first parthenogenetic "New Woman" to become the "Queen-Priestess-Mother" of a "new race" expresses his author's desire for an enlivening encounter with such a goddess.[21]

Interestingly, although Gilman's *Herland* is set in a wild and largely unexplored continent at least as fictive as the Africa of Sexton's poem, the "Marching stateliness" of its "great mothers" may owe a good deal to the iconographic obsessions of her former husband, the painter Charles Walter Stetson, for in the years from 1892 to 1910 this fin de siècle fantasist produced a series of images of ecstatic communities of women whose rituals seem to parallel those of, say, Harrison's Maenads or Coleridge's "wild white women" even while they foreshadow the independence of Gilman's Herlanders. Both more hellenic and more hedonistic than his sometime wife's women, the subjects of such Stetson paintings as *Pagan Procession* (1892), *In Praise of Dionysius* [sic] (1899), *Procession and Moonrise* (1900), *Girls with Banner* (1901), and *Moonlight and a Dance* (1901) march, dance, bathe, and embrace in a nakedly female rapture that illustrates not only the "long, long dances" of *The Bacchae* and Isadora Duncan but also the fruitful feminism of Herland. That such images may have been expressions of a male voyeurism (or anxiety) about the emerging Furies of the suffrage movement is true but beside the point here, for they also functioned to inspire Gilman's own dreams of womanly communion and of a community like that of Monique Wittig's *Les Guérillères* in which the powers of the goddess are multiplied almost indefinitely in order both to inspire women and to immolate men.

The annihilation of sexual categories implied by the parthenogenesis of Herland points toward yet another, and even more paradoxical kind of fantasy facilitated by the concept of the Great Mother: the fantasy of gynandry, a state of being in which, with the male generative abilities subsumed into the Great Vessel of the goddess's womb, childbearing can become itself divine as well as a metaphor for the divine because it has been stripped of its literal associations with "blood, mucus, discharge, purulent offensive discharge." Though they differ significantly from each other, two major texts of such gynandrous (pro)creativity are Virginia Woolf's *Orlando* and Ursula LeGuin's *The Left Hand of Darkness,* both ostensibly fictive speculations about transsexuality which nevertheless include obliquely articulated meditations on the elements of female sexuality.

In the first, Orlando—based on the real-life figure of Woolf's own lesbian lover, Vita Sackville-West—is a man who becomes a woman who then becomes (almost in a subordinate clause) one of the mother protagonists in Woolf's oeuvre—albeit a very different one from, say, *To the Lighthouse*'s Mrs. Ramsay. That Orlando's effortless childbearing coincides with the completion (after centuries of composition) of her prize-winning poem "The Oak Tree," with the end of the Victorian age, with the absence of her husband, and with the glittering advent of "the present moment" makes a key point about its symbolic centrality as well as its matriarchal implications. Becoming fully female, reproducing with fantastic autonomy, Orlando also becomes a uniquely womanly artist, whose majestic possession of her own house and of all English history is finally signaled in the book's suggestively moonlit conclusion by the uncanny arrival of a dead queen—Queen Elizabeth as the Great Mother/ Muse of English Literature:

> All was still now. It was near midnight. The moon rose slowly over the weald. Its light raised a phantom castle upon earth. There stood the great house with all its windows robed in silver. Of wall or substance there was none. All was phantom. All was still. All was lit as for the

coming of a dead Queen. Gazing below her, Orlando saw dark plumes tossing in the courtyard, and torches flickering and shadows kneeling. A Queen once more stepped from her chariot.

Almost at the same moment that such female royalty manifests itself, Orlando's husband returns in a magic airplane and, as if to stress his status as attendant/muse, as if, indeed, to incorporate the powers of his body and mind into her own being, she bares "her breast to the moon . . . so that her pearls [glow] like the eggs of some vast moon-spider, guiding him in out of the clouds." Obliterating the threat of the male by assimilating his energies, this queenly hero/heroine recuperates what Neumann calls the "mysterious creative character" of the matriarchal vessel "that brings forth the male in itself and from out of itself."

Different as it is from *Orlando* or, for that matter, from *Herland*, LeGuin's *The Left Hand of Darkness* similarly posits gynandry, here by redistributing the powers of the mother to an entire society of females who are also males—thus defying and denying the powers of the father. Some feminists have taxed the author of this fantasy for her use of the pronoun "he" to describe her androgynes, but in fact it may well be LeGuin's willed reiteration of "he" and "his" in connection with "the king's pregnancy" or the Orgota Creation Myth in which "the nations of men [were] born . . . out of Edondurath's womb" that produces the most dramatic effect of uncanniness. For on the planet of Winter everyone has a womb and therefore everyone called "he" is really, in our sense, a "she," so that "the masculinity that rapes and the femininity that is raped" have been "eliminated." Indeed, while Genly Ai, the bemused narrator—a "normal" human man—contemplates his friend Estraven with an anxiety born of his own sexual stereotypes, musing that "it was impossible to think of him as a woman, that dark, ironic, powerful presence . . . and yet whenever I thought of him as a man I felt a sense of falseness . . ." Estraven contemplates him with affectionate pity: "There is a frailty about him. He is all unprotected, exposed, vulnerable, even to his sexual organ which he must carry always outside himself . . ." In this society, where because everyone bears children no one feels subordinated or "enslaved to the species," the power of the womb has been so purified of negative connotations that a merely masculine being like Ai can be considered a "pervert." At the same time, in a remarkable visionary passage Ai recounts the séance of a band of Foretellers, in which at the climactic moment of prophecy their leader, "Faxe the Weaver," manifests himself in all his power as "a woman dressed in light . . . an armored woman with a sword." Behind or beyond the gynandry of Winter's people, this epiphany suggests, gleams the lunar luminosity of the womb.

If in works like *Orlando* and *The Left Hand of Darkness* the luminosity of the womb is empowered precisely because it is multiplied, distanced, redistributed to all and each in fluent revisions of female sexuality that redefine the woman while deifying her, such strategies are important not just in themselves but because they recapitulate in fictional form the tactics deployed in some crucial feminist meditations on the issue with which I began my consideration of all of these texts: the metaphor of literary maternity. To be sure, a few women writers seem to have appropriated this metaphor intact from the roster of male thinkers that Terry Castle reviews in "Lab'ring Bards." Anaïs Nin's insistence, for instance, that "woman's creation . . . must be exactly like her creation of children, that is it must come out of her own blood, englobed by her womb, nourished with her own milk" foreshadowed Hélène Cixous' claim that woman must write in "white ink" because there is always a little of "that good mother's milk in her." Similarly, Anne Sexton's "In Celebration of My Uterus" praises the "singing" made possible for her by the "sweet weight" of her womb:

> *Sweet weight,*
> *in celebration of the woman I am*
> *and of the soul of the woman I am*
> *and of the central creature and its delight*
> *I sing for you. I dare to live.*

For H. D., however, the case was not quite so simple; like the most dramatic fantasists mentioned here, she sought to transform the exigencies of biology in order to valorize the imagination's womb. Thus, her late posthumously published *Hermetic Definition* enacts a pregnancy that leads to the paradoxical "birth" of its dead subject; Lionel Durand, the man she loves, is reborn and resurrected through the art of her literary maternity. "In September," she explains, "you were on the way," and adds that "it was . . . a little over nine months to the day" since her first meeting with this "muse" who inspired her sequence, "at Christmas time / that you were born." Ultimately, though, even after making herself into a literary Virgin Mary, the (re)producer of a Christmas child/text/man, she rejects the fantasy child her womb has brought forth in order to affirm herself and the virgin womb of her imagination. Thus, her vision emphasizes the independent authority of the goddess/maker rather than her tender attendance upon the "Dionysos Liknites" of her creation.

In much the same way, Denise Levertov's *The Poet in the World* plays with the metaphor of literary maternity while apparently withdrawing from it. Beginning with the notation that "the poet is in labor . . . and the child is pushing and sliding out of her, insistent, a poem," she dissolves and resolves her pronouns into masculinity in order, like LeGuin and Woolf, to appropriate and incorporate the powers of masculinity, of fatherhood and sonhood, all of which are implicit in the primordial power of the poet/mother. "The poet is a father," she explains, and the poem is "the remote consequence of a dream of his, acted out nine months before," and also "the poet is being born . . . he is . . . aware of a new world around him, the walls of the womb are gone . . ." Like the protagonist of Adrienne Rich's more anxious and ambivalent "The Mirror In Which Two Are Seen as One," Levertov imagines herself as poet/mother giving birth to her/himself as divine poet/child, her "two hands grasping [her] head / drawing it down against the blade of life / [her] nerves the nerves of a midwife / learning her trade." But unlike the anguished, laborious pregnancy Rich describes, which includes a vision of a "mother dying in childbirth over and over," Levertov's poetic maternity is blissfully complete, self-generating, self-enclosed, self-fulfilling, for—again like Neumann's Great Vessel—she possesses every aspect of the "mysterious creative power." The product of her art is not fictive or mystic to her, for it has ripened in her imagination's womb; at the same time, her relation to it is not passive, for she has begotten it in and of herself; finally, she need not lose it, for she *is* it, it is her.

If Levertov's deployment of the metaphor of literary maternity is as fantastic as any of Woolf's or LeGuin's redefinitions of sexuality, however, it is prosaic in comparison to the concept of "womb vision" that H. D. elaborated in "Notes on Thought and Vision." In a radical yet firmly confident series of comments, H. D. comes here to terms with the terms of female sexuality by formulating a fantasy of (pro)creativity that simultaneously detaches the womb from the body and deifies what she defines as its special epistemological powers. There are "three states or manifestations of life—body, mind, over-mind," H. D. observes at the beginning of her "Notes," and it seems at first as if she will go on to develop a theory of *chakras* like the Yogic ideology at the center of Lawrence's *Fantasia of the Unconscious* or a theory of personality like the one that constitutes Yeats' *A Vision*. But she moves quickly to more daring claims: "Vision is of two kinds—vision of the womb and vision of the brain," she writes, observing that "vision of the womb or love-vision," located in the body, is as special as "vision of the brain" or "over-mind," and wondering whether it may be "easier for a woman to attain this state of consciousness [i.e., womb vision] than for a man," and whether we should "be able to think with the womb and feel with the brain."

Significantly, her answers to these questions, while oblique, take her back to the "Elusinian mysteries [*sic*]" that "had to do with sex" and toward what is essentially a *thriambos* to "Dionysius Anthico—god in a flower . . . Dionysius Zagreus—the flower torn," as well as to an affirmation that "no man may speak your name, O Goddess." For her, she explains, Euripides is "a white rose—lyric, feminine, a spirit," and the "mystery of Demeter, the Earth Mother" is crucial to the workings of creativity even as "Christ and his father, or as the Eleusinian mystic would have said, his mother, were one . . . [for Christ] was the body of nature, the vine, the Dionysius, as he was the soul of nature," and the poem, the creative product, is "an incarnation of the womb, the flesh *and* spirit of the female not unlike Christ himself."

The power of the womb translated into a power of the mind, the world's vision of the womb transformed into the womb's vision of the world: such radical variations upon the old theme of literary maternity could only have been possible in an age whose biomythology had reimagined maternity and redefined the madwoman who haunted the attics of the nineteenth century as mystical Maenads with "miraculous magnetic powers" of literal and literary (pro)creation. Just as the husbands and fathers of Macedonia were, Harrison tells us, *"frighten[ed] out of their senses [sic]"* by their Dionysian wives and daughters, the male contemporaries of these newly Maenadic artists were daunted by such women's claims to empowerment. In *Kangaroo,* Lawrence observed that his autobiographical protagonist, Richard Somers, "feared and wondered over" the verse of a "poetess" who is a thinly disguised version of H. D. In 1942 Phillip Wylie struggled to put "mom" back in her place by defining her as a "five-and-ten-cent-store Lilith," and as recently as 1976 Harold Bloom, quoting the Zohar's account of the primacy of "Lilith, a hot and burning female" who was Adam's legendary first wife, came to terms with the masculine anxiety such a figure inspires by explaining that "filthy myths of Lilith actually are filthy myths of the male dread of female otherness, and of what the male envies as female proximity to origins." But Bloom's conclusion was dark and exhausted: "All men are belated in their stance towards all women." Against such exhaustion, however, H. D. and other female fantasists had already set a redemptive vision of female authority. The priestess of the *Bona Dea* who appears at the end of *Tribute to the Angels* possesses herself in patience, awaiting and inspiring the new age dreamed by women from Harrison and Gilman to Plath and Rich. Though she is "immaculate" as "the Lamb's Bride," "the Lamb [is] not with her, / either as Bridegroom or Child; / her attention is undivided, / we are her bridegroom and lamb; / *her book is our book*" (italics mine).[22]

—1986, 1999

NOTES

PART I: Finding Atlantis—and Growing into Feminism

Becoming a Feminist Together—and Apart: Notes on Collaboration and Identity

1. "Auden on opera, detective writers, wit, politics, the camera, drugs, poets and poetry," interviewed by Brendan Kennelly, in *Swarthmore College Bulletin,* alumni issue, May 1972, p. 5.
2. "Click": see Jane O'Reilly, "The Housewife's Moment of Truth," *New York Magazine* ([*Ms.* insert], December 20, 1971); "making a woman inferior": see Dworkin, chap. 7.
3. Lawrence, "The Spirit of Place," *Studies in Classic American Literature,* p. 31. Added Lawrence in a few sentences that further illuminated our guest's assertions, "The proper function of a critic is to save the tale from the artist who created it" [because] "an artist usually intellectualizes on top, and his dark under-consciousness goes on contradicting him beneath."
4. Valenti, pp. 175–76.
5. Baumgardner and Richards, p. xxi.
6. See Chodorow, passim, and also, for more general theories about collaboration in, for instance, multiple psychic processes, see Ogden, esp. chap. 1, "On Becoming a Subject." I am grateful to Claire Kahane for calling this work to my attention; and for further thoughts on collaboration I also thank the other members of the Betty Roszak soirée.

Finding Atlantis: Thirty Years of Exploring Women's Literary Traditions in English

1. Christine de Pizan, II.36.1–4, pp. 153–55.
2. Gage, vol. 1, pp. 28–29.
3. Lanson, pp. 166–67, as cited and translated in Laennec, p. 47. See also http://www .fabula.org/actualites/article8040.php for the prospectus of a recent conference held at the University of Liège, January 2005, on "Christine de Pizan: A Woman of Science, a Woman of Letters."
4. See Curnow, and Christine de Pizan. For a more recent translation, see Rosalind Brown-Grant (1999).
5. See Quilligan; and for a problematizing of Christine's feminism, see Delany, "Mothers to Think Back Through."

6. Austen, *Northanger Abbey,* chap. 5; Barrett Browning to H. F. Chorley, January 7, 1845, *Letters,* vol. 1, pp. 230–32; Dickinson, *Poems,* J. 593, p. 291. All Dickinson texts are from *The Complete Poems of Emily Dickinson,* ed. Thomas Johnson. Where necessary, citations will be given as here, by "Johnson" number—i.e., as numbered in this edition.

7. Austen to James Edward Austen, December 16–17, 1816, *Letters,* p. 323; Brontë to Robert Southey, March 16, 1837, *Letters,* pp. 168–69; Brontë, *Tales of Angria,* p. 452, and *Legends of Angria,* p. 316.

8. Shelley, *Frankenstein,* p. 186; Rossetti to William Rossetti, December 10, 1888, *Letters,* vol. 4, p. 103; Dickinson to T. W. Higginson, June 7, 1862, *Letters,* vol. 2, pp. 408–9; Eliot to Mrs. Charles Bray, November 8, 1843, *Letters,* vol. 1, p. 164.

9. Bradstreet, "The Prologue," pp. 7–8; Winchilsea, "The Spleen," p. 250, and "The Introduction," p. 6; Newcastle, p. 136.

10. Behn, epilogue to *Sir Patient Fancy,* vol. 6, p. 85; Woolf, *A Room of One's Own,* pp. 75–76; Plath to Aurelia Schober Plath, February 24, 1957, *Letters Home,* p. 297.

11. Eliot, "Silly Novels by Lady Novelists," *Selected Essays,* p. 149; Plath to Aurelia Schober Plath, April 29, 1956, *Letters Home,* pp. 243–44.

12. Sayers, p. 116; Behn, preface to *The Lucky Chance,* vol. 7, p. 217; Dickinson to Mrs. J. G. Holland, early March 1866, *Letters,* vol. 2, p. 449; Woolf, *A Room of One's Own, Orlando*; astonishingly enough, even Christine appears to have believed this, at least intermittently. "I am a man," she once wrote, adding *"I am not lying"*: cited and translated in Beer, p. 125.

13. Gilbert and Gubar, *The Norton Anthology of Literature by Women,* pp. 618 (Bishop) and 542 (Riding).

14. Christine de Pizan, II.36.1, p. 153; Astell, pp. 18 and 24; Wollstonecraft, *A Vindication of the Rights of Woman,* in *Political Writings,* pp. 107 and 277; Cooper, "The Higher Education of Coloured Women," *The Voice of Anna Julia Cooper,* p. 73; Woolf, *The Complete Shorter Fiction,* p. 147.

15. Fern, p. 286.

16. Rich, *Diving into the Wreck,* pp. 23–24.

What Do Feminist Critics Want? Or, A Postcard from the Volcano

1. This essay is adapted from a talk given at the 1980 summer seminar of the Association of Departments of English in Spokane, Washington, soon after the eruption of Mount St. Helens in Oregon.

2. Kizer, "Pro Femina," p. 116.

3. See Woolf, *A Room of One's Own*; Rich, "When We Dead Awaken"; Heilbrun, *Reinventing Womanhood*; Kelly-Gadol, p. 4.

4. See Gilbert and Gubar, *The Madwoman in the Attic,* esp. "Toward a Feminist Poetics"; see also Ortner.

5. Hopkins, p. 133.

6. Dickinson, J. 1677.

7. Woolf, *A Room of One's Own,* p. 64.

8. See Gilbert and Gubar, *The Madwoman in the Attic,* pp. 45–92.

9. Woolf, *A Room of One's Own,* p. 94.

10. See Winchilsea, "The Introduction," pp. 4–5.
11. Heilbrun, "Feminist Criticism," p. 35.
12. Robinson, p. 19.
13. Miller, "The Function of Rhetorical Study at the Present Time," p. 12.
14. Greg, *Why Are Women Redundant?*
15. Dickinson, J. 175 and J. 601.
16. Vincent Barabba, quoted in the *San Francisco Chronicle,* May 20, 1980, p. F5; for an analysis of this massive cultural "forgetting" of the First Wave of feminism, see Theodore Roszak.
17. Bloom, *A Map of Misreading,* p. 33.
18. Ong, pp. 249–50.
19. See, e.g., Irwin, p. 163; see also Gubar, " 'The Blank Page.' "

The Education of Henrietta Adams

1. Adams, p. 762.
2. Fancher, pp. 60–61.
3. Adams, p. 755.
4. Adams, pp. 341, 737, 770, and 774.
5. Adams, pp. 582–83, 523, and 1042.
6. Adams, p. 1042; Kaledin, p. 57; Woolf, *A Room of One's Own,* p. 46.
7. Adams, p. 1042.
8. Kaledin, pp. 14, 241, and 224.

A Tarantella of Theory: Hélène Cixous' and Catherine Clément's *Newly Born Woman*

1. Cixous and Clément, pp. 21, 20, and 22.
2. Cixous and Clément, pp. 136 and 117.
3. Ortner, pp. 73, 76, 85, and 86.
4. Woolf, *Three Guineas,* p. 129; Barrett Browning, *Letters,* pp. 231–32; Dickinson, J. 593.
5. Fauré, p. 86; Jones, p. 368.
6. Lawrence, *Lady Chatterley's Lover,* pp. 174–75.

Reflections on a (Feminist) Discourse of Discourse, or, Look, Ma, I'm Talking!

1. Jardine, p. 97.
2. Jardine, pp. 107–8.
3. Kristeva, *Revolution in Poetic Language,* pp. 27 and 30.
4. Irigaray, p. 543; emphases mine.
5. Lodge, pp. 322 and 323.
6. See chap. 5, "Sexual Linguistics," of Gilbert and Gubar, *No Man's Land,* vol. 1, *The War of the Words,* pp. 227–75.
7. Kristeva, "Oscillation Between Power and Denial" (interview by Xavière Gauthier), pp. 117–18.
8. Woolf, *A Room of One's Own,* pp. 117–18.

PART II: Reading and Rereading Women's Writing

"My Name Is Darkness": The Poetry of Self-Definition

1. Rosenthal, pp. 15 and 61.
2. Bloom, *The Anxiety of Influence,* esp. "Introduction: A Meditation upon Priority," pp. 5–16.
3. All from Plath, *Ariel.*
4. All from Wakoski, *Inside the Blood Factory* and *Dancing on the Grave of a Son of a Bitch.*
5. All from Rich, *Poems: Selected and New, 1950–1974.*
6. All from Sexton, *Love Poems, The Book of Folly,* and *The Death Notebooks.*
7. All from Levertov, *O Taste and See* and *The Sorrow Dance.*
8. Winchilsea, "The Introduction," pp. 4–6.
9. Rich, "Has Nature": "Snapshots of a Daughter-in-Law"; "an instrument": "Planetarium," *Poems,* pp. 49 and 148; Plath, *The Bell Jar,* p. 68; "rules": "A Birthday Present," *Ariel,* p. 42; Rich, "thinking woman": "Snapshots," *Poems,* p. 42; Plath, "What am I": "Poppies in October," *Ariel,* p. 19.
10. Lowell, "Man and Wife," *Life Studies,* p. 87; Snodgrass, "These Trees Stand," *Heart's Needle,* p. 36; Levertov, "Stepping Westward," *The Sorrow Dance,* p. 15; Plath, "Tulips," *Ariel,* p. 10.
11. Sexton, "Third Psalm," *The Death Notebooks,* p. 82; Rich, "The Stranger," *Diving into the Wreck,* p. 19; Wakoski, "The Diamond Merchant," "The Mirror of a Day Chiming Marigold," and "In the Secret Room East of the Sun . . . ," *Dancing on the Grave of a Son of a Bitch,* pp. 118, 23, and 22.
12. Levertov, "In Mind," *O Taste and See,* p. 71.
13. Sexton, "The Other," *The Book of Folly,* pp. 30–31. On Sexton's use of Christopher Smart, see Gilbert, "Jubilate Anne."
14. Plath, "Fever 103°," *Ariel,* pp. 54–55; "Elm," p. 16; Sexton, *Love Poems,* p. 29; Rich, "Ghazals: Homage to Ghalib," *Poems,* p. 125; Wakoski, "This King: The Tombed Egyptian One," "Water Shapes," "Blue Monday": *Inside,* pp. 33, 23, and 10–11.
15. Plath, "Stings," *Ariel,* p. 63; Levertov, "The Wings," *The Sorrow Dance,* p. 12.
16. Rich, "When We Dead Awaken," *Poems,* p. 187; "Song," *Diving into the Wreck,* p. 20.
17. Rich, "From the Prison House," *Diving into the Wreck,* pp. 17–18; Lawrence, "Humiliation," *Complete Poems,* vol. 1, p. 215.
18. Yeats, "He and She," from "Supernatural Songs," *Collected Poems,* p. 285; Rukeyser, "The Poem as Mask," *The Speed of Darkness,* p. 3.

"A Fine, White Flying Myth": The Life/Work of Sylvia Plath

1. "Den of Lions," pp. 127 and 144–45.
2. Foreword to *Ariel,* p. ix.
3. See Moers, pp. 90–110.
4. See Ellis, pp. 9 and 15.
5. See Lewes.
6. Newman, "Candor Is the Only Wile," in *The Art of Sylvia Plath,* p. 48.
7. Hughes, "Notes on the Chronological Order of Sylvia Plath's Poems," in Newman,

The Art of Sylvia Plath, p. 188; Stade, introduction to Steiner, *A Closer Look at "Ariel,"* p. 9.

8. *Ariel,* pp. 63 and 27; *The Bell Jar,* pp. 58 and 68.

9. Brontë, *Jane Eyre,* chap. 2.

10. "Ocean 1212-W," in Newman, *The Art of Sylvia Plath,* p. 272.

11. Dickinson, "It was not Death, for I stood up," J. 510, and "The Soul has Bandaged moments—," J. 512, *The Complete Poems of Emily Dickinson.*

12. "The Fifty-ninth Bear," p. 20.

13. *The Bell Jar,* p. 60.

14. Beauvoir, p. 467.

15. Shelley, *Mary Wollstonecraft Shelley's Frankenstein,* p. 177; Sexton, "Third Psalm," *The Death Notebooks,* pp. 83–84.

16. Beauvoir, pp. 468 and 464.

17. Otto Plath, *Bumblebees and Their Ways;* "our local midwife": quoted in Douglas Cleverdon, "On Three Women," in Newman, *The Art of Sylvia Plath,* p. 228.

18. Lawrence, "The Song of a Man Who Has Come Through," *The Complete Poems of D. H. Lawrence,* vol. 1, p. 250; Hughes, p. 192; "glassy music": quoted in Alvarez, "Sylvia Plath," in Newman, *The Art of Sylvia Plath,* p. 59; see Bly, pp. 39–43.

19. "Context," pp. 45–46.

The Wayward Nun Beneath the Hill: Emily Dickinson and the Mysteries of Womanhood

1. Todd, in Leyda, vol. 2, p. 357; "fiery mist": see T. W. Higginson to ED in Dickinson, *Letters,* vol. 2, p. 461: "I have the greatest desire to see you, always feeling that perhaps if I could once take you by the hand I might be something to you; but till then you only enshroud yourself in this fiery mist & I cannot reach you, but only rejoice in the rare sparkles of light."

2. For a newspaper story about a real "New England Nun" whose career would have been known to Dickinson, see Leyda, vol. 1, p. 148; for a fictionalized account of a "New England Nun" that mythologizes female domesticity in a way partly (though not wholly) comparable to Dickinson's own, see Freeman, "A New England Nun"; Leyda, vol. 2, pp. 576 and 151.

3. *The Boston Cooking-School Magazine,* June–July 1906; quoted by James Reeves in an Introduction to *Selected Poems of Emily Dickinson* reprinted in Sewall, p. 119.

4. Keats to George and Georgiana Keats, February 18, 1819, in *Letters.*

5. Leyda, vol. 1, pp. 131 and 135.

6. Dickinson, *Letters,* vol. 2, p. 460.

7. "conversion": J. 593.

8. "Though I than He—may longer live / He longer must—than I— / For I have but the power to kill / Without—the power to die—"

9. J. 165, 281, and 175.

10. Dickinson, *Letters,* vol. 2, p. 404.

11. Rich, "Vesuvius at Home"; J. 285: "Without the Snow Tableau / Winter, were lie—to me— / Because I see—New Englandly."

12. See Gilbert and Gubar, *The Madwoman in the Attic,* pp. 613–21.

13. Dickinson, *Letters,* vol. 2, p. 412.

14. See Gilbert and Gubar, *The Madwoman in the Attic*, pp. 613–21.

15. For Mabel Todd on Dickinson's similarity to "Miss Haversham" [*sic*], see Leyda, vol. 2, p. 377.

16. See *Aurora Leigh* in Barrett Browning, *Poetical Works* (1891), pp. 21, 28, 149; Nancy Rexford, costume curator at the Northampton Historical Society, has assured me that the white Dickinson dress at the Amherst Homestead is a comparatively "ordinary" cotton day dress—what we would now, perhaps, call a "housedress," or at least a dress designed for casual wear—fashioned in the style of the 1870s or 1880s, the period when Dickinson would have worn it regularly. She also notes, however, that it was not at that time at all "ordinary" for such a garment to be made in *white* unless it was a child's dress or a summer costume designed for wearing at the seaside (which Dickinson's plainly was not).

17. See Carlyle, book 2, chap. 8, "Natural Supernaturalism." Carlyle's picture, incidentally, was one of three portraits that hung on ED's bedroom wall. The other two were of Eliot and Barrett Browning.

18. Leyda, vol. 2, p. 482.

19. Ransom, "Emily Dickinson," in Sewall, p. 89.

20. Austen, *Northanger Abbey*, chap. 14; Woolf, "Modes and Manners of the Nineteenth Century," *Books and Portraits*, p. 23; Dickinson to Mrs. J. G. Holland, 1884, *Letters*, vol. 3, p. 849.

21. Austen, *Letters to Her Sister Cassandra and Others*, pp. 468–69; see J. 1651; for a related, but differently designed, discussion of "A Word made Flesh" and its implications for Dickinson's own sense of herself as somehow divine, see Homans, pp. 212–14; see "Käthe Kollwitz" ("What would happen if one woman told the truth about her life? / The world would split open"), in Rukeyser, *The Speed of Darkness*; Leyda, vol. 2, p. 481.

22. Leyda, p. 483; "esoteric sips": see J. 1452.

23. Homans, analyzing this phenomenon, argues differently (but to the same end) that Dickinson deliberately exploits language's potential for ambiguity, duplicity, and fictiveness (Homans, pp. 165–214, passim).

24. J. 392, 24, 140, 392, 258, 956, and 1099.

25. See, for instance, Ortner, and Neumann, *The Great Mother*.

26. Dickinson, *Letters*, vol. 3, p. 783.

Jane Eyre and the Secrets of Furious Lovemaking

1. Cited in Gilbert and Gubar, *The Madwoman in the Attic*, pp. 173–77; Mozley, p. 423; Oliphant, p. 557.

2. Millett, p. 147; Rich, "When We Dead Awaken," pp. 35–36; Dworkin, p. 100; Plath, *Collected Poems*, p. 223.

3. Nudd, p. 140; Lerner, p. 199.

4. Indeed, if *Jane Eyre* dramatizations are added to *Wuthering Heights* dramatizations and Brontë family history dramatizations, they constitute such a major industry that one "Wilella Waldorf" once wrote a comic editorial calling for a "National Society for the Suppression of Plays about the Brontës" (Nudd, p. 137); on "romantic thralldom," see DuPlessis, "Romantic Thralldom in H. D."

5. See, for example, Bret Harte's "Miss Mix by Ch–l–tte Br–nte" (1867), in which the

smugly virtuous heroine leaves her childhood home at "Minerva Cottage" forever to enter the service and the arms of "Mr. Rawjester," the polygamous master of "Blunderbore Hall"; Showalter, p. 115.

6. In reviewing these stories, along with those implicit in Brontë's representations of her male characters, I am drawing heavily on a talk entitled "Plain Jane Goes to the Movies" that I coauthored and delivered with Susan Gubar at the University of South Carolina in the spring of 1997. For the contribution that work has made to this section of my essay, as well as the part her incisive thinking has played throughout this piece, I am (as I have so often been throughout my career) deeply indebted and very grateful to my longtime collaborator.

7. See Gilbert, "Plain Jane's Progress"; and Gilbert and Gubar, *The Madwoman in the Attic.*

8. For "postcolonial" readings of *Jane Eyre,* see, among others, David, pp. 77–117; Donaldson; Meyer, pp. 69–95; Perera; Sharpe, pp. 26–53; Spivak; and Young.

9. In *The Education of the Senses,* Gay rejects as "derisive" and "little-challenged" the "tenacious misconceptions . . . of Victorian culture as a devious and insincere world in which middle-class husbands slaked their lust [with mistresses and prostitutes] . . . while their wives . . . were sexually anaesthetic" (p. 6); on Acton, see Showalter, p. 120; for Duncan and Stanton, see Gay, pp. 134 and 119.

10. I am particularly indebted to conversations with Susan Gubar for these observations about the textual function of Richard Mason as well as for a number of other points about the ways in which Brontë represents and interrogates received notions about male sexuality.

11. Act II, Scene 2: "Isolde: No more Isolde! / Tristan: No more Tristan! / Both: No more naming, / no more parting" (Wagner, *Tristan and Isolde,* pp. 19–20). For a further comment on this phenomenon (and the darkness of the *Liebestod* it often entails), see Bataille: "Only the beloved, so it seems to the lover . . . can in this world bring about what our human limitations deny, a total blending of two beings, a continuity between two discontinuous creatures . . . For the lover, the beloved makes the world transparent. Through the beloved appears . . . full and limitless being unconfined within the trammels of separate personalities, continuity of being, glimpsed as a deliverance through the person of the beloved" (pp. 20–21). The rhetoric of mystical communion that marks the orgasmic moments when Jane and Rochester "hear" each other's calls is best explained in this context, as is Rochester's declaration in chapter 23 that "my bride is here . . . because my equal is here, and my likeness"; for a brief discussion of the Minnegrotte as an implied trope in *Jane Eyre,* see Lerner, p. 190.

12. For a different perspective on the authority (or lack of it) associated with Jane's/Joan Fontaine's gaze in the 1944 Stevenson movie, see Ellis and Kaplan: "Cinematically, Jane is placed as Rochester's observer . . . We retain [her] point of view, but her gaze is fixed on Rochester as object of desire, an odd reversal of the usual situation in film where the male observes the woman as object of desire in such a way that the audience sees her that way too. Interestingly, the reversal of the look does not give Jane any more power: Rochester comes and goes, commands and manages, orders Jane's presence as he wishes. Jane's look is of a yearning, passive kind as against the more usual controlling male look at the woman." (I should confess, in response to this comment, that I have trouble understanding the distinction between a "yearning" look and a "controlling" look.)

The Key to Happiness: On Frances Hodgson Burnett's *The Secret Garden*

1. Quoted in Bixler, p. 4.
2. Burnett, pp. 312 and 325.
3. Bixler, p. 9.
4. See Bixler, pp. 11 and 4–5.
5. *The New York Journal and Advertiser,* quoted in Thwaite, p. 190.
6. "forced and blackguarded": quoted in Thwaite, p. 191; on Maytham Hall and Plandome: see Thwaite, pp. 178–84, 217, and 227.
7. "a passionate gardener": Bixler, p. 15; *In the Garden*: quoted in Bixler, p. 102.
8. Blake, "Infant Joy": *Songs of Innocence and of Experience*; "hidden laughter": Eliot, "Burnt Norton," *Four Quartets.*
9. Bewick.
10. Burnett's novel also, of course, lent its title to Nancy Friday's *My Secret Garden* (1981), a book of erotic fantasies, but serious critical cases have been made for its influence on Lawrence and Eliot in, for instance, Verduin; Lindskoog, pp. 98–103; and White.

"Dare You See a Soul *at the White Heat*?": Thoughts on a "Little Home-keeping Person"

1. Both of my "Dickinson poems" appear in Gilbert, *Emily's Bread.*
2. See my discussion of this poem in *Death's Door,* pp. 353–55.
3. Gilbert, *Kissing the Bread,* pp. 108–9.

PART III: Mother Rites: Maternity, Matriarchy, Creativity

From *Patria* to *Matria*: Elizabeth Barrett Browning's *Risorgimento*

1. All of the quotations from *Aurora Leigh* in this essay come from Barrett Browning, *Aurora Leigh and Other Poems*. All references to *Casa Guidi Windows* are to Barrett Browning, *Casa Guidi Windows*. I am deeply grateful to Elliot Gilbert for critical insights that have been helpful throughout this essay. In addition, I am grateful to Susan Gubar and Dorothy Mermin for useful comments and suggestions. Finally, I want to thank my mother, Angela Mortola, for inspiring me to think about Italy. This paper is dedicated to her, with love.
2. "Poetic pitch": quoted by Markus in *Casa Guidi Windows,* pp. xvi–xvii; "Poetic Aberrations"; *Blackwood's* 87 (1860): 490–504; Barrett Browning, "Napoleon in Italy," *Poetical Works,* p. 412. In a brilliant essay on the Brownings and Italian politics, Flavia Alaya notes the connections among the regeneration of Aurora Leigh, the reunification of Italy, and Barrett Browning's personal sense of rebirth after her flight with Browning from England to Italy. But Alaya's study emphasizes the literary dialectic between two major poets who were, as she puts it, "quite literally political bedfellows," for she shows through a close reading of *The Ring and the Book* how Browning's Pompilia constitutes a revision of both Elizabeth and Italy, so that the husband's complex set of dramatic monologues is in some sense a response to the wife's earlier, apparently more naïve and personal epic of a heroine's *risorgimento*. In addition, through close readings of Barrett Browning's letters and some of her poems,

Alaya vigorously defines and defends this woman poet's often misunderstood (and frequently scorned) political stance.

3. "Female Sexuality," p. 195. Though Alaya sees Browning/Romney as the "father" of Elizabeth/Aurora's reborn self, an opinion I disagree with, she does also suggest that "a mother-quest played a much more dominant role in [Barrett Browning's] psychic life" than is usually thought (Alaya, p. 30 n. 18).

4. For a discussion of Aurora's vision of her mother's portrait, see Gilbert and Gubar, *The Madwoman in the Attic*, pp. 18-20.

5. Rogers, p. 301; Eliot, *Middlemarch*, book 2, chap. 15; Wharton, *Italian Backgrounds*, p. 3.

6. "Niobe": *Childe Harold*, canto 4, stanzas 2, 78, and 79; Ruskin, "Paradise of cities": *Diaries*, vol. 1, p. 183, *Letters*, p. 128; Ouida, *Pascarel*, quoted in Churchill, p. 163. Alaya also discusses this pervasive trope of Italy as a tragic woman and the political function of the image in the *risorgimento*, and Ruskin describes the way the pillars of the porches of San Marco "half refuse and half yield to the sunshine, Cleopatra-like, 'their bluest veins to kiss'" (*Letters*, p. 128). For a discussion of woman as Galatea, see Gilbert and Gubar, *The Madwoman in the Attic*, pp. 12-13.

7. *Letters*, vol. 1, pp. 341-43. Elsewhere Barrett Browning remarks that "[we] can dine our favorite way . . . with a miraculous cheapness . . . the prophet Elijah or the lilies of the field took as little thought for their dining, which exactly suits us" (*Letters*, vol. 1, p. 303).

8. *Letters*, vol. 1, p. 332.

9. Barrett Browning to Mr. Boyd, p. 176; Staël, *Corinne*, "l'image": book 2, chap. 2, p. 50; "langue maternelle": book 7, chap. 2, p. 183; "tout était langage": book 6, chap. 1, p. 141; "Tuscan musical/vowels": *Casa Guidi Windows*, 1.1188-90. For a useful analysis of *Corinne's* significance to nineteenth-century women writers, and especially to Barrett Browning, see Moers, pp. 173-210; on *Corinne's* Italy as a "land of women," see Gutwirth, pp. 208-15, and Peel, esp. pp. 34-64. I am grateful to Ellen Peel for sharing this material with me.

10. *Casa Guidi Windows*, pp. 66 and 67; *Flush*, pp. 75 and 78-79.

11. For "the rigid North," see "Enrica" and *Casa Guidi Windows*, 1.1173; it is possible, even likely, that Rossetti borrowed the phrase from Barrett Browning. For "the sweet South," see Rossetti's "Italia, Io Ti Saluto," pp. 378-79.

12. Barrett Browning, *Letters*, vol. 1, pp. 288 and 291.

13. Barrett Browning, *Letters*, vol. 1, p. 291.

14. Barrett Browning, *Letters*, vol. 2, pp. 190 and 193; *Casa Guidi Windows*, 2.638-39 and 649-51.

15. Until recently, few critics have dealt directly with *Aurora Leigh*; major modern writers on the subject include Woolf, "*Aurora Leigh*"; Moers, esp. 201-7; Cooper, "Working into Light"; Cora Kaplan, introduction to Barrett Browning, *Aurora Leigh*; Gelpi, "*Aurora Leigh*"; Steinmetz; Rosenblum; Plath, "Tulips," *Ariel*, p. 12.

16. *Letters*, vol. 1, p. 134.

17. Tennyson, p. 130.

18. The name Marian Erle evokes Goethe's "Erlkönig," the uncanny and elfish forest spirit who is a manifestation of nature rather than of culture.

19. Freud, *Totem and Taboo*, pp. 915-19.

20. Marchand, vol. 1, p. 396; for Barrett Browning's ambivalent feelings toward Byron, see Taplin, pp. 15 and 103.

21. See Barrett Browning, *Aurora Leigh,* pp. 23–24. Dorothy Mermin has pointed out to me the resemblances between Romney Leigh and St. John Rivers, a likeness Taplin also takes up (pp. 316–17). Interestingly, as Romney becomes more like Rochester, he also becomes, in a sense, more Byronic; at the same time, however, his kinship to St. John Rivers mutes (and thus makes acceptable) his Byronic qualities.

22. Immersed in Browning's very name is a wordplay on "Bro's" fate: "Browning" suggests a conflation of "Bro" and "drowning."

23. See Barrett Browning, *Casa Guidi Windows,* 2.399–405:

> *I love no peace which is not fellowship,*
> *And which includes not mercy. I would have*
> *Rather, the raking of the guns across*
> *The world, and shrieks against Heaven's architrave;*
> *Rather the struggle in the slippery fosse*
> *Of dying men and horses, and the wave*
> *Blood-bubbling . . .*

24. Barrett Browning, "A Thought on Thoughts," *Complete Works,* vol. 6, pp. 352–59.

25. Quoted in Chevigny, pp. 435 and 453.

26. "Imagined possibility": quoted in Chevigny, p. 375. Chevigny ascribes this comment to W. H. Hurlbut, who thought Ossoli an "underdeveloped and uninteresting Italian." In any case, the parallels between Barrett Browning and Fuller are interesting. Although Barrett Browning makes Romney older than Aurora, both Ossoli and Browning were considerably younger than their mates, as though Fuller and Barrett Browning had each half consciously decided that in a utopian rearrangement of the relationship between the sexes men should be younger than their wives in order symbolically to free women from the bonds of daughterhood. In addition, both Fuller and Barrett Browning, quite late in life and rather unexpectedly, had children in Italy, and the private experience of maternity may well have reinforced their mutual hopes for a public experience of matriarchy; "Bologna": Chevigny, pp. 427–28; as Susan Gubar has pointed out to me, the conclusion of George Eliot's *Romola* (1863) imagines a kind of private matriarchy secretly existing behind the patriarchal façade of fifteenth-century Florence.

27. Bachofen, pp. 28–29.

28. H. D., *Tribute,* p. 111; Goethe, *Faust,* Part 2, Act I, lines 6215–21.

29. *Casa Guidi Windows,* 2.776; *Aurora Leigh,* 9.949.

30. As Chevigny notes, Fuller's experiences during the *risorgimento* were marked by similar—and more dramatically personal—ambiguities, for motherhood simultaneously empowered and weakened her. While Ossoli was fighting in Rome, she was in Rieti, absorbed in child care, and "in their letters [during this period] they came near assuming conventional sex roles" (p. 385).

31. Nightingale, pp. 44 and 50.

32. Gubar, "She in Herland," p. 140; Lawrence, *Italy,* p. 44.

33. It is interesting that she wrote this poem to honor a literary man, Hans Christian Andersen, who had produced such visions of redemptive (but self-renouncing) femaleness as "The Snow Queen" and "The Mermaid."

"Life's Empty Pack": Notes Toward a Literary Daughteronomy

1. See Gilbert and Gubar, "Tradition and the Female Talent" and "'Forward Into the Past,'" *No Man's Land*.
2. "First woman": Woolf to Lady Robert Cecil, January 26?, 1919, *Letters*, vol. 2, p. 322; the historian Sheldon Rothblatt called George Eliot a "Man of Ideas" (paper delivered at the George Eliot Centenary Conference, Rutgers University, September 1980); and see Stephen; "frightens me": Showalter, *A Literature of Their Own*, p. 108; Elizabeth Robins, *George Mandeville's Husband*, quoted in Showalter, *A Literature of Their Own*, p. 109.
3. Eliot had said that *Silas Marner* "came to me first of all, quite suddenly, as a sort of legendary tale" (Eliot to John Blackwood, February 24, 1861, quoted in Haight, p. 341); "Doom of Fruit": Dickinson to Thomas Niles, April 1883, *Letters*, vol. 3, pp. 769–70.
4. Wharton, review of *George Eliot* by Leslie Stephen, pp. 251 and 250.
5. Eliot, "Prelude," *Middlemarch*, p. 26; Lacan, "On a Question Preliminary to Any Possible Treatment of Psychosis," *Écrits*, p. 199. Anika Lemaire succinctly summarizes this Lacanian position:

> Society and its structures are always present in the form of the family institution and the father, the representative of the law of society into which he will introduce his child by forbidding dual union with the mother (the register of the imaginary, of nature). By identifying with the father, the child receives a name and a place in the family constellation; restored to himself, he discovers that he is to be made in and by a world of Culture, language and civilization.
> (Lemaire, p. 92)

Elsewhere Lacan observes: "That the woman should be inscribed in an order of exchange of which she is the object, is what makes for the fundamentally conflictual, and, I would say, insoluble character of her position: the symbolic order literally submits her, it transcends her" (Lacan, "Seminar 2" [1954–55], quoted in Rose and Mitchell, p. 45).

6. For female "anxiety of authorship" and women's corollary need for matrilineal legitimation, see Gilbert and Gubar, *The Madwoman in the Attic*, chap. 2; Eliot, "Silly Novels by Lady Novelists," *Writings*, vol. 22, p. 209. In a study of Eliot's stance toward paternal authority, Dianne F. Sadoff makes a point similar to this one, noting that Eliot seeks "to usurp [paternal authority] as the discourse of a male narrator, the authority of a male author" (Sadoff, p. 3).
7. Eliot to Blackwood, January 12, 1861, quoted in Redinger, p. 436. As Susan Gubar has suggested to me, the resonant image of the "packman" may be associated with the figure of Bob Jakin in *The Mill on the Floss* (which Eliot had just completed), the itinerant pack-bearing peddler who brings Maggie Tulliver a number of books, the most crucial of which is Thomas à Kempis' treatise on Christian renunciation (so that its subject metaphorically associates it with *Silas Marner*'s pack full of emptiness). Redinger, p. 439; Eliot, "Finale," *Middlemarch*, p. 896.
8. For "liminal zone," see Turner, "Passages, Margins, and Poverty: Religious Symbols of Communitas," *Dramas, Fields, and Metaphors*, pp. 231–71, and "Betwixt and

Between: The Liminal Period in *Rites de Passage,*" *The Forest of Symbols,* pp. 93–111.

9. Eliot herself consciously exploits the text-textile analogy in *Silas Marner,* refer-ring to the "tale" of cloth Silas weaves and letting Silas accuse William Dane of having "woven a plot" against him (*Silas Marner,* part 1, chap. 2, p. 1). For discus-sions of her more general use of webs, weaving, and spinning as metaphors, see Gilbert and Gubar, *The Madwoman in the Attic,* pp. 522–28; Stump, pp. 172–214; and Miller, "Optic and Semiotic in *Middlemarch,*" pp. 125–45. On Eliot's own ten-dency to avarice—an inclination that, at least in the view of Blackwood, her pub-lisher, became problematic just at the time she was composing *Silas Marner*—see Dessner, pp. 258–59; see Ortner; in connection with Silas' "female" qualities, it is interesting that the villagers respond to his herbal knowledge by trying to make him take the place of "the Wise Woman," a role he at first vigorously resists (see *Silas Marner,* part 1, chap. 2).

10. Eliot, quoted in Haight, p. 336. U. C. Knoepflmacher has pointed out that Silas, like Shakespeare's Pericles, will become "another passive Job . . . redeemed through the miraculous gift of a daughter" (Knoepflmacher, p. 229).

11. In a psychoanalytic study of Eliot's work, Laura Comer Emery points out "the con-nection of [Silas'] guineas" to a solipsistic "anality" (Emery, pp. 62 and 63).

12. See Sigmund Freud's observation that, as the girl enters the Oedipal stage, her "libido slips into a new position by means—there is no other way of putting it—of the equa-tion 'penis = child.' She gives up her wish for a penis and puts in place of it a wish for a child" ("Some Psychological Consequences of the Anatomical Distinction between the Sexes" [1925], in Freud, *Sexuality and the Psychology of Love,* p. 191). On the spe-cial qualities of a boy-child, see Chodorow, pp. 107 and 131–32.

13. See Lévi-Strauss, *The Elementary Structures of Kinship,* pp. 115–16: "Even with regard to our own society, where marriage appears to be a contract between persons . . . the relationship of reciprocity which is the basis of marriage is not established between men and women, but between men by means of women, who are merely the occa-sion of this relationship."

14. See Isaiah 62:4 and 5; for "daughter" see Eliot, *A Writer's Notebook,* p. 98, where Eliot looks at Grimm's law, which traces the evolution of *dhugh* into "daughter." The theme of the daughter as treasure is, in addition, one that Eliot might have picked up from Honoré de Balzac's *Eugénie Grandet* (1833), a novel which treats the relationship of a miserly father and a "treasured" only daughter far more cynically than *Silas Marner* does.

15. It is arguable that the very name "George Eliot" represents Mary Anne Evans' own concern with this question. Unable legally to marry the man to whom she felt herself to be married, she still wanted, like a dutiful wife, to "take" his name. Since George Henry Lewes' surname was not available to her—his first "wife" had preempted it— she had to content herself with his Christian name. In this way, though she was osten-sibly a lawbreaker, she was able symbolically to signal that even "so substantive and rare a creature" as Mary Anne Evans had been properly (if only partially) "absorbed into the life of another," as, according to the laws of her society, every woman ought to be (Eliot, "Finale," *Middlemarch,* p. 894). Emery observes that at the end of *Silas Marner* "it is almost as though Eppie and her father were being married" (Emery, p. 70). Similarly, Sadoff suggests that Eliot "portrays . . . daughterly desire as fabled fantasy in *Silas Marner* and *Felix Holt,*" adding in a general analysis of the (father-

daughter) "scene of seduction" that "the story the daughter relates about this scene, this moment in her history, symbolizes the emergence of her sexuality expressed as desire for her father and represents her attempt to solve this enigma of childhood history" (Sadoff, pp. 78, 104). Although Sadoff cites an early, unpublished version of my "Life's Empty Pack" essay as making some of the same points she makes, we differ radically in our interpretation of the meaning that the female Oedipus complex has for Eliot and other culture-mothers. Sadoff takes as a given the "emergence" of female sexuality and its inevitable expression as "daughterly desire"; I am interested in the coercive cultural construction of "daughterly desire," a point Mitchell emphasizes when she remarks that "the father, so crucial for the development of femininity, and the men that follow him, so essential for the preservation of 'normal' woman-hood, are only secondary figures, for pride of place as love-object is taken by the mother for both sexes [so that] in a sense, the father is only second-best anyway" (Mitchell, p. 111).

16. "Deutera": Haight, p. 49; "little sister": Eliot, "Brother and Sister," *Poems,* pp. 356 and 357.

17. Joyce, *Ulysses,* p. 205; on the significance of the name "Cass," see Knoepflmacher, p. 239.

18. Because of her metonymic as well as coincidental connection with the gold stolen by Godfrey Cass' brother Dunstan, Eppie represents the law in yet another way, reinforcing our sense that its curses as well as its blessings cannot be averted. The place in society that Silas' false brother, William Dane, stole from him is ironically restored to him through an act of theft perpetrated by Godfrey's false brother, Dunstan Cass. Though he has tried to flee culture on the horse Wildfire, moreover, Dunstan falls inexorably into the Stone-pits of damnation—the abyss the law has prepared for him. Similarly, his God-free brother, who tries to flee his cultural responsibility as father, loses not one but all children and inherits an empty house, a mere shell or box (a "case," so to speak) devoid of meaning because devoid both of sons who can carry on its name and daughters who can link it into society. Even his refusal to be his prodigal brother's keeper eventually brings about Godfrey's nemesis, for it is the discovery of Dunstan's skeleton in the Stone-pits that causes this rejecting father to make his rejected proposal to Eppie. In all of these cases, essentially, the machinations of murderous brothers dramatize failures of just those Mosaic laws of the Father which should make transactions between man and man both orderly and faithful.

19. Freud, "Female Sexuality" (1931), *Sexuality and the Psychology of Love,* p. 195.

20. According to Freud, the Oedipus complex means for the girl an attachment to the father which parallels the boy's attachment to his mother; but for the girl, her attachment to the father is a "positive" phenomenon that succeeds an earlier "negative" phase in which she experiences the same "first mother-attachment" that the boy feels. When the girl learns that her mother has not "given" her a penis, however—i.e., in Lacan's sense, that the mother has not given her the power represented by the "Phallus"—she turns in disgust and despair to the father, the one who has the phallus and may therefore be able to give her some of its power (see Freud, "Female Sexuality," pp. 195, 199, passim, and "Some Psychological Consequences of the Anatomical Distinction between the Sexes"). Interestingly in this regard, Sadoff observes that a "pattern of the displaced mother occurs throughout Eliot's novels and serves the story of father-daughter seduction" (Sadoff, p. 69).

21. Observing that "a boy's repression of his Oedipal maternal attachment (and his pre-Oedipal dependence) seems to be *more* complete than a girl's"—in part, no doubt, because the boy can look forward to a future in which he will "have" at least a figure of the mother—Chodorow quotes Alice Balint's assertion that "the amicable loosening of the bond between daughter and mother is one of the most difficult tasks of education" (Chodorow, p. 130).

22. Aeschylus, p. 169; this is Apollo's argument.

23. Cixous, "Sorties," p. 92.

24. James to Wharton, December 1912, quoted in Bell, p. 274.

25. On the analogy between nature ("raw") and culture ("cooked"), see Lévi-Strauss, *The Raw and the Cooked*.

26. Plath, "The Colossus," *Collected Poems*, p. 129; "The Beekeeper's Daughter," *Collected Poems*, p. 118; and see "Electra on Azalea Path," pp. 116–17.

27. See Cummins, *The Lamplighter*; a major bestseller in its day, it tells the story of orphaned Gerty's daughterly devotion to the adoptive father, Trueman Flint, who rescued her from poverty and starvation. For a discussion of the book's appeal in its day, see Baym, pp. 164–69.

28. Andrea Hammer's remark was made in an unpublished paper on *Summer*. Wolff notes that Charity Royall's feelings for Lucius Harney are "explicitly sexual" and her view of him "inescapably phallic" (introduction to Wharton, *Summer*, p. xi).

29. It is possible that in recounting Charity's desire for Lucius Harney, Wharton is recording nostalgic details of her affair with Morton Fullerton (see Lewis, pp. 203–328). In addition, by implying that Charity at first experiences her passion for Lucius Harney as a desire for a brotherly equal, she may be meditating on Fullerton's long erotic relationship with his cousin Katherine, who had been brought up to believe she was his half-sister (see pp. 200–203). Further resonance might have been added to the relationship by the brother-sister romance of Siegmund and Sieglinde in Richard Wagner's *Die Walküre*, a work Wharton surely knew.

30. Wharton, "Beatrice Palmato," in Lewis, p. 548; and see pp. 544–48. For a related analysis of father-daughter incest in *Summer* and "Beatrice Palmato," see Elizabeth Ammons' suggestion that *Summer* is "Wharton's bluntest criticism of the patriarchal sexual economy" and her ensuing discussion of the two texts (Ammons, p. 133; and see pp. 133–43). I agree with many points in Ammons' reading of *Summer* but do not believe that Wharton was consciously "criticizing" the "patriarchal sexual economy"; rather, like Eliot, she was transcribing a myth that nonjudgmentally (if painfully) "explains" woman's position in patriarchal culture.

31. Aeschylus, p. 169; and see Lewis, p. 397.

32. Browning, *Aurora Leigh*, book 1, 11.622–23, p. 57; Dickinson, J. 722. For a more general discussion of maternal images in the works of Barrett Browning, see Gilbert, "From *Patria* to *Matria*," in this volume; for a discussion of Dickinson's use of such imagery, see Gilbert and Gubar, *The Madwoman in the Attic*, pp. 642–50.

33. Olivier, p. 149; my translation (*"Or dans [le miroir tendu par l'homme] la femme ne voit pas son image mais celle que l'homme a d'elle. Jocaste a imprimé au coeur de l'homme sa trace indélébile car ce miroir ne contient que l'image d'une femme 'morte'"*).

34. Freud, *Sexuality and the Psychology of Love*, p. 199; Deutsch, vol. 1, p. 252.

35. In his essay "Fathers and Daughters," the psychoanalyst Joseph H. Smith makes a similar case for the inevitability of what I am calling "resignation" in women; see

Smith, "Fathers and Daughters," esp. pp. 391 and 395. For a different formulation of the same point, see Freud, "Analysis Terminable and Interminable" (1937), in *Therapy and Technique,* esp. pp. 268–71. Freud's note 14, a quotation from Sándor Ferenczi, is particularly telling in this regard: "In every male patient the sign that his castration-anxiety has been mastered . . . is a sense of equality of rights with the analyst; and every female patient . . . must have . . . become able to submit without bitterness to thinking in terms of her feminine role" (p. 270 n. 14).

36. Wharton, quoted in *Summer,* p. xv.

37. Chesler, p. 76; Herman, p. 110.

38. Chodorow, p. 132; Chodorow also notes that "sociologist Robert Winch reports that marked attachment to the opposite gender parent retards courtship progress for male college students and accelerates it for females" (p. 133); thus the father-daughter bond is actually "healthful" for women while the mother-son bond is "unhealthy" for men.

39. Freud, *Sexuality and the Psychology of Love,* p. 199.

40. Deutsch, vol. 1, p. 252; Lamb, Owen, and Chase-Lansdale, p. 94.

41. Herman, pp. 12, 87, 60, and 61.

42. Sadoff, p. 68; Mannoni, p. 45; Mitchell, p. 9.

43. Freud to Wilhelm Fliess, May 31, 1897, in *The Origins of Psycho-Analysis,* p. 206; Freud to Fliess, October 3, 1897, *Origins,* p. 219; and see the dreams and memories reported on pp. 215–25; Freud to Fliess, September 21, 1897, *Origins,* pp. 215–16.

44. Mitchell, p. 75; an article in *Newsweek* in 1981 reported interviews with a number of scholars who speculated, on the basis of recently discovered documents relating to the Freud family and unpublished portions of the letters to Fliess, that Freud's anxiety about his own father "prevented him from recognizing the primal guilt of Laius"—that is, of all fathers (Gelman, p. 67; and see pp. 64–70); as Kris points out in a footnote to the Fliess letters, Freud later observed that "seduction still retains a certain aetiological importance, and I still consider that some of the psychological views expressed [in the first theory] meet the case" (Freud, *Origins,* p. 217 n. 1). Herman declares that "Freud falsified his incest cases," that he named uncles instead of fathers as seducers in several instances, because he wanted to exercise "discretion" (Herman, p. 9). The *Newsweek* article asserts that "in unpublished passages of the Fliess letters [Freud] continued to describe cases of sexual brutality by fathers" (Gelman, p. 67). In a pioneering essay on this subject, Robert Seidenberg and Evangelos Papathomopoulos discuss the pressures put on late-Victorian daughters by ill or tyrannical fathers and the implications of those pressures for *Studies on Hysteria* (see Seidenberg and Papathomopoulos, esp. pp. 135–39).

45. Seidenberg and Papathomopoulos, p. 150; they observe, in addition, that "the word, *Kore,* is also used to designate the female figures who act as supports, the Caryatids of the Holy Temples" (p. 150).

46. Graves, quoted in Seidenberg and Papathomopoulos, p. 151.

47. Shelley, *The Cenci,* Act 5, Scene 4, 11.60–61, in *Poetical Works,* p. 332. For discussions of Eliot's views of Antigone, see Gilbert and Gubar, *The Madwoman in the Attic,* p. 494, and Redinger, pp. 314–15 and 325; both of these analyses emphasize the rebellious heroine of *Antigone,* but significantly, Eliot had the eponymous heroine of *Romola* sit for a portrait of Antigone at Colonus—the dutiful daughter.

48. Rich, "Sibling Mysteries," *The Dream of a Common Language,* p. 49.

49. "Allerleirauh," in Grimm, pp. 326–27.

50. In a brief discussion of this tale, Herman argues that "Allerleirauh" is a version of "Cinderella"; see Herman, p. 2. Even more interestingly, the folklorist Alan Dundes argues a connection between the plot of this story ("tale type 923, Love Like Salt"), "Cinderella," and *King Lear*, although he claims—as perhaps Sadoff would—that this basic plot functions as "a projection of incestuous desires on the part of the daughter" (Dundes, pp. 355 and 360).

51. Psychologically speaking, in fact, Allerleirauh's flight could even be compared to the seizures of hysteria suffered by so many of Freud's and Josef Breuer's patients, daddy's girls who sought to escape the imprisonment of the father by rejecting not only the modes and manners but also the language of "his" culture and speaking instead through a more "natural" body language.

52. To be sure, in, e.g., *Romola* and *Middlemarch* and in, e.g., *The Age of Innocence*, Eliot and Wharton, respectively, embed fantasies of female, and sometimes even matriarchal, autonomy, fantasies which clearly function as covertly compensatory gestures toward liberation from the father-daughter scripts elaborated in works like *Silas Marner* and *Summer*.

53. This essay was researched and written with the assistance of grants from the Rockefeller and Guggenheim Foundations, to both of which I am very grateful. In addition, I have profited greatly from criticisms and suggestions offered by many friends and colleagues, including (as always) Susan Gubar and Elliot Gilbert, as well as Andrea Hammer, Susan Lurie, Elyse Blankley, Peter Hays, Suzanne Graver, and Michael Wolfe. Finally, I have learned much from audiences at a number of institutions where this paper was "tried out" in various forms, among them helpful and incisive respondents at the Rutgers University George Eliot Centenary Conference, and at Harvard University, the University of Colorado, the University of Washington, Yale University, the University of Southern California, and Princeton University.

Potent Griselda: Male Modernists and the Great Mother

1. Lawrence, "Matriarchy," *Phoenix II*, p. 549.

2. Lawrence, "Benjamin Franklin," *Studies in Classic American Literature*, p. 23; Joyce, *Ulysses*, p. 205; Duncan, p. 275; H. D., *The Gift*.

3. See Stein, "Patriarchal Poetry" (1927), *The Yale Gertrude Stein*, pp. 106–46; Gilbert, "Literary Paternity"; also see Gilbert and Gubar, *The Madwoman in the Attic*, pp. 3–44 (chap. 1); Hopkins, p. 133.

4. "The hymen [as an] always folded . . . space," etc., is Gayatri Spivak's succinct summary of the theories presented in Derrida's *La double séance* in her translator's preface to Derrida, *Of Grammatology*, p. lxvi, but for an extended discussion of the point, see Derrida, "The Double Session," in *Dissemination*, especially pp. 209–85; for "the phallic pen" and the "virgin page," as well as a discussion of "the phallic generative power of the creative imagination," see Irwin, p. 163; for a feminist perspective on this material, see Gubar, "The Blank Page."

5. For a summary and discussion of this theory, see Oppenheimer, p. 121; for a useful analysis of the ways in which "procreation theories" can be seen both "as creation mythemes" and as projective representations of sexual dominance/subordination, see James Hillman, "On Psychological Femininity," in Hillman, esp. pp. 217–54. For

a late and anxiously formulated vision of woman as empty vessel, see Joyce, *Ulysses*, p. 282, where Leopold Bloom, meditating on his wife's "chamber music," decides that "empty vessels make most noise"; later in the same chapter ("Sirens") he thinks, "Blank face. Virgin should say: or fingered only. Write something on it: page," and, tellingly, broods that "goddess I didn't see" (p. 285).

6. Oppenheimer, p. 130; Wordsworth's conceit, elaborated in the "Intimations of Immortality" ode, is significant because it implies that Nature, "the homely Nurse," and the "Mother," are comparably inferior "prison-house[s]" when set against the patriarchal God in whom the soul originates and whose generative energy is both "the fountain-light of all our day" and "a *master*-light of all our seeing" (emphasis added). Aeschylus, pp. 169–70; Neumann, *The Great Mother*, p. 63.

7. Chaucer himself, of course, withdraws in a kind of repugnance from "The Clerk's Tale" in "Lenvoy de Chaucer," where he admonishes "noble wyves, ful of heigh prudence," to "Lat noon humilitee youre tonge naille," and so forth; Neumann, *The Great Mother*, p. 62.

8. Lawrence, "Making Love to Music," *Phoenix II*, p. 160; Neumann, *The Great Mother*, p. 62; for a discussion of this point, see Briffault, p. 27.

9. Taylor, introduction to Briffault, p. 10.

10. Bachofen, p. 113; Campbell, introduction to Bachofen, p. lv; Harrison, pp. 261 and 497.

11. Bachofen, p. 108; see Balinsky, pp. 14–15.

12. Bachofen, pp. 25 and 29; Harrison, p. 626; Hopkins, p. 133.

13. Castle; for a sweeping but different analysis of the childbirth metaphor as deployed by both male and female writers, see Friedman, "Creativity and the Childbirth Metaphor," passim.

14. Bachofen, introduction, passim; see Neumann, *The Origins and History of Consciousness*, and "The Negative Elementary Character," *The Great Mother*, pp. 147–210; for the "Minoan-Mycenaean" stage in psychosexual development, see Freud, "Female Sexuality" (1931), in *Sexuality and the Psychology of Love*, p. 195; for the vagina as "non-existent," see the same essay, p. 197; for the vagina as "an asylum for the penis," see "The Infantile Genital Organization of the Libido" (1923) in the same volume, p. 175; for a perceptive analysis of Freud's inheritance from such misogynistic precursors as Galen and Aristotle, see Hillman, pp. 238–43.

15. Adams, p. 523; and for a commentary on this subject, see Dye, p. 17; Graves, *The White Goddess*; Wylie, esp. pp. 194–217; Lawrence, "Matriarchy," *Phoenix II*, p. 550; Bachofen, p. 156; Lawrence, "A Propos of 'Lady Chatterley's Lover,'" *Phoenix II*, p. 490.

16. Smith, "A New Adam and a New Eve," p. 25; a similar point, including a comparable (but very different) reading of "The Ladybird," is offered in Ruderman, a book that has only become available to me since this essay was completed.

17. See Weiss; Lawrence, "The Real Thing," p. 196.

18. For the connections between Lawrence, the *kosmiche Runde*, and Bachofen, see Green, esp. pp. 73, 84, and 343. Smith also observes that Frieda's principles were consistently matriarchal, quoting her remark in *Not I, But the Wind* that "a man is born twice: first his mother bears him, then he has to be reborn again from the women he loves," as well as her equally important insight that "in his heart of hearts [Lawrence] always dreaded women, felt that they were in the end more powerful than

men" (Smith, p. 37); Bruce Clarke, "'The Woman Not Fit to Be Seen': D. H. Lawrence and the Maternal Sublime," p. 5; I am grateful to Clarke for sharing this interesting essay with me.

19. Lawrence, "The Ladybird," *Four Short Novels*, p. 60.
20. Leavis, p. 56.
21. See Lawrence, *Studies in Classic American Literature*, p. 90.
22. See George Boas, preface to Bachofen, pp. xx–xxi.
23. Frazer, p. 420; Harrison, pp. 461 and 403; later Harrison observes, "The interesting thing about Dionysos is that, develop as he may, he bears to the end, as no other god does, the stamp of his matriarchal origin. He can never rid himself of the throng of worshipping women, he is always the nursling of his Maenads" (p. 561).
24. Harrison, p. 267.
25. See Grimm, "The Six Swans," pp. 232–37.
26. Bachofen, p. 56.
27. Goethe, *Faust*, Part 2, Act I, lines 6223–24 and 6265–66.
28. Lawrence, *Sons and Lovers*, p. 288; Lawrence, *Collected Letters*, vol. 1, p. 291; Lawrence, *Women in Love*, p. 238.
29. Lawrence, "The Captain's Doll," *Four Short Novels*, pp. 262 and 264.
30. Lawrence, "Purple Anemones," *Complete Poems*, vol. 1, pp. 307–9.
31. Lawrence, "Figs," *Complete Poems*, vol. 1, pp. 282–84.
32. Lawrence, *The Escaped Cock*, pp. 41 and 45; quoted by Lacy in *The Escaped Cock*, p. 136.
33. Lawrence, *Lady Chatterley's Lover*, p. 193.
34. Lawrence, *Etruscan Places, D. H. Lawrence and Italy*, pp. 14, 45, 29–30, 13, 53, 54, 51, and 59.
35. W. B. Yeats, "The Crazed Moon," *Complete Poems*, pp. 237 and 301–2.
36. Yeats, *Collected Poems*, p. 285.
37. Joyce, *A Portrait of the Artist as a Young Man*, p. 217; *Selected Letters*, p. 169.
38. Ellmann, pp. 297 and 475; Graves, *Goodbye to All That*, p. 31.
39. Bachofen, p. 109.
40. Quoted by Conrad Aiken in Aiken, p. 233.
41. Stevens, *Collected Poems*, pp. 507, 406, and 388; Bly, "The Teeth Mother Naked at Last," *Sleepers Joining Hands*, pp. 18–28.
42. Lawrence, "The Woman Who Rode Away," *Complete Short Stories*, vol. 2, p. 581; Lawrence, "Invocation to the Moon," *Complete Poems*, vol. 2, pp. 695–96.

Mother Rites: Maternity, Matriarchy, Creativity

1. Shelley, *The Last Man*, pp. 1–4; Brontë, *The Professor*, p. 155. Though, as Virginia Woolf once suggested, the author of *Paradise Lost* was the "first of the masculinists" in his contempt for Eve, the "Mother of Mankind," Brontë drastically revised his imagery, de-emphasizing the generative power of the patriarchal poet and stressing the powerful womb of the matriarchal muse. Barrett Browning, *Aurora Leigh*, 3.245–47, 6.782; Dickinson, J. 1651, J. 956, and J. 722. N.B.: Many texts quoted in this chapter are not cited by page numbers, since they are relatively easy to find, but all are included in the bibliography.

2. Auerbach, p. 14; for Seidenberg, p. 4; Eliot, *Letters*, vol. 1; and Ortner; for more on these works, see Part III of this book: "From *Patria* to *Matria*" and "Potent Griselda."

3. Harrison, *Reminiscences*, pp. 72 and 88; she recorded this pleasure in 1925, the year Woolf told her diary that she had just "thought out . . . *To the Lighthouse*."

4. Ellmann, pp. 489 and 490; but note Weaver's remark on p. 491: "I must ask you once more not to pay the slightest attention to any foolish remark I may make," etc.

5. For another analysis of these issues, see Friedman, "Creativity and the Childbirth Metaphor."

6. Deutsch, p. 27; Freud ("no 'place'").

7. Duncan, p. 119.

8. Harrison, *Prolegomena*, pp. 409, 411, and 445.

9. Harrison, *Prolegomena*, pp. 388–89, 395, 402, 285, and 401.

10. Harrison, *Prolegomena*, pp. 392, 397–99, and 400; for an interesting analysis of the revisionary politics behind *The Prolegomena*, see Peacock, esp. pp. 187–88, passim.

11. Harrison, *Prolegomena*, p. 395.

12. M. E. Coleridge, p. 212; she herself insisted in a note to the poem that it was based on "a legend of Malay, told by Hugh Clifford."

13. See Kroll, p. 239; Graves, *The White Goddess*, p. 373, and, expressing his own anxiety about contemporary women and "Dionysiac religion," p. 376: "I have witnessed it myself in helpless terror."

14. Graves, *The White Goddess*, p. 372; Plath, *Journals*, p. 266.

15. Harrison, *Prolegomena*, pp. 442–43.

16. Harrison, *Prolegomena*, p. 407.

17. H. D., *The Gift*, p. 60; see, for instance, Susan Stanford Friedman's *Psyche Reborn*, passim.

18. To be sure, Rich's poem is not strictly a transformation of *The Bacchae* since it was also shaped by the surrealistic vision of female "Hell's Angels" that Jean Cocteau presented in his film *Orphée*.

19. See Orenstein, pp. 41, 45, and 47.

20. Bachofen, pp. 206–7.

21. For a discussion of this, see Gubar, "She in Herland."

22. Bloom, pp. 268, 272, and 273.

BIBLIOGRAPHY

Adams, Henry. *Novels, Mont Saint Michel, The Education.* New York: Library of America, 1983.

Aeschylus. *The Oresteian Trilogy.* Trans. Philip Vellacott. Harmondsworth, UK: Penguin, 1959.

Aiken, Conrad. *Ushant.* New York: Duell; Boston: Little, Brown, 1952.

Alaya, Flavia. "The Ring, the Rescue, and the Risorgimento: Reunifying the Brownings' Italy." *Browning Institute Studies* 6 (1978): 1–41.

Alvarez, A. *The Savage God: A Study of Suicide.* 1st ed. New York: Random House, 1972.

Amiran, Minda Rae. "What Women's Literature?" *College English* 39 (1978): 653–61.

Ammons, Elizabeth. *Edith Wharton's Argument with America.* Athens: University of Georgia Press, 1980.

Astell, Mary. *A Serious Proposal to the Ladies.* Ed. Patricia Springborg. London: Pickering & Chatto, 1997.

Atwood, Margaret. *The Handmaid's Tale.* Boston: Houghton Mifflin, 1986.

——. *Surfacing.* New York: Simon and Schuster, 1972.

Auden, W. H. *The Collected Poetry of W. H. Auden.* New York: Random House, 1946.

Auerbach, Nina. *Communities of Women: An Idea in Fiction.* Cambridge, Mass.: Harvard University Press, 1978.

Austen, Jane. *Jane Austen's Letters.* Ed. Deirdre Le Faye. Oxford and New York: Oxford University Press, 1995.

——. *Jane Austen's Letters to Her Sister Cassandra and Others.* 2nd ed. London: Oxford University Press, 1952.

Bachofen, J. J. *Myth, Religion, and Mother Right: Selected Writings of J. J. Bachofen.* Trans. Ralph Manheim. Princeton, N.J.: Princeton University Press, 1967.

Balinsky, B. I. *An Introduction to Embryology.* Philadelphia: W. B. Saunders, 1960.

Barrett Browning, Elizabeth. *Aurora Leigh and Other Poems.* Introduction by Cora Kaplan. London: The Women's Press, 1978.

——. *Casa Guidi Windows.* Ed. Julia Markus. New York: Browning Institute, 1977.

——. *The Complete Works of Elizabeth Barrett Browning.* Ed. Charlotte Porter and Helen A. Clarke. 6 vols. New York: Crowell, 1900; facsimile, New York: AMS Press, 1973.

——. *Elizabeth Barrett to Mr. Boyd.* Ed. Barbara McCarthy. New Haven, Conn.: Yale University Press, 1955.

——. *The Letters of Elizabeth Barrett Browning.* Ed. Frederic G. Kenyon. New York: Macmillan, 1898.

——. *The Poetical Works of Elizabeth Barrett Browning.* Ed. Harriet Waters Preston.

Cambridge: 1900; repr. with an introduction by Ruth M. Adams, Boston: Houghton Mifflin, 1974.

Bataille, Georges. *Erotism: Death and Sensuality*. Trans. Mary Dalwood. San Francisco: City Lights, 1986.

Baumgardner, Jennifer, and Amy Richards. *Manifesta: Young Women, Feminism, and the Future*. New York: Farrar, Straus and Giroux, 2000.

Baym, Nina. *Woman's Fiction: A Guide to Novels by and about Women in America, 1820–1870*. Ithaca, N.Y.: Cornell University Press, 1978.

Beauvoir, Simone de. *The Second Sex*. New York: Bantam, 1961.

Beer, Jeanette M. A. "Stylistic Conventions in *Le Livre de la Mutacion de Fortune*." In Richards, *Reinterpreting Christine de Pizan*, pp. 124–36.

Behn, Aphra. *The Works of Aphra Behn*. Ed. Janet Todd. Columbus: Ohio State University Press, 1992.

Bell, Millicent. *Edith Wharton & Henry James: The Story of Their Friendship*. New York: George Braziller, 1965.

Bercovitch, Sacvan, ed. *Reconstructing American Literary History*. Cambridge, Mass., and London: Harvard University Press, 1986.

Bernikow, Louise. *The World Split Open: Four Centuries of Women Poets in England and America, 1552–1950*. New York: Vintage, 1974.

Bewick, Thomas. *A History of British Birds*. Newcastle, UK: Longman, 1823.

Bixler, Phyllis. *Frances Hodgson Burnett*. Boston: Twayne, 1984.

Bloom, Harold. *The Anxiety of Influence*. New York: Oxford University Press, 1973.

————. *A Map of Misreading*. New York: Oxford University Press, 1975.

Bly, Robert. *Sleepers Joining Hands*. New York: Harper & Row, 1973.

Bradstreet, Anne. *The Complete Works of Anne Bradstreet*. Ed. Joseph R. McElrath Jr. and Allan P. Robb. Boston: Twayne, 1981.

Briffault, Robert. *The Mothers*. Abridged by Gordon Rattray Taylor. New York: Atheneum, 1977.

Brontë, Charlotte. *Jane Eyre*. Harmondsworth, UK: Penguin, 1986.

————. *Legends of Angria*. Ed. Fannie E. Ratchford and William Clyde De Vane. New Haven, Conn.: Yale University Press; London: H. Milford and Oxford University Press, 1933.

————. *The Letters of Charlotte Brontë: With a selection of letters by family and friends*. Ed. Margaret Smith. Oxford: Clarendon Press, 1995.

————. *The Professor and Emma: A Fragment*. Ed. Margaret Lane. London: Dent & Sons, 1974.

————. *Tales of Angria*. Ed. Heather Glen. London: Penguin, 2006.

Browning, Elizabeth Barrett. See Barrett Browning, Elizabeth.

Buckley, Jerome H., ed. *The Worlds of Victorian Fiction*. Cambridge, Mass.: Harvard University Press, 1975.

Burnett, Frances Hodgson. *Little Lord Fauntleroy*. New York: Scribner, 1910.

————. *The One I Knew the Best of All*. 1893; repr., New York: Arno, 1980.

————. *The Secret Garden*. New York: Lippincott, 1911.

Carlyle, Thomas. *Sartor Resartus*. Ed. Kerry McSweeney and Peter Sabor. Oxford: Oxford University Press, 2008.

Castle, Terry. "Lab'ring Bards: Birth *Topoi* and English Poetics, 1660–1820." *Journal of English and Germanic Philology* 78 (April 1979): 193–208.

Cather, Willa. *The Professor's House*. New York: Knopf, 1925.

————. *The Song of the Lark*. Boston: Houghton Mifflin, 1915.

Chesler, Phyllis. "Rape and Psychotherapy." In Connell and Wilson, *Rape*, pp. 76–81.

Chevigny, Bell Gale. *The Woman and the Myth: Margaret Fuller's Life and Writings*. Old Westbury, N.Y.: Feminist Press, 1976.

Chodorow, Nancy. *The Reproduction of Mothering: Psychoanalysis and the Sociology of Gender*. Berkeley: University of California Press, 1978.

Churchill, Kenneth. *Italy and English Literature, 1764–1930*. London: Macmillan, 1980.

Cixous, Hélène. "Sorties." In Marks and Courtivron, *New French Feminisms*, pp. 90–99.

————, and Catherine Clément. *The Newly Born Woman*. Trans. Betsy Wing. With an introduction by Sandra M. Gilbert. Minneapolis: University of Minnesota Press, 1986.

Claudius, Matthias. *Werke*. Stuttgart, Ger.: J. G. Cotta, 1954.

Connell, Noreen, and Cassandra Wilson, eds. *Rape: The First Sourcebook for Women*. New York: New American Library, 1974.

Cooper, Anna Julia. *The Voice of Anna Julia Cooper: including "A Voice from the South" and other important essays, papers, and letters*. Ed. Charles Lemert and Esme Bhan. Lanham, Md.: Rowan & Littlefield, 1998.

Cooper, Helen. "Working into Light: Elizabeth Barrett Browning." In Gilbert and Gubar, *Shakespeare's Sisters*, pp. 65–81.

Costello, Bonnie. "Response to Gilbert and Gubar." In Sussman, *Literary History*, pp. 28–31.

Culler, Jonathan. *On Deconstruction: Theory and Criticism after Structuralism*. Ithaca, N.Y.: Cornell University Press, 1982.

Cummins, Maria S. *The Lamplighter*. Boston: J. P. Jewett, 1854.

Curnow, Maureen. "The *Livre de la Cité des Dames*: An Introduction and Critical Edition." Ph.D. diss., Vanderbilt University, 1975.

Daly, Mary. *Gyn/Ecology: The Metaethics of Radical Feminism*. Boston: Beacon Press, 1999.

David, Deirdre. *Rule Britannia: Women, Empire, and Victorian Writing*. Ithaca, N.Y.: Cornell University Press, 1995.

Delany, Paul. *D. H. Lawrence's Nightmare*. New York: Basic Books, 1978.

Delany, Sheila. "Mothers to Think Back Through: Who Are They? The Ambiguous Example of Christine de Pizan." In Finke and Shichtman, *Medieval Texts and Contemporary Readers*, pp. 177–97.

Derrida, Jacques. *Dissemination*. Trans. Barbara Johnson. Chicago: University of Chicago Press, 1981.

————. *Of Grammatology*. Trans. Gayatri Spivak. Baltimore, Md.: Johns Hopkins University Press, 1976.

Dessner, Lawrence Jay. "The Autobiographical Matrix of *Silas Marner*." *Studies in the Novel* 11 (Fall 1979): 251–82.

Deutsch, Helene. *The Psychology of Women: A Psychoanalytic Interpretation*. 2 vols. New York: Grune & Stratton, 1944–45.

Dickinson, Emily. *The Complete Poems of Emily Dickinson*. Ed. Thomas H. Johnson. Boston: Little, Brown, 1960.

————. *The Letters of Emily Dickinson*. Ed. Thomas H. Johnson. Cambridge, Mass.: Belknap Press of Harvard University Press, 1986.

————. *The Poems of Emily Dickinson*. Ed. R. W. Franklin. Cambridge, Mass.: Belknap Press of Harvard University Press, 1999.

Dinesen, Isak. *Out of Africa*. New York: Vintage, 1965.

Dinnerstein, Dorothy. *The Mermaid and the Minotaur: Sexual Arrangements and Human Malaise*. New York: Harper & Row, 1977.

Donaldson, Laura E. *Decolonizing Feminisms: Race, Gender and Empire Building*. Chapel Hill: University of North Carolina Press, 1992.

Doolittle, Hilda. See H. D.

Duncan, Isadora. *My Life*. New York: Liveright, 1927.

Dundes, Alan. " 'To Love My Father All': A Psychoanalytic Study of the Folktale Source of *King Lear*." *Southern Folklore Quarterly* 40 (September–December 1976): 353–66.

DuPlessis, Rachel Blau. "Romantic Thralldom in H. D." In Friedman and DuPlessis, *Signets*, pp. 406–29.

————, and Susan Stanford Friedman. "Woman Is Perfect: H. D.'s Debate with Freud." *Feminist Studies*, vol. 7, no. 3 (Fall 1981): 417–30.

Dworkin, Andrea. *Intercourse*. New York: Free Press, 1987.

Dye, Nancy Schrom. "Clio's American Daughters: Male History, Female Reality." In Sherman and Beck, *The Prism of Sex*, pp. 9–31.

Eldredge, Charles C. *Charles Walter Stetson: Color and Fantasy*. Lawrence: Spencer Museum of Art, University of Kansas, 1982.

Eliot, George. *The George Eliot Letters*. Ed. Gordon S. Haight. New Haven, Conn.: Yale University Press, 1954–78.

————. *Middlemarch*. Ed. W. J. Harvey. Harmondsworth, UK: Penguin, 1965.

————. *The Poems of George Eliot*. New York: T. Y. Crowell, 1884.

————. *Selected Essays, Poems and Other Writings*. Ed. A. S. Byatt and Nicholas Warren. London: Penguin, 1990.

————. *Silas Marner: The Weaver of Raveloe*. Ed. Q. D. Leavis. Harmondsworth, UK: Penguin, 1967.

————. *A Writer's Notebook, 1854–1879, and Uncollected Writings*. Ed. Joseph Wiesenfarth. Charlottesville: University Press of Virginia, 1981.

————. *The Writings of George Eliot*. 25 vols. Boston and New York: Houghton Mifflin, 1907–8.

Eliot, T. S. *The Letters of T. S. Eliot*, vol. 1, 1898–1922. Ed. Valerie Eliot. New York: Harcourt Brace Jovanovich, 1988.

Ellis, Kate, and E. Ann Kaplan. "*Jane Eyre*: Feminism in Brontë's Novel and Its Film Versions." In Klein and Parker, *The English Novel and the Movies*, pp. 83–94.

Ellis, Mrs. Sarah Stickney. *The Family Monitor*. New York: Henry G. Langley, 1844.

Ellmann, Richard. *James Joyce*. New York: Oxford University Press, 1982.

Emery, Laura Comer. *George Eliot's Creative Conflict: The Other Side of Silence*. Berkeley: University of California Press, 1976.

Euripides. *Alcestis*. Trans. Richard Aldington. London: Chatto & Windus, 1930.

————. *The Bacchae*. Trans. Gilbert Murray. In *The Complete Greek Drama*, ed. Whitney J. Oates and Eugene O'Neill Jr. 2 vols. New York: Random House, 1938.

Faderman, Lillian. *Surpassing the Love of Men: Romantic Friendship and Love Between Women from the Renaissance to the Present*. New York: Morrow, 1981.

Fancher, Robert T. "English Teaching and Humane Culture." In Finn and Fancher, *Against Mediocrity*, pp. 49–69.

Farr, Judith, ed. *Emily Dickinson: A Collection of Critical Essays.* Upper Saddle River, N.J.: Prentice Hall, 1996.

Fauré, Christine. "The Twilight of the Goddesses, or, The Intellectual Crisis of French Feminism." *Signs,* vol. 7, no. 1 (Autumn 1981): 81–86.

Fern, Fanny (Sarah Willis Parton). *Ruth Hall and Other Writings.* Ed. Joyce W. Warren. New Brunswick, N.J.: Rutgers University Press, 1986.

Fetterley, Judith. *The Resisting Reader: A Feminist Approach to American Fiction.* Bloomington: Indiana University Press, 1978.

Finke, Laurie A., and Martin B. Shichtman, eds. *Medieval Texts and Contemporary Readers.* Ithaca, N.Y.: Cornell University Press, 1987.

Finn, Chester E., Jr., Diane Ravitch, and Robert T. Fancher, eds. *Against Mediocrity: The Humanities in America's High Schools.* New York: Holmes & Meier, 1984.

Fowler, Jeanette D., and Merv Fowler. *Chinese Religions: Beliefs and Practices.* Brighton, UK, and Portland, Ore.: Sussex Academic Press, 2008.

Frazer, Sir James. *The New Golden Bough.* New York: Mentor, 1954.

Freeman, Mary Eleanor Wilkins. *A New England Nun, and Other Stories.* New York: Harper & Brothers, 1891.

Freud, Sigmund. *The Basic Writings of Sigmund Freud.* Trans. and ed. A. A. Brill. New York: Modern Library, 1938.

————. *The Origins of Psycho-Analysis: Letters to Wilhelm Fliess, Drafts and Notes, 1887–1902.* Ed. Marie Bonaparte, Anna Freud, and Ernst Kris. Trans. Eric Mosbacher and James Strachey. New York: Basic Books, 1977.

————. *Sexuality and the Psychology of Love.* Ed. Philip Rieff. New York: Collier, 1963.

————. *Therapy and Technique.* Ed. Philip Rieff. New York: Collier, 1963.

Friedman, Susan Stanford. "Creativity and the Childbirth Metaphor: Gender Difference in Literary Discourse." *Feminist Studies,* vol. 13, no. 1 (Spring 1987): 49–82.

————. *Psyche Reborn: The Emergence of H. D.* Bloomington: Indiana University Press, 1981.

————, and Rachel Blau DuPlessis, eds. *Signets: Reading H. D.* Madison: University of Wisconsin Press, 1990.

Gage, Matilda Joslyn, Elizabeth Cady Stanton, and Susan B. Anthony. *History of Woman Suffrage.* New York: Fowler & Wells, 1881–1922.

Gay, Peter. *The Education of the Senses.* New York: Oxford University Press, 1984.

Gelman, D. "Finding the Hidden Freud." *Newsweek,* November 30, 1981, pp. 64–70.

Gelpi, Albert. "Hilda in Egypt." *The Southern Review,* vol. 18, no. 2 (Spring 1982): 233–50.

Gelpi, Barbara. "Aurora Leigh: The Vocation of the Woman Poet." *Victorian Poetry,* vol. 19, no. 1 (1981): 35–48.

————, and Albert Gelpi, eds. *Adrienne Rich's Poetry and Prose.* New York: W. W. Norton, 1993.

Gennep, Arnold van. *The Rites of Passage.* Trans. Monika B. Vizedom and Gabrielle L. Caffee. Chicago: University of Chicago Press, 1960.

Gilbert, Sandra M. "The American Sexual Poetics of Walt Whitman and Emily Dickinson." In Bercovitch, *Reconstructing American Literary History,* pp. 123–54.

————. *Death's Door: Modern Dying and the Ways We Grieve.* New York: W. W. Norton, 2006.

————. *Emily's Bread.* New York: W. W. Norton, 1984.

————. "In Yeats's House: The Death and Resurrection of Sylvia Plath." In Wagner, *Critical Essays on Sylvia Plath*, pp. 207–19.

————. "Jubilate Anne." *The Nation*, September 14, 1974, pp. 214–16.

————. *Kissing the Bread: New and Selected Poems, 1969–1999*. New York: W. W. Norton, 2000.

————. "Literary Paternity." *Cornell Review* 6 (Summer 1979): 54–65.

————. "Mephistopheles in Maine: Rereading Robert Lowell's 'Skunk Hour.' " In Kuzma, *A Book of Rereadings*, pp. 254–64.

————. " 'My Name Is Darkness': The Poetry of Self-Definition." *Contemporary Literature* 18 (1977): 443–57.

————. "Plain Jane's Progress." *Signs*, vol. 2, no. 4 (Summer 1977): 779–804.

————, and Susan Gubar. *The Madwoman in the Attic: The Woman Writer and the Nineteenth-Century Literary Imagination*. New Haven, Conn.: Yale University Press, 1979.

————. *No Man's Land: The Place of the Woman Writer in the Twentieth Century*. 3 vols. New Haven, Conn.: Yale University Press, 1988–94.

————, eds. *The Norton Anthology of Literature by Women*. New York: W. W. Norton, 2007.

————, eds. *Shakespeare's Sisters: Feminist Essays on Women Poets*. Bloomington: Indiana University Press, 1979.

Gilman, Charlotte Perkins. *Herland*. 1915; repr., New York: Pantheon, 1979.

————. *The Yellow Wallpaper*. 1892; Old Westbury, N.Y.: Feminist Press, 1973.

Ginsberg, Allen. *Howl*. San Francisco: City Lights, 1956.

————. *Kaddish*. San Francisco: City Lights, 1961.

Graves, Robert. *Goodbye to All That*. New York: Doubleday, Anchor Books, 1957.

————. *The White Goddess*. New York: Creative Age Press, 1948.

Green, Martin. *The von Richthofen Sisters: The Triumphant and the Tragic Modes of Love*. New York: Basic Books, 1974.

Greg, William Rathbone. *Why Are Women Redundant?* London: N. Trübner, 1869.

Griffin, Susan. *Woman and Nature: The Roaring Inside Her*. London: Women's Press, 1994.

Grimm, J. L. K., and W. K. Grimm. *The Complete Grimm's Fairy Tales*. Trans. Margaret Hunt and James Stern. New York: Pantheon, 1972.

Gubar, Susan. " 'The Blank Page' and the Issues of Female Creativity." *Critical Inquiry*, vol. 8, no. 2 (Winter 1981): 243–63.

————. "The Echoing Spell of H. D.'s *Trilogy*." *Contemporary Literature*, vol. 19, no. 2 (Spring 1978): 196–218.

————. "She in Herland: Feminism as Fantasy." In Slusser, Rabkin, and Scholes, *Coordinates*, pp. 139–49.

Gutwirth, Madelyn. *Madame de Staël, Novelist: The Emergence of the Artist as Woman*. Urbana: University of Illinois Press, 1978.

H. D. *Bid Me to Live: A Madrigal*. Redding Ridge, Conn.: Black Swan Books, 1983.

————. *Collected Poems, 1912–1944*. Ed. Louis L. Martz. New York: New Directions, 1983.

————. *The Gift*. New York: New Directions, 1982.

————. *Hermetic Definition*. New York: New Directions, 1972.

————. *HERmione*. New York: New Directions, 1981.

—————. *Notes on Thought and Vision & The Wise Sappho.* London: Peter Owen, 1982.

—————. *Tribute to Freud: Writing on the Wall, Advent.* New York: McGraw-Hill, 1975.

—————. *Trilogy.* New York: New Directions, 1973.

Haight, Gordon S. *George Eliot: A Biography.* New York: Oxford University Press, 1968.

Hardwick, Elizabeth. "Sylvia Plath." In *Seduction and Betrayal.* New York: Random House, 1973.

Harrison, Jane. *Prolegomena to the Study of Greek Religion.* New York: Meridian, 1955.

—————. *Reminiscences of a Student's Life.* London: Hogarth Press, 1925.

Harte, Bret. "Miss Mix by Ch–l–tte Br–nte." In *The Luck of Roaring Camp and Other Stories and Sketches,* pp. 103-112. Boston: Houghton, Mifflin, 1921.

Hartman, Geoffrey H. *Saving the Text: Literature, Derrida, Philosophy.* Baltimore, Md.: Johns Hopkins University Press, 1981.

Heilbrun, Carolyn. "Feminist Criticism: Bringing the Spirit Back to English Studies." *The State of the Discipline, 1970s–1980s: A Special Issue of the ADE Bulletin,* no. 62 (September–November 1979): 35–38.

—————. *Reinventing Womanhood.* New York: W. W. Norton, 1979.

Herman, Judith Lewis, with Lisa Hirschman. *Father-Daughter Incest.* Cambridge, Mass.: Harvard University Press, 1981.

Hillman, James. *The Myth of Analysis: Three Essays in Archetypal Psychology.* Evanston, Ill.: Northwestern University Press, 1972.

Hoeveler, Diane Long, and Beth Lau, eds. *Approaches to Teaching Brontë's* Jane Eyre. New York: Modern Language Association of America, 1993.

Holbrook, David. *Sylvia Plath: Poetry and Existence.* London: Athlone, 1976.

Holland, Norman. *Poems in Persons.* New York: W. W. Norton, 1973.

Homans, Margaret. *Women Writers and Poetic Identity: Dorothy Wordsworth, Emily Brontë, and Emily Dickinson.* Princeton, N.J.: Princeton University Press, 1980.

Hopkins, Gerard Manley. *The Correspondence of Gerard Manley Hopkins and Richard Watson Dixon.* Ed. C. C. Abbott. London: Oxford University Press, 1935.

Horney, Karen. *Feminine Psychology.* New York: W. W. Norton, 1967.

Howe, Florence, ed. *Tradition and the Talents of Women.* Urbana: University of Illinois Press, 1991.

—————, and Ellen Bass, eds. *No More Masks!* New York: Doubleday, 1973.

Hughes, Ted. "Notes on the Chronological Order of Sylvia Plath's Poems." In Newman, *The Art of Sylvia Plath,* pp. 187–95.

Irigaray, Luce. *Speculum of the Other Woman.* Trans. Gillian C. Gill. Ithaca, N.Y.: Cornell University Press, 1985.

Irwin, John. *Doubling and Incest, Repetition and Revenge.* Baltimore, Md.: Johns Hopkins University Press, 1975.

Jardine, Alice. "Opaque Texts and Transparent Contexts: The Political Difference of Julia Kristeva." In Miller, *The Poetics of Gender,* pp. 96–116.

Jones, Ann Rosalind. "Writing the Body: Toward an Understanding of l'Écriture féminine." In *The New Feminist Criticism: Essays on Women, Literature, and Theory,* ed. Elaine Showalter. New York: Pantheon, 1985.

Jong, Erica. *Fear of Flying.* New York: New American Library, 1973.

Joyce, James. *A Portrait of the Artist as a Young Man.* 1916; repr., New York: Viking, 1969.

—————. *Selected Letters.* Ed. Richard Ellmann. New York: Viking, 1975.

—————. *Ulysses.* New York: Random House, 1934.

Juhasz, Suzanne. *Naked and Fiery Forms: Modern American Poetry by Women.* New York: Octagon, 1976.

Kaledin, Eugenia. *The Education of Mrs. Henry Adams.* Philadelphia: Temple University Press, 1981.

Keats, John. *The Letters of John Keats, 1814–1821.* Ed. Hyder Edward Rollins. Cambridge, Mass.: Harvard University Press, 1958.

Kelly-Gadol, Joan. "The Social Relations of the Sexes: Methodological Implications of Women's History." *Signs: Journal of Women in Culture and Society* 1 (Summer 1976): 809–23.

Kennard, Jean E. *Victims of Convention.* Hampton, Conn.: Shoe String Press, 1978.

Kenner, Hugh. "Sincerity Kills." In Lane, *Sylvia Plath,* pp. 33–44.

Kizer, Carolyn. *Cool, Calm, Collected: Poems, 1960–2000.* Port Townsend, Wash.: Copper Canyon Press, 2001.

Klein, Michael, and Gillian Parker, eds. *The English Novel and the Movies.* New York: Frederick Ungar, 1981.

Knoepflmacher, U. C. *George Eliot's Early Novels: The Limits of Realism.* Berkeley: University of California Press, 1968.

Kolodny, Annette. "The Feminist as Literary Critic." *Critical Inquiry* 2 (1976): 821–32.

Kopp, Claire B., ed. *Becoming Female: Perspectives on Development.* New York: Plenum Press, 1979.

Kramer, Heinrich, and Jacob Sprenger. *Malleus Maleficarum.* Trans. Montague Summers. New York: B. Blom, 1970.

Kristeva, Julia. "Oscillation Between Power and Denial." Trans. Marilyn A. August. In Marks and Courtivron, *New French Feminisms,* pp. 165–67.

————. *Revolution in Poetic Language.* Trans. Margaret Waller, with an introduction by Leon S. Roudiez. New York: Columbia University Press, 1984.

Kroll, Judith. *Chapters in a Mythology: The Poetry of Sylvia Plath.* New York: Harper & Row, 1976.

Kuzma, Greg, ed. *A Book of Rereadings.* Crete, Neb.: Best Cellar Press, 1979.

Lacan, Jacques. *Écrits: A Selection.* Trans. Alan Sheridan. New York: W. W. Norton, 1977.

Laennec, Christine Moneera. "Unladylike Polemics: Christine de Pizan's Strategies of Attack and Defense." *Tulsa Studies in Women's Literature,* vol. 12, no. 1 (Spring 1993): 47–59.

Lamb, Michael E., Margaret Tresch Owen, and Lindsay Chase-Lansdale. "The Father-Daughter Relationship: Past, Present, and Future." In Kopp, *Becoming Female,* pp. 89–112.

Lane, Gary, ed. *Sylvia Plath: New Views on the Poetry.* Baltimore, Md.: Johns Hopkins University Press, 1979.

Lanson, Gustave. *Histoire de la littérature française.* 1895; Paris: Hachette, 1952.

Larsen, Nella. *Quicksand.* 1928; Westport, Conn.: Greenwood Press, 1969.

Lawrence, D. H. *The Collected Letters of D. H. Lawrence.* Ed. Harry T. Moore. New York: Viking, 1962.

————. *The Complete Poems of D. H. Lawrence.* Ed. Vivian de Sola Pinto and Warren F. Roberts. 2 vols. New York: Viking, 1964.

————. *The Complete Short Stories.* 3 vols. London: Heinemann, 1960–63.

————. *D. H. Lawrence and Italy: Twilight in Italy. Sea and Sardinia. Etruscan Places.* New York: Viking, 1972.

————. *The Escaped Cock.* Ed. Gerald M. Lacy. 1929; repr., Santa Barbara, Calif.: Black Sparrow, 1978.

————. *Four Short Novels of D. H. Lawrence.* 1923; repr., New York: Viking, 1965.

————. *Kangaroo.* 1923; New York: Viking, 1960.

————. *Lady Chatterley's Lover.* The Hague, Neth.: Heinemann, 1956.

————. *Phoenix: The Posthumous Papers of D. H. Lawrence.* Ed. Edward D. McDonald. New York: Viking, 1936.

————. *Phoenix II; Uncollected, Unpublished, and Other Prose Works.* Ed. Warren Roberts and Harry T. Moore. New York: Viking, 1968.

————. *Psychoanalysis and the Unconscious, and Fantasia of the Unconscious.* New York: Viking, 1965.

————. *Sons and Lovers.* New York: Random House, 1922.

————. *Studies in Classic American Literature.* 1923; repr., New York: Penguin, 1977.

————. *Women in Love.* 1920; repr., New York: Penguin, 1978.

Leavis, F. R. *D. H. Lawrence: Novelist.* London: Chatto & Windus, 1955.

Le Guin, Ursula. *The Left Hand of Darkness.* New York: Walker, 1969.

Lemaire, Anika. *Jacques Lacan.* Trans. David Macey. London and Boston: Routledge & Kegan Paul, 1977.

Lerner, Laurence. *Love and Marriage: Literature and Its Social Context.* London: Edward Arnold, 1979.

Levertov, Denise. *Candles in Babylon.* New York: New Directions, 1982.

————. *The Freeing of the Dust.* New York: New Directions, 1975.

————. *Here and Now.* San Francisco: City Lights, 1957.

————. *The Jacob's Ladder.* New York: New Directions, 1961.

————. *Life in the Forest.* New York: New Directions, 1978.

————. *Light Up the Cave.* New York: published for James Laughlin by New Directions, 1981.

————. *O Taste and See.* New York: New Directions, 1964.

————. *Oblique Prayers: New Poems with 14 Translations from Jean Joubert.* New York: New Directions, 1984.

————. *The Poet in the World.* New York: New Directions, 1973.

————. *Relearning the Alphabet.* New York: New Directions, 1970.

————. *The Sorrow Dance.* 1963; repr., New York: New Directions, 1966.

————. *The Speed of Darkness.* New York: Random House, 1968.

————. *With Eyes at the Back of Our Heads.* New York: New Directions, 1959.

Lévi-Strauss, Claude. *The Elementary Structures of Kinship.* Trans. James Harle Bell, John Richard von Sturmer, and Rodney Needham. Ed. Rodney Needham. Boston: Beacon Press, 1969.

————. *The Raw and the Cooked.* Trans. John and Doreen Weightman. New York: Harper & Row, 1969.

Lewes, G. H. "The Lady Novelists." *Westminster Review,* n.s. 2 (July 1852): 129–41.

Lewis, R. W. B. *Edith Wharton: A Biography.* New York: Harper & Row, 1975.

Leyda, Jay. *The Years and Hours of Emily Dickinson.* 2 vols. New Haven, Conn.: Yale University Press, 1960.

Lindskoog, Kathryn. "Roots and Fruits of the Secret Garden: George MacDonald, Frances Hodgson Burnett, Willa Cather, and D. H. Lawrence." In *Surprised by C. S. Lewis, George MacDonald, & Dante: An Array of Original Discoveries,* pp. 98–103. Macon, Ga.: Mercer University Press, 2001.

Lodge, David. *Small World.* New York: Penguin, 1995.

Lorde, Audre. *The Collected Poems of Audre Lorde.* New York: W. W. Norton, 1997.

Lowell, Robert. *Life Studies, and For the Union Dead.* New York: Farrar, Straus and Giroux, 1967.

Mahl, Mary, and Helene Koon, eds. *The Female Spectator: English Women Writers before 1800.* Bloomington: Indiana University Press/Feminist Press, 1978.

Mannoni, Octave. *Freud.* Trans. Renaud Bruce. New York: Vintage, 1971.

Marchand, Leslie. *Byron: A Biography.* 3 vols. New York: Knopf, 1957.

Marks, Elaine, and Isabelle de Courtivron, eds. *New French Feminisms.* New York: Schocken, 1981.

McGann, Jerome J., ed. *Historical Studies in Literary Criticism.* Madison: University of Wisconsin Press, 1985.

Meyer, Susan. *Imperialism at Home: Race and Victorian Women's Fiction.* Ithaca, N.Y.: Cornell University Press, 1996.

Miller, Cristanne. *Emily Dickinson: A Poet's Grammar.* Cambridge, Mass., and London: Harvard University Press, 1987.

Miller, J. Hillis. "The Function of Rhetorical Study at the Present Time." *The State of the Discipline, 1970s–1980s:* A Special Issue of the *ADE Bulletin,* no. 62 (September–November 1979): 10–18.

———. "Optic and Semiotic in *Middlemarch.*" In Buckley, *The Worlds of Victorian Fiction,* pp. 125–45.

Miller, Nancy K. "Emphasis Added: Plots + Plausibilities in Women's Fiction." *PMLA,* vol. 96, no. 1 (1981): 36–48.

———, ed. *The Poetics of Gender.* New York: Columbia University Press, 1986.

Millett, Kate. *Sexual Politics.* New York: Avon, 1969.

Mitchell, Juliet. *Psychoanalysis and Feminism.* New York: Pantheon, 1974.

Moers, Ellen. *Literary Women.* New York: Doubleday, 1976.

Moore, Harry. *The Priest of Love: A Life of D. H. Lawrence.* New York: Farrar, Straus, and Giroux, 1974.

Morgan, William W. "Feminism and Literary Study: A Reply to Annette Kolodny." *Critical Inquiry* 2 (1976): 807–16.

Morris, Adalaide. "Reading H. D.'s 'Helios and Athene.' " *The Iowa Review,* vol. 12, nos. 2–3 (Spring–Summer 1981): 155–63.

Morrison, Toni. *Sula.* New York: Knopf, 1973.

Mozley, Anne. *The Christian Remembrancer* 25 (June 1853): 423–43.

Murray, Michele. *The Great Mother and Other Poems.* New York: Sheed and Ward, 1974.

Neumann, Erich. *The Great Mother: An Analysis of the Archetype.* Trans. Ralph Manheim. Princeton, N.J.: Princeton University Press, 1955.

———. *The Origins and History of Consciousness.* Trans. R. F. C. Hull. New York: Pantheon, 1954.

Newcastle, Margaret Cavendish, Duchess of. *Paper Bodies: A Margaret Cavendish Reader.* Ed. Sylvia Bowerbank and Sara Mendelson. Peterborough, Ont.: Broadview Press; Hadleigh, UK: BRAD, 1999.

Newman, Charles, ed. *The Art of Sylvia Plath*. Bloomington: Indiana University Press, 1971.

————. "Candor Is the Only Wile." In Newman, *The Art of Sylvia Plath,* pp. 21–55.

Nightingale, Florence. *Cassandra*. Old Westbury, N.Y.: Feminist Press, 1979.

Nin, Anaïs. *The Diary of Anaïs Nin, 1934–1939*. Ed. Gunther Stuhlmann. New York: Harcourt Brace, 1967.

Nudd, Donna Marie. "Rediscovering *Jane Eyre* Through Its Adaptations." In Hoeveler and Lau, *Approaches to Teaching Brontë's* Jane Eyre, pp. 139–47.

Oates, Joyce Carol. "The Death Throes of Romanticism: The Poetry of Sylvia Plath." In *New Heaven, New Earth: The Visionary Experience in Literature*. New York: Fawcett, 1974.

Ogden, Thomas H. *Subjects of Analysis*. Northvale, N.J.: Jason Aronson, 1977.

Oliphant, Margaret. "Modern Novels—Great and Small." *Blackwood's* 77 (May 1855): 544–68.

Olivier, Christiane. *Les Enfants de Jocaste*. Paris: Denoël/Gonthier, 1980.

Olsen, Tillie. *Silences*. New York: Delacorte Press/Seymour Lawrence, 1978.

Ong, Walter. *The Presence of the Word: Some Prolegomena for Cultural and Religious History*. New Haven, Conn.: Yale University Press, 1967.

Oppenheimer, Jane M. *Essays in the History of Embryology and Biology*. Cambridge, Mass.: MIT Press, 1967.

Orenstein, Gloria F. "The Women of Surrealism." *The Feminist Art Journal,* vol. 2, no. 2 (Spring 1973): 15–21.

Ortner, Sherry. "Is Female to Male as Nature Is to Culture?" In Rosaldo and Lamphere, *Women, Culture, and Society*, pp. 68–87.

Otto, Walter Friedrich. *Dionysus: Myth and Cult*. Trans. Robert F. Palmer. Bloomington: Indiana University Press, 1965.

Peacock, Sandra J. *Jane Ellen Harrison: The Mask and the Self*. New Haven, Conn.: Yale University Press, 1988.

Peel, Ellen. "Both Ends of the Candle: Feminist Narrative Structures in Novels by Staël, Lessing, and Le Guin." Ph.D. diss., Yale University, 1982.

————, and Nanora Sweet. "*Corinne* and the Woman as Poet in England: Hemans, Jewsbury, and Barrett Browning." In *The Novel's Seductions: Staël's "Corinne" in Critical Inquiry,* ed. Karyna Szmurlo. Lewisburg, Pa.: Bucknell University Press, 1999, pp. 204–20.

Perera, Suvendrini. *Reaches of Empire: The English Novel from Edgeworth to Dickens*. New York: Columbia University Press, 1991.

Perloff, Marjorie. "Sylvia Plath's 'Sivvy Poems': A Portrait of the Poet as Daughter." In Lane, *Sylvia Plath,* pp. 155–78.

Perry, Ruth. *The Celebrated Mary Astell: An Early English Feminist*. Chicago: University of Chicago Press, 1986.

Pizan, Christine de. *The Book of the City of Ladies*. Trans. Rosalind Brown-Grant. New York: Penguin, 1999.

————. *The Book of the City of Ladies*. Trans. Earl Jeffrey Richards. New York: Persea Books, 1982.

Plath, Otto. *Bumblebees and Their Ways*. New York: Macmillan, 1934.

Plath, Sylvia. *Ariel*. New York: Harper & Row, 1965.

————. *The Bell Jar*. New York: Bantam, 1972.

————. *The Collected Poems.* Ed. Ted Hughes. New York: Harper & Row, 1981.

————. *The Colossus.* New York: Vintage, 1968.

————. "Context." *London Magazine,* February 1962.

————. "Den of Lions." *Seventeen,* May 1951, pp. 127 and 144–45.

————. "The Fifty-ninth Bear." *London Magazine,* February 1961.

————. *The Journals of Sylvia Plath.* Ed. Frances McCullough. New York: Dial, 1982.

————. *Letters Home: Correspondence, 1950–1963.* Ed. Aurelia Schober Plath. New York: Harper & Row, 1975.

————. *The Unabridged Journals of Sylvia Plath, 1950–1962.* Ed. Karen V. Kukil. New York: Anchor Books, 2000.

————. *Winter Trees.* New York: Harper & Row, 1972.

"Poetic Aberrations." *Blackwood's* 87 (1860): 490–504.

Quilligan, Maureen. *Allegory of Female Authority: Christine de Pizan's "Cité des Dames."* Ithaca, N.Y.: Cornell University Press, 1991.

Quinn, Vincent. "H. D.'s 'Hermetic Definition': The Poet as Archetypal Mother." *Contemporary Literature,* vol. 18, no. 1 (Winter 1977): 51–61.

Ransom, John Crowe. "Emily Dickinson: A Poet Restored." In Sewall, *Emily Dickinson,* pp. 88–100.

Redinger, Ruby V. *George Eliot: The Emergent Self.* New York: Knopf, 1975.

Rich, Adrienne. *Blood, Bread, and Poetry: Selected Prose 1979–1985.* New York: W. W. Norton, 1986.

————. *Diving into the Wreck: Poems, 1971–1972.* New York: W. W. Norton, 1973.

————. *The Dream of a Common Language: Poems, 1974–1977.* New York: W. W. Norton, 1978.

————. *The Fact of the Doorframe: Poems Selected and New, 1950–1984.* New York: W. W. Norton, 1984.

————. "Jane Eyre: The Temptations of a Motherless Woman." In Rich, *On Lies, Secrets, and Silence,* pp. 89–106.

————. *Of Woman Born: Motherhood as Experience and Institution.* New York: W. W. Norton, 1986.

————. *On Lies, Secrets, and Silence: Selected Prose, 1966–1978.* New York: W. W. Norton, 1979.

————. *Poems: Selected and New, 1950–1974.* New York: W. W. Norton, 1974.

————. *Twenty-One Love Poems.* Emeryville, Calif.: Effie's Press, 1976.

————. "Vesuvius at Home: The Power of Emily Dickinson." In Gilbert and Gubar, *Shakespeare's Sisters,* pp. 99–121.

————. "When We Dead Awaken: Writing as Re-Vision." In Gelpi and Gelpi, *Adrienne Rich's Poetry and Prose,* pp. 166–177.

Richards, Earl Jeffrey, ed. *Reinterpreting Christine de Pizan.* Athens: University of Georgia Press, 1992.

Riddel, Joseph. "H. D.'s Scene of Writing—Poetry as (and) Analysis." *Studies in the Literary Imagination,* vol. 12, no. 1 (Spring 1979): 41–59.

Rigney, Barbara Hill. *Madness and Sexual Politics in the Feminist Novel: Studies in Brontë, Woolf, Lessing, and Atwood.* Madison: University of Wisconsin Press, 1978.

Robinson, Lillian. *Sex, Class, and Culture.* Bloomington: Indiana University Press, 1978.

Rogers, Samuel. *The Complete Poetical Works of Samuel Rogers.* Ed. Epes Sargent. Boston: Phillips, Sampson, 1854.

Rosaldo, Michelle Zimbalist, and Louise Lamphere, eds. *Woman, Culture, and Society.* Stanford, Calif.: Stanford University Press, 1974.

Rose, Jacqueline, and Juliet Mitchell, eds. *Feminine Sexuality: Jacques Lacan and the "école freudienne."* Trans. Jacqueline Rose. New York: W. W. Norton, 1985.

Rose, Phyllis. *Woman of Letters: A Life of Virginia Woolf.* New York: Oxford University Press, 1978.

Rosenblum, Dolores. "Face to Face: Elizabeth Barrett Browning's *Aurora Leigh* and Nineteenth-Century Poetry." *Victorian Studies,* vol. 26, no. 3 (1983): 321–38.

Rosenthal, M. L. *The New Poets: American and British Poetry Since World War II.* New York: Oxford University Press, 1967.

Rossetti, Christina. *The Letters of Christina Rossetti.* Ed. Antony H. Harrison. Charlottesville: University Press of Virginia, 1997.

————. *The Poetical Works of Christina Georgina Rossetti.* Ed. William Michael Rossetti. London: Macmillan, 1928.

Roszak, Betty, and Theodore Roszak, eds. *Masculine/Feminine: Readings in Sexual Mythology and the Liberation of Women.* New York: Harper & Row, 1969.

Roszak, Theodore. "The Hard and the Soft: The Force of Feminism in Modern Times." In Roszak and Roszak, *Masculine/Feminine,* pp. 87–104.

Ruderman, Judith. *D. H. Lawrence and the Devouring Mother.* Durham, N.C.: Duke University Press, 1984.

Rukeyser, Muriel. *The Collected Poems of Muriel Rukeyser.* New York: McGraw-Hill, 1982.

————. *The Speed of Darkness.* New York: Random House, 1968.

Ruskin, John. *The Diaries of John Ruskin.* Ed. J. Evans and J. H. Whitehouse. Oxford: Oxford University Press, 1956.

————. *Ruskin's Letters from Venice, 1851–1852.* Ed. J. L. Bradley. New Haven, Conn.: Yale University Press, 1955.

Sadoff, Dianne F. *Monsters of Affection: Dickens, Eliot, and Brontë on Fatherhood.* Baltimore, Md.: Johns Hopkins University Press, 1982.

Sayers, Dorothy. *Unpopular Opinions.* London: Victor Gollancz, 1946.

Seidenberg, Robert, and Evangelos Papathomopoulos. "Daughters Who Tend Their Fathers: A Literary Survey." *Psychoanalytic Study of Society* 2 (1962): 135–60.

Sewall, Richard Benson, ed. *Emily Dickinson: A Collection of Critical Essays.* Englewood Cliffs, N.J.: Prentice Hall, 1963.

Sexton, Anne. *The Book of Folly.* Boston: Houghton Mifflin, 1972.

————. *Collected Poems.* Boston: Houghton Mifflin, 1981.

————. *The Death Notebooks.* Boston: Houghton Mifflin, 1974.

————. *Love Poems.* Boston: Houghton Mifflin, 1969.

Sharpe, Jenny. *Allegories of Empire: The Figure of Woman in the Colonial Text.* Minneapolis: University of Minnesota Press, 1993.

Shelley, Mary. *The Last Man.* Ed. Hugh J. Luke Jr. Lincoln: University of Nebraska Press, 1965.

————. *Mary Wollstonecraft Shelley's Frankenstein; or, The Modern Prometheus.* Ed. Susan J. Wolfson. New York: Pearson Longman, 2007.

Shelley, Percy Bysshe. *Poetical Works.* London: Oxford University Press, 1970.

Sherman, Julia A., and Evelyn Torton Beck, eds. *The Prism of Sex: Essays in the Sociology of Knowledge.* Madison: University of Wisconsin Press, 1977.

Showalter, Elaine. "Critical Cross-Dressing." *Raritan* 3 (1983): 130–49.

————. "Feminist Criticism in the Wilderness." *Critical Inquiry*, vol. 8, no. 2 (1981): 179–205.

————. *A Literature of Their Own: British Women Novelists From Brona to Lessing.* Princeton, N.J.: Princeton University Press, 1977.

Sigourney, Lydia. *The Weeping Willow.* Charleston, S.C.: Nabu Press, 2010.

Simpson, Eileen. *Poets in Their Youth.* New York: Vintage, 1983.

Sinclair, May. *Mary Olivier: A Life.* New York: Macmillan, 1919.

Slusser, George E., Eric S. Rabkin, and Robert Scholes, eds. *Coordinates: Placing Science Fiction and Fantasy.* Carbondale: Southern Illinois University Press, 1983.

Small, Judy Jo. "A Musical Aesthetic." In Farr, *Emily Dickinson*, pp. 206–24.

Smith, Anne, ed. *Lawrence and Women.* London: Vision, 1978.

————. "A New Adam and a New Eve—Lawrence and Women: A Biographical Overview." In Smith, *Lawrence and Women.*

Smith, Joseph H. "Fathers and Daughters." *Man and World: An International Philosophical Review* 13 (1980): 385–402.

Snodgrass, W. D. *Heart's Needle.* New York: Knopf, 1961.

Spivak, Gayatri Chakravorty. "Three Women's Texts and a Critique of Imperialism." *Critical Inquiry* 12 (1985): 243–61.

Staël-Holstein, Anne Louise Germaine de. *Corinna, or Italy.* 1807. Ed. and trans. Avriel H. Goldberger. New Brunswick, N.J.: Rutgers University Press, 1987.

————. *Corinne, ou, l'Italie* (1807). Ed. Claudine Herrmann. Paris: Des Femmes, 1979.

Stein, Gertrude. *Bee Time Vine.* New Haven, Conn.: Yale University Press, 1953.

————. *The Yale Gertrude Stein: Selections.* Ed. Richard Kostelanetz. New Haven, Conn.: Yale University Press, 1980.

Steiner, Nancy Hunter. *A Closer Look at "Ariel."* New York: Harper's Magazine Press, 1972.

Steinmetz, Virginia. "Beyond the Sun: Patriarchal Images in *Aurora Leigh*." *Studies in Browning and His Circle*, vol. 9, no. 2 (1981): 18–41.

Stephen, Leslie. *George Eliot.* London: Macmillan, 1902.

Stetson, Charles Walter. See Eldredge, Charles C.

Stevens, Wallace. *The Collected Poems and Prose.* New York: Library of America, 1997.

————. *The Collected Poems of Wallace Stevens.* New York: Knopf, 1955.

Stoneman, Patsy. *Brontë Transformations: The Cultural Dissemination of* Jane Eyre *and* Wuthering Heights. Hemel Hempstead, UK: Prentice Hall/Harvester Wheatsheaf, 1996.

Stump, Reva. *Movement and Vision in George Eliot's Novels.* Seattle: University of Washington Press, 1959.

Sussman, Herbert L., ed. *Literary History: Theory and Practice.* 2 vols. Boston: Northeastern University Press, 1984.

Taplin, Gardner B. *The Life of Elizabeth Barrett Browning.* New Haven, Conn.: Yale University Press, 1957.

Tennyson, Alfred. *The Princess: A Medley.* London: Strahan, 1869.

Thwaite, Ann. *Waiting for the Party: The Life of Frances Hodgson Burnett, 1849–1924.* London: Secker & Warburg, 1974.

Turner, Victor Witter. *Dramas, Fields, and Metaphors: Symbolic Action in Human Society.* Ithaca, N.Y.: Cornell University Press, 1974.

————. *The Forest of Symbols; Aspects of Ndembu Ritual.* Ithaca, N.Y.: Cornell University Press, 1967.

Valenti, Jessica. *Full Frontal Feminism: A Young Woman's Guide to Why Feminism Matters.* Emeryville, Calif.: Seal Press, 2007.

Verduin, Kathleen. "Lady Chatterley and the Secret Garden: Lawrence's Homage to Mrs. Hodgson Burnett." *D. H. Lawrence Review,* vol. 17, no. 1 (Spring 1984): 61–66.

Villon, François. *Complete Poems.* Ed. and trans. Barbara N. Sargent-Baur. Toronto: University of Toronto Press, 1994.

Vivien, Renée. *The Muse of the Violets: Poems.* Trans. Margaret Porter and Catharine Kroger. Bates City, Mo.: Naiad Press, 1977.

Wagner, Linda, ed. *Critical Essays on Sylvia Plath.* Boston, Mass.: G. K. Hall, 1984.

Wagner, Richard. *Tristan and Isolde: Opera in Three Acts.* Trans. Stewart Robb. New York and London: G. Schirmer, n.d.

Wakoski, Diane. *Dancing on the Grave of a Son of a Bitch.* Los Angeles: Black Sparrow Press, 1975.

————. *Inside the Blood Factory.* New York: Doubleday, 1968.

Weiss, Daniel. *Oedipus in Nottingham: D. H. Lawrence.* Seattle: University of Washington, 1962.

Wharton, Edith. *Italian Backgrounds.* New York: Scribner, 1905.

————. Review of *George Eliot* by Leslie Stephen. *Bookman* 15 (May 1902): 247–50.

————. *Summer.* 1917; repr., with an introduction by Cynthia Griffin Wolff, New York: Harper & Row, 1980.

White, Alison. "Tap-Roots in a Rose Garden." *Children's Literature* 1 (1972): 74–76.

Whitman, Walt. *Leaves of Grass.* Ed. Sculley Bradley and Harold W. Blodgett. New York: W. W. Norton, 1973.

Winchilsea, Anne, Countess of. *The Poems of Anne, Countess of Winchilsea.* Ed. Myra Reynolds. Chicago: University of Chicago Press, 1903.

Wittgenstein, Ludwig. *Philosophical Investigations.* Trans. G. E. M. Ascombe. Oxford: Blackwell, 1953.

Wittig, Monique. *Les Guérillères.* Boston: Beacon Press, 1985.

Wolff, Cynthia. *A Feast of Words: The Triumph of Edith Wharton.* Oxford: Oxford University Press, 1977.

Wollstonecraft, Mary. *Political Writings.* Ed. Janet Todd. Toronto and Buffalo, N.Y.: University of Toronto Press, 1993.

Woolf, Virginia. "Aurora Leigh." In *The Second Common Reader,* pp. 182–92.

————. *Books and Portraits: Some Further Selections from the Literary and Biographical Writings of Virginia Woolf.* New York: Harcourt Brace Jovanovich, 1978.

————. *The Complete Shorter Fiction of Virginia Woolf.* Ed. Susan Dick. San Diego: Harcourt Brace Jovanovich, 1989.

————. *Flush: A Biography.* New York: Harcourt Brace, 1933.

————. *The Letters of Virginia Woolf.* Ed. Nigel Nicolson and Joanne Trautmann. 6 vols. New York: Harcourt Brace Jovanovich, 1975–1980.

————. *Orlando: A Biography.* New York: Harcourt Brace, 1928.

————. *A Room of One's Own.* 1929; repr. Orlando, Fl.: Harcourt Brace Jovanovich, 2005.

————. *A Room of One's Own, and Three Guineas.* Ed. Morag Shiach. Oxford: Oxford World Classics, 1992.

————. *The Second Common Reader*. New York: Harcourt Brace, 1932.

————. *Three Guineas*. 1938; repr. Orlando, Fl.: Harcourt Brace Jovanovich, 2006.

————. *To the Lighthouse*. New York: Harcourt Brace, 1927.

————. *The Voyage Out*. New York: Harcourt Brace, 1920.

Wylie, Philip. *Generation of Vipers*. New York: Rinehart, 1955.

Yeats, W. B. *The Complete Poems of W. B. Yeats*. New York: Macmillan, 1955.

Young, Robert J. C. *Colonial Desire: Hybridity in Theory, Culture and Race*. New York: Routledge, 1995.